Imagining China

RHETORIC AND PUBLIC AFFAIRS SERIES

IMAGINING CHINA

RHETORICS OF NATIONALISM
IN AN AGE OF GLOBALIZATION

EDITED BY

Stephen J. Hartnett, Lisa B. Keränen,
and Donovan Conley

MICHIGAN STATE UNIVERSITY PRESS • *East Lansing*

Michigan State University Press
East Lansing, Michigan 48823-5245

Printed and bound in the United States of America.

26 25 24 23 22 21 20 19 18 17   1 2 3 4 5 6 7 8 9 10

LIBRARY OF CONGRESS CATALOGING-IN-PUBLICATION DATA
Names: Hartnett, Stephen J., editor. | Keranen, Lisa B., editor. | Conley, Donovan S., editor.
Title: Imagining China : rhetorics of nationalism in an age of globalization
/ edited by Stephen J. Hartnett, Lisa B. Keranen, and Donovan S. Conley.
Description: East Lansing, Michigan : Michigan State University Press, 2017.
| Series: Rhetoric and public affairs series | Includes bibliographical references and index.
Identifiers: LCCN 2016057847| ISBN 9781611862577 (pbk. : alk. paper)
| ISBN 9781609175399 (pdf) | ISBN 9781628953084 (epub) | ISBN 9781628963083 (kindle)
Subjects: LCSH: Rhetoric—Political aspects—China. | Discourse analysis—Political aspects—China.
| Nationalism—China. | United States—Foreign relations—China. | China—Foreign relations—United States.
| Intercultural communication. | Nationalism—China.
Classification: LCC P302.77 .I524 2017 | DDC 302.20951—dc23 LC record available at https://lccn.loc.
gov/2016057847

Book design by Charlie Sharp, Sharp Des!gns, East Lansing, MI
Cover design by Erin Kirk New
Cover image of Shanghai Skyline is © Jeremy Make and used
courtesy of the photographer. All rights reserved.

Visit Michigan State University Press at *www.msupress.org*

Contents

———◄O►———

INTRODUCTION

A Gathering Storm
or a New Chapter?

———•◆•———

I n the summer of 2013, China's President Xi Jinping flew to southern
California to engage in a "shirtsleeve summit" with U.S. President
Barack Obama at the historic Sunnylands estate. The former man-
sion of Walter H. Annenberg, who bequeathed the property to the city
of Rancho Mirage, Sunnylands has been called the "Camp David of the
West" and has served as a political refuge and diplomatic hosting site
for Presidents Eisenhower, Nixon, Ford, Reagan, George H. W. Bush,
Clinton, and George W. Bush.[1] In this case, the location fulfilled two
purposes. First, by meeting President Xi outside of Washington, D.C.,
President Obama sought to create more intimate working conditions free
from the usual pressures of balancing the needs of D.C. insiders, White
House personnel, swarming media, and invitation-seeking lobbyists and
elected officials. Second, and more importantly, President Obama sought
to send a clear message about life in America. For, as prominent Chinese
intellectual Wang Jisi has observed, imagining the United States "as a

declining hegemon is almost a form of political correctness in China."[2]
Sunnylands offered the perfect antidote to this perception, for it enabled
President Obama to draw upon the setting's magnificent views, clean air,
stunning architecture, manicured grounds, and world-class art collection
to portray an elegant, relaxed, urbane, and prosperous United States.

The tranquil setting belied the fact that Presidents Obama and Xi
met amid rising global tensions. Prefaced by months of conflict between
the two nations regarding alleged cyberattacks on each other's military,
economic, and intellectual infrastructure, differing perspectives on how
to contain North Korea's and Iran's nuclear ambitions, contested territorial claims in the South China Sea, heated exchanges concerning China's
artificially deflated currency and the United States' perpetually increasing national debt, and ongoing differences regarding human rights, free
speech, and norms of governance, the stakes of the meeting were high.
Writing in the *New York Times*, David Sanger framed the goals of the
summit in preventative terms, as if the best anyone could hope for was
averting embarrassment or, worse, an escalation of conflict. President
Obama, Sanger argued, needed to avoid a series of looming "pitfalls"
in order to prevent the two nations from "descending into a Cold War
mentality."[3] Sanger's gloomy outlook reflects a deep-seated U.S. unease
about China's rise, a concern expressed in Ian Bremmer's warning that
the United States and China face a "gathering storm."[4]

Both nations' leaders did their part at Sunnylands to counter the perception that U.S.–China conflict is inevitable. After a series of one-on-one
meetings, close-quarter meals, and leisurely walks staged to demonstrate
collegial and intimate conversation, the two presidents entered the press
conference of June 8 smiling and looking relaxed. President Obama spoke
first, pointing to what he called "very constructive conversations on a whole
range of strategic issues"; President Xi echoed that cordial line, noting that
the discussions at the summit were "in depth, sincere, and candid."[5] While
the U.S. press took a wary tone with the summit, the Chinese press was
ebullient, with the *People's Daily* celebrating "a forward thrust in Sino–US
relations" and "a new chapter in China–U.S. relations."[6]

Despite the cheerful location, the tight scripting, and the positive
press coverage out of Beijing, many observers could not help but watch
the "shirtsleeve summit" with a sense of trepidation, for U.S.–China

relations have been marked for more than sixty years by entrenched misunderstandings, unproductive communication patterns, and simmering rivalries.[7] These cumulative tensions infuse Bill Gertz's call to crisis, *China Threat*; they fuel Martin Jacques's predictions of what will happen *When China Rules the World*; they underwrite the prognostications of Stefan Halper's *The Beijing Consensus: How China's Authoritarian Model Will Dominate the Twenty-First Century*; and they drive the "global call to action" offered in Peter Navarro and Greg Autry's *Death by China*.[8] Combined with the warnings of the U.S. Congressional-Executive Commission on China, the Defense Science Board, various think tanks, and multiple U.S. intelligence agencies, this collection of voices expresses what Stephen J. Hartnett has called "the rhetoric of war-hawk hysteria," an anxiety-producing form of threat construction meant to escalate tensions with China (and others), thus ensuring continued spending on the military and intelligence projects that are justified as responses to these inflated tensions.[9] Suspicion, it would seem, is—if nothing else—at least politically productive. For these professional threat-constructors, engaging in prudential, balanced, respectful discourse with and about China amounts to naïveté at best, national suicide at worst.

It is important to foreground a sense of multiplicity, however, for as this brief survey of recent discourse suggests, while some commentators envision China becoming a New World master at the cost of the United States' security, a contrary view imagines China suffering a catastrophic collapse.[10] While some observers eagerly await China evolving into a democracy,[11] fueled by the rise of a digitally mediated civil society,[12] others point toward a nation haunted by traumatic nationalism and seeking to compensate for past injuries by driving hard toward a renewed sense of imperial entitlement.[13] The Communist Party of China (CPC or the Party) itself, meanwhile, seems to oscillate from a terrified siege mentality to a confident, nationalist swagger. Amid this multitude of juxtaposing positions, we find Presidents Obama and Xi, shirtsleeves rolled up, drinks in hand, California sun melting into the chocolate-colored mountains, proclaiming their commitments to diplomacy and partnership even as the intelligence agencies of both nations publish documents pointing to an increasingly intense rivalry that could, under certain adverse conditions, erupt into conflict.[14]

Thus, while the rhetoric of mutual threat construction and war-hawk hysteria represents one prominent vein of discourse about U.S.–China relations, such discourse appears amid a multivalent tapestry of voices, positions, and perspectives, including those who configure China and the United States as uneasy allies, reluctant partners, and behemoths with shared interests and entwined futures. This torrent of voices configuring, contesting, and speculating about U.S.–China relations should lead even the casual observer to wonder: How do state officials, ordinary citizens, and media outlets addressing the United States and China speak about, to, with, and/or against one another? Such questions about our shared political imaginings are fundamentally questions about *communication*: about how the United States and China envision each other and how such interlinked imaginaries create both opportunities and obstacles for greater understanding. We begin this volume with these overarching questions about how communication drives our imagined communities because the authors whose work fills the pages herein are convinced that relations between the United States and China will continue to play a significant role in shaping the twenty-first century. Representing the world's two largest economies, marshaling the world's two largest armies, holding enormous stockpiles of nuclear weapons and natural resources, and serving as the media generators for billions of image consumers around the world, the two nations are positioned to influence notions of governance, nationalism, citizenship, human rights, health care, environmental sustainability, and global markets for the foreseeable future.

Despite the significance of this relationship, many observers have noted how communication between the United States and China is based not only on misunderstandings but on flagrant misrepresentations, amounting in James Mann's words to *The China Fantasy*, and in James Bradley's words to *The China Mirage*.[5] Rather than assuming such "fantasies" and "mirages" are fundamentally wrong, however—Mann calls them "an elaborate set of illusions"[6]—the chapters in this book chronicle how a wide range of global discourses (including those authored by the CPC) configure "China" across a broad swath of cultural texts. Moreover, our analyses demonstrate how such "illusions" can, at times, be empowering and ennobling, just as they can, at other times, prove hurtful and even deadly. By diving into the rhetorical processes that produce this discourse, we hope to make sense of what we will hereafter call the social imaginary. A symbolic process that is historically constitutive and collectively invented, the social imaginary is both tangible, as it participates in creating things like institutions and highways and schools, and fictive, because it is not closed or finished but open to endless interpretation and revision. As Dilip Gaonkar observes, "what is crucial here is not that human beings always eat, raise children, tinker with the established ways, and tell stories, but that they do so in such a variety of ways. Therein lies the hold of the social imaginary. Our response to material needs, however technically impoverished, is always semiotically excessive. We lean on nature but are steered by the social imaginary."[17] Indeed, we reimagine and rearticulate our collective fates every morning, perpetually engaging in the production and re-production of personal "stories" that reflect, contradict, or reinforce social imaginations about those things called "nations." It is important to note that this process of imagining often occurs via definition by contrast: a group's sense of who they are is influenced as much by who and what they imagine themselves *not* to be as by their unique and evolving histories, memories, and forgettings. Moreover, we argue that such constructions of national identity are never monolithic; rather, they are multilayered, contested, and produced in vernacular and official sources alike.

Imagining China: Rhetorics of Nationalism in an Age of Globalization therefore provides an in-depth rhetorical analysis of how official and vernacular discourses on both sides of the Pacific configure China, in large part by imagining and reimagining a new sense of Chinese nationalism and by making sense of how that Chinese nationalism impacts the United States and other international players. The purpose of this volume then, is to examine the global rhetorical work of imagining China from the perspectives of discourses that cross the Pacific to and from the United States and then back to Beijing, Hong Kong, Tibet, and beyond. Engaging in this critical work entails our willingness to look at selected rhetorical fragments as if they represent larger political and/or historical entities. For example, if we look back over the discourse leading up to Sunnylands, we find individual rhetors, government agencies, and media outlets responding to specific political moments as if they function, almost magically, as truth statements about the larger entities called nation-states and the even more mysterious notion of nationalism. Both analyzing and relying upon this representational strategy, the contributors to this volume note in the chapters that follow how one exiled Chinese lawyer has positioned himself as a barometer for global debates about human rights; how breastfeeding mothers writing in online forums have made arguments about the health of Chinese women and, thus, the health of the Chinese nation; how one Chinese artist's dissident gesture has been turned by art aficionados into a referendum on the possible futures of the CPC; even of how a stuffed animal has been adopted by proponents of the Umbrella Revolution as a playful symbol of the anger and hopes of a new generation of democracy-hungry Hong Kongers. In each example, some social part is imagined as pointing toward a political whole, some instance is turned into the emblem of an epoch, some fragment is portrayed as a window into a projected totality. Within rhetorical and literary studies, this process of conversion is known as *synecdoche*—it is the basic symbolic mechanism of the social imaginary, as we shall demonstrate later in this introduction.

In order to shed light on how China is being constructed, contested, understood, and mobilized by a cacophony of players, in the remainder of this introduction we sketch out some of the competing constructions of U.S.–China relations, address the central critical concepts that are threaded through the book—nationalism, imagined community, and synecdoche—and outline our methodological approaches. We turn first, however, to some representative examples of how China is being imagined by the CPC, by multiple parties in the United States, and by concerned observers around the globe, thus tracing the broad parameters of rhetorical work that is, taken as a whole, imagining both contemporary and historical China.

Pivots, Threats, and Dreams; or, Reimagining U.S.–China Relations

In contrast to the producers of war-hawk hysteria, many practitioners of public political discourse—the White House, the State Department, various cultural liaison groups, etc.—have sought to create a sense of mutual respect and an evolving partnership between the United States and China.[18] For example, President Obama and Secretary of State Hillary Clinton rolled out the idea of a U.S. "pivot" to Asia in November 2011; framed as a rebalancing of U.S. foreign policy following the Bush administration's militarized, post-9/11 actions, the pivot was explicitly linked to the goals of building expanded and bipartisan communication pathways between the United States and China.[19] As National Security Advisor Tom Donilon repeated in speech after speech, the pivot was intended to "rebalance our posture in the world" while recognizing that "America's success in the 21st century is tied to the success of Asia" in general and, most importantly, is based upon "pursuing a stable and constructive relationship with China."[20] As seen here, "the success of Asia" was a foundational premise of the pivot; no longer seen as either a doormat or a threat, Asia is portrayed in pivot rhetoric as a rising region of networked forces to be reckoned as economic, diplomatic, cultural, and military partners. Thus, speaking at a summit about the pivot in 2014, Emanuel Pastreich, director of the influential Asia Institute in New York City, observed:

> We no longer look at a backwards Asia. . . . We are looking now at nations in East Asia that are peers, and often ahead of the United States in certain sectors. We must have an equal relationship in our discussions in which we are learning as much as we are teaching. . . . So the relationship must be one between equals, akin to what we have seen in Europe over the last fifty years.[21]

As seen in the speeches and writings of President Obama, former Secretary of State Clinton, National Security Advisor Donilon, and Asia Institute Director Pastreich, the rhetoric of the pivot—like the communication produced at Sunnylands—has been prudent, respectful, and cautiously optimistic: *the relationship must be one between equals.*

Nonetheless, even while high-level leaders from the United States and China sought to create stronger communicative bonds, they were buffeted by what appear to be cottage industries in both nations committed to manufacturing extremism and escalating tensions. Indeed, popular discussions about our relations swing between two poles: from predictions of a coming Chinese century—*When China Rules the World*—wherein the United States becomes an indebted vassal backwater ruled by bankers in Shanghai, to equally exaggerated suggestions of a coming Chinese collapse, wherein the hinterlands rebel, the urban megacities explode in violence, and the Chinese finally bury Chairman Mao's legacy while reeling from the effects of a rapidly falling Chinese market. For an example of the first pole, consider a blog post following an article published by Radio Free Asia about some of President Obama's comments on Tibet, wherein a Chinese respondent predicts that "in the next twenty years, America will be [en]slaved to China."[22] This comment captures a popular sentiment in China that is much feared and loudly rejected in the United States: that America is a declining empire soon to be eclipsed by a rising China. At the other pole, in *World Affairs*, Gordon Chang celebrates "The Coming Collapse of China." Pointing to "banks with unacknowledged bad loans . . . trade frictions arising from mercantilist policies, a pandemic of defective products and poisonous foods . . . a rising tide of violent crime, a monumental environmental crisis, [and] ever worsening corruption," Chang concludes that China's complications amount to a "dagger pointed at the heart of the country's one-party state."[23] This argument captures a sentiment popular in the United States and much feared in China: that the People's Republic of China (PRC) is a "fragile" power teetering on the brink of explosion.[24] Both poles—*the United States will collapse* vs. *China will collapse*—offer hyperbolic scenarios that the authors in this book work to ameliorate through empirical rigor and analytic precision. Rather than engaging in overblown threat-construction, the chapters offered herein provide detailed and prudent engagements with specific moments of intercultural and transnational communication, thus offering analyses of actually existing communication dynamics and, hopefully, roadmaps toward strengthened relations.

Whereas the interpretive frames noted above focus on coming collapses, epic implosions, and imminent conflicts, a different picture appears in the work of Guobin Yang, who argues that because of the advent of the Internet, the "Chinese people have created a world of carnival, community, and contention in and through cyberspace," hence fueling "the slow and limited institutionalization of government transparency and citizen input."[25] Yang's argument reflects the hopes of international cyber-activists who champion the political power of emerging digital networks.

Eric Schmidt and Jared Cohen, the CEO of Google and the director of Google Ideas, respectively, go so far as arguing that "any person with access to the Internet, *regardless of living standard or nationality*, is given a voice and the power to effect change" in the new "interconnected estate."[26] As a Google spokesperson said recently, Google holds onto "a profound optimism about the potential for technology to improve the world."[27] These corporate titans are thus pushing the technophile dream of happy globalization, wherein burgeoning free markets bring joy and beauty to the masses and healthy returns to the investing class, all while developing green technology and spreading democracy by wiring up the downtrodden.

While Yang envisions the Internet fueling the slow but steady rise of informed and engaged civil society in China, and whereas Schmidt, Cohen, and the Google luminaries envision salvation through expanded Wi-Fi access, a different glimpse into China's wired future may be found in a set of links offered by the *People's Daily*, the CPC's English-language newspaper.[28] Following a routine statement on the latest "totally ground-less and irresponsible" comments about China coming from the United States, readers are invited to peruse such titles as "Baby Alien Found by Mexican Farmer," "Which Country Has the Most Beautiful Women?" and "Indian Media Stinks Up Public Opinions."[29] This kind of mundane media programming is countered in China's blossoming web-spheres, however, by a rising rhetoric of hard-line nationalism. In fact, Rachel Lu reports that the most-circulated Internet story in China in the autumn of 2013 was a "nationalist screed against western encroachment."[30] Travers-ing blogs and websites, and reposted by the Xinhua News Agency, *People's Daily*, *Global Times*, and other Party-run media outlets, the postings, Lu observes, capture a prominent (and Party-endorsed) trope within con-temporary Chinese culture, wherein the ghosts of former humiliations at the hands of the United Kingdom, the United States, and especially Japan drive the population toward a fevered nationalism that veers dan-gerously close to xenophobia, Han exceptionalism, and even, particularly as regards Japan, war-mongering triumphalism. Hartnett has diagnosed this rhetorical trope as a form of "traumatized nationalism," wherein "the wounds of [China's] history as a colonial victim" drive the impulse for "a new chest-thumping bravado."[31]

For example, in May and June 2014, the Party-run papers offered a concatenation of articles portraying the United States as a Cold War–style aggressor seeking to contain China;[32] China's ethnic others as terrorists committed to destroying the motherland, thus necessitating a "People's War" against separatists and "splittists";[33] Vietnam and the Philippines as unreasonable and hostile neighbors seeking to grab territory (in the South China Sea) rightfully controlled by China;[34] and global hackers, led by the United States, seeking to undermine China's stability by waging cyberwar.[35] As portrayed in virtually daily installments in *China Daily*, the *People's Daily Online*, and the *Global Times*, the vultures were circling. Still, even as the Party produced this brew of China under attack from all corners, it simultaneously fostered a sense of aggrandizing nationalism. For example, while a bold headline in *China Daily* announced "U.S. Must Get Used to China's Rise," each of the stories cited above about Vietnam and the Philippines indicated that China would not negotiate over territory it rightly held, instead sending a flotilla of vessels, including military ships, to occupy the contested territory.[36] The rhetoric of traumatized nationalism circles around these two tropes: of China as the innocent victim of meddling by both foreign powers and internal traitors seeking to destroy the motherland, and of China as a muscular and rising power demanding respect on both regional and global stages. As numerous chapters herein argue, this combination of wounded humiliation and rising nationalism makes for a shaky, internally contradictory rhetoric with little room for public negotiation. Moreover, in China as in the United States, vested interests have garnered vast power by stoking the fears that fuel this CPC version of war-hawk rhetoric. As a prominent human rights activist in Hong Kong observed in an interview, the CPC has created "a social-stability-industrial complex . . . they've built such an enormous infrastructure around maintaining stability that they need to blow up the threat to justify their own existence."[37]

Still, much as with the rhetoric of war-hawk hysteria in the United States, we need to be clear that the rhetoric of traumatized nationalism in China by no means represents anything like a national credo; rather, it amounts to one line of argumentation, advanced by a set of interested parties, with multiple counterarguments representing multiple perspectives flowing in from every direction. It is worth repeating the earlier comment that social imaginaries are neither closed nor finished. Rather, the chapters offered herein illustrate how approaching U.S.–China relations from a communication perspective enables our authors to address daily and ongoing constructions and contests over the meanings, values, and directions of our shared tomorrows. Given this perspective, the chapters in this book are written with a sense of urgency, for the stakes are high when trying to understand the rhetorical workings of the social imaginaries that underwrite our senses of ourselves, our communities, our nations, and our relationships with others. To offer more detailed comments on the rhetorical methods underwriting this project, we turn now to an exposition of the intellectual traditions that help us make sense of imagined communities in the United States, China, and beyond.

Synecdoche, Nationalism, and the Rhetorical Work of Imagining Communities

In his classic *A Handlist of Rhetorical Terms*, Richard Lanham observes how the synecdochic "understanding one thing with another" via the "substitution of part for whole" depends in large part on processes of "scale-change" and "magnification."[38] Similarly, in *A Rhetoric of Motives*, Kenneth Burke discusses a hypothetical worker who, in traditional Marxist fashion, "can think of himself as representing not only the interests of that class alone, but the grand design of the entire historical sequence." In this way, Burke argues, synecdoche "scale-changes" a particular "moment" into an all-telling representation of "a universal movement."[39] Whether it is a Marxist conversion of a worker into the harbinger of a universal movement, or of an individual into a member of a nation, Burke notes that the psychological satisfaction of participating in the process hinges on the individual being able to feel as if he or she is "communicating directly with [some] universal logic, or ultimate direction."[40] You "can call it fallacious if you want," Burke notes, but the key point is that engaging in this "magnification" enlarges one's sense of self, providing everyday life with the power of purpose, even calling.[41] As each of the chapters in this book demonstrates, perhaps no form of calling is as grand

and compelling, or as strange and ambiguous, as imaging one's self a part of the larger political entities we have come to call nations.

Indeed, throughout this book, we frame our individual case studies as rhetorically informed microanalyses situated within this larger, macroanalytic framework, wherein the rhetorical process of synecdoche—as utilized by activists, politicians, scholars, artists, and others—converts individual texts, materials, images, and actions into representations of the larger work of nations. As we demonstrate, this rhetorical work of conversion requires participants to envision themselves as part of a nation that is conceived of as both historical and contemporary, as both embodied and ethereal, as both standing for a series of beliefs and against perceived enemies. The chapters contained herein demonstrate how this rhetorical work of imagining and magnification takes place in the contested spaces of daily life. To explain this thesis in more detail, it is important to weave our way, albeit briefly, through this notion of nations, the nationalisms that envelop and sustain them, and the complicated synecdochal work that facilitates the imagining of oneself as a part of this historically recent configuration called a nation. Indeed, as a guiding theme, complicating question, and pressing political problem, we see this book as contributing to ongoing scholarly debates about how imagined communities are called into being, how they are perpetually reinvented, and how they both stitch individuals and communities into and weave other individuals and communities out of the multilayered fabric of the nation.

We begin by noting that thinking about nations and nationalisms has changed dramatically over the years. For example, as the foundational text of one dominant strain of thought, consider the version of synecdoche, nations, and nationalisms offered in Karl Marx's 1848 *Communist Manifesto*, which portrays "the history of all hitherto existing society" as being driven by "class struggles."[42] Writing amid the Industrial Revolution and its attendant encircling of the globe by new forms of production, consumption, and political and military power—the stepchildren of that monster entity called "Modern Industry"—Marx envisioned a rising bourgeoisie scrambling "over the whole surface of the globe" in the delirious attempt to "establish connexions everywhere."[43] For Marx, the propulsive force of modern industry was so great, the pull of new wealth so overwhelming, and the "enforced destruction" unleashed by these powers so explosive that this new army of globalizing capitalists was sure to crush all prior forms of belief, daily life, and political order, meaning "national one-sidedness and narrow-mindedness [would] become more and more impossible" as modernity and capitalism washed across the globe.[44] Because of this war of the mechanized New against everything already existing, and because of the unstoppable and homogenizing force of "that single, unconscionable freedom, Free Trade," Marx argued that Old World nationalisms and provincialisms must die; as a consequence, "all that is solid melts into air, all that is holy is profaned."[45] For Marx and the generations of radicals who followed in his footsteps, globalizing capitalism would crush nationalism, slowly but surely melding the world together into one seamless market driven by exploitation. Marx welcomed these processes, as he envisioned them leading to the unrest and alienation that would unleash revolutions everywhere, leading eventually to the universal spread of communism. Thus, when Marx referred to nations and nationalisms, he portrayed them in what can only be called mocking tones, aligning them alongside such relics of a fast-dying past as "the idiocy of rural life," "aristocracy," "feudal absolutism," and the provincial thinking that drove successive emperors to leave the Middle Kingdom's economy hostage to the mercantilism that kept out European traders by building "Chinese walls."[46] Cheering the dissolution of these Old World practices, Marx imagined modern capitalism rolling over ancient tribalisms and nationalisms, meaning that the synecdochic conversion of part to whole, of an agent ascribing allegiance to a larger political entity, would henceforward be driven not by religion or nation but by the hard, cold, irrefutable logic of the market.

This Marxist belief that class allegiances would trump Old World nationalisms was so deeply embedded in late nineteenth- and early twentieth-century Europe that in the days leading up to World War I, many continental socialists assumed that soldiers would refuse to fight for corrupt monarchies. But as Eric Hobsbawm laments in *The Age of Empire*, the dissolution of old ways of living at the hands of modern capitalism did not drive a generation of workers toward revolution; instead, "the imaginary community of 'the nation'" was deployed to "fill this void." Thus, when the war broke, "the people of Europe, for however brief a moment, went lightheartedly to slaughter and be slaughtered."[47] As these comments indicate, World War I made it clear that an emerging sense of nationalism was stronger than the pull of socialism or Marxism: working-class Englishmen were only too willing to kill working-class Germans. Whether embedded in flags or military uniforms or folk songs, or in culinary traditions and languages, or in some perceived connection to ancient pasts, it was clear that Europeans imagined themselves as parts of nations, regardless of class boundaries. Contrary to Marx's belief that a rational analysis of economics would drive one's political consciousness, it was becoming clear that nationalism was in fact a deeply held belief, a construction of immense complexity, not so much a burden to be tossed off as a comforting skin that is both inherited and invented. In short, the colossal destruction of World War I showed that the sense of nations and nationalisms was, for lack of a better word, *rhetorical*.

Writing from the relative safety of the United States, and deeply immersed in studying both the immense arc of intellectual history and the specific political dilemmas of a Europe again working toward war, Kenneth Burke sought to understand the mysteries of how rhetorical imaginings could lead to allegiances so deep and unwavering as to produce the carnage of World War I and, subsequently, the rising threat of fascism in Germany. And so, in his 1937 *Attitudes toward History*, Burke returned to much older forms of allegiance and imagination to argue—contrary to Marx and his followers—that imagined communities hinged not on rational class alliances but on the rhetorical work of "forming and reforming congregations."[48] Continuing with the metaphor of "identification" as a form of religion, Burke observed how William James's writings about public life in America amounted to a "secular kind of prayer."[49] Whereas we have already seen Burke suggest above that such identifications with transcendent immensities—whether the nation, or revolution, or God, or Hitler—can be "fallacious" in the empirical sense, here he calls them a "gorgeous subterfuge" that "lends dignity to the necessities of existence."[50] From this perspective, the rhetorical work of imagining communities, of deploying synecdoche to convert alienation into belonging, the self into a member of the nation, is both politically and psychologically necessary, for without such "scale-changes" the individual would be lost in a sea of uncertainty and confusion, adrift on the absurd currents of time without purpose.

A keen student of both Marx and Burke, communication scholar Michael Calvin McGee made a breakthrough in this line of thinking in 1975, when he argued that this synecdochic conversion of part to whole was based on a previously unrecognized sleight of hand. Prior thinkers argued about how agents (organic, preformed, discreet entities) aligned with nations and classes (likewise assumed to be wholly formed bodies), thus reducing political analysis to the trenches of persuasion. Tweaking this line of thought, McGee argued that the very notions of agents, or classes, or nations, were in themselves rhetorical constructions forever under revision. And so, McGee argued, "'The people' are not objectively real in the sense that they exist as a collective entity in nature; rather, they are a fiction dreamed by an advocate and infused with an artificial, rhetorical reality by the agreement of an audience."[51] Instead of preexisting realities that would occasionally collide with or elide each other given particular political needs, each part of our social world—individuals, groups, classes, parties, and nations—was perpetually in the process of rhetorical invention, meaning "'the people' are more *process* than *phenomenon.*"[52] From this perspective, an imagined national community was not simply a finished product that persuaded already formed individuals to support or attack it, but rather an ongoing and unstable process of rhetorical invention. Although perhaps disturbing to realize at the time, McGee was saying that nations and nationalisms are giant tautologies, machines of invention and revision, collective fantasies that, as they are called into being, create their audiences and histories.

The post-Marxist literary critic Fredric Jameson brought many of these intellectual threads together in 1981 in his *Political Unconscious,* where he argued that our sense of reality hinges on our accessing and interpreting textual constructions—novels, plays, laws, speeches—that themselves are constructions made up from prior narratives. This means, for Jameson, that "texts come before us as the always-already-read; we apprehend them through sedimented layers of previous interpretations."[53] These "sedimented layers" are so historically deep, so politically complicated, so formally multifaceted, Jameson argues, that they can sometimes feel to us almost pregiven, for their "prior textualization" renders them as part of our collective "political unconscious."[54] The U.S. Pledge of Allegiance, for example, seems timeless, as if it has always been there, calling out to generation after generation of school children who memorize its rhymes before understanding any of its claims. Likewise, Jameson argues that the "great fantasms of the various nationalisms" come to the individual with a sense of being wholly formed, as if America or Britain or Russia or China are prehistorical entities, always-already-existing nations, not relatively recent rhetorical inventions.[55] Nonetheless, and echoing Burke, Jameson concluded his *Political Unconscious* by noting that no subject would assent to participate in such "fantasms" if they were not deeply satisfying. And so, alongside the usual "demystifying vocation to unmask" how imagined communities enable exploitation, racism, oppression, and other "forms of false consciousness," Jameson posited a second, equally important critical function: to understand how imagined communities offer "Utopian" promises and "symbolic affirmations."[56]

This line of thinking about the deep rhetorical processes (and unconscious longings) that underwrite nations and nationalisms then took another tremendous leap in 1983, when Benedict Anderson published *Imagined Communities: Reflections on the Origin and Spread of Nationalism*, which offered a galvanizing thesis about the sheer *constructedness* of nationalism.[57] Anderson began his analysis by flagging three central "paradoxes" within the rhetorical processes of "magnification" that lead to the building of nations and nationalisms. First, the contrast between the "objective modernity of nations" (as driven by the same factors addressed by Marx) and the "subjective antiquity" of those who imagine their "nations" as somehow ancient, prehistorical entities (an issue that, as the chapters herein address again and again, is crucial to the evolving imagined communities of China). Second, the contrast between "the formal universality of nationality," which is imagined as spreadable across space, and the "irremediable particularity" of the innumerable local entities that must be enveloped within the nation, but which still retain their prenational flavor (thus, for example, as Stephen John Hartnett's chapter illustrates, making China's claims over Tibet so complicated). Third, the contrast between the immense "political power of nationalisms" to mobilize masses, as seen in World Wars I and II, for example, and the "philosophical poverty and even incoherence" of notions of nationalism (thus, for example, as Xing Lu's chapter indicates, accounting for post-Maoist China's search for a political language strong enough to unite the nation).[58] In short, Anderson argued that the sense of nationalism involved *temporal slippage* between the lived present and the longed-for past, *geographic slippage* between the originating source of a nation and its longed-for expansions across space, and *political slippage* between the arousing glory of nationalism and the realization that behind the flag or the uniform or the gun, all we find is a rhetorical construction, what we saw Burke call an "identification," and what we saw McGee call "a collective fantasy." Perhaps most importantly, Anderson realized that the sense of "fraternity," "community," and "deep, horizontal comradeship" holding the nation together worked "regardless of the actual inequality and exploitation" found in particular communities.[59] Contrary to Marx, then, and echoing Burke's notion of identifications that are "fallacious" and, as Jameson argued, even "utopian," Anderson wrote that the rhetorical work of imagining nationalism was, by its very nature, illogical and subjective, perhaps even working against one's economic interests.

Given the clear overlap between Anderson's arguments and those made previously by Burke, McGee, and Jameson, it comes as no surprise to learn that it was not long before this notion of *imagined communities* seeped into communication studies more broadly. Trying to indicate how the rhetorical work of imagined communities involves not simply persuasion between preexisting social categories but the simultaneous production of them, Maurice Charland argued in 1987—in work culled from a dissertation advised by McGee—that such rhetorical work is "constitutive rhetoric, for it calls its audience into being."[60] Like Anderson, Charland observed how constitutive rhetoric engages in a historical sleight of hand, for even as it "constitutes the identity" of a group seeking new political rights and privileges, thus engaging in the work of forward-looking invention, so "it simultaneously presumes" this new category reflects some "pre-given and natural" entity "existing outside of rhetoric," thus engaging in the work of looking backward.[61] In this "perfectly tautological" formulation, an already formed past identity is presented as predating the rhetorical work of imagining that calls the present identity into being.[62] A "gorgeous subterfuge" indeed.

There is no better example of this rhetorical tautology than the revolutionary United States, where the invocation of "We the People" sought both to form and to presume as already formed a united public that was, in fact, badly fractured.[63] The "constitutive" work of the *Federalist Papers*, for example, touched upon four key maneuvers, described by James Jasinski in 1998 as follows: "in addition to self-constitution and the formation of subjectivity, discourse functions to organize and structure an individual's or a culture's expectations of time and space, the norms of political culture, and the experience of communal existence."[64] Given the enormous complexity of this rhetorical imagining, Ronald Greene argued in 1998 that communication scholars should be devoting their energies toward building "a cartography of deliberative rhetoric," thus mapping the vectors of creation, influence, revision, and rebuttal that overlap while creating "a functioning network of power."[65] Within this metaphor of rhetorical criticism as mapping, Greene asked his colleagues to realize that "the imaginary relationship to the real is not to be confused with a distortion of reality," meaning that the rhetorical work of imagining communities, regardless of its relationship to objective, economic factors, always feels "real" to those authors of the fiction.[66]

This trajectory of scholarship—bringing together Marxism and cultural studies, rhetorical criticism and studies of nationalism, work that was historical, contemporary, and theoretical—had become so ubiquitous by the end of the twentieth century that communication studies in particular saw an explosion in works mining this vein. In 2002, Robert James Branham and Stephen John Hartnett published *Sweet Freedom's Song: "My Country 'Tis of Thee" and Democracy in America*, arguing that the rhetorical work of imagining a national community was aided greatly during the American Revolution by the embodied practice of singing political songs in public.[67] By 2005, Mary Stuckey was arguing that this rhetorical work of imagining—still ongoing during the 2004 presidential conventions that she studied—involved nothing less than "a contest for the moral future of the nation."[68] In 2010, Jennifer Mercieca applied many of these same principles to the founding period of U.S. history, arguing in *Founding Fictions* that the nation's emerging sense of itself as a "democracy" was driven by a complex series of debates that hinged on how different factions imagined the nation's (mostly fictional) past and its (hotly contested) rise toward continental power.[69] By 2010, Derek Sweet and Margaret McCue-Enser were arguing that such rhetorical work amounted to President Obama's chief mission, wherein he sought "to reconstitute the U.S. electorate's understanding of 'the people.'"[70]

While each of these works deployed the notions of synecdoche, imagined communities, and constitutive rhetoric to study how individual actors and larger movements created themselves while shuttling between public assertions of assent and dissent, Jeremy Engels added another layer to this school of thought when he published *Enemyship* in 2010.[71] Having studied the ways early U.S. political discourse was infused with anger, and even hatred, directed toward a coterie of perceived enemies—whether slaves, or pirates, or Native Americans, or the immigrant Irish, etc.—Engels concluded that hating outsiders galvanized political subjects (some of whose allegiance was dubious) into united forces of nationalist aggression. The next year, Hamilton Bean, Lisa Keränen, and Margaret Durfy explored how conceptions of resilience propped up visions of enduring British nationalism in the wake of the London 7/7 bombings, thus paving the way for a new round of militarized national policies targeting those dangerous Others perceived as threatening the nation.[72] From the perspective of these works—and echoing a wave of post-9/11 scholarship about the usefulness of enemies—cultural fictions, political fictions, and constitutive rhetorics are often most successful in imagining a coherent national community when they are conceived in opposition to some loathed Other.[73] The rhetorical work of imagining a national community is often concerned, then, at least in part, with imagining other national communities, other bodies, other ways of being deemed less noble, or less kind, or less worthy of approbation. Indeed, as the chapters herein demonstrate, the rhetorical work of imagining communities is always relational: any sense of an emerging new Chinese national identity is being formed, in part, in contrast to the perceived injustices foisted upon the nation by foreign powers over the centuries. Likewise, thinking in the United States about China continues to be formed, in part, by a relational logic that imagines the Chinese as inferior to typical Americans; as observed by Kent A. Ono and Joy Yang Jiao in their essay on "China in the US Imaginary," centuries of racism percolate through these contemporary imaginings.[74]

If the rhetorical work of imagining the nation is often set against some perceived Other, it can also proceed with the goal of bridging national differences, thus trying to establish a sense of leadership and vision. Much work has been done along these lines regarding the 2008 Beijing Olympics, for example, wherein scholars have addressed how the CPC sought to turn that massive, international spectacle of sports into a vehicle not only for new national imaginings but for projecting a sense of China on a global scale.[75] As these Olympic studies demonstrate, and as Anderson, McGee, Charland, and others discussed above argued, the rhetorical work of imagining the nation, both as a discreet entity and as a part of larger international communities, often entails revising history, thus projecting an envisioned future on the back of some assumed historical grounding.[76] To underline the significance of a sense of history within these processes of imagining, we offer below a series of cautionary comments regarding the troubled history of how some Western observers have imagined China.

Methodological Caution; or, Humility amid the "Heathens"

Having offered a brief overview of the intellectual underpinnings of synecdoche and how it underwrites our thinking about the rhetorical work of imagining national communities, it is important now to step outside of that lineage and into another, for our sense is that there is no way to begin this collection of essays without addressing the obvious problem of Orientalism. Edward Said popularized the term in 1978, when he analyzed how centuries of European scholars, poets, artists, government officials, and military leaders had portrayed the Middle East—with that term used in its broadest, most encompassing sense—as a hotbed of uncivilized heathens in need of either salvation or destruction. Said argued that "we need not look for correspondence between the language used to depict the Orient and the Orient itself, not so much because the language is inaccurate but because it is not even trying to be accurate." Rather, what such discourse sought to create was an "imaginative geography" that would justify, facilitate, and help to manage European conquests. And so, despite that region's remarkable complexity, to say nothing of its internal divisions, such Orientalist discourse played a homogenizing, totalizing, and simplifying role: "Since it was commonly believed that the whole Orient hung together in some profoundly organic way, it made perfectly good hermeneutical sense for the Orientalist scholar to regard the material evidence he dealt with as ultimately leading to some better understanding of such things as the Oriental character, mind, ethos, or world-spirit."[77] Such an "imaginative geography" amounted, for Said, to a racism-driven political fiction, a constitutive rhetoric deployed in the name of imperialism.

While Said was concerned with the colonization of the Middle East, his term is painfully applicable to the history of Western encounters with China as well. As Kent Ono and Joy Yang Jiao note, "the position of China within the US imaginary" is colored by both "time-worn orientalist images" and "mounting Sinophobic discourse."[78] It is important to note, however, that the routes of misunderstanding also include Romanticization, in which long-standing "China nightmares" are contrasted with "American Dreams" about China; as Jeff Wasserstrom observes, our "spectral visions" about China include both "dismay" and "hope."[79] Similarly, James Bradley's *China Mirage* details how Western missionary visions about China's coming Christian conversion fooled presidents and policymakers alike from the Opium Wars through World War II, in part because Westerners wanted to see themselves reflected in their Chinese compatriots.[80] While the essays in this collection seek to avoid the traps described by Said, Ono and Jiao, Wasserstrom, and Bradley, it will be instructive to observe how some prior works contributed to this tradition of Orientalism; if nothing else, a brief detour into the rhetorical histories of Orientalist discourses will provide some methodological inoculation against repeating the same old mistakes, thus providing a sense of the distance between the self-reflexive efforts of the authors in this book and the romantic fantasies and xenophobic nightmares that have all too often animated discourses about China and the United States.[81]

For example, consider Athanasius Kircher's *China Illustrata*, which landed in Amsterdam in 1667 complete with text describing and images portraying a strange land full of flying turtles (he apparently mistranslated the word for *furry* into *flying*). Kircher's imaginarium included a gorgeous image of Chinese picnickers dining in an exotic garden, where they enjoyed a jackfruit the size of a packing chest; one such fruit, conveniently cut in half in the image's forefront, displays the jackfruit's symmetrical inner anatomy, all tidy rows of tasty black seeds surrounded by juicy, white fruit. For Kircher, Chinese foliage, beasts, and fruit indicate a land of wonders and mysteries enjoyed by elegant ladies and gentlemen robed in Confucian splendor.[82]

Or consider Nathum Tate's *Poem Upon Tea*, published in London in 1702. In Tate's long poem, his protagonist, Palaemon (perhaps named after an ancient mythological God of the sea, whom Euripedes called "the guardian of ships") resolved to explore the world. Upon completing his epic voyage, Palaemon reported that "none he found, his gentle Soul to please / Like the Refin'd and Civiliz'd *Chinese*."[83] In this early example of European romanticism for an idealized Orient, Tate depicts a minor god finding the Chinese as among the Earth's superior beings. For both Kircher and Tate, the Chinese were not so much like them as better than them; for these early European rhetors, the Oriental Other was envisioned as strange, foreign, and wondrous—an *imagined community* indeed.

We do not want to simplify the remarkably long and complicated histories of Western fascination with China—trails littered with what Timothy Billings calls "wacky misapprehension"[84]—but will suggest that it is a short conceptual step from Tate's and Kircher's early examples of Orientalist Romanticism to the technophile dreams addressed above, wherein the Chinese encounter the same technologies readily available to Americans only to turn them, as we so decisively have not, toward achieving revolutionary goals. Yang's and Chang's Web dreams repeat the Orientalist impulse of Tate and Kircher, albeit with the added twist of rebel-rousing technology. For such postmodern Orientalists, even though the Web has left many (if not most) Americans paralyzed by prurient puffery, the romanticized Oriental Other will turn this same technology to wondrous purposes. In contrast to this romantic version of Orientalism, we have noted earlier in this essay how certain think tanks in the United States have produced a cottage industry of threat constructors whose jobs appear to consist of portraying China as the End of Everything: this is the uglier, fear-based, xenophobic branch of Orientalist discourse. Whether practicing the romantic or the xenophobic version of Orientalism, such rhetoric is driven by a relentless urge to simplify.

For an example of this Orientalist and simplifying communication pattern from a different historical era, consider the rhetoric of Dean Acheson, one of the chief architects of Orientalism in U.S. foreign policy in the post–World War II era, when he served as undersecretary of state and then secretary of state during the Roosevelt and Truman administrations. In his memoirs, Acheson notes that the U.S. merchants who "raced to the Orient" to feast upon its market possibilities "also carried missionaries to educate the minds and heal the bodies as well as save the souls of the heathen Chinese."[85] Such frank talk reveals the racist and exceptionalist assumptions that drove U.S. foreign policy during the early Cold War: American Christians would save Chinese heathens, at gun point if necessary, while getting rich in the process.[86] Few leaders in Washington would use such language today, but it is a short step from Acheson's Cold War talk of converting the "heathens" to Christianity to today's champions of U.S.-style and tech-savvy democracy, who envision equally millennial conversions forthcoming in China: convert to Christianity, convert to Democracy, convert to Capitalism . . . *convert, convert, convert*. Moreover, Tani E. Barlow has noted that while Acheson and his fellow Cold War elites were producing this missionary rhetoric of conversion, so the postwar founders of modern China studies—she sites Marion Levy, Lucian Pye, and John K. Fairbank as exemplars—were crafting an academic field that served the interests of empire. By embedding Orientalism in U.S. universities, Barlow argues, Cold War–era China studies scholars provided intellectual justifications for U.S. containment projects throughout Asia, in part by erasing histories of colonialism and imperialism to make room for a benevolent discourse of modernization.[87]

These examples from Kircher in 1667, Tate in 1702, Acheson in the mid-1940s, and early China studies in the 1950s—and of course more examples could be found from other historical periods, including the explosion of texts surrounding the First Opium War in 1839 to the raft of anticommunist propaganda that flooded the United States up until 1989—demonstrate the remarkable resilience of the two communication patterns noted herein: of either demonizing or romanticizing China, and in both cases by simplifying, flattening, or all-out forgetting the complexities of Chinese politics, history, and communication patterns. Such rhetorical politics continue today. For example, in the spring of 2014, when Chinese tech giant Alibaba announced that it would sell public shares—with the company's worth estimated by some observers to be in excess of $200 billion—the U.S. press resorted to long-standing stereotypes to convey the story. As part of this barrage, the front page of the *New York Times*'s business section included an image of an ancient Chinese dragon storming into New York City, complete with the dramatic title "The Dragon Makes Its Entrance."[88] Viewers will notice that the tail of the dragon stretches back not to one of the hundreds of glistening skyscrapers that dominate the stunning skylines of Shanghai, Beijing, or Shenzhen, but to a stereotypical Confucian edifice linked to the Great Wall; viewers might also suspect that the invading dragon is about to eat the tiny Statue of Liberty floating off on the right-hand side of the image. How this icon, so ubiquitous in Dragon Boat Festival imagery, to say nothing of ancient Chinese calligraphy and imperial prints, explains the postmodern world of transnational technology firms launching stock blowouts is anyone's guess.

It is important to note that these rhetorical patterns are just as prevalent within Chinese discourse about America, which has long been characterized in lurid, romantic, escalatory, and paranoid ways. For example, in a political cartoon from *China Daily* during the summer of 2014, Uncle Sam was caricatured as an oddly old-fashioned yet tech-armed cyber snoop assaulting a puzzled Chinese panda, who wants only to be left alone to rock out with music headphones. The sketch provides visual evidence of the trope of "traumatized nationalism," in which China—the slump-shouldered bear, all innocence and minding its own business—is portrayed as the target of Western aggression. Such a portrayal, if the valences were reversed, would certainly raise charges of racism, xenophobia, and yellow fever–mongering in the Chinese media, yet such images of the United States appear virtually daily in CPC-controlled outlets.[89] As these examples indicate, and as Engels feared, it would appear that the rhetorical work of imagining national communities in both the United States and China is based, in part, on stigmatizing and simplifying images that portray the Other as an enemy.

• • •

Against this historical and rhetorical backdrop, it is imperative for scholars who strive to think globally while eschewing any lingering Orientalist fantasies to jettison facile notions of either China or the United States as simplistic and coherent, either historically backward or superadvanced, comprised either of heathens or saints, or as amounting in any other way to places somehow outside of or above the same historical dilemmas, political complications, and economic forces that impact the rest of the world. Rey Chow has argued that the first step in thinking creatively about China is "to disengage from the monolithic notion that China is one culture,"[90] but surely that same recognition of complexity should be applied regarding the United States as well. This is why, in the following chapters, our authors strive to convey the awesome complexity of China, to say nothing of the United States, or India, or Tibet, or the other nations discursively configured in relation to China in the pages herein. Indeed, following a host of scholarship on nationalism(s) in the postmodern era, the authors in this collection, even when using condensing signifiers like "China" or "the United States," work from the assumption that nation-states are rhetorical constructions that overlay the massive complexities of daily life.[91] As noted by Louisa Schein in her ethnography of the Miao within China, scholars who speak of nationalities and cultures do so with the understanding that such concepts are always "produced, contingent, and deployable."[92]

And so the chapters included in this book address China and the United States not as monolithic, romanticized, feared, or incomprehensible Others, but as imagined communities made up of multilayered political conundrums, complex and often inchoate cultural appropriations, and wonderful communication opportunities. Building upon this commitment, the chapters in this book are unified by a rhetorical approach to national imaginaries, one that, reflecting broader trends within humanities scholarship, draws from a variety of methodological positions to address discourses of identity and belonging.[93] In so doing, whether the chapters use the conventional rhetorical method of hermeneutics, or close reading of primary texts, or computer-driven content analysis, whether the chapters offer analyses of visual rhetorics or present statistical summary, they each approach their subject matter with an eye toward the discourses that animate U.S.–China imaginaries. Drawing on multiple methods that derive from the nature of their questions, each chapter tracks "how specific symbolic patterns structure meaning and action" in relation to imagining China.[94]

Alongside the ethical commitments and methodological practices noted above, it is also important to address our relationships to national languages. Several of our authors study texts in Chinese, only to then write about them in English; some use texts they have translated from Chinese to English; others use commercially made English-language translations of Chinese texts; still others rely upon CPC-created English-language texts (as is the case with *People's Daily*, *China Daily*, and many of the other CPC-run sources cited throughout this study, which are pro-Chinese, English-based sources meant for foreign consumption). Consider the case of the exiled Tibetans addressed in Stephen Hartnett's chapter, for example, as their leaders have learned to publish their key documents in Tibetan, Chinese, and English at the same time, thus acknowledging their multiple, global audiences. Or consider the case of Ai Weiwei's provocations, which often hinge on his Chinese audiences being scandalized by their ability to interpret his works via the meanings embedded in them by what Chinese characters might mean or sound like when rendered in English. In these cases, the rhetorical work of imagining community hinges on an assumed transnational hybridity, on the circulation of ideas and images across multiple languages and cultural traditions. While some readers may wonder what gets lost within these processes of translation and influence, we want both to acknowledge the power dimensions involved in translation and to underscore that we always already live in the Tower of Babel in two key ways.[95] First, we stress that any assumption that one's analysis of texts written in their native tongue is somehow innately accurate is deeply flawed, as John Durham Peters has illustrated in his trenchant critiques of the transmission model of communication.[96] In short, all artifacts are polysemic, slippery, and multifaceted, regardless of the language in which they are rendered. Second, globalization has intensified the circulation of translations themselves, meaning that we are almost always already working within translational zones of encounter—being global citizens means working in and across a labyrinth of language games and interpretive models, none of which are, by definition, any more or less accurate than others.[97] Consider, for example, how generations of scholars have come to rely upon English-language translations of key critical theory scholars: How many authors citing Foucault can read him in French? How many authors citing Marx have read him in German? How many colleagues enraptured by Umberto Eco have read him in Italian? How many fans of Liu Xiaobo's polemics have read them in Chinese? As these questions indicate, we scholars have come to accept the use of translations—in a variety of forms and styles—as one of the inevitable tools for thinking across national language barriers. Rather than framing these issues as a "lack" or "problem," we see them as part of the invigorating work of thinking across national boundaries and as exercises in good will. And so, to promote transparency, our authors position themselves in relation to the translation practices they deploy while acknowledging their own subjective interpretive understandings and discussing how their varying translation practices circumscribe and/or enrich the nature of their claims.

We should note that the authors of these chapters represent a remarkable cross section of subject positions within our age of globalization. Some of our authors were born in China and now work and/or study in the United States and China, rotating between the two (Zhuo Ban, Xing Lu, Huiling Ding, and Jingwen Zhang); some of our authors were born and trained in the United States and now either work on and/or study in some capacity in China (Elizabeth Brunner, Stephen Hartnett, Leonard Hawes, Lisa B. Keränen, Kirsten Lindholm, Kent Ono, Jared Woolly, and Michelle Murray Yang); one of our authors was born to Taiwanese and American parents, raised and trained in the United States, and is now working full time in China (Patrick Shaou-Whea Dodge); one of our authors was born in India, trained in the United States, and now works in Singapore (Mohan Dutta); one of our authors was born in Canada, trained in the United States, and has worked in China and Singapore (Donovan Conley). The authors in this volume therefore embody globalization in practice and bring to their chapters many years of experience working in and on the United States, China, India, Tibet, Singapore, and Taiwan. Our chapters are therefore infused not only with concerns about and hopes for improved transnational communication, but also—and most importantly—with a deep love for the places we write about and live in.

•   •   •

Taken as a whole, the book offers readers insights into how a rising nation is imagining itself and others in an age of globalization, and how communication about the United States and China configures both nations at a time when the (alleged) security needs of states, the economic goals of transnational capitalism, the political hopes of nongovernmental organizations and cosmopolitan activists, the cultural aspirations of marginalized peoples, and the health risks that bind us come crashing together. While our political perspectives, methods of rhetorical analysis, and proposed routes forward may diverge, the authors in this volume believe these big issues will be the drivers of future U.S.–China communication, which in turn will impact the evolution of twenty-first-century global leadership. The daunting challenge that drives this project, then, is trying to make sense of the rhetorical work of imagining national communities, which can be compensatory and misguided, and/or empowering and ennobling, and/or infused with a sense of fear and loathing toward imagined Others. While these imaginings may be "perfectly tautological," as we saw Charland call them earlier, they can also be "utopian," as Jameson called them, meaning we enter our analyses with a sense of wonder, confusion, and hope.

Indeed, built on the concepts of mutual respect and intercultural friendship, and embodied in the transnational lives many of us lead, we proceed with the belief that creating better communication patterns in and about the United States, China, and our global neighbors will contribute to reducing the Orientalism, imperialism, and constant threat-construction paradigms that have soured U.S.–China relations for so long. At the Global China Summit, a business affair held in Washington, D.C., to discuss the future of U.S.–China economic cooperation, Cheng Lixin, a Shenzhen-based technology leader noted, *"the most important thing for us is communication. . . .* Telling Americans who we are, why we are here, and what we can bring to America."[98] This book encapsulates that ethic while expanding its scope of intentions: by offering readers rich case studies of communication in action, we hope to prompt informed debate about such questions as *what competing images of self and other can bring to the world.* In this way, *Imagining China* hopes to trigger a new round of rhetorical work wherein we collectively begin to imagine new and different national and perhaps even global communities.

NOTES

1. "Shirtsleeve summit" was the phrase used to market while downplaying the event; see the Sunnylands website (http://sunnylands.org), which contains photographs of Presidents Obama's and Xi's meeting as well as images from past diplomatic events at the site; and see Adam Nagourney, "A Retreat for the Rich and Powerful Is Opening Its Doors to the World," *New York Times*, January 23, 2012.

2. Wang Jisi, "Letter to the Editor," *Foreign Policy* 198 (January/February 2013): 8–9.

3. David Sanger, "Xi and Obama See Pitfalls that Might Be Difficult to Avoid," *New York Times*, June 10, 2013, A8; for rhetorical analysis of the diplomatic summit that launched modern U.S.–China relations, see Michelle Murray Yang, "President Nixon's Speeches and Toasts during His 1972 Trip to China: A Study in Diplomatic Rhetoric," *Rhetoric & Public Affairs* 14 (2011): 1–44.

4. Ian Bremmer, "Gathering Storm: America and China in 2020," *World Affairs*, July/August 2010.

5. "Remarks by President Obama and President Xi Jinping of the People's Republic of China after Bilateral Meeting," June 8, 2013, http://obamawhitehouse.archives.gov.

6. "A Forward Thrust in Sino–US Relations," *People's Daily*, June 8, 2013 and "Commentary: Xi–Obama Summit Opens New Chapter in China–U.S. Relations," *People's Daily*, June 10, 2013. *The Global Times* and *China Daily* coverage was similar.

7. For overviews of evolving U.S.–China relations, see Xing Lu, "From 'Ideological Enemies' to 'Strategic Partners': A Rhetorical Analysis of U.S.–China Relations in Intercultural Contexts," *Howard Journal of Communications* 22 (2011): 336–57, and James Mann, *The China Fantasy: Why Capitalism Will Not Bring Democracy to China* (New York: Penguin, 2007).

8. Bill Gertz, *The China Threat: How the People's Republic Targets America* (New York: Regency, 2000); Martin Jacques, *When China Rules the World* (New York: Penguin, 2009); Stefan Halper, *The Beijing Consensus: How China's Authoritarian Model Will Dominate the Twenty-First Century* (New York: Basic Books, 2010); Peter W. Navarro and Greg Autry, *Death by China: Confronting the Dragon—A Global Call to Action* (New York: Pearson Prentice Hall, 2011).

9. On "the rhetoric of war-hawk hysteria," see Stephen John Hartnett, "Google and the 'Twisted Cyber Spy' Affair: U.S.–China Communication in an Age of Globalization," *Quarterly Journal of Speech* 97 (2011): 411–34; the Congressional-Executive Commission on China's materials are accessible at https://www.cecc.

gov/; the Defense Science Board's website (http://www.acq.osd.mil/dsb/index.htm) offers reports along these lines; on the DSB as a premier threat-constructor, see Stephen John Hartnett and Gregory Goodale, "The Demise of Democratic Deliberation: The Defense Science Board, the Military-Industrial Complex, and the Production of Imperial Propaganda," in *Rhetoric and Democracy: Pedagogical and Political Practices*, ed. David Timmerman and Todd McDorman (East Lansing: Michigan State University Press, 2008), 181–224.

10. Gordon G. Chang, "The Party's Over: China's Endgame," *World Affairs*, March/April 2010; for a dire view on China's coming environmental catastrophe, see Richard Smith, "Creative Destruction: Capitalist Development and China's Environment," *New Left Review* I/222 (March–April 1997): 3–41.

11. See Andrew Nathan, Larry Diamond, and Mac Plattner, eds., *Will China Democratize?* (Baltimore, MD: Johns Hopkins University Press, 2013), and Bruce Gilley, *China's Democratic Future: How It Will Happen and Where It Will Lead* (New York: Columbia University Press, 2004).

12. See Guobin Yang, *The Power of the Internet in China: Citizen Activism Online* (New York: Columbia University Press, 2009).

13. For a review of this literature, see Hartnett, "Google and the 'Twisted Cyber Spy' Affair."

14. For a high-level and bipartisan report focused on rising tensions, see Kenneth Lieberthal and Wang Jisi, *Addressing U.S.–China Strategic Distrust* (Washington, D.C.: Brookings Institution, 2012); for a typical production of U.S. government insiders, see Bryan Krekel, George Bakos, and Christopher Barnett, *Capability of the People's Republic of China to Conduct Cyber Warfare and Computer Network Exploitation* (Washington, D.C.: U.S.–China Economic and Security Review Commission/Northrop Grumman, 2009). China's political elite also includes professional threat-constructors, in this case shrouded under the heading of fighting against "separatism," as argued in Wang Lixiong, "Independence after the March Incident," in *The Struggle for Tibet*, ed. Wang and Tsering Shakya (London: Verso, 2009), 223–51; his list of such Chinese institutions is on 224–25.

15. Mann, *China Fantasy*; James Bradley, *The China Mirage: The Hidden History of American Disaster in Asia* (New York: Little, Brown, 2014).

16. Mann, *China Fantasy*, xiii.

17. Dilip Gaonkar, "Toward New Imaginaries: An Introduction," *Public Culture* 14 (2002): 1–19, 7.

18. This amounts to the party line for the Obama administration, as seen in the posts

on the White House webpage (now located at http://obamawhitehouse.archives.
gov); for a public example of this line, see Vice President Joseph R. Biden Jr.,
"China's Rise Isn't Our Demise," *New York Times*, September 8, 2011, A25; for
an analysis of how China's leaders have sought to distance themselves from the
strident rhetoric of the Mao years, see Xing Lu and Herbert Simons, "Transitional
Rhetoric of Chinese Communist Party Leaders in the Post-Mao Reform Period:
Dilemmas and Strategies," *Quarterly Journal of Speech* 92 (2006): 262–86.

19. The key texts announcing the pivot are Secretary of State Clinton's "America's
Pacific Century," *Foreign Policy*, October 11, 2011, http://www.foreignpolicy.com,
and "Remarks by President Obama to the Australian Parliament," November
17, 2011, http://obamawhitehouse.archives.gov; for an overview, see Kenneth
Lieberthal, "The American Pivot to Asia," *Foreign Policy*, December 21, 2011,
http://www.foreignpolicy.com.

20. "Remarks by National Security Advisor Tom Donilon—As Prepared for Delivery,"
November 15, 2012, http://obamawhitehouse.archives.gov; and see "Remarks by
Tom Donilon, National Security Advisor to the President: 'The United States
and the Asia-Pacific in 2013,'" March 11, 2013, speech to the Asia Society, http://
obamawhitehouse.archives.gov; on the "pivot," see *Pivot to the Pacific? The Obama
Administration's "Rebalancing" Toward Asia* (Washington, D.C.: Congressional
Research Service, 2012).

21. Emanuel Pastreich, "Director Pastreich Statement for the 'United States Re-
Balancing in East Asia Seminar,'" speech of March 26, 2014, posted by the Asia
Institute, http://www.asia-institute.org.

22. The anonymous threat was posted on November 21, 2009, following "Obama
Calls for Tibet Talks," *Radio Free Asia*, November 18, 2009, http://www.rfa.org; on
the stalemate between China, the United States, and Tibet, see Stephen John
Hartnett, "'Tibet Is Burning': Competing Rhetorics of Liberation, Occupation,
Resistance, and Paralysis on the Roof of the World," *Quarterly Journal of Speech*
99 (2013): 283–316.

23. Chang, "The Party's Over"; for a dire view on China's coming environmental
catastrophe, see Smith, "Creative Destruction."

24. While more nuanced than Gertz, the title is nonetheless suggestive in Susan
Shirk, *China: Fragile Superpower* (Oxford: Oxford University Press, 2008).

25. Yang, *Power of the Internet in China*, 1, 221.

26. Eric Schmidt and Jared Cohen, "The Digital Disruption: Connectivity and the
Diffusion of Power," *Foreign Affairs* 89, no. 6 (November/December 2010).

27. The new "interconnected estate" will apparently include various products and services being streamed into the world's households via Google's private Air Force, for in April 2014 the technology giant acquired Titan Aerospace, the maker of "high-altitude, solar-powered drones." The passage quoted here is from the article announcing this sale: James O'Toole, "Google Buys Drone Maker Titan Aerospace," *CNN Money*, April 14, 2014, http://money.cnn.com.

28. For analysis of the *People's Daily*'s roles in Chinese life, written by a former editor of the paper, see Guoguang Wu, "Command Communication: The Politics of Editorial Formulation in the *People's Daily*," *China Quarterly*, no. 137 (1994): 194–211; in *Socialism Is Great! A Worker's Memoir of the New China* (New York: Anchor Books, 2008), Lijia Zhang notes that during her childhood in China, people joked that "the paper was so dull . . . it worked quicker than sleeping pills" (27).

29. Quotations from and links to stories following "U.S. Assertions of China Military Threat 'Groundless, Irresponsible,'" *People's Daily*, September 18, 2009; all *People's Daily* stories are archived at http://english.people.com.cn, but only back through 2010, so we can provide no live link for this story.

30. Rachel Lu, "China's Viral, Nationalist Screed against Western Encroachment," *ChinaFile*, December 6, 2013, https://www.chinafile.com.

31. Hartnett, "Google and the 'Twisted Cyber Spy' Affair," 413; and see Evan Medeiros, "Is Beijing Ready for Global Leadership?" *Current History* 108 (2009): 250–56.

32. We return to this Cold War–obsessed and anti-U.S. rhetoric below; for examples, see "Heart of the Pacific Matter," *China Daily*, May 21, 2014; Ruan Zongze, "Rising to the Security Challenges," *China Daily*, May 19, 2014, 9; Zhao Shengnan, "Experts Blast Hagel over 'Destabilizing' Accusations," *China Daily*, June 1, 2014, 1; and Zhao Shengnan, "West Still Can Hardly Get Used to China's Rise," *China Daily*, June 2, 2014, 2.

33. The "People's War" was announced by the Party and covered in Gu Liyan, "Fight Terrorism on All Fronts," *China Daily*, May 7, 2014, 9; the "3/11" terrorist attack at the railway station in Kunming, which injured over 140 and killed 29 innocent Chinese, had, by summer, led to wide support for this "People's War" against terrorists from Xinjiang. For a sampling of the fear and anger triggered by these attacks, see the blog postings listed under "Liveblog: Attack in Kunming," hosted by *China Digital Times*, http://chinadigitaltimes.net.

34. Territorial disputes in the South China Sea dominated news coverage and included some fantastical accusations of "plots" against Chinese sovereignty, as

in "ASEAN Leader 'Sends Wrong Signals on Conflict,'" *China Daily*, May 20, 2014, and Luo Yongkun, "Manila, Hanoi's Plots on South China Sea Will Never Succeed," *China Daily*, June 2, 2014, 4.

35. For representative stories, see "Cyberthief Crying Wolf," *China Daily*, May 21, 2014; Philip Cunningham, "The Pot Calls the Kettle Black," *China Daily*, May 23, 2014, 9; and Kong Chushan, "US's Industrial Cyber Espionage," *China Daily*, May 28, 2014, 9.

36. See Zhao Shengnan, "US Must Get Used to China's Rise," *China Daily*, May 22, 2014, and the stories in notes 32–35.

37. Interview with the authors, in Hong Kong, June 2014; all interviewees quoted in this chapter are cited anonymously to protect them from political retribution; the interviews were conducted in compliance with the terms established by the Colorado Multiple Institution Review Board protocol # 13-1348, as approved in May 2013 and renewed in May 2014.

38. Richard A. Lanham, *A Handlist of Rhetorical Terms*, 2nd ed. (Berkeley: University of California Press, 1991), 148.

39. Kenneth Burke, *A Rhetoric of Motives* (Berkeley: University of California Press, 1969), 190–91.

40. Ibid., 196.

41. Ibid., 197.

42. Karl Marx, *The Communist Manifesto*, ed. Frederick Bender, Norton Critical Edition (New York: W. W. Norton, 1988), 56.

43. Ibid., 57, 58.

44. Ibid., 61, 59; on the link between globalization and destruction, see Tyler Cowen, *Creative Destruction: How Globalization Is Changing the World's Cultures* (Princeton, NJ: Princeton University Press, 2004), and Stephen John Hartnett and Laura Ann Stengrim, *Globalization and Empire: The U.S. Invasion of Iraq, Free Markets, and the Twilight of Democracy* (Tuscaloosa: University of Alabama Press, 2006).

45. Marx, *Communist Manifesto*, 57, 58; and see the classic study that takes its name from this line, Marshall Berman, *All That Is Solid Melts into Air* (New York: Penguin, 1988).

46. Marx, *Communist Manifesto*, 59, 64, 66, 59.

47. Eric Hobsbawm, *The Age of Empire, 1875–1914* (London: Verso, 1987), 148, 326.

48. Kenneth Burke, *Attitudes toward History*, 3rd ed. (Berkeley: University of California Press, 1984), i.

49. Ibid., 7; on James's roles in helping to form a sense of the intellectual in public life, see Paul Stob, *William James and the Art of Popular Statement* (East Lansing: Michigan State University Press, 2013).

50. Burke, *Attitudes toward History*, 16, 35.

51. Michael C. McGee, "In Search of 'The People': A Rhetorical Alternative," *Quarterly Journal of Speech* 61 (1975): 235–49, 240.

52. Ibid., 242.

53. Fredric Jameson, *The Political Unconscious: Narrative as a Socially Symbolic Act* (Ithaca, NY: Cornell University Press, 1981), 9.

54. Ibid., 35.

55. Ibid., 79.

56. Ibid., 291.

57. Benedict Anderson, *Imagined Communities: Reflections on the Origin and Spread of Nationalism*, rev. ed. (London: Verso, 2006).

58. Ibid., 5.

59. Ibid., 7.

60. Maurice Charland, "Constitutive Rhetoric: The Case of the *Peuple Québécois*," *Quarterly Journal of Speech* 73 (1987): 133–50, 134.

61. Ibid., 137.

62. Ibid., 140.

63. See Michael Warner, "Textuality and Legitimacy in the Printed Constitution," *Proceedings of the American Antiquarian Society* 97 (1987): 59–84.

64. James Jasinski, "A Constitutive Framework for Rhetorical Historiography: Toward an Understanding of the Discursive (Re)constitution of 'Constitution' in *The Federalist Papers*," in *Doing Rhetorical History: Concepts and Cases*, ed. Kathleen J. Turner (Tuscaloosa: University of Alabama Press, 1998), 72–92, 75.

65. Ronald Walter Greene, "Another Materialist Rhetoric," *Critical Studies in Mass Communication* 15 (1998): 21–41, 22.

66. Ibid., 26.

67. Robert James Branham and Stephen John Hartnett, *Sweet Freedom's Song: "My Country 'Tis of Thee" and Democracy in America* (Oxford: Oxford University Press, 2002); and see Kelly Jakes, "*La France en Chantant*: The Rhetorical Construction of French Identity in Songs of the Resistance Movement," *Quarterly Journal of Speech* 99 (2013): 317–40.

68. Mary Stuckey, "One Nation (Pretty Darn) Divisible: National Identity in the 2004 Conventions," *Rhetoric & Public Affairs* 8 (2005): 639–56, 640.

69. Jennifer R. Mercieca, *Founding Fictions* (Tuscaloosa: University of Alabama Press, 2010); and see Joan Didion's book *Political Fictions* (New York: Vintage, 2002).

70. Derek Sweet and Margaret McCue-Enser, "Constituting 'the People' as Rhetorical Interruption: Barack Obama and the Unfinished Hopes of an Imperfect People," *Communication Studies* 61 (2010): 602–22, 603.

71. Jeremy Engels, *Enemyship: Democracy and Counter-Revolution in the Early Republic* (East Lansing: Michigan State University Press, 2010).

72. Hamilton Bean, Lisa Keränen, and Margaret Durfy, "'This Is London': Cosmopolitan Nationalism and the Discourse of Resilience in the '7/7' Terrorist Attacks," *Rhetoric & Public Affairs* 14 (2011): 427–64.

73. See Robert L. Ivie and Oscar Giner, "Hunting the Devil: Democracy's Rhetorical Impulse to War," *Presidential Studies Quarterly* 37 (2007): 580–98; Robert L. Ivie, "Fighting Terror by Rite of Redemption and Reconciliation," *Rhetoric & Public Affairs* 10 (2007): 221–48; and Donovan S. Conley, "The Joys of Victimage in George W. Bush's War of Totality," *Cultural Studies ⬄ Critical Methodologies* 10 (2010): 347–57.

74. Kent A. Ono and Joy Yang Jiao, "China in the US Imaginary: Tibet, the Olympics, and the 2008 Earthquake," *Communication and Critical/Cultural Studies* 5 (2008): 406–10.

75. Along with Ono and Jiao's piece from above, see Jie Gong, "Re-Imaging an Ancient, Emergent Superpower: 2008 Beijing Olympic Games, Public Memory, and National Identity," *Communication and Critical/Cultural Studies* 9 (2012): 191–214, and Le Han, "'Lucky Cloud' Over the World: The Journalistic Discourse of Nationalism beyond China in the Beijing Olympics Global Torch Relay," *Critical Studies in Media Communication* 28 (2011): 275–91.

76. For one example of this work, see C. Pan, C. Lee, J. Chen, and C. So, "Orchestrating the Family-Nation Chorus: Chinese Media and Nationalism in the Hong Kong Handover," *Mass Communication and Society* 4 (2001): 331–47.

77. Edward Said, *Orientalism* (New York: Pantheon, 1978), 71, 255; for additional discussion of Said and the postcolonial debates triggered by his work, see the first two chapters in this book.

78. Ono and Jiao, "China in the US Imaginary," 406, 407; for an antidote to such "Sinophobic" discourse, see the travel narratives in Peter Hessler, *Oracle Bones: A Journey through Time in China* (New York: Harper Perennial, 2006).

79. Jeff Wasserstrom, "A Century of American Dreams and Nightmares of China," *China Story* (blog), September 22, 2013, http://www.thechinastory.org.

80. Bradley, *China Mirage*.

81. For a case study of Orientalism at work, in this case in the contemporary fashion industry, see Anjali Vats and LeiLani Nishime, "Containment as Neocolonial Visual Rhetoric: Fashion, Yellowface, and Karl Lagerfeld's 'Idea of China,'" *Quarterly Journal of Speech* 99 (2013): 423–47.

82. Athanasius Kircher, *China Illustrata* (Amsterdam, 1667), as excerpted in Timothy Billings, "Strange Fruit and Fast Friends," *Folger Magazine*, Fall 2009, 8–17, 14–15; Kircher's rare book was displayed in *Imagining China: The View from Europe, 1550–1700*, an exhibition hosted by the Folger Shakespeare Library, Washington, D.C., December 2009.

83. Nathum Tate (1652–1715), *A Poem Upon Tea* (London: J. Nutt, 1702), 2.

84. Billings, "Strange Fruit and Fast Friends," 10.

85. Dean Acheson, *Present at the Creation: My Years in the State Department* (New York: W. W. Norton, 1969), 8; Bradley, *China Mirage*.

86. See Stephen John Hartnett, "The Folly of Fighting for Providence; or, the End of Empire and Exceptionalism," *Cultural Studies ⟺ Critical Methodologies* 13 (2013): 201–14, and Bradley, *China Mirage*.

87. Tani E. Barlow, "Colonialism's Career in Postwar China Studies," in *Formations of Colonial Modernity in East Asia*, ed. Barlow (Durham, NC: Duke University Press, 1997), 373–411.

88. The image appeared on the *Times*'s webpage first, under the byline of Vindu Goel, Michael J. De La Merced, and Neil Gough, "Chinese Giant Alibaba Will Go Public, Listing in U.S.," *New York Times*, May 6, 2014; it then landed on the front page of the business section alongside Peter Eavis, "Big Profits at Alibaba, But Filing Has Gaps," *New York Times*, May 7, 2014, B1—this version of the story included the headline, splayed atop the image, "The Dragon Makes Its Entrance."

89. See Wang Xiaoying's political cartoon from *China Daily*, May 23, 2014, 9; for an archive of such images, see http://www.chinadaily.com.cn/opinion/cartoon/.

90. Rey Chow, "Can One Say No to China?" *New Literary History* 28 (1997): 150; along these lines, see Susan K. McCarthy, "The State, Minorities, and Dilemmas of Development in Contemporary China," *Fletcher Forum of World Affairs* 26 (2002): 107–18; and Ralph Litzinger, "Theorizing Postsocialism: Reflections on the Politics of Marginality in Contemporary China," *South Atlantic Quarterly* 101 (2002): 33–55.

91. This literature is addressed in Michelle Murray Yang's chapter; for background, see Kent Ono, "Problematizing 'Nation' in Intercultural Communication

Research," in *Communication and Identity across Cultures*, ed. Dolores V. Tanno and Alberto Gonzalez (Thousand Oaks, CA: Sage, 1998), 193–202.

92. Louisa Schein, *Minority Rules: The Miao and the Feminine in China's Cultural Politics* (Durham, NC: Duke University Press, 2000), 13.

93. For work that discusses the combination of rhetorical and social science methods, see J. Blake Scott, Judy Z. Segal, and Lisa Keränen, "The Rhetorics of Health and Medicine: Inventional Possibilities for Scholarship and Engaged Practice," *POROI: An Interdisciplinary Journal of Rhetorical Analysis and Invention* 9, no. 1 (2013), Article 17.

94. Lisa Keränen, "'This Weird, Incurable Disease': Competing Diagnoses in the Rhetoric of Morgellons," in *Health Humanities Reader*, ed. Therese Jones, Delease Wear, and Les D. Friedman (New Brunswick, NY: Rutgers University Press, 2012), 36.

95. For a fascinating take on the transnational idiom and "World English," see Marco Jacquemet, "Transidiomatic Practices: Language and Power in the Age of Globalization," *Language & Communication* 25 (2005): 257–77.

96. John Durham Peters, *Speaking into the Air: A History of the Idea of Communication* (Chicago: University of Chicago Press, 2001).

97. Along these lines, see Robert Batchelor, *London: The Selden Map and the Making of a Global City, 1549–1689* (Chicago: University of Chicago Press, 2014).

98. Quoted in Tan Yingzi, "Chinese Businesses Want a Wider Door to the U.S.," *China Daily*, September 28, 2011.

Rhetorical Histories, Contested Nationalities, and Emerging Transcultures

Preface to Part One

Leonard C. Hawes

I n their introduction to this collection of essays, Stephen Hartnett, Lisa Keränen, and Donovan Conley propose three questions about the dilemmas and opportunities of U.S.–China communication in an age of globalization: What are the directions of these relations? What do we know about the ways we speak about, to, and against one another? And what are the forces driving those intercultural communication patterns? The editors suggest that framing the questions in terms of the "interlinked imaginaries" of the two nation-states provides opportunities to think about qualitatively different questions and projects. The "imaginary" is Jacques Lacan's name for the creation of a dual relationship in which each subject invents and misidentifies the other, confusing the Imaginary and the Real.[1] The three chapters that constitute Part One of this book can be read as offering three ways of making sense of the material and discursive relations that constitute these colossal "interlinked imaginaries," for they address how the world's two largest

economies—with massive armies and nuclear arsenals, plentiful but definitely finite natural resources, and the most sophisticated global media
technologies—invent the Other and then love, fear, and sometimes hate
its Other. Rather than doing the arduous intellectual and cultural work of
coming to know China on its own paradoxical terms, and thereby creating
different communication relations, many in the United States insist on
maintaining the imaginary while at the same time remaining steadfastly
unwilling to acknowledge their own constitutive paradoxes, a reluctance
China is more than willing to highlight as hypocrisy. The converse is the
case as well, as many in China too appear committed to portraying the
United States in terms more imaginary and fantastical than real. The
interlinked imaginaries discussed herein can be seen, then, as blocking
the kinds of authentic, genuine, fruitful encounters that could lead to
better U.S.–China communication.

Within this framework, the following three essays examine the rhetorical histories, contested nationalities, and emerging transcultures that
drive the interlinked imaginaries of the United States and China, which
appear to have produced sixty years of entrenched misunderstandings,
dangerously dysfunctional communication patterns, simmering rivalries,
and dramatically different conceptions of human rights. To address these
questions from within China, in the first chapter, Xing Lu maps several
long-standing rhetorical patterns within China and addresses the dilemmas President Xi Jinping and the Communist Party of China (CPC or
the Party) face as they try to cling to Mao-style rhetoric while building
a supercharged, globally linked, hypercapitalist economy. The rhetorical
exigency is spiritual as well, for since the late 1970s, China has been experiencing a religious awakening of arguably historic proportions, manifesting not only as relatively new religious groups such as the Falun Gong,
but as a reawakening of Buddhism, Daoism, Christianity, and Islam as
well, with each belief system standing in possible tension with Party
claims to legitimacy. This religious reawakening, and the Party's discom-
forts because of it, can be attributed in measure to the CPC's insistence
that Confucianism not be viewed as a religion in China.[2] The political
and rhetorical problematics in this regard for the CPC consist in managing the intersections of religious discourse, human rights discourse, and
Confucian discourse on the one hand, while at the same time reconciling

Maoist communist principles with its burgeoning market-capitalist global economy on the other. To make sense of this moment, Xing Lu listens to the ways President Xi Jinping and other Chinese intellectuals invoke Mao and his writings, particularly Mao's *Little Red Book*; she concludes with a provocative argument about the waning force of the rhetorical, philosophical, and certainly political voice of Mao in contemporary China. In this way, Xing Lu begins the book by offering us a sweeping overview of the rhetorical traditions that underwrite contemporary national imaginings in China.

In the second chapter, Michelle Murray Yang maps the dilemmas and opportunities of U.S.–China communication relations along the disputed and staunchly defended lines drawn by the dissident discourses of the human rights debate. Yang focuses on the recent controversy surrounding Chinese dissident Chen Guangcheng's internal critique of the CPC and his journey from China to the United States, on the one hand, and, on the other hand, Chen's growing dissatisfaction with and his eventual critique of U.S. hypocrisy in terms of allowing economic relations to trump human rights. By tracking Chen's movements from China to the United States, and by analyzing his dissident rhetoric against and within both nations, Yang demonstrates how some imaginings—in this case about supposedly transnational human rights—leap across national boundaries and traditional cultures, creating a new space of globalizing aspirations.

Switching from U.S.–Chinese debates about human rights to an examination of these questions on China's disputed southern border, in the third chapter Stephen Hartnett analyzes Tibet's alternative modernity under China's repressive occupation. Hartnett notes how China is modernizing itself and its Tibetan colony in accord with both its long-standing imaginary relation to Tibetan culture and the materially real model of axiomatic capitalism (more on this in a moment), thus building an alternative modernity that Tibetans refuse to recognize as anything other than colonialism, which in turn drives their struggle for freedom. Hartnett emphasizes the disorienting disjuncture between what China imagines it is doing in and to Tibet and what Tibetans claim is being done to them. Indeed, in both Yang's and Hartnett's chapters, we see how the imaginary creates communicative relations that are stifling, even oppressive, yet also laced with possibility, particularly as static notions about nationality weave into emerging notions of global civil society, what these authors call "transculture."

As foreshadowed in the introduction to this book, these chapters are deeply concerned with the unstable notion of nationalism. In China, the interlinked imaginaries have produced (among myriad other effects) China's long-standing rhetoric of what Hartnett, Keränen, and Conley call "traumatized nationalism," what Xing Lu diagnoses as the nation's current "Mao fever," and the post-Mao and post–Cold War dilemmas of reconciling China's expanding market economy with its Marxist-Maoist ideals of socialism and its occupation of Tibet. For the United States, the interlinked imaginary sounds and looks like a paranoid rhetoric of "war-hawk hysteria," which at times is articulated to rhetorics of "happy globalization" and, as Yang argues, to the Obama administration's controversial pivot to Asia. As these chapters illustrate, the imaginary can be fear-filled, as the issues raised here are often cloaked within rhetorics of "America [as] a declining empire" and a "coming Chinese century."

Thinking transculturally, these chapters illustrate how China struggles to articulate a CPC version of Mao-style communist political ideology to its economic model of axiomatic capitalism (which I will define below). For the United States, one of its key international challenges revolves around reconciling the contradictions between individual rights, liberties, and protections for each citizen, on the one hand, with collective guarantees of equal protection under the law and equal opportunity and access, on the other. Both the United States and China are witnessing an accelerating redistribution of wealth and a growing chasm between rich and poor, meaning both nations are struggling to argue for leadership models that appear linked to economic inequality. For example, Xing Lu examines some of the ways President Xi Jinping recuperates and deploys select Mao(ist) phrases in the interest of articulating a nostalgia for the clarity and directness of the principles and lessons gleaned from Mao's *Little Red Book*, while at the same time leading the nation into the murky waters of global capitalism. As all three chapters indicate, the age of globalization finds local rhetorical habits, moments, and artifacts—like Mao's *Little Red Book*, or Chen's claims regarding human rights, or Tibetan charges about cultural autonomy—jostling up against international forces, thus creating new, and global, means of persuasion and obliteration.

The relentless production of these interlinked imaginaries in and between the United States and China are similar in several significant respects. Most importantly, both nation-states are at work reconciling contradictions between their respective political ideologies and axiomatic capitalism. For Gilles Deleuze and Félix Guattari, world capitalism is axiomatic to the extent that it is a formal mechanism of distribution without political content or ideological substance.[3] Think of axiomatic capitalism as a system that is entirely operational, completely flexible, and multiply realizable—it is productivity and consumption on its own terms, without recourse to ethics, religion, or culture. China, for example, is in the process of reconciling its Maoist-communist values, principles, and practices to its new model of axiomatic capitalism, while the United States continues its efforts to reconcile liberal-democratic values, principles, and practices to its evolving model of axiomatic capitalism—in both cases dressing up axiomatic capitalism as if it reflects values that are long gone, or at least deeply compromised. I am suggesting, then, that we think of the United States and China as substantively different worlds with respective historical trajectories, cultural practices, and political ideologies that are nonetheless competitively struggling to appropriate the same formal (i.e., axiomatic) system, all while mistaking differences in degree between "democracy" and "communism" for a qualitative difference in kind. Yet each party is unwilling to acknowledge the common formative logic of the other's axiomatic model of global capitalism. My sense of the matter, however, is that what I am calling "axiomatic capitalism" is capable of absorbing virtually any qualitative ideological substance (whether democracy, or communism, or elite pluralism, etc.) while continuing to accelerate the circulation and distribution of commodities. Reframing U.S.–China communication patterns along these lines opens up different registers for deliberation and different logics of settlement and agreement. Indeed, approaching both the United States and China as equally important cogs in the international networks of axiomatic capitalism may provide a different and potentially rich and valuable way of reimagining U.S.–China relations.

What if the focus of the U.S.–China communication research agenda were to map deliberations and debates along the lines of a world-capitalist axiomatic logic of globalization? I would like to think that if such a research agenda were pursued, there would be more scholarly work along the lines of the following essays. Michelle Murray Yang traces a bit of China's invention of a U.S.-style democracy, manifested as living democratic principles of individual inalienable rights protected by a bill of rights and a constitution and exercised freely in daily life. The trajectory of Chen Guangcheng traces the arc of one Chinese human rights activist's conflict between his imaginary U.S.-style democracy and his eventual critique of its actual practices in the United States. In Chen's case, his protesting China's repression of individual human rights was fed by his interlinked imaginary with/of the United States. His expectations were made both rational and reasonable by means of the imaginary inventions of U.S.-style democracy and Chinese-style communism, but when the political economics of realpolitik violated Chen's expectations—in the pushing and shoving between the CPC's collectivist conception of rights and the U.S.'s individualist conception of rights—he became angry and felt betrayed when political economics trumped human rights. This same process, in which imaginary expectations crash against real practices, is confusing and enraging for many in the United States and China, thus rendering Chen's story a representative anecdote of intercultural misunderstanding.

Likewise, Hartnett's chapter vividly animates the frenetic "storm of progress" launched by China's colonizing of Tibet, including China's invention of Tibet as a Maoist-capitalist colony and its brutalizing a militarily defenseless country in the name of national defense. In this case, seemingly unregulated market capitalism manifesting in social and cultural chaos—even if coded as "progress" by the CPC—illustrates the costs of axiomatic capitalism. And this may be one of the several qualitatively different discourses available in and through which pragmatically necessary arrangements and agreements can be crafted. How do economic, philosophical, political, religious, scientific, and artistic discourses articulate to the actual and virtual empirical conditions of the material world? How do the discourses of liberal democracy and Maoist communism actually articulate to axiomatic capitalism in ways that account for its contradictions and paradoxes? And how do these questions impact local cultures, like Tibet, when they begin to enter the global networks of axiomatic capitalism? Responses to these interdependent questions go a long way toward addressing the question about whether China's immersion in axiomatic capitalism can ever bring liberal, U.S.-style democracy to China, Tibet, or Hong Kong.

While that last question is currently in vogue, I want to make clear that there are no necessary relations that articulate discourses of democracy to axiomatic capitalism. Moreover, if there are no necessary or automatic relations between the Imaginary and the Real, then axiomatic capitalism can articulate to democratic discourse as readily as it can to communistic discourse. In this sense, to question whether China's immersion in axiomatic capitalism will yield a U.S.-style democracy makes little, if any, sense, for the point of axiomatic capitalism is to convert its practitioners not to democracy but to capitalism. Indeed, models of axiomatic capitalism can assume a variety of material forms and contents; consider, for example, that global capitalism enmeshes the neoliberal models of the United States and Britain, the totalitarian model of Putin's Russia, and Xi Jinping's evolving Chinese model. So as long as the discourse remains on the plane of political philosophy—and the political philosophy of the United States is the product of Jeffersonian, desiring-individuality, while the political philosophy of China is a Confucian, desiring-collectivity— there appears to be little likelihood of any significant shift of comprehension, policy, or practice between the two nations. The interlinked imaginaries remain reciprocally locked in perpetual discord. The United States persists in reinventing a new-liberal democratic capitalist Chinese nationality predicated on individual rights (without much consideration of the attending obligations and responsibilities), which China does not recognize; and China continues reinventing a Confucian capitalist nationality predicated on collective rights, and the responsibilities, duties, and obligations that, when met, materialize as collective rights. Moreover, for reasons having to do less with axiomatic capitalism than with long-standing imaginary stereotypes, each side invents its Other in the least generous and most sinister terms possible, thus making it difficult to work through the rhetorical baggage toward something like mutual respect and understanding.

Another confusion contributing to the misidentifications bedeviling this imaginary is that both the United States and China are working more or less frantically in different ways to paper over their respective shames and traumas: the shame of the United States for having built its model of axiomatic capitalism on the backs and with the bodies of slaves, and on a land cleared and cleansed of its native populations, and the trauma, humiliation, and shame of China's colonial history with Japanese occupation, British intervention, and bloody civil wars. Hartnett, Keränen, and Conley describe these interlinked histories of shame, fear, and ambition as leading to China's rhetoric of "traumatized nationalism" and the U.S.'s rhetoric of "war-hawk hysteria." As the essays in Part One indicate, the sixty-year history of entrenched misunderstandings is working itself out in symmetrically variable but precipitously dangerous ways considering the scale of the two nations' economies, militaries, nuclear arsenals, natural resources, and media networks. The stakes are enormous. Nonetheless, the rhetorical problems and the questions that give rise to them can be addressed productively with critically informed responses such as the three chapters that follow.

NOTES

1. Jacques Lacan, *The Four Fundamental Concepts of Psycho-Analysis* (New York: W. W. Norton, 1978), 279–81.

2. For a brief discussion of this phenomenon, see Sébastien Billioud and Joël Thoraval, "*Jiaohua*: The Confucian Revival Today as an Educative Project," *China Perspectives* 4, no. 72 (2007): 4–20, and David Ownby, "Kang Xiaoguang: Social Science, Civil Society, and Confucian Religion," *China Perspectives* 4, no. 80 (2009): 101–11; for a more in-depth analysis, see Daniel Bell, *China's New Confucianism* (Princeton, NJ: Princeton University Press, 2008).

3. On axiomatic capitalism, see Gilles Deleuze and Félix Guattari, *A Thousand Plateaus: Capitalism and Schizophrenia* (Minneapolis: University of Minnesota Press, 1987), 460–73.

The *Little Red Book* Lives On: Mao's Rhetorical Legacies in Contemporary Chinese Imaginings

Xing Lu

During the height of his popularity, Mao Zedong, the founding father of the People's Republic of China (PRC), was revered as the "red sun" shining all over China and as the nation's savior from its semifeudal and semicolonial past. Before his death in 1976, and especially during China's Cultural Revolution (1966–76), books, films, songs, and theatrical performances were produced to adulate him; his portrait hung in every Chinese household; and his quotation book, known as the *Little Red Book*, was read every day by everyone. In all of these texts, Mao was celebrated for his contribution to establishing a communist China that touted equality, unity, independence, and a better life. I lived in China during this time and remember clearly how Mao was elevated to the status of a living god, resulting in mass hysteria, blind faith, absolute obedience, and cultish behavior among the Chinese people. Fervent devotion to his teachings and the absence of any alternative views made Mao the final arbiter of truth and knowledge, which ultimately led to acts of destruction and cruelty in the name of revolution and continued revolution.[1] Ironically, tragically, and maybe inevitably, Mao's extremism eventually destroyed the revolutionary legacy he had so painstakingly built; he created glory for China, but by the time of his death he also brought the country into chaos and to the brink of collapse. Succeeding leaders attempted to demystify Mao, evaluating him as "70 percent right and 30 percent wrong."[2] The assessment partially blamed Mao for the chaos and atrocities of the Cultural Revolution but still suggested his achievements for China far outweigh his failure. Thus, now almost seventy years since the communist revolution of 1949, Mao remains a colossal rhetorical influence on life in contemporary China. If the work of imagining nations depends, in part, on appropriating rhetorical resources inherited from prior generations, then Mao stands among the most important, even foundational, figures for helping China make sense of itself. Imagining China hinges on reimagining Mao.

Since Mao's death in 1976, China has moved toward Westernization and economic reform, resulting in a booming economy and the rapid improvement of living standards for the Chinese people.[3] However, at the same time, China has experienced alarming corruption and moral decline in the post-Mao era. In such contexts, Mao has been resurrected in various popular cultural forums as an emblem of all that China has lost because of its rapid modernization; especially among older Chinese, a sense of nostalgia for Mao's era has become popular. Indeed, what some observers call the "Mao fever" has risen so quickly that Mao is once again worshipped: taxi drivers hang Mao's portrait in their cars; Mao's badges are again worn by ordinary civilians; books, shows, and songs under the theme of "red classics" have again become popular. As observed by Melissa Schrift, "Mao, in spirit if not in body (his crystal-encased corpse in Tiananmen aside), is, indeed, alive and well in contemporary China."[4] In the celebration of Mao's 120th birthday, on December 26, 2013, thousands of people in Shaoshan (Mao's hometown) ate noodles together, sharing a traditional birthday meal while celebrating Mao's longevity.[5] In addition, the government media has published a large number of books and articles on Mao's life, while films and TV series have applauded Mao's infallible leadership during China's anti-Japanese war and civil war. These nostalgic and heroic tributes to Mao tend to extol his personal charisma, wisdom, and eloquence.[6] Because of the influence of Mao's writings, one can still hear Mao's sayings repeated in everyday conversations and online communications among the Chinese people. As Ross Terrill said vividly, "The real Mao has melded with China's body, like yeast in a loaf already baked."[7] In sum, even as China is emerging as a power with global reach, Mao's *Little Red Book* lives on.

In the post-Mao period of economic and political reforms, the Communist Party of China (CPC or the Party) has moved from Mao's ideological dogmatism toward pragmatism, as is evident in the nation's relaxed economic and foreign policies as well as the Party's increasingly de-radicalized rhetoric.[8] However, the CPC still faces the challenge of addressing the rhetorical exigencies caused by rising inequality, rampant corruption, alleged moral decline, and the wave of social unrest that has followed in the aftermath of the reforms. Indeed, it has been reported that strikes, protests, and petitions in both rural and urban areas have intensified throughout China: according to a report from the Europe China Research and Advice Network (ECRAN), public protests in China in 2012 ranged from a low of 180,000 events to as many as 230,000. The reasons for these protests vary from land disputes to economic inequality, from social injustice to environmental degradation, and from anger over rising prices to concerns about corruption.[9] Within this context, the post-Mao leaders of China face the dilemma of sustaining remarkable economic growth—achieved by transitioning from a central-planning, state-owned economy to a market economy—while simultaneously trying to appear to adhere to the Marxist-Maoist ideals of socialism. It should come as no surprise, then, to learn that the CPC's leaders have addressed this rhetorical exigency by invoking Mao's discourse, in essence by calling upon his legacy for the purposes of justifying the CPC's legitimacy, even while simultaneously breaking away from Mao's radical and utopian rhetoric. From this perspective, even economic reforms and political programs in 2016 are framed, justified, and debated in terms that invoke Mao and his complicated legacy—imagining a new China runs though Mao, even while appropriating his words and images in strange ways.

Thus, in this chapter, I attempt to make sense of the many ways Mao's rhetorical legacy lives on in contemporary China. To do so, I first identify the major characteristics of Mao's revolutionary rhetoric,

clarifying his main themes and styles. Then I trace Mao's rhetorical legacies as they have been appropriated by Chinese leaders in the post-Mao
period. In the next section, I address President Xi Jinping's speeches, as
his rhetorical tactics resemble closely those used by Mao. Throughout my
analysis, I contend that the CPC's current leaders use Mao's rhetorical
themes and styles as powerful means of persuasion, especially because
Mao's heroic legacy and anticolonial nationalism appeal strongly to a new
generation of Chinese citizens eager to see their nation as a rising global
power. Nonetheless, I propose that in order to sustain the CPC's legitimacy as the sole leading party of China, post-Mao Chinese leaders must
not just mimic certain useful aspects of Mao's rhetoric but should go
beyond Mao's legacy to engage and adapt to politically diverse as well as
rhetorically sophisticated audiences both at home and abroad. Indeed, in
my conclusion I argue that basing contemporary Party rhetoric on Mao's
legacy is placing significant rhetorical constraints on improving China's
communication with the world. Mao has been useful up to now, I argue,
but the time has come for a new era of rhetorical invention—the creative
work of imagining China needs to move past Mao.

Chinese Official Discourse

Traditionally, Chinese official discourse was used in the imperial courts
in exchanges between the emperor and ministers on state issues, in pro-
posals or arguments presented to the emperor in written or spoken form,
in a number of ritualized state settings, and in formal government decrees
or announcements. Within this highly structured imperial court context,
Chinese official language was characterized by its formality, observation
of courtesy, and conciseness. Such formal language was reserved for the
educated elites and government officials trained in the intricacies of Confucianism and diplomacy. In contrast, ordinary Chinese people spoke in
local vernaculars (*baihua*) and regional dialects (*fangyan*) in an informal
manner wedded to long-standing oral traditions. As Perry Link argues,
Chinese official language's "distinctive features separated it clearly from
everyday talk," which ordinary people preferred to use.[10]

During Mao's years, and especially during the Cultural Revolution, official, state language and private, vernacular languages were supposed to merge, as the Chinese people were expected to be politically correct, ideologically aligned, and linguistically enveloped within the CPC's discourse. In his seminal book, *Imagined Communities*, Benedict Anderson explains how the use of language evolved with and in part drove the construction of new forms of national consciousness in early modern Europe.[11] Although happening a century later, China's new communist version of nationalism was based in part on a similar process. Indeed, as part of this post-1949, Mao-led ideological and linguistic consolidation, Chinese citizens were encouraged—and, in many cases, forced—to fill their everyday language with quotations from Mao's *Little Red Book*. This communist indoctrination was so complete that ordinary people were expected to use official, Marxist/Maoist phrases to express their most private thoughts, such as in family conversations, personal diaries, and private letters. In a nation of abundant cultural and symbolic resources, Mao-era Chinese citizens were told to speak in and write with set phrases and political formulae meant to consolidate a new, Party-approved, national imagination. As this politicized language infiltrated people's private lives, many learned to monitor their choice of words, for they feared they would be persecuted if they said anything ideologically incorrect. For example, Mao's notion of "class struggle" divides people into the proletarian and bourgeois classes. According to Mao, everything must be viewed through the lens of class struggle, even love. In Mao's words, "it is a basic Marxist concept that being determines consciousness, that the objective realities of class struggle and national struggle determine our thoughts and feelings. . . . Now as for 'love' in a class society, there can be only class love."[12] And so, for the reasons noted above, "class struggle" became the dominant discourse that everyone was expected to use and conform to during Mao's years.

In fact, during the Cultural Revolution, the fear of violating language protocols was so great that partners wrote their love letters filled with revolutionary slogans on class struggle. In one example, a man wrote to his lover: "Nowadays class struggle is extremely complicated. There are all kinds of people in this world. You should stand firmly on your revolutionary ground. Never trust glib tongues and do not let class enemies take advantage of you. You should always tighten the string of class struggle when interacting with people at workplace and in social contexts." The woman replied: "I pledge in the name of revolution that I will stand firmly on my ground in facing complicated class struggle embedded in human relationships. I will handle well any kind of relationships. Please feel at ease."[3] As the letters indicate, "class struggle" became a banal slogan that moved from Chinese political discourse into private communication. By participating in this linguistic homogenization and political indoctrination, many Mao-era Chinese people turned themselves into what George Orwell has called the "thought police." In Orwell's imagined police state, words and sentences are carefully crafted for political purposes while the population is monitored to make sure it adheres to ideologically correct language habits.[4]

Because such public uses of Mao are not—and, some would argue, cannot be—criticized, Link has called this new Party rhetoric "officialese."[5] Link cautions, however, that such "officialese" is more than just an Orwellian means of repression, for, as noted above, within Chinese history there is a long tradition of approaching official language as a necessary and even noble means of conveying moral values.[6] Even as he sought to destroy the "olds" of ancient China—which Mao thought held the PRC back—he appropriated this traditional belief in the moralizing power of language for his purpose of achieving national unity. Thus, as was true in imperial and Confucian times as well, during Mao's years in power, speaking in and with the Party's line, or referencing Mao's words, indicated that the speaker was a moral person, a properly revolutionary citizen, and a strong nationalist.

However, the effectiveness of official language has dwindled severely in the post-Mao era, for the Chinese people are increasingly cynical about state-imposed revolutionary rhetoric and have even begun—in private, of course—to make fun of the CPC's official discourse. Such rhetorical inventions often use one of Mao's widely employed sayings, which are then ridiculed or changed for comical effect. This sly rhetorical creativity shows how many of Mao's sayings are believed to be outdated; at the same time, however, there are also still many public situations wherein Mao's sayings are deployed because they are seen as relevant and applicable. This ambiguity regarding how Mao's sayings fit (or not) within the changing context of contemporary China often leads to comic moments. For example, Perry Link offers the example of when a waiter at a Beijing restaurant jokingly said "serve the people"—a classic line from Mao—while serving food to Link and his Chinese friends, who all laughed at the insertion of a heroic communist phrase into the daily functions of a restaurant. As Link observes, "the Maoist slogan was highly incongruous, and therefore funny, to insert into such a relaxed and informal context."[17] In this sense, people in China sometimes approach Mao's slogans via what Kenneth Burke calls "the comic frame," thus enabling them, by poking fun at Mao, to criticize China's rigid political system.[18] It is important to note, however, that appropriating Mao's sayings for comic effect only takes place in private settings. In fact, when Mao is quoted in official, public contexts, the speaker, usually a Party official, tries to marshal Mao's sayings as unimpeachable evidence of the righteousness of his or her arguments, to present him- or herself as an ethical and properly nationalist leader, and to invoke the heroic legacy of Mao as the ultimate champion of the people. Thus, even as the Chinese strive to imagine a new nation, they call upon the legacies of Mao as rhetorical resources.

Indeed, even in the post-Mao context, the CPC's official language is still used by government-controlled media outlets—including newspapers, radio, TV, political meetings, websites, and speeches—to set the tone and range of agreed-upon jargon that is then regurgitated throughout other official channels and Party apparatus. These Party propositions and policy announcements are usually structurally rigid and repetitive, often rely on moral appeals that feel like clichés, avoid policy details for vagueness, and use euphemisms. Michael Schoenhals thus describes Chinese Party rhetoric as a "formalized language" that relies upon mind-numbing jargon to reproduce state-supporting dogma. Schoenhals argues that far from the Confucian model of deploying elegant language in teaching morality, this formalized Party language has become a tool of coercion meant to impose severe limits on creative political debate.[19] Still, as I demonstrate below, the current Chinese official language has lost much of its persuasive effectiveness for the ironic reason that it has failed to carry on Mao's rhetorical legacy.

Imagining a Revolutionary Nation; or,
the Major Characteristics of Mao's Rhetoric

Having lived in China during the Cultural Revolution and having studied Mao's writings closely, I have come to believe that Mao's revolutionary rhetoric provides the foundation for the banality of current Chinese official language. In other aspects, however, the current Chinese official language has lost its persuasive effectiveness precisely because it has failed—in the great rush to become an economically powerful nation—to carry on Mao's rhetorical legacy, particularly his commitment to equality, as embodied in his well-known call to "serve the people." To make sense of this complicated rhetorical context, I will describe here the four major goals of Mao's rhetoric: to advocate for the moral legitimacy of Marxism-Leninism; to call upon the Party and all revolutionary Chinese to serve the people; to engage in criticism and self-criticism; and to construct a triumphant sense of nationalism. Once I have established the contours of Mao's rhetoric, I will then, in subsequent sections of analysis, discuss how his legacy has been appropriated by succeeding Chinese leaders. As my analysis demonstrates, imagining China by appropriating Mao amounts to a delicate balancing act, where leaders strive to honor Mao's known ideals even while shading them toward new meanings.

The first major thrust of Mao's rhetoric, portraying the moral legitimacy of Marxism-Leninism, depicts Marxism as the only historically accurate, politically sound, and morally tenable ideology for the Chinese people. However, to make this foreign, Western-inspired, radical ideology acceptable for China, Mao needed to present a convincing argument that Marxism was indeed applicable not only to Europe's already industrialized nations but to China's mostly agrarian situation as well. Thus, in 1938, Mao proposed "to apply Marxism concretely in China so that its every manifestation has an indubitably Chinese character."[20] In other words, Marxism would be reinterpreted and adapted to the Chinese context and measured by Chinese values. This "sinification of Marxism," as Nick Night argues, was "an attempt to establish a formula by which a universal theory such as Marxism could be utilized in a particular national context and culture without abandoning the universality of that theory."[21] This appropriation of Marxism enabled Mao to build a Communist Party with

Chinese characteristics, thus leading the revolution by incorporating the traditional Chinese values of hierarchy, loyalty, and self-cultivation.

While he adapted radical European doctrines to the Chinese situation, there is no doubt that Mao was an ardent believer in Marxism, especially its theory of class struggle. He was inspired by the Soviet Revolution of 1917 and was a good student of Lenin, adhering throughout his life to the Soviet doctrine of social transformation led by a proletarian dictatorship. Indeed, Mao devoted his life to preaching and executing the Marxist theory of class struggle, and he accordingly—despite China's largely preindustrial status up through the revolution—divided the Chinese people into two classes: proletarians and bourgeoisie. For Mao, the former embodied an advanced and correct consciousness, earned through the hard lessons of lifetimes of labor and exploitation, and thus were entitled to exercise political leadership; the latter represented a corrupt bureaucratic-capitalist class that was morally defective, aligned with a history of colonialism, and doomed to defeat at the hands of communism. This Marxist version of change was so attractive to Mao's view of social development that he assumed "all other countries will inevitably take" this same path.[22] Throughout his life, as a consequence of this theory of inevitable and constant struggle, Mao fought with external threats and internal class enemies. External threats consisted mainly of American and Japanese imperialists and Chiang Kai-shek (whom the U.S. government supported, as part of its Cold War efforts against communism), while internal enemies were intellectuals, high-ranking officials who threatened Mao's rule, and any vestiges of the bourgeoisie within the nation. Guided by conspiracy theories and this dualistic thinking, Mao constantly fought with real or imagined "class enemies," creating a culture of constant danger, backroom purges, and countless persecutions. The rhetorical work of imagining the nation often hinges on the production of enemies. Thus, at the core of Mao's rhetoric, we find a lifelong commitment to eliminating enemies, justifying the need for class struggles, and portraying all political life as warfare.

Even when deploying the trope of "democracy," Mao stressed the centrality of struggle. In their article "The Constitutive Rhetoric of Democratic Centralism: A Thematic Analysis of Mao's Discourse on Democracy," Canchu Lin and Yuen-Ting Lee posit that "Mao's concept of democracy was linked with his notion of class struggle" and was "associated with Communism as opposed to capitalism."[23] For Mao, only the proletarian or working class was entitled to practice democracy. The bourgeoisie or bureaucratic-capitalist class only deserved the proletarian dictatorship and thus had no right to practice democracy. But Mao's categories of these two classes constantly changed. A person could be a member of the proletarian class one day, yet be charged as a member of the bourgeoisie the next day simply because he or she said something against the Party or challenged Mao's doctrines. Nonetheless, in many places, Mao claimed that fighting for democracy was the main task of his Party; he often promised a democratic China under his leadership.[24] Still, Canchu and Lee observe that "Mao's idea that democracy does not apply to counter-revolutionaries reveals the dictatorial nature of his proletarian democracy."[25]

If the first key part of Mao's rhetoric offers communist versions of revolution and democracy adapted to the Chinese context, the second theme of his rhetoric is "serving the people." Coming from a peasant family background, Mao claimed to be a representative of the "working class," whom he argued made up the vast majority of Chinese people (even though they were not, technically speaking, part of a European-style working class). Throughout his writings, Mao emphasizes the message of "serving the people wholeheartedly," requesting Party members and intellectuals to abandon their elitist attitudes and mingle with the masses.[26] Mao was so convinced of the moral superiority of the working class that he called upon Party members and intellectuals to learn from workers, peasants, and soldiers and to glorify their life experiences. As a logical corollary to this Marxist version of class struggle, Mao stated that "all our literature and art are for the masses of the people, and in the first place for the workers, peasants and soldiers."[27] He devoted a number of his speeches and writings to how to serve people, how to connect with people, and how to use their language to identify with and persuade them. This concept of serving the people is a rhetorical strategy to ensure a "Mandate of Heaven" in governing, a concept rooted in the Confucian tradition. Mencius, in particular, coined the notion that "those who win the hearts of people will win the world."[28] Mao was keenly aware that he would not be able to win the revolution and lead the nation without the support of the majority of Chinese people, including elites, experts, or intellectuals, yet he hoped to transform their thinking and work habits into supports for proletarian consciousness. This explains why, in many places in his writing, Mao warns Party members to be modest, to endure hardship, to be thrifty, and to never separate themselves from the masses.[29] At its core, this trope of "serve the people" calls for a radical shift in the social hierarchy and the mindset driving class relations, all while singing the tune of Confucian values to pursue communist notions of a harmonious collective. Ironically, Mao's authoritarian leadership did not allow the Chinese people to voice dissenting views. From this perspective, the rhetorical work of imagining a new, revolutionary China hinged, in part, on controlling the masses, who were not meant to invent, or contribute to inventing, new narratives, but rather, to follow the new imaginings authored by Mao and the Party.

The third theme of Mao's rhetoric is the employment of criticism and self-criticism as an approach to becoming a "new communist person." Because of his literary habits and training in Chinese classics, Mao was, to a large degree, a Confucianist. A major component of Confucian teaching is self-cultivation, which is the rudimentary quality for maintaining a good family and strong relationships with others and for making a contribution to one's own country and subsequently to the rest of the world.[30] Mao approached the idea of moral perfection by teaching how one can become a "new communist person."[31] In its ideal Confucian and early Maoist phases, the process involved a diligent study of moral exemplars, constant self-introspection, and engagement of criticism and self-criticism.[32] Once in power, however, such self-criticism became a central component of repressive communist politics, as millions of Party members, intellectuals, and ordinary Chinese people were forced to participate in criticism and self-criticism sessions—often called "struggle sessions"—during countless political campaigns. In a typical criticism and self-criticism session, intellectuals and Party members were expected to denounce their past "selfish thought," "immoral behavior," and/or "erroneous views."[33] On the surface, these moral qualities resonate with the Confucian notion of becoming a gentleman, but Mao politicized these values for specific purposes. For example, intellectuals were expected to report how they would work hard to overcome their "ideological disease," thus moving closer to becoming a new communist person under Mao's guidance. Millions of them were deprived of their dignity and were forced to fabricate their purported crimes as well as the wrongdoings of others. Betraying friends and family members was common. The "new communist person" was to be selfless, loyal to Mao and the Party, and willing to sacrifice for the country, yet these goals often shaded into political repression, naming names, and fabricating evidence; in the name of moral improvement, millions of lives were crushed.

The fourth theme of Mao's rhetoric is nationalism. Many Chinese people agree that Mao is a national hero. The key to Mao's version of nationalism was eliminating the shame caused by the "century of humiliation" brought upon China by unfair treaties and foreign military invasions.[34] Story-telling is one of the rhetorical techniques Mao used to construct Chinese nationalism. In "On the People's Democratic Dictatorship," Mao begins his narrative of China's victimization by Western aggression. He asserted that China's modernization was interrupted by Western military powers and colonization and that Chiang Kai-shek's government had failed to lead China. Thus, China had no choice but to adopt Marxism-Leninism, and the CPC was the only legitimate force for building China's future.[35] In such stories, as is consistent with Marxism broadly, the end is known from the beginning: the nation will be saved by a communist revolution. In contrast to the sometimes impenetrable density of Marx's writings, however, or to the high theory of Lenin's, Mao's narrative version of communist nationalism was folksy, accessible, and highly visionary. For example, in one piece Mao makes this emotional plea: "All comrade commanders and fighters of our army! We are shouldering the most important, the most glorious task in the history of our country's revolution. We should make great efforts to accomplish our task. Our efforts will decide the day when our great motherland will emerge from darkness into light and our beloved fellow-countrymen will be able to live like human beings and to choose the government they wish."[36] Mao's nationalistic rhetoric recounts China's humiliating past as a prelude to envisioning a bright future made possible by making hard choices in the present.

Mao also personified nationalism through his tough rhetoric on foreign relations, where Mao took a strong stand against the United States and later against the Soviet Union, in both cases refusing to bend to the demands of the two powerful rivals.³⁷ In his words, "China must be liberated, China's affairs must be decided and run by the Chinese people themselves, and no further interference, not even the slightest, will be tolerated from any imperialist country."³⁸ Mao's nationalism was so strong that even when China was struggling to rebuild after World War II and its own long civil war, he vowed that China would surpass the Western world in economic output and military power.³⁹ As Mao wrote on September 16, 1949, "Of all things in the world, people are the most precious. Under the leadership of the Communist Party, as long as there are people, *every kind of miracle* can be performed. . . . We believe that *revolution can change everything*, and that before long there will arise a new China with a big population and a great wealth of products, where life will be abundant and culture will flourish."⁴⁰ As the italicized passages indicate, Mao's nationalism contained a sense of hope and promise bordering on the miraculous. By embodying this optimism, Mao established himself as an admired leader and an inspiration to many in the Third World, simultaneously railing against imperialism while dreaming of building a powerful and prosperous China. Mao's rhetoric of hope and promise, and his use of earthy language and emotional appeals, was tremendously effective for agitating nationalistic sentiments among the Chinese. Indeed, as we will see below, Mao's revolutionary and miraculous nationalism remains one of the most popular aspects of his rhetorical legacy.

The Post-Mao Imaginings of Deng Xiaoping, Jiang Zemin, and Hu Jintao

Mao died in 1976, bringing the turbulent Cultural Revolution and his radical doctrine to an end. As observed by Andrew Walder, "Mao Zedong left China in a quiet crisis, an unsettled state and society very much in flux."⁴¹ The primary tasks of the new Chinese leaders were to rescue a devastated economy, demystify Mao's god-like image, and begin to build a functional government. By this time, many if not most of the Chinese people had lost faith in Mao's utopianism—and especially the unending cycle of political movements—and were longing for a better life, particularly in light of a decade of Cultural Revolution, when China's economy collapsed, the CPC faced severe challenges to its legitimacy and felt the strong need to provide incentives for economic development. The problem, however, was that Mao's revolutionary mission and commitment to communism meant the CPC could not claim that China would take the route of capitalism, even though capitalism has proved to be a more effective system for economic development. In the midst of this ideological crossroad—with post-Mao China needing to learn the lessons of capitalism, the former enemy—the new Chinese leaders were compelled to remap the rhetorical route for the Party, to redefine the rhetorical situation, and to come up with rhetorical strategies that could pave the way for post-Mao national imaginings. To do so, the CPC launched unprecedented reforms, which ultimately affected all areas of day-to-day life in China, particularly regarding the economy and foreign policy. To explain these reforms to the people, the CPC's post-Mao leaders crafted new slogans and linguistic formulations to legitimize the reforms and consolidate the CPC's rule. Still, hemmed in by Mao's enormous influence, the Party had to reimagine Chinese "officialese" while not appearing to break with Mao's legacy. Thus, over four successive generations of post-Mao leadership, each top official coined his own slogans in a way that separated himself from Mao while simultaneously appropriating Mao's rhetoric to maintain political legitimacy; these leaders struggled to be seen as both apart from and a part of Mao's legacy. This explains how China's leaders, since 1976, have all emphasized the Maoist ideals of living a moral life, serving the people, and building a strong nation, even as they sought to justify the dynamic—and clearly not communist or revolutionary—ways China embraced capitalism to secure economic reforms.[42]

For twenty-seven years (1949–76) under Mao's rule, China claimed itself as a socialist country with a communist ideology, yet by the end of the Cultural Revolution, China was in chaos and at the brink of economic collapse.[43] The Chinese people were disillusioned about the communist ideology and were uncertain about China's future. Deng Xiaoping, the first paramount leader in the post-Mao period, faced the rhetorical exigency of the CPC's crisis in legitimacy, triggered in large part by the people's demands for a better life. In response, Deng coined the term "socialism with Chinese characteristics," which he first used at a July 1981 meeting with Jin Yong, a fantasy book writer and the head of the Hong Kong weekly journal *Ming Bao*. The term signaled a departure from the Maoist utopian path within an acceptable framework of socialist norms. The phrase then entered widespread usage following a meeting with a Japanese delegation, when Deng gave a speech titled "Building Socialism with Chinese Characteristics."[44] Deng justified this ambivalent yet strategic position with a famous Mao quote: "Practice is the sole criterion for measuring truth," implying that change was necessary given the imminent demands for a better life.[45] He also emphasized that the change of direction was aligned with Mao's political ambition in building a strong, independent, and prosperous China. In short, Deng appropriated Mao's nationalism while jettisoning his radical commitment to communism.

Even while making this political turn, Deng showed his loyalty to Mao's commitment to socialism and his aversion to capitalism. In practice, he encouraged borrowing and learning from capitalist countries in science, technology, investment, and management, yet in his public comments Deng asserted that "a capitalist system is profit-driven; it cannot rid itself of exploitation, pillage, and economic crisis."[46] In another speech, Deng reiterated that "China must adhere to socialism. Capitalism will not work in China. If China took the path of capitalism, its chaotic situation would never end; its poverty would never be changed."[47] At this point in the early 1980s, many Chinese people still held Mao's belief that only socialism could guarantee equality and prevent exploitation. Because fears over the evils of capitalism, as proclaimed in Mao's discourse, still lingered, Deng's response sought to address the necessity for change while not deviating too much from Maoist ideals. Thus, by employing the fear of capitalism and the rhetoric of promise for a better life, Deng sustained Mao's moral legitimacy while sanctioning a new market economy and expanded international trade.

Deng's coinage of the term "socialism with Chinese characteristics" is an example of what Fengyuan Ji calls linguistic engineering, "the attempt to change language in order to affect attitudes and beliefs."[48] Indeed, Deng's term was strategically ambiguous and rhetorically paradoxical, encouraging capitalist innovations and private ownership while retaining segments of the former, state-owned economy and ongoing Party control. In the cities, people were given the freedom to start their own business, workers were encouraged to buy stocks of their factories, and foreign investors were allowed to launch joint-venture enterprises. In rural areas, peasants were encouraged to grow crops for sale in local markets, the People's Communes were dismantled, and peasants were allowed to migrate to the cities to work. These changes in daily life overturned Mao's dualistic philosophy, which divided economic life into warring social classes, and integrated formerly segregated levels of production into an evolving capitalist economy. In a significant way, Deng's phrase was designed to rescue the CPC from its weakening mandate and reset the political agenda in China: in fact, by moving away from Mao's rhetorical purity to the practical improvement of the material well-being of the Chinese people, Deng's "socialism with Chinese characteristics" enabled the nation to move forward. In this sense, Deng's language engineering is a prime example of what Donald Bryant defines as the function of rhetoric: "adjusting ideas to people and people to ideas."[49]

Deng Xiaoping passed away in 1997, leaving China with a rapidly growing capitalist economy, but also, as Mao and the communists had feared, increased corruption, mounting unemployment, environmental degradation, and a widening gap between the rich and poor. For example, according to Reuters reporter Kim Kyung-Hoon, by 2013 there were 2.7 million millionaires and 251 billionaires in China while 12 percent of Chinese people still lived on less than $1.25 per day.[50] Deng's reforms had triggered a historically unprecedented period of economic growth yet also led to China's economy, like that in the United States, creating patterns of gross inequality. Moreover, many businessmen and businesswomen who acquired new wealth from engaging in China's new market economy were recruited into the Party, tying their business interests to the political clout of the Party, thus creating the sense that the CPC was not catering to the needs of the people. The moral legitimacy of the CPC, which under Mao was linked to serving the masses, was therefore severely questioned by those who thought Deng's reforms had gone too far down the road of capitalism.

Jiang Zemin, Deng's successor, bore the burden of justifying the Party's rule and appeasing the rising tide of discontent. To do so, Jiang proposed "The Three Represents" as the key to the Party's post-Deng pursuit of moral legitimacy.[51] Within this model, the Party represents the demands for the development of advanced productive forces, the forward direction of advanced culture, and the fundamental interests of the great majority of Chinese people. The coinage was first introduced in a speech on February 25, 2000, during his trip to Guangdong Province.[52] Part of Jiang's rhetorical dilemma was that as Deng's economic reforms had created new wealth, so the Party had to find ways to represent itself as the vanguard of both the working class and the new entrepreneurs/capitalists: from proposing class warfare between the proletariat and the bourgeoisie, the Party now needed to play the role of mediator between and champion of both classes. At the same time, Jiang was still expected to pay lip service to Marxist-Maoist rhetoric by acknowledging Mao's and Deng's heroic contributions to the well-being of the nation.[53] For example, in his speech at the Sixteenth Party Congress in 2001, Jiang said that "Whatever difficulties and risks we may come up against, we must unswervingly abide by the Party's basic theory, line, and program. We should persist in arming the entire Party membership with Marxism-Leninism, Mao Zedong Thought, and Deng Xiaoping Theory, and use them to educate our people."[54] By invoking Mao, Deng, and Marxism-Leninism, and by using the military notion of "arming" the Party and the masses, Jiang sought to justify an era of capitalist development while simultaneously wrapping himself within Mao's nationalistic discourse.

In this context, the first two "represents," as coined by Jiang, served as code phrases for the Party's mandate to continue with economic reform and Westernization. "Representing advanced productive force" implied the Party's determination to continue free market economic development; "representing advanced culture" could be interpreted as arguing for the adoption of cultural forces (science, entertainment, education, and so on) from outside China. "Representing the vast majority of Chinese people" is meant to reiterate Mao's pledge of the Party to serve the people, thus ensuring that the first two represents will be employed for nationalist purposes and the benefit of the people. In this sense, Jiang continued Mao's legacy of justifying the Party's actions as always focusing on strong nation-building and providing a better life for the Chinese people: Jiang waved the flags of his predecessors when justifying new imaginings.[55]

Hu Jintao succeeded Jiang Zemin as the Party's general secretary in November 2002, becoming the third president of China in the post-Mao era. While China's economy continued to boom under Hu's leadership, the nation paid the heavy price of increased disparity between the rich and poor, rampant corruption among high-level Party officials, and moral decline in society. As Kerry Brown notes, "The question facing Hu when he came into office was what to do about the huge differences between the rich and the poor across the country."[56] As mentioned earlier in the chapter, these conditions gave rise to a wave of Mao nostalgia, wherein many Chinese citizens sought refuge from the new world of uncertainty and inequality by recalling memories of Mao's "iron rice bowl" society. In response to this rhetorical exigency, Hu made repeated references to the Confucian phrase "putting people first" and stressed Mao's legacy of serving the people. For example, in a speech celebrating the eighty-second birthday of the CPC, Hu expounded this concept to Party members:

> Party officials at every level should solidly establish the mindset of serving the people and the spirit of honesty to and responsibility for the people. They must exercise their power for the people, build an emotional bond with the people, and seek benefits for the people. They must solve concrete problems for the people, make every effort to handle difficult situations for them, persistently doing good deeds for the sake of people, and always place people's interest above everything else.[57]

By 2001, however, such appeals to Maoist promises and Confucian values were beginning to sound hollow; as the gap continued to expand between the Party's rhetorical appeals to Mao's communism and the daily reality of capitalism gone wild, the people became restive, again putting CPC legitimacy in question.

Recognizing the difficulty of the situation, Hu traveled in December 2002 to Xibanpo, Mao's revolutionary base, where he used both traditional and Maoist slogans in calling for "arduous struggle" and "plain living." Hu quoted Mao's "two musts": "[The Party members] must keep the virtues of modesty, caution, humbleness, and calmness; [they] must continue to maintain the party's tradition of plain living and arduous struggle."[58] Mao gave these admonitions to Party officials when he took control of China in 1949. Hu's visit to Xibanpo sent a warning about corruption among

Party members, thus showing his alignment with Maoist values while also invoking the Confucian norms of "modesty, caution," and plain living. More than Mao, Deng, or Jiang, Hu thus signaled a willingness to use the rhetoric of his predecessors while also looking even farther back into Chinese history, and so Hu began to move further away from portraying China as a revolutionary, communist, and anti-imperial state, instead seeing the nation in an even longer, civilizational lens rooted in Confucian values. In Hu's hands, the rhetorical work of imagining the nation meant fashioning a postcommunist China that was indebted to Mao yet also to Confucius.

In *The Ideal Chinese Political Leader: A Historical and Cultural Perspective*, Xuezhi Guo notes that "in modern Chinese political thought, the notion of benevolent government is related to at least three central components: social equality, wealth of the people, and national greatness."[59] These were among the foundations of Mao's promises to the Chinese people when he founded the PRC in 1949. As shown here, versions of these themes have infused the post-Mao rhetoric of Deng, Jiang, and Hu as well, even as they have slowly tried to steer the nation away from Mao's version of revolutionary communism. Within this lineage, Hu's rhetoric of "putting people first" is an effort to redirect national priorities from economic growth at any price to developmental balance, from encouraging entrepreneurship to crackdowns on corruption. Hu's efforts were not as successful as the Party hoped, however, which meant that when Xi Jinping assumed leadership in 2012, he inherited a rhetorical legacy increasingly depleted, fractured, and out of step with daily life in China.

President Xi Jinping's Renewed Nationalism

Since he took office as China's president in November 2012, Xi Jinping has delivered a number of speeches to domestic and international audiences making it clear that Xi is not a charismatic speaker, like Mao, yet he has built a reputation for being calm, down-to-earth, hardworking, and deeply committed to renewing China's sense of its central place in global politics. He is, above all else, a strong nationalist. His father was

a high-ranking official and contemporary of Mao Zedong who was persecuted during Mao's era; as a young man, Xi was sent to a poverty-stricken
village to labor for seven years, leading Ho Pin to speculate that Xi's "past
sufferings will most likely make him an advocate of ordinary people's
interests."[60] He then held a number of local and provincial leadership
posts in the post-Mao era, meaning that President Xi has experienced
many aspects of the transformation of China from Mao's era to Deng's
period of economic reform. Cheng Li believes that Xi's "arduous and
humbling experiences," like other fifth-generation Chinese leaders, will
help him to "cultivate valuable traits such as endurance, adaptability,
and humility."[61]

Although China still faces problems of rampant corruption, inequality, moral decline, and social injustice in the aftermath of the economic
reforms, many Chinese believe that Xi Jinping has the courage and capability to tackle these issues. Because of his family history, and his record
of accomplishments, he is considered a good "princeling."[62] Unlike his
predecessors, as observed by William Overholt, Xi "has the confidence
that comes from being a princeling and from having some military background."[63] Also unlike his immediate predecessor, Hu Jintao, Xi carries
more political clout among the Chinese Party officials and appears more
at ease in speaking his own mind. More importantly for my argument, it
is striking to observe that Xi hardly makes any references to the political
slogans of his predecessors—Deng Xiaoping, Jiang Zemin, and Hu Jintao—as would be expected within the tight protocols of CPC leaders;
instead, the only predecessor Xi refers to with any regularity is Mao. As
Willy Wo-lap Lam puts it "He's much more a disciple of Mao Zedong than
Deng Xiaoping," and "Xi will continue to hold up Mao Zedong's teachings
as the guiding principle of the country."[64] To pursue this claim, I analyze twelve of Xi's speeches from 2008 to 2013 (including two ceremonial
speeches: a New Year address and a speech commemorating Mao's 120th
birthday). My analysis is divided into three parts: Xi's use of metaphors;
his references to authoritative texts; and his habit, like Mao, of telling
nationalist stories. Given both Mao's history of authoritarian rule and the
rising tide of Mao fever in China, it would appear that Xi has calculated
that appropriating Mao's nationalist themes and rhetorical style will serve
him well as he steers China on a course of renewed nationalism.

USE OF METAPHORS

Using metaphors was a predominant feature of Mao's rhetoric, which was often elliptical, aphoristic, and literary; at the same time, Mao was famous for his blunt talk—oscillating between the two patterns was one of Mao's key rhetorical habits. Xi Jinping appears to be mimicking this strategy, as I will demonstrate below. Regarding the use of metaphors, Xi's rhetoric tends to fall into dream metaphors, animal metaphors, hygiene metaphors, medicine metaphors, journey metaphors, and nature metaphors. These categories of metaphors add up to Xi's major rhetorical trademark, the "Chinese dream." As Xi defines it, the Chinese dream "is about the rejuvenation of China as a nation. It has been the greatest dream of Chinese people. . . . History has taught us, every person's fate is closely linked to the future fate of the nation. Only when the nation is good, [can] our life be good."[65] The "dream" is therefore a forward-looking wish for renewed greatness wrapped in the standard flag of Maoist nationalism. While dream metaphors may have a universal appeal, Xi's dream metaphor differs from the American dream, where individual happiness is the primary goal; in Xi's hands, the Chinese dream puts the nation first. Xi thus celebrates a modern, capitalist sense of striving and advancement—the dream of improvement and forthcoming power—while clearly invoking Mao's reverence for China's collectivistic and nationalist values and echoing with Mao's vision of building a strong and powerful China. Indeed, to avoid any linkage of the "Chinese dream" with the "American dream," which is premised on a good material life in a capitalistic society, Xi argues that "the realization of the Chinese dream depends on taking the Chinese road, reviving the Chinese spirit, and gathering China's strength."[66] This statement implies that China will not follow the model of Western democracies, for China has its own historical, material, and human resources to draw upon as it marches toward greatness.

Much like Mao, Xi is deeply concerned with cleansing the Party of perceived traitors, who are often referred to via the animal metaphors of "tiger" and "fly"; tigers are high-ranking officials engaged in corruption, while flies are lower-ranking officials who commit petty crimes.[67] While the terms reentered Chinese discourse via Xi's speeches, they have become adopted as part of CPC "officialese," wherein the metaphors are frequently used to express the government's determination to curb the problems of hedonism and corruption among Party members. Such metaphors hearken back to Mao's era; in 1951, Mao launched an anticorruption movement known as "The Three-Anti Campaign and Five-Anti Campaign."[68] Those who were charged with corruption crimes were called "tigers" at the time. Thus, the metaphor is nothing new to the Chinese people. Now the word has become a metaphor for high-ranking Party leaders who have been charged with corruption or economically related crimes.[69] On another occasion, Xi emulated Mao by quoting from an ancient philosopher: "Many worms will disintegrate wood, and a big enough crack will lead to the collapse of a wall."[70] Similar to Mao, Xi is concerned about the Party's moral legitimacy to rule if corrupt Party officials are not removed or punished. While Xi's anticorruption campaign has been successful, some interpret it as a strategic move to eliminate his political opponents. In Lam's remark, "He's following Mao Zedong's playbook of using anticorruption as a weapon against his enemies in the Party."[71] Following Mao's steps, Xi appears to be determined to root out corruption at all levels and to make Party members morally pure and righteous by catching the flies and tigers who erode the body of the CPC and threaten the legitimacy of Party rule.

While Xi uses images of flies, tigers, and worms to speak about corruption and/or integrity within the Party, he also uses a wide range of metaphors about cleanliness to point toward issues of moral behavior. In one speech, he told Party members to "look at yourself in the mirror, groom your clothes, take a bath, and cure your disease."[72] Xi explained that the mirror refers to the Party constitution; clothes refer to the Party members' image; taking a bath is to clean off any wrongdoings through Mao-style criticism and self-criticism; and curing the disease refers to helping the corrupted officials return to good behavior, either through education or punishment.[73] Xi's rhetoric clearly echoes with one of Mao's famous lines about Party corruption, in which he said, "If a member of our Party acts in this way [being corrupt or wavering in loyalty] . . . and his face is caked with the dust of bureaucracy, [he] needs a good wash in a basin of hot water."[74] In the same speech, Mao observed that "As our faces are apt to get dirty, we must sweep it every day; as the floor is apt to gather dust, we must sweep it every day."[75] For Mao, these references to cleaning the house and washing the body were meant to be folksy, agrarian indications that communism was a moral endeavor linked to long-standing Confucian notions of honor and dignity. For Xi to so explicitly and repeatedly appropriate this rhetorical trope indicates that he, like Mao, sees his role as the Party's and the nation's healer, literally as the figure who will wash the nation clean of its corruption.

Xi's rhetoric of catching corrupt and dangerous animals and cleaning dirty bodies and dusty houses points toward the central Maoist theme of self-criticism as a necessary means of rectifying Party members. Xi often describes this Maoist tradition of engaging in criticism and self-criticism as "good medicine" that can "prevent disease." In his words, "Medicine is bitter and does not sound good to the ears, but it is good for health." He diagnoses the cause of Party members' corruption as contracted "osteo-malacia" and "lack of calcium."[76] Much like those aspects of Xi's rhetoric addressed above, here too his language is based on careful invocations of Mao. For example, Xi quotes Mao a number of times on having a "correct attitude" toward criticism and self-criticism, stating that "party members must listen to any sharp criticism. Correct your action if criticism applies; take a caution if criticism does not apply."[77] This rhetoric of criticism can shade into a paranoid, surveillance mode, such as when Mao said to Party members in 1945 that they should "say all you know and say it without reserve"; "blame not the speaker but be warned by his words"; "correct mistakes if you have committed them and guard against them if you have not." Mao continued, "This is the only effective way to prevent all kinds of political dust and germs from contaminating the minds of our comrades and the body of our Party."[78] As many observers have noted, in this way Xi appears to be leaning dangerously close to some familiar Maoist actions, including imposing mandatory versions of criticism and self-criticism as ways to maintain Party control. Still, as Celia Hatton from the *BBC News* notes, while "China's current leader is clearly copying Mao Zedong's style, he'll have to create his own solutions to address the rampant corruption and disillusionment that was inconceivable in China's Communist heyday."[79]

While Xi's Mao-style rhetoric of criticism is therefore cause for alarm, his metaphors of journeys and travel point toward the more hopeful side of his "China dream." For example, he said "a thousand miles begins from the feet," thus invoking Mao's famous "long march" to remind Chinese listeners that there is still a long way to go toward realizing the Chinese dream, and that the Chinese people must take a step at a time to face the challenges.[80] In his meeting with U.S. Vice President Joe Biden, President Xi used three journey metaphors to portray China's strategic partnership with the United States. He first used Deng Xiaoping's iconic phrase, "cross the river by feeling the stone," to imply that there is no clear path ahead for U.S.–China relations, which will need to be created carefully, as if by feeling a stone in the water. He then used a metaphor from a traditional Chinese play, *Orphans of the Zhao*: "When confronted by mountains, one finds a way through. When blocked by a river, one finds a way to bridge to the other side," indicating that China would take action when the time comes for U.S.–China mutual benefits and interests. Finally, Xi used the lyric "May I ask where the path is? It is where you take your first step," which is from *Journey to the West*, a popular television show based on a Chinese classical novel. Here Xi encourages his strategic partners to be creative and adventurous in their endeavors to build healthy U.S.–China relations. As was true of Mao's rhetoric as well, what is striking in these instances of Xi's version of international diplomacy is his drawing from classical sources (an opera), popular culture (a TV show), and a former leader's appropriation of folk culture to weave together a rhetoric that is both folksy and learned, both obscure but also pointed. As Robert Lawrence Kuhn observes, Xi is a pragmatist: "Xi is goal-oriented, not ideologically constrained. He seeks to enhance the overall well-being of the Chinese people and to build the overall vitality of the Chinese nation."[81] A good relationship with the United States is crucial for China's economic development. Just as Mao used ping-pong diplomacy to invite Nixon to China, Xi's journey metaphors imply that he will be flexible and strategic regarding foreign relations.

In keeping with Confucian traditions, the final key metaphorical tool in Xi's rhetoric regards his repeated use of nature imagery. At the Boao Forum for Asia, Xi quoted a Chinese poem, "a single flower does not make spring while one hundred flowers in full bloom bring to the garden," to call for cooperation in moving towards the common good by pulling together the resources of Asia to substantiate economic development. He used "the ocean is vast because it admits hundreds of rivers" to suggest that Asian countries have the right to choose their own political system and economic model.[82] In his 2014 New Year address, Xi used a common

Chinese saying, "we must sow before we can reap," to encourage Chinese people to work hard and "we are in the same boat" to symbolize national unity.[83] In an interview at a BRICS conference, Xi said "to make a mountain by accumulating soil; to create an ocean by accumulating water," to express his continued commitment to cooperate with other developing nations. He also told his audience, "mountains and oceans cannot separate those who have the same ambition."[84] To some readers, such phrases may sound idiomatic and clichéd, yet Xi's rhetorical habits in these speeches are grounded in the Chinese tradition of using metaphors and analogies as persuasive practices; in particular, animal and nature metaphors were frequently employed in China's ancient classics.[85] Fully versed in this tradition, Mao also employed dream metaphors, hygiene metaphors, and journey metaphors in his writings and speeches. Xi's renewed nationalism, then, even while imagining a rising China, is rooted in these ancient Confucian and modern Maoist rhetorical traditions.

REFERENCES TO AUTHORITATIVE TEXTS

In his visit to Mexico, Xi referenced Zhuangzi, a Chinese classical thinker: "If water is not thick enough, big boat cannot float on it." Then he continued: "Let the friendship between the peoples of China and Mexico fill with immense water so that the boat of our cooperation can forge ahead through winds and waves."[86] Taking inspiration from the *Book of Poetry*, one of the oldest Chinese classics, Xi cited a common phrase, "as if facing the cliff, as if walking on thin ice," to instruct Party members to integrate themselves with common people and place the interests of people above everything else, a slogan that Mao often repeated to Party members.[87] These instances of Xi's nature metaphors all draw from Chinese common sayings or Chinese classics, thus embedding Xi's policies within the centuries-old march of Chinese civilization, in this way giving his rhetoric a sense of historical depth and rootedness and also portraying him as a well-learned man.

Indeed, like Mao, one of Xi's trademark rhetorical strategies is his situating his comments within the epic sweep of Chinese history. This strategy is evident in his many references to classical philosophical texts written by Confucius, Mencius, Xunzi, Han Feizi, Laozi, and Zhuangzi;

to classical poetry from texts such as the *Book of History*, the *Book of Poetry* and assorted poems composed in the Tang and Song dynasties; and to the sayings of famous Chinese heroes as enshrined in classical Chinese texts. Moreover, as noted here, Xi has supplemented his sense of China's historical grandeur with repeated references to Mao's sayings, thus folding Mao, who is usually thought of as offering a violent rupture in Chinese history, into the longer, seamless march of Chinese history.[88] In both Mao's and Xi's hands, that historical past points toward inevitable national greatness. As Xi said in one of his speeches honoring Mao, "Once the fate of China is in the hands of its people, China will be like the sun rising from the east that shines throughout the earth with its radiance." "We Chinese have the spirit of fighting with our enemy until the end," he said, "we have the determination to be independent; we have the ability to stand high in the world." Just as Mao once predicted, so Xi says the "Chinese people have the will and competence to catch up and surpass the advanced countries in the world."[89] As these examples indicate, when Xi imagines the nation, he appropriates Mao's imagery, wraps it in a grand, civilizational sense of Chinese history, and foretells an age when the Chinese dream will become a global dream.

TELLING NATIONALIST STORIES

As was true of Mao's rhetoric as well, Xi's narrative of greatness includes a sense of struggle, victimization at the hands of foreigners, and heroic effort. In one speech to Party leaders, for example, Xi reviewed modern Chinese history since the Opium Wars, saying:

> After the Opium War, China became a semicolonial and semifeudal society. Chinese history is a history of imperialist oppression, humiliation, and suffering. Almost all the imperialist countries in the world have invaded and bullied China. . . . They slaughtered Chinese people, forced China to sign a series of unequal treaties, sabotaged China's sovereignty, [and] set up their territories. . . . They extorted us to pay unfair reparation, pillaged our wealth, stole our treasures, [and] controlled China's economy. All these have brought unfathomable miseries to Chinese people.[90]

China's humiliating story did not end there, as Xi went on to list a series of resistances, reforms, and revolutionary movements all aimed at
reclaiming Chinese dignity from its century of humiliation. These movements include the Taiping Rebellion, the Hundred Day's Reform, the
Boxing Rebellion, and the 1911 Revolution. Xi praises the leadership of
the CPC during the anti-Japanese war and Chinese civil war and re-
minds his audience how many Party members sacrificed their lives for
the cause of creating an independent and prosperous China, culminating
in the establishment of the PRC in 1949. In his historical narrative, Xi
skips over the period of Mao's China and does not mention his mistakes,
instead praising the Party's leadership of post-Mao economic reforms. In
this way, the horrors of the Cultural Revolution are avoided, and Mao's
revolutionary communism is situated as part of the long, slow progress
of China as a great, modern nation. This telling and retelling of China's
history of victimization and triumphant resistance is a recurring theme in
Mao's writings and much contemporary Chinese rhetoric. Stephen Hartnett has called this rhetorical form "traumatized nationalism," arguing
that it breeds resentment and hostility toward Western countries, fuels
the determination to make China a strong military power, and stokes
an aggressive sense of Chinese nationalism.[91] Indeed, as I have shown
here, President Xi is an expert practitioner of the rhetoric of "traumatized
nationalism," but he is also remarkably adept at invoking Confucian classics, folksy idioms, and a wide range of animal and nature metaphors,
all while wrapping himself in the lineage of Mao's revolutionary communism, albeit switched now from an anticapitalist fervor to a strident
form of Chinese nationalism.

Conclusion

Historically, Chinese political leaders' speeches have contributed significantly to the formation of official Chinese discourse. Still today, top
leaders' speeches and writings are studied at Party meetings, read by local
Party officials, and debated among the people. As was true in both imperial and communist China, Party officials are still expected to use political
jargon and set phrases from these speeches in all political and public

situations, thus showing conformity and loyalty to the CPC's leadership. As one of the most prominent leaders of the twentieth century, Mao Zedong exerted tremendous influence on Chinese rhetoric, particularly on the official language used by subsequent Chinese leaders in the post-Mao regime. Drawing from Mao's rhetorical resources, these leaders—Deng, Jiang, Hu, and now Xi—have preached Mao's moral ideals of socialism, even while building a capitalist giant; they have repeated Mao's charge to "serve the people" while facing increasing corruption within the Party; they have built a strong sense of nationalism and imagined great glory for China's future; and they have given new life to Mao's notion of self-cultivation through criticism and self-criticism. In this way, Mao's *Little Red Book* lives on as a key rhetorical resource for contemporary China.

On the other hand, China's post-Mao leaders' speeches have deviated from Mao's rhetorical style in several aspects. First, they do not use radical words and have abandoned Mao's revolutionary ideology, particularly his divisive rhetoric of class struggle. Instead, their speeches call for unity rather than division, harmony rather than conflict. In a speech delivered at the celebration of the fiftieth anniversary of Sino-French diplomatic relations in Paris, Xi remarks, "Napoleon Bonaparte once said that China 'is a sleeping lion,' and 'when China wakes up, the world will shake.' In fact, the lion of China has awoken, but what the world sees now, is a peaceful, amiable, civilized lion."[92] Moreover, when they talk about China's modern history of humiliation, these post-Mao leaders offer an account of what has already happened, rather than attacking former colonizers and invaders. In this way, the century of humiliation is giving way to an age of expected greatness; Mao's nationalist aspiration has become Xi's "Chinese dream."

It is unlikely that China will go back to Mao's radical era, but Xi's leadership has shown a form of neoauthoritarianism by concentrating his power and using tough rhetoric both at home and abroad. Indeed, given the complexity of China's problems and challenges, he may need near-absolute powers to push through social changes in China while retaining the Party's legitimacy. This means the Western model of intertwining capitalism and democracy will not take place in the near future in China, as Mao's legacy lives on in Xi's leadership. Still, even while appropriating Mao's rhetorical themes and styles, the CPC leaders face the challenges of establishing a national imagination compelling enough to enthuse Party members while responding to the increasing demands from Chinese people for a truly civil, equal, and democratic China. As the following chapters in this section illustrate, part of the materials infusing this new national imagination may come from China's neighbors, Tibet and India, or from exiles living in the United States, for in these cases the emerging sense of Chinese nationalism and greatness is folded into emerging global conversations about human rights, democracy, and cultural autonomy.

NOTES

1. For more information on this period, see Xing Lu, *Rhetoric of the Chinese Cultural Revolution: The Impact on Chinese Thought, Culture, and Communication* (Columbia: University of South Carolina Press, 2004).

2. The CPC's assessment of Mao was issued in "The Resolution of the Sixth Plenum of the 11th Central Committee of the Communist Party of China," in June 1981; the English version of the document can be found in *Beijing Review* 27 (July 6, 1981).

3. Since the 1980s, China has become the world's fastest-growing economy as "its GDP has increased by an average of almost 10% a year for the past 30 years." Pam Woodall, "The Dragon Still Roars," *The Economist: The World in 2010*, November 13, 2009, 61.

4. Melissa Schrift, *Biography of a Chairman Mao Badge: The Creation and Mass Consumption of a Personality Cult* (New Brunswick, NJ: Rutgers University Press, 2001), 2; also see Geremie R. Barmé, *Shades of Mao: The Posthumous Cult of the Great Leader* (Armonk, NY: M. E. Sharpe, 1996), and Edward Friedman, "Democracy and 'Mao Fever,'" *Journal of Contemporary China* 6 (1994): 84–95.

5. "China Marks Mao's Birth with Noodles and Songs," YouTube video, 0:45, posted by AFP news agency, December 26, 2013, https://www.youtube.com.

6. Examples of such shows are *Long March* and *In Praise of Yan'an*.

7. Ross Terrill, *A Biography, Mao* (New York: Harper & Row, 1980), 434.

8. On the move away from radical rhetoric, see Xing Lu and Herbert Simons, "Transitional Rhetoric of Chinese Communist Party Leaders in the Post-Mao Reform Period: Dilemmas and Strategies," *Quarterly Journal of Speech* 92 (2006): 262–86.

9. See Christian Göbel and Lynette H. Ong, "Social Unrest in China," Europe

China Research and Advice Network Report, 2012; "A Dangerous Year," *The Economist*, January 28, 2012; and Tom Orlik, "Unrest Grows as Economy Booms," *Wall Street Journal*, September 26, 2011.

10. Perry Link, *An Anatomy of Chinese: Rhythm, Metaphor, Politics* (Cambridge, MA: Harvard University Press, 2013), 13.

11. Benedict Anderson, *Imagined Communities: Reflections on the Origin and Spread of Nationalism* (London: Verso, 1983), 67–82.

12. Mao Tse-Tung, "Talks at the Yenan Forum on Literature and Art," *Selected Works of Mao Tse-Tung* (Beijing: Foreign Language Press, 1967), 3:73–74.

13. The letter was accessed at http://blog.rbc.cn/html/28/528-291.html on January 30, 2014, but it has since been pulled down.

14. George Orwell, *1984* (New York: Signet Classics, 1977), 2; and also see Xing, *Rhetoric of the Chinese Cultural Revolution*.

15. Link, *An Anatomy of Chinese*, 13.

16. Perry Link , *Ban yang suibi* [Notes across the ocean] (Taibei: Sanmin shuju, 1999).

17. Link, *An Anatomy of Chinese*, 238.

18. Kenneth Burke, *Attitudes toward History* (Berkeley: University of California Press, 1959), 171.

19. Michael Schoenhals, *Doing Things with Words in Chinese Politics* (Berkeley: Center for Chinese Studies, University of California, 1992), 14–15.

20. Mao, "The Current Situation and the Party's Tasks," *Selected Works*, 2:299; in this regard, Mao's task in China was not unlike the dilemmas faced by the leaders of other developing nations, who also needed to reframe Marxism for agrarian, peasant societies.

21. Nick Night, "The Form of Mao Zedong's 'Sinification of Marxism,'" *Australian Journal of Chinese Affairs*, no. 9 (January 1983): 17–33, 18.

22. Mao, "On Contradiction," *Selected Works*, 1:334; in this regard, revolutionary communism stands among the key, early moments in what we call today "globalization"; this notion would eventually become explicit in the 1955 Bandung Conference, where a global coalition of developing nations came together under the banner of anticolonial self-advancement. In traditional Daoist concept, things in the universe are never static; instead, they change and evolve in different fashions. This change is not necessarily in the upward direction, but in a dialectical and interrelated way. Mao's thinking on social change was influenced by Daoist teaching; see Lao Tsu, *Tao Te Ching*, trans. Gia-fu Feng and Jane English (London: Vintage Books, 1989).

23. Canchu Lin and Yuen-Ting Lee, "The Constitutive Rhetoric of Democratic Centralism: A Thematic Analysis of Mao's Discourse on Democracy," *Journal of Contemporary China* 22 (2013): 148–65,155.

24. Mao, "New-Democratic Constitutional Government," in *Selected Works*, 2:407; Mao, "On Coalition Government," in *Selected Works*, 3:229.

25. Canchu and Lee, "Constitutive Rhetoric of Democratic Centralism," 156.

26. Mao, "Talks at the Yenan Forum on the Literature and Art," in *Selected Works*, 3:73–74.

27. Ibid., 84.

28. Mencius, *Mengzi* (Beijing: China Books, 1992), ch. 14.

29. Mao, "Report to Second Session of Seventh Central Committee," *Selected Works*, 4:374.

30. Confucius, *Lun Yu* (The Analects) (Beijing: China Books, 1992), ch. 1.

31. Mao, "Win the Masses in their Millions," *Selected Works*, 1:291. For Mao, a new communist person must be versed in Marxism-Leninism, willing to sacrifice for others and the nation, and selfless.

32. Moral exemplars include Comrade Zhang Side, to whom Mao wrote a tribute for his sacrificing spirit, and Norman Bethune, a Canadian doctor who came to China and helped the CPC during the Anti-Japanese War. Mao wrote an essay in memory of him: "In Memory of Norman Bethune," in *Selected Works*, 2:337–38; Mao "Serve the People," in *Selected Works*, 3:177–78, and 73–74.

33. For more details on these sessions, see Gao Hua, *Hongtaiyang shi zenyang shengqide: Yan'an zhengfeng de lailongqumai* (How does the red sun rise: The story of Yan'an rectification movement) (Hong Kong: Chinese University Press, 2002). Also see Robert Lay Lifton. "Thought Reform: The Cultural Perspectives," in *Communist China: A System-Functional Reader*, ed. Yung Wei (Columbus: Charles E. Merrill, 1972), 163–73.

34. See Mao Zedong, "Essays on the Sense of Shame," in *Mao's Road to Power: Revolutionary Writings, 1912–1949*, vol. 1, ed. Stuart Schram (Armonk, NY: M. E. Sharpe, 1992), 66.

35. Mao, "On the People's Democratic Dictatorship," in *Selected Works*, 4:411–23.

36. Mao, "Manifesto of Chinese People's Liberation Army," *Selected Works*, 4:151–52.

37. The U.S. government did not recognize the legitimacy of the PRC and imposed political isolation and economic sanctions against China throughout the 1950s and 1960s. While occasional allies, the USSR and PRC had a rocky relationship punctuated by repeated conflict and even border skirmishes. When U.S.

President Nixon opened dialogue with Mao in 1972, he sought to drive a wedge between the USSR and PRC; see W. Cohen, *America's Response to China: A History of Sino-American Relations*, 4th ed. (New York: Columbia University Press, 2000).

38. Mao, "Address to New Political Consultative Conference," *Selected Works*, 4:407.

39. Mao Zedong, *Jianguo yilai Mao Zedong wengao* (Mao Zedong's documents after the founding of the PRC), vol. 7 (Beijing: Zhongyang wenxian chubanshe, 1999), 236.

40. Mao, "Bankruptcy of Idealist Conception of History," *Selected Works*, 4:454 emphasis added.

41. Andrew G. Walder, *China Under Mao: A Revolution Derailed* (Cambridge, MA: Harvard University Press, 2015), 341.

42. Hua Guofeng was appointed by Mao as the chairman of the CPC before his death and was the top leader in China for two years before stepping down. Since the Third Plenum of the CPC in 1978, China ended the system of life-long tenure of top leadership; now, every ten years, there is a change of top leadership. See Deng Xiaoping, "Guance tiaozheng fangzhe, baozheng anding tuanjie" (Carry on with adjustment, guarantee stability and unity), in *Deng Xiaoping wenquan* (Works of Deng Xiaoping), vol. 2 (Beijing: The People's Press, 1994), 360.

43. China's GDP growth was in the double digits in most of Mao's years. For example, GDP growth was 15 percent in 1956 and 17 percent in 1965. Production was undermined during the Cultural Revolution. By 1976, when the Cultural Revolution ended, China's GDP growth fell to -1.6 percent (see the data at National Bureau of Statistics of China, http://data.stats.gov.cn/english/). I lived through the Cultural Revolution, when the economy was so bad that shelves in shops were nearly empty; we had little to eat; everything was rationed. During this period, it was common for three generations to live together in a small room.

44. Deng Xiaoping, "Building Socialism with Chinese Characteristics," in *Deng Xiaoping wenquan*, 3:62–66.

45. Mao, "Party Unity and Party Traditions," *Selected Works*, 5:316.

46. Deng Xiaoping, "Stick to the Four Cardinal Principles," in *Deng Xiaoping wenquan*, 2:167.

47. Deng, "Building Socialism with Chinese Characteristics," *Deng Xiaoping wenquan*, 3:63.

48. Fengyuan Ji, *Linguistic Engineering: Language and Politics in Mao's China* (Honolulu: University of Hawai'i Press, 2004), 3.

49. Donald Bryant, "Rhetoric: Its Functions and Its Scope," *Quarterly Journal of Speech* 39 (1953): 401–24, 413.

50. Kim Kyung-Hoon. "Documenting the Wealth Gap in China," Reuters, Photographers' Blog, September 5, 2013, http://blogs.reuters.com.

51. Jiang Zemin, *Jiang Zemin Wenxuan* (Selected works of Jiang Zemin) (Beijing: The People's Press, 2006), 3:28.

52. The term "represent" is a direct translation of *daibiao* from Chinese, meaning "on behalf of someone or something"; here, Jiang uses the term to mean the CPC is the voice of the Chinese people, speaking and acting on behalf of the Chinese people.

53. It has been the norm within CPC speeches that each leader has to acknowledge the merits of his predecessors and has to articulate a correct ideological line to demonstrate the consistency in their leadership. Because speaking and acting against predecessors is a moral taboo in Chinese culture, there are strong rhetorical impediments against social transformation.

54. Jiang Zemin, "Jiang Zemin's Speech at the 16th Party Congress," *People's Daily*, August 9, 2001, 1.

55. See John Wang and Zheng Yongnian, "Embracing the Capitalists: The Chinese Communist Party to Brace Itself for Far-Reaching Changes," in *Damage Control: The Chinese Communist Party in the Jiang Zemin Era*, ed. Wang Gungwu and Zheng Yongnian (London: Eastern Universities Press, 2003), 365–76.

56. Kerry Brown, "Hu Jintao's Legacy," *Foreign Policy*, November 8, 2012, http://www.foreignpolicy.com.

57. Hu Jintao, "Speech at the 82nd Birthday of the Chinese Communist Party," *People's Daily*, July 2, 2003, 1.

58. Hu Jintao, "Speech at the Visit of Xibanpo," *People's Daily*, December 9, 2002, 1.

59. Xuezhi Guo, *The Ideal Chinese Political Leader: A Historical and Cultural Perspective* (Westport, CT: Praeger, 2002), 18.

60. Ho Pin, "China's Heir Apparent," *New York Times*, February 12, 2012.

61. Cheng Li. "China's Fifth Generation: Is Diversity a Source of Strength or Weakness?" *Asian Policy*, no. 6 (July 2008): 53–93, 66–67.

62. The princelings, also translated as the Crown Prince Party, are the sons and daughters of high-ranking Chinese Communist officials. The term is usually derogative, as the princelings receive benefits and privileges due not to their own merits but to their connections and the influence of their parents.

63. William H. Overholt, "Reassessing China: Awaiting Xi Jinping," *Washington*

Quarterly 35, no. 2 (2012): 123. In terms of his military background, Xi's father was a Red Army general, and Xi himself served as the chairman of the Central Military Commission of the PRC.

64. Ian Johnson, "Willy Wo-Lap Lam on 'Chinese Politics in the Era of Xi Jinping,'" *Sinosphere* (blog), June 1, 2015, http://sinosphere.blogs.nytimes.com. Lam is the author of *Chinese Politics in the Era of Xi Jinping: Renaissance, Reform, or Retrogression?* (London: Routledge, 2015).

65. Xi Jinping, *Dang de shibada yilai xi jinping tongzhi de zhongyao jianghua huibian* (Important speeches of Comrade Xi Jinping since Party's 18th Congress) (Compiled by the office of Communist Youth Association of Fujian Province, 2013), 23, http://www.fjrtvu.cn/gqtw/; hereafter "Xi, *Important Speeches*."

66. Xi, *Important Speeches*, 76–77.

67. Ibid., 53.

68. The Three-Anti Campaign was launched in 1951 and targeted anticorruption, antiwaste, and antibureaucracy. The Five-Anti Campaign followed in 1952 to address antibribery, anti–theft of state property, anti–tax evasion, anti–cheating on government contracts, and anti–stealing of state economic information. The campaigns appeared to address moral and economic issues, but were targeted at wealthy capitalists and political dissidents. See Theodore His-En Chen and Wen-Hui C. Chen, "The 'Three-Anti' and 'Five-Anti' Movements in Communist China," *Pacific Affairs* 26 (1953): 3–23.

69. Since Xi took office, a large number of "tigers" (provincial and central level Party officials) have been charged with various kinds of crimes, with Bo Xilai (former member of the Political Bureau of the Central Committee of the CPC and the secretary of the CPC's Chongqi branch) and Zhou Yongkang (former member of the Politburo Standing Committee of the CPC and the secretary of the Central Political and Legislative Committee) on the top of the list. See Mamta Badkar, "China's President Has Only Begun to Take Down the Tigers and Swat the Flies in His Historic Corruption Crackdown," *Business Insider*, July 26, 2014, http://www.businessinsider.com.

70. Roderick MacFarquhar, "China: The Superpower of Mr. Xi," *New York Review of Books*, August 13, 2015.

71. Johnson, "Willy Wo-Lap Lam on 'Chinese Politics in the Era of Xi Jinping.'"

72. Xi, *Important Speeches*, 132.

73. Ibid.

74. Mao, "Get Organized," *Selected Works*, 3:158.

75. Ibid., 3:160.

76. Xi Jinping, "Jinjin weirao jianchi he fazhan zhongguo tese shehui zhuyi" (Closely centered around adherence and developing socialism with Chinese characteristics), in *Shibada fudao duben* (18th Party congress study book) (Beijing: People's Press, 2012), 1–12, 10.

77. Xi, *Important Speeches*, 59.

78. Mao, *Selected Works*, 3:266–67.

79. Celia Hatton, "Can Xi Jinping's Mao-style Clean-up Campaign Revive Public Trust?" *BBC News*, October 26, 2013.

80. Xi, *Important Speeches*, 113.

81. Robert Lawrence Kuhn, "China's Xi Jinping Isn't a Reformer, He's a Pragmatist," *Christian Science Monitor*, November 18, 2013.

82. Xi Jinping, "Full Text of Xi Jinping's Speech at the Opening Ceremony of the Boao Forum for Asia AC 2013," Boao Forum for Asia, April 7, 2013, http://english. boaoforum.org.

83. Xi Jinping, "New Year Address" (2014), http://edu.sina.com.cn/en/2014-01-02/145878636.shtml.

84. Xi, *Important Speeches*, 93.

85. See examples from Xing Lu, *Rhetoric in Ancient China, Fifth to Third Century B.C.E.* (Columbia: University of South Carolina Press, 1998), 121–24.

86. Xi, *Important Speeches*, 127.

87. Xi, "Speech at the Opening Ceremony of the Boao Forum."

88. See Xi Jinping, "Mao Was Not a God, but His Spirit . . . ," *AsiaNews*, December 27, 2013, http://www.asianews.it.

89. Ibid.

90. Xi, *Important Speeches*, 241–42.

91. Stephen J. Hartnett. "Google and the 'Twisted Cyber Spy' Affair: U.S.–China Communication in an Age of Globalization," *Quarterly Journal of Speech* 97 (2011): 411–34, 413.

92. The speech was delivered on March 27, 2014, http://www.chinadaily.com.cn/language_tips/auvideo/2014-04/02/content_17400426.htm.

Chen Guangcheng and the Rhetorical Politics of Dissent: Imagining Human Rights in U.S.–Sino Relations

Michelle Murray Yang

The situation had all the makings for a compelling melodrama: after years of being confined to house arrest and forced to endure countless beatings, an activist deftly scales a wall in the dark of night in a daring escape to freedom. To elude his captors, he threads his way through the maze of cornfields and ravines surrounding his village until he reaches a coconspirator, who takes him under the cover of night to Beijing, where the intrepid man seeks and is given refuge within the U.S. embassy. The story is made even more compelling by the fact that the protagonist is blind, his affliction the result of a severe fever suffered during his childhood. In this harrowing tale of dissent from oppression and escape from captivity, we find a synecdochical representation—a compelling part that figures a larger whole—of the dangers faced by those who criticize the Communist Party of China (CPC or the Party) in the name of human rights.

After serving eighteen months under house arrest, Chen Guangcheng escaped from guards at his home in Shandong Province on April 22, 2012. He fled to the U.S. embassy in Beijing where he would stay for six days before checking into a Beijing hospital for an injury he sustained to his foot during his escape. After heated negotiations between U.S. and Chinese officials, a representative for the Chinese Foreign Ministry in Beijing issued a statement in early May 2012 that if Chen wanted to study outside of China, he was able to do so "like any other Chinese citizen."[1] While Chen was given a fellowship to study law at New York University and he and his immediate family were allowed to leave China, his extended family and friends, some of whom aided his escape, remained in jeopardy. In fact, in the wake of Chen's flight from house arrest, his nephew, Chen Kegui, was arrested. He was later found guilty of "intentional infliction of injury" and sentenced to three years and three months in prison for defending his family from officials who forcibly searched their home after his uncle's escape.[2] According to Human Rights Watch, Chen Kegui's trial was "widely seen as retribution against Chen Guangcheng and fell short of international standards."[3] Thus, as in the case of Liu Xiaobo's family, the CPC engaged not only in the persecution of Chen but in the harassment and eventual imprisonment of his family members as well.[4]

Prior to his escape from China in 2012, Chen Guangcheng earned notoriety as the "barefoot lawyer" in the late 1990s as a result of his legal activism involving China's one-child policy and the CPC's use of forced abortions to punish those who violated the policy. "Barefoot lawyer" is a contemporary expression that can be traced back to the term "barefoot doctor," which was used during the Cultural Revolution to denote rural peasants whom the government allowed to receive rudimentary medical training.[5] In comparison, "barefoot lawyers" refers to self-educated legal activists in China who challenge unfair governmental practices through litigation and by offering free legal services to impoverished citizens. As Chen explains in his memoir, "the crucial difference" between these terms is that the Chinese government "has never supported barefoot lawyers."[6] In 2005, he filed a class-action lawsuit in China suing local officials in Shandong's Linyi prefecture on behalf of poor women who claimed to be victims of forced abortions and sterilizations. He was subsequently tried and found guilty in 2006 of "organizing a mob to disturb traffic" as part of a protest and was sentenced to four years and three months in prison.[7]

Upon his release from prison in September 2010, Chen remained under house arrest with his wife, children, and mother.

While this record of activism left Chen largely unknown outside of China, his daring escape from local authorities quickly made him an international hero among human rights supporters, making his fate a complicated issue for U.S. and Chinese leaders to navigate. Indeed, the U.S. media lauded Chen for his courageous defiance of the Chinese government. For example, a May 2012 editorial in the *New York Times* praised the escaped activist as "a man of extraordinary courage";[8] four days later, the paper characterized Chen's desire to ultimately return to China rather than seek asylum in the United States as "a brave choice and a bold challenge to China's government."[9] The *Washington Post* also bestowed praise upon the activist, describing Chen as "one of China's best-known and bravest human rights activists."[10] His determination earned him the title "Rebel of the Year" by GQ magazine.[11] If the rhetorical work of imagining nations relies, in part, on portraying the nation as a montage of its more compelling characters, then here was the ideal figure for those Western observers who hoped to see more daring dissent from Chinese citizens; indeed, Chen was so quickly and firmly embraced by the U.S. media and political elite because he stood for them as a representative anecdote, a synecdochical icon, of U.S.-style human rights in action.

Nearly a year after arriving in the United States, however, Chen made headlines for a very different reason. The activist published an editorial in the *New York Times* claiming NYU was forcing him to leave the university. Alleging that Chinese government officials were pressuring the school to compel the activist's exit, Chen declared that NYU leaders were concerned that his continued presence could jeopardize the future of the school's new satellite campus in Shanghai. Explaining "the work of the Chinese Communists within academic circles in the United States is far greater than what people imagine," he warned that "academic independence and academic freedom in the United States are being greatly threatened by a totalitarian regime."[12] Chen also claimed that NYU personnel had repeatedly tried to prevent him from engaging with conservative advocacy groups. Vigorously disputing these allegations, NYU representatives expressed sadness and dismay in their responses to Chen's claims. Mattie J. Bekink, a translator provided by NYU for Chen during his fellowship, denied that the school had restricted access to the activist. Professor Jerome Cohen explained that he and others at NYU had cautioned Chen that both Democratic and Republican organizations—with both parties desperate to appear tough on China—would attempt to co-opt his support leading up to the 2012 presidential election. Cohen, Bekink, and other NYU officials therefore urged Chen to learn more about the U.S. political system before getting involved with members from either party. However, Cohen and others refuted claims that the university had prevented him from meeting with other activists or that they had experienced pressure from Chinese leaders seeking to force his exit from the school.[13] Instead, they claimed that the terms of Chen's fellowship always stipulated that it would be for one year. The controversy played out in the U.S. media and, at least for some, soured the image of Chen as the triumphant human rights advocate. While a wealthy donor initially offered to fund a three-year position at Fordham University for Chen, the offer was withdrawn after the NYU controversy unfolded. While Chen's initial flight from China thrilled the world because of its symbolic clarity—man fights for rights, is persecuted, but wins his freedom!—his spat with NYU offered a much cloudier story of clashing ambitions, political naïveté, and fouled intercultural communication.

Chen's disagreement with NYU coincided with his turn to prophetic rhetoric in his public statements. While Chen was initially hopeful that the Chinese government would keep its word and investigate the abuse his family had suffered, this optimism steadily faded, for after living in the United States for a year, he had seen no evidence that the Chinese government would mount an investigation. As Chen became increasingly frustrated with Chinese officials' inaction, U.S. political leaders' unwillingness to hold China accountable for these broken promises, and NYU's treatment of his family, his discourse became progressively more divisive and uncompromising. Examining Chen's prophetic turn illustrates the radical progression of his rhetoric as he transitioned from demanding that the Chinese government conduct a proper investigation to insisting that the United States help overthrow the CPC.[14] Chen's evolution from peace activist to war hawk illustrates the conflicting perceptions and misinterpretations that often plague the social imaginings that underpin U.S.–Sino relations.

Chen's story, as it was portrayed in U.S. media outlets and in the activist's own words, therefore raises important questions for and provides significant insights into the fraught communication patterns between the United States and China and the complications within the national imaginings that drive the countries' relationship. Indeed, I argue that Chen functions as a synecdoche—a part for whole conversion—of the continual misinterpretations that occur within imaginings of U.S.–Sino relations. These misinterpretations are embodied in the United States' "pivot to Asia" policy and in Chinese leaders' public criticism of Western democracy and constitutionalism.[15] For example, interpreting territorial conflicts between China and its neighbors as evidence of increasing Chinese aggression, the Obama administration has strengthened military and economic ties with Pacific nations as part of its pivot to Asia policy. But these actions have, in turn, led to increased suspicion among Chinese leaders, who view the pivot as a revised form of Cold War containment. In response to U.S. efforts to strengthen military relations with Australia as part of the pivot, a People's Liberation Army official likened the alliance to "an expression of a Cold War mentality," which violates "the trend of peace, development, and cooperation."[16] As these responses indicate, the United States and the CPC appear to be locked in a dance of mutual miscomprehension in which each views the other as a threat to its respective economic, military, and national stability. This chapter therefore speaks to the complexities of contemporary international relations, which require political and economic engagement between great powers in the midst of continued and deeply rooted historical distrust.

These rising tensions regarding military posturing and possibly clashing intentions in the China Sea dovetail with China's long-standing concerns regarding the threat posed by Western-style democracy to the stability of the CPC. In April 2013, the Government Office of the CPC Central Committee articulated these threats in a report (to which I return below) titled *Document No. 9*.[17] In conjunction with this report, high-ranking CPC officials have made repeated criticisms of Western democracy in public statements and newspaper articles, pointing to the continued chaos and violence in Egypt and Libya to support their claims regarding the dangers of Western-style democracy. Some Chinese intellectuals such as Zhang Wei and Wang Jisi, of Beijing University, have also been vocal in their criticism of democracy, citing the continued tumult in developing nations that have tried to implement political change as evidence of democracy's limitations. As Wang explains, "many developing countries that have introduced Western values and political systems are experiencing disorder and chaos."[18]

From this perspective, Chen's story stands synecdochically as the part so compelling that it encapsulates the larger pattern of misinterpretations that haunt U.S.–Sino relations. Indeed, U.S. media outlets characterized the Chinese activist as a heroic synecdoche for besieged human rights in China, while the CPC portrayed him as the poster child of all that is wrong with both democracy in general and the United States in particular. Analyzing *New York Times* and *Washington Post* coverage of the activist's ordeal, I argue that U.S. media outlets positioned Chen as a synecdochical representation of the status of human rights within China and as a representation of the issue of human rights in the United States' relationship with China. For example, rather than addressing the Chen case as a particularly complicated moment within evolving U.S.–China relations, the *New York Times* and *Washington Post* portrayed the Obama administration's response to the Chen crisis as a litmus test of the United States' commitment to human rights and democratic values. I argue that casting Chen as a synecdochical representation for China's handling of human rights and characterizing the United States' negotiation of his release as a measure of the United States' dedication to human rights simplified a complex issue by ignoring the efforts of numerous other activists in China as well as the many human rights problems that continue to plague the United States. As a result of this rhetorical flattening and Orientalist perspective—the U.S. press's championing of Chen and, simultaneously, its celebration of the United States' role in safeguarding his freedom and flight from Chinese oppression—the Chen case ended up portraying the United States in a superior moral position, thus continuing the cycle of transnational animosity.

The White House and U.S. press did not act alone in this regard, however, for Chen repeatedly and vigorously constructed the United States as a synecdoche for some dream version of democratic ideals: Chen too was pursuing his own national imaginings. Analyzing interviews and public statements given by Chen after his escape from house arrest and during his first year in the United States, I conclude that he appears to have believed that the United States would make serious revisions in its relationship with China as a result of his plight, even going so far as to privilege human rights over economic concerns, military matters, and ongoing diplomatic negotiations. Repeatedly depicting the United States as a "beacon for democracy," he positioned the human rights debate between the United States and China as a battle between good and evil, thereby obscuring the messy realities of democracy in practice as well as the components necessary to the workings of democracy: dialogue, dissenting voices, and negotiation. By taking a stance of moral absolutism and employing discursive elements of prophetic rhetoric, Chen adopted an increasingly radical rhetorical approach that left no room for compromise. Demanding that the CPC must be taken out of power and that the United States must help in this endeavor if it is to safeguard the survival of freedom and democracy, Chen privileged a confrontational approach to U.S.–Sino relations predicated upon impossible demands and naive expectations. Both U.S. media outlets' equation of Chen with China's treatment of human rights issues in general and Chen's conflation of the United States with the democratic ideal constituted gross oversimplifications of complex transnational issues. From this perspective, I argue that Chen's case was turned from a complex series of specific factors into a symbolic blank-slate upon which both U.S. and Chinese media and political leaders hoped to write stories confirming their national imaginings.

To pursue these arguments, this chapter begins by examining distrust and misinterpretations within U.S.–Sino relations. From there, it transitions into a discussion of prophetic rhetoric and its use in Chinese dissident rhetoric, particularly as regards human rights–based arguments. This is followed by a rhetorical analysis of the *New York Times* and *Washington Post*'s coverage of Chen Guangcheng's flight from house arrest and an analysis of Chen's discourse during his first year in the United States, including his turn toward prophetic rhetoric. Finally, this chapter concludes by exploring the implications of attempting to use such synecdochical representations as weapons either in favor of or opposed to human rights and democratic ideals. I argue that both U.S. media outlets' coverage of the controversy and Chen's discourse during his first year in the United States projected naive understandings of the complexities underlying U.S.–Sino relations; when combined, these discourses assert the supremacy of U.S. democratic ideals over all other forms of governance, thus perpetuating an outdated perspective on U.S.–Sino relations while ignoring the well-chronicled post-9/11 human rights problems plaguing the United States.[19] Ultimately, then, I suggest that the case of the "barefoot lawyer" demonstrates how relying upon synecdochical representations to make sense of the complicated national imaginings in and between China and the United States only clouds our analysis of ourselves, each other, and our entwined fates.

Rhetorics of Distrust in U.S.–Sino Relations: The Pivot to Asia and Document No. 9

There is perhaps no better example of the United States' misreading of China than President Obama's pivot to Asia policy. Announced in 2011, the pivot signaled a significant change in U.S. foreign policy from focusing on the Middle East to shifting attention to economic, military, cultural, and diplomatic opportunities in the Pacific region. In order to interlink the U.S. economy more seamlessly with the growing prosperity of Pacific economies, the United States fostered expanded engagement with the region by strengthening its connections to the Association of Southeast Asian Nations (ASEAN) and backing the Trans-Pacific Partnership (TPP), which involved Singapore, New Zealand, Malaysia, Chile, Bruni Darussalam, Australia, Peru, and Vietnam.[20] The pivot to Asia policy also includes bolstering military ties between the United States and Japan, South Korea, and the Philippines, in part by extending the U.S. Navy's Pacific presence and establishing a rotating operation of marines in Australia. Additionally, the United States has cultivated closer relationships with Indonesia and Vietnam while simultaneously pursuing reengagement with Burma. Secretary of State Hillary Clinton emphasized the pivot's significance to U.S. economic and diplomatic policy, explaining that "one of the most important tasks of American statecraft over the next decade will therefore be to lock in a substantially increased investment—diplomatic, economic, strategic, and otherwise—in the Asia Pacific region."[21]

The U.S. pivot to Asia policy came about in part due to escalating tensions in the Pacific region. It is no coincidence that many of the countries the United States has increased economic and military engagement with have been involved in territorial disputes with China. After Shintaro Ishihara, governor of Tokyo, announced plans to purchase several of the Senkaku Islands in April 2010, simmering hostilities over the sovereignty of the islands, which have historically been a source of contention between China and Japan, boiled over. China was mired in another territorial conflict two years later after the Philippines took eight Chinese fishing vessels into custody, alleging they had traversed into disputed waters. As a result of these confrontations, China asserted it had sovereignty over the majority of the South China Sea, claiming its territory stretched from the People's Republic of China (PRC) and traced the coasts of Vietnam, Malaysia, the Philippines, and Taiwan.[22] The U.S. State Department disparaged China's territorial claims, stating that the Treaty of Mutual Cooperation and Security stipulated that the United States must help protect Japan from military aggression.[23] As is typical of this pattern of misunderstanding and threat escalation, Chinese officials interpreted such statements not as evidence of the United States making prudent commitments to its allies but as creeping U.S. interference in China's affairs. Suspicious that U.S. leaders were trying to capitalize on the volatile situation, the Chinese Foreign Ministry questioned "the true intention of the U.S. side."[24] Similarly, the *People's Daily*, a newspaper overseen by the Chinese government, questioned the motives underlying the U.S. response, accusing the country of augmenting the tensions by "fanning [the] flames" of conflict.[25]

Along with this series of highly charged confrontations involving Chinese territorial claims, U.S. political leaders also interpreted other actions as evidence of the eastern country's rising aggression. For example, at the 2009 U.N. Climate Change Conference, Chinese leaders refused to compromise in negotiations, alleging that U.S. efforts to limit greenhouse gases were, in fact, covert attempts to stymie China's economic development.[26] In January 2010, China suspended security talks with the United States after U.S. leaders sold military arms to Taiwan.[27] Additionally, China's continued incarceration of the 2010 Nobel Peace Prize laureate, Liu Xiaobo, did little to quell concerns regarding the country's human rights record.[28] U.S. leaders interpreted these actions not as attempts to protect China's national interests but as evidence that China was becoming increasingly hostile and uncompromising in domestic, regional, and international affairs. Thus, to some Americans, these developments confirmed prior fears that a rising China would lead to escalating military threats and tensions.[29] While the United States and PRC thus fueled the pattern of mutual miscomprehension, some of America's East Asian allies wondered if the financially crippled United States "could contend with a seemingly more confident and capable China."[30] Faced with a credibility crisis in its international affairs, the Obama administration implemented the pivot to Asia policy, in part, as a means of reassuring Asian allies while simultaneously containing what it interpreted as increasing Chinese aggression in the region.[31]

China analysts have disputed the soundness of the Obama administration's rationale for the pivot. Robert Ross and Justin Logan contend the very events that the administration points to as evidence of escalating Chinese hostilities are actually indicators of increased Chinese insecurity. Claiming U.S. leaders have misinterpreted Chinese foreign policy, Ross and Logan argue that the series of Pacific conflicts involving China indicate that Chinese leaders are facing increased insecurity and pressure as a result of growing financial instability and high profile corruption scandals involving Chinese politicians.[32] Patrick Mendis, a senior fellow and affiliate professor at George Mason University's School of Public Policy, asserts that Chinese leaders perceive the pivot as a revised form of Cold War containment, much like the strategy implemented by the United States against the Soviet Union. According to Mendis, the Chinese government views the pivot as an "attempt to comprehensively contain China and to counterbalance a perceived China threat."[33] As the comments from Ross, Logan, and Mendis indicate, China watchers continue to be split between those who see China as an emboldened and confident rising power and those who see it as a paper tiger trying to bluff its way to superpower status; likewise, the U.S. pivot is seen by some observers as a prudent response to complicated issues, while others see it as a foolish return to Cold War threat escalation.

Viewing the pivot as a means for the United States to undermine China's sovereignty by interfering in territorial conflicts, Chinese leaders distrust the policy and the motives underlying it. Explaining how China interprets the pivot as an effort to augment "conflict between China and other regional states," Ely Ratner, a former State Department officer, states that Chinese leaders see the policy as "actively pressuring and encouraging countries to challenge China."[34] Chinese suspicions that the United States is actively working to obstruct China's rise as a world power is not a new phenomenon. Rather, it can be traced to deep historical distrust of Western powers fueled by memories of what the Chinese term "the century of humiliation."[35] From 1839 to 1949, this period was marked by the repeated humiliation of China and its people at the hands of Western and Japanese imperialisms. "The century of humiliation" continues to profoundly influence PRC leaders' views, which have culminated in the rhetorical pattern of "traumatized nationalism," whereby Chinese leaders interpret any Western policy that seems to impede Chinese economic or political interests as evidence that the West seeks China's subjugation.

While Chinese leaders are suspicious of the United States' pivot to Asia policy, they are also wary of the subversive potential of Western-style democracy. According to Kenneth Lieberthal, director of the John L. Thornton China Center at the Brookings Institution, and Wang Jisi, director of the Center for International and Strategic Studies at Peking University, "America's democracy promotion agenda is understood in China as designed to sabotage the Communist Party's leadership."[36] Due to the historical precedent of humiliation and subjugation at the behest of foreign powers, Chinese leaders are deeply suspicious of U.S. intentions; the PRC's elite believe that the United States' aim "is to maintain its global hegemony," and "they conclude that America will seek to constrain or even upset China's rise."[37]

Chinese distrust of U.S. efforts to promote democracy, which are seen by the CPC as covert attempts to undermine domestic stability within China, and of the United States' pivot, which is perceived as a Cold War–style attempt to stymie China's rise as an economic and political power, fueled the creation of *Document No. 9*. Issued in April 2013 by the Government Office of the CPC Central Committee, *Document No. 9* enumerates the dangers posed by Western-style democracy to the power and stability of the CPC. Indeed, the threat at the top of the list is "advocating Western constitutional democracy. Seeking to negate the current leadership and the government system of socialism with Chinese characteristics." Additionally, the report warns Chinese leaders of six other threats to the CPC, including advancing "universal values" in order to replace Chinese ideals with Western values, advocating for the restructuring of China's economic system, disassembling Chinese State-owned Enterprises, undermining the CPC's oversight of the press, and refuting the history of the PRC and the CPC as well as the "scientific value and guiding role of Mao Zedong Thought." The report accuses "anti-China forces in Western countries and domestic dissidents" of "infiltrating China's ideological domain and challenging mainstream ideology." The directive goes on to warn that "Western forces hostile to China and dissidents within the country are still constantly infiltrating the ideological sphere." While denouncing constitutionalism and civil society, *Document No. 9* also addresses the inflammatory tensions in Tibet, alerting officials to subversive attempts to "manipulate and stir up Tibetans to self-immolate, create violent and terrorist incidents in Xinjiang, [and] use ethnic and religious issues for separatist and disruptive activities."[38] By accusing Western democratic countries of trying to infiltrate Chinese society via democratic ideology and to undermine the PRC's political control, *Document No. 9* illustrates the suspicion, paranoia, and cynicism underlying Chinese leaders' views of the West.

Suspicions that the United States is sponsoring subversive actions to undermine CPC power and control are hardly new. Former president Hu Jintao pointed to the "Shadow Internet" as evidence that the United States was actively trying to ignite political instability within China. In an essay that appeared in the January 2012 edition of the CPC magazine *Qiu Shi*, President Hu warned "we must clearly see that international hostile forces are intensifying the strategic plot of westernizing and dividing China, and ideological and cultural fields are the focal areas for their long-term infiltration."[39] To counter these subversive efforts, he claimed there was a need to "take forceful measures to be on guard and respond."[40] While *Document No. 9* is clearly a response to these fears among the CPC leadership regarding the subversive efforts of Western governments and organizations to destabilize the Party, it also points to a burgeoning debate within China regarding the merits of adopting constitutional governance in China. As a response to these debates, proponents of constitutionalism have been censored and silenced. For example, censors first rewrote and then deleted an editorial titled "The Chinese Dream Is the Dream of Constitutionalism," which was slated to appear in the Guangzhou newspaper the *Southern Weekend*.[41] Likewise, Zhang Xuezhong, a professor at East China College of Politics and Law and an advocate for constitutionalism, was prohibited from teaching and later fired.[42]

While the incidents noted above point to censorship and harassment, the CPC has also launched its own public relations attack against democracy. Indeed, CPC officials have issued public statements and CPC affiliated publications have published articles detailing the threats posed by Western democracy and constitutionalism. Such works repeatedly cast suspicion on the motives compelling Western nations such as the United States to advocate for China to implement constitutionalism and to adopt Western democratic values. For example, Renmin University professor Wang Tingyou claims that Western countries urging China to adopt constitutionalism actually seek to "progressively abolish [the] CPC's leadership and socialism system."[43] Directly challenging the concept of "universal values," an anonymous article in the publication *Qiu Shi* argues that such norms do not refer to values "shared by all humans, rather, it particularly refers to Western political ideas and systems." When Western countries promote "universal values," they actually intend to engage in "foreign expansions" in order to "conquer the world." Cataloguing the limitations and dangers of implementing Western democracy, the article explains that such conceptualizations of democracy are predicated upon the games of "competition and election," which, when applied in "non-Western countries and regions often brings . . . non-stop political dispute, unstable political systems, and weak government." Deeming this phenomenon a "democracy trap," the article connects the disastrous consequences of adopting Western-style democracy with the true intentions of the United States, declaring "the more countries have internal chaos . . . the better for America to dominate the world." The article pointedly questions "if Western democracy is really a good thing . . . would the Western anti-China forces be so eager to export this to China?"[44] Western democracy, like all political systems, is plagued by problems and unrealized ideals; however, the anonymous author of the *Qiu Shi* article belies his or her paranoid worldview by crafting conspiratorial fantasies that place the United States and China in a zero-sum conflict for world domination. Instead of facilitating informed debate on the merits and limitations of different political systems, both the anonymous author's diatribe and Wang Tingyou's more reasoned critique ultimately construct democracy as a straw man against which they privilege the superiority of CPC rule. As these examples demonstrate, the national imaginings driving contemporary CPC leaders point to the likely perpetuation of hostilities between the two nations.

Within this framework, I argue that the continual misinterpretation and distrust within U.S.–Sino relations pervaded the case of Chen Guangcheng. As an advocate of constitutionalism, Chen was perceived by the PRC's leaders as a symbol of the threat posed by universal values to the internal governance of China. In contrast, according to many American journalists, Chen represented the status of human rights within China as well as the ability of the United States to spread Western democratic values. And so, while U.S. media outlets exulted Chen as a model of courage and determination, Chinese political leaders and government publications cited the activist's growing disenchantment with American politicians and the U.S. political system as evidence of democracy's limitations. As we shall see, U.S. media outlets constructed Chen as a synecdochical representation of human rights in China, thereby eliding the intricate complexities of such issues. In turn, Chen's reliance on prophetic rhetoric and his synecdochical conflation of the United States with a dreamy version of democracy further fueled the misconceptions hamstringing U.S.–Sino relations.

Prophetic Rhetoric, Human Rights, and Synecdochical Representation

Illuminating the intricacies of prophetic rhetoric, James Darsey has chronicled how the "rhetorics of radical reform . . . exhibit similarities with the discursive tradition of the Old Testament prophets."[45] According to Darsey, both radical reformers and prophets aim to align practice with higher principles, craft a clear mission, and remain unyielding to compromise.[46] For example, the Hebrew prophet Ezekiel proclaimed

God had called him to become a prophet, and he unceasingly prophesied that Jerusalem and its temple would be destroyed. Rhetorical scholars have shown how prophetic rhetoric is most effective when directed at an audience that shares the rhetor's beliefs and sense of purpose. As Darsey explains, "it is only in the presence of a viable community that the declaratory impulse in prophecy has adequate credibility to insist on engagement."[47] Similarly, Robert Terrill notes "the voice of prophecy is most vibrant when common ideals are shared among its audience."[48] Following Darsey and Terrill, Stephen Hartnett has examined the use of prophetic discursive practices by Chinese dissident Liu Xiaobo. Analyzing Liu's political manifesto, *Charter 08*, Hartnett illustrates the dual outcomes of the activist's use of prophetic rhetoric: Liu's use of blistering diatribes and prophetic language to espouse a universalist conceptualization of human rights gained the activist international recognition and support; however, despite successfully appealing to international audiences that shared Liu's vision and beliefs, his discourse was "a dismal rhetorical failure" within China and did nothing to persuade "the CPC to change its ways."[49] Grounding Liu's divisive rhetoric within the cultural particularities endemic to life under CPC rule, Hartnett explains how the activist's fiery discourse can "be understood as the consequence of living in a state that outlaws political debate."[50] As a result of blocking avenues for the expression of political dissent, Hartnett argues, CPC "repression from above creates rhetorical escalation from below."[51]

Having cut his teeth on the same political system as Liu, it seems reasonable to argue that Chen's prophetic rhetoric, like Liu's, represents his frustrations with China's closed rhetorical options. Just as Liu and Chen share certain similarities in terms of their domestic frustrations, so both activists have become recognized as representative figures of larger movements. Indeed, Hartnett describes how Liu became a synecdoche for a global human rights debate between "international human rights advocates and local dissidents," who support a universalist conceptualization of human rights, and the CPC, which espouses "a particularist and Communist" understanding of rights.[52] The conflict between these human rights perspectives has fueled a rhetorical stalemate between the United States and China, in which neither party seeks "common ground, instead provoking each other to alarming levels of nationalist chest-thumping."[53]

In this sense, Chen's case closely parallel's Liu's, with both figures illustrating how observers in both the United States and China respond to
individual political figures and/or scenarios through long-held and deeply
felt national imaginings that question the legitimacy and intentions of
what they perceive as the other's commitments.

Chen's case is particularly complicated, for scholars have illustrated
the contested and confusing nature of human rights–based arguments.
For example, tracing contradictory conceptualizations of human rights,
Mark Tushnet highlights the abstract, unstable, and indeterminate nature of rights.[54] Due to these limitations, he explains that rights-based
arguments often result in obfuscating spirals rather than fostering social
progress. Likewise, Leonard Hawes illustrates how rights-based arguments often function as "trumps, as rhetorically self-evident truths and
transcendent positions that stand above and beyond contestation"; as a
result, such arguments escalate conflicts "by claiming the unassailable
moral high ground."[55] In that same vein, Michael Ignatieff discounts the
ability of human rights to "define a higher realm of shared moral values
that will assist in finding common ground," declaring such a belief an
"illusion."[56] As these scholars demonstrate, the rhetoric of human rights
is contested, contradictory, and often counterproductive, especially when
such rights claims veer into the realm of prophecy and moral absolutism.

Despite these observations, after living in the United States for nearly
a year, Chen adopted more radical approaches in his human rights discourse, thus pushing his claims—like Liu's prophetic rhetorical practices
in *Charter 08*—toward absolutist demands. This rhetorical turn toward
prophecy may have been the product, in part, of Chen reading about
himself in the Western press, for just as Hartnett details how Liu became
a synecdoche for a global human rights debate, I argue that the *New York
Times* and *Washington Post* cast Chen Guangcheng as a heroic synecdoche for the struggle for human rights in China. Additionally, the papers
characterized the United States' handling of Chen's ordeal as a synecdoche for how the issue of human rights is approached in U.S.–Sino
relations. In both cases—Chen's own language and the press's comments
about him—the key parties seemed committed to a relentless process
of simplification. Kenneth Burke defines synecdoche as "part for the
whole, whole for the part, container for the contained, sign for the thing

signified, material for the thing made, cause for effect, effect for cause, genus for species, species for genus."[57] According to Burke, the term "representation" can be used as a substitution for synecdoche. He explains how representative government constitutes an example of "synecdochic form," as it entails "some part of the social body (either traditionally established, or elected, or coming into authority by revolution) is held to be 'representative' of the society as a whole."[58] While Burke acknowledges discord over determining what portion of society should be represented and how this representation is enacted, he states that such disagreements do not detract from the fact that "in a complex civilization any act of representation automatically implies a synecdochic relationship (insofar as the act is, or is held to be, 'truly representative')."[59] The problem, of course, which Burke elides, but which the case of the "barefoot lawyer" highlights in painful detail, is determining which "parts" represent which "wholes." What authority underwrites claims to be representative? And can "society as a whole" ever be represented in a way that does not entail massive simplifications, multiple erasures, and politically motivated choices? As we shall see below, when one man fighting one legal battle becomes represented as a synecdoche of an entire nation (China), or a global cause (human rights), or a nation's foreign policy (the United States' toward China), then we are in the realm of political theater, not reasoned debate.

Imagining a Hero: Chen Guangcheng in the New York Times and Washington Post

The *Washington Post* repeatedly positioned the Chen crisis as a test of the United States' dedication to human rights. This test was predicated upon U.S. officials taking a stronger approach to China by assuming responsibility for Chen's welfare and intervening on his behalf with Chinese leaders. From the outset of Chen's escape in late April 2012, the *Post* maintained that the Obama administration had an obligation to safeguard Chen, grant him "refuge if he seeks it, and refuse to allow his return to state custody." Depicting the U.S. response to Chen's plight as a test, the paper claimed "the administration's handling of this affair may tell the new Chinese leadership, and the rest of the world, whether the United States is serious about defending those who seek to push China toward that different path."[60] The *New York Times* also conveyed that the United States had a responsibility to ensure Chen's safety. Noting the sensitive nature of the situation as U.S. and Chinese leaders prepared to convene in Beijing for the nations' annual Strategic and Economic Dialogue, the paper acknowledged, "the United States needs to work with Beijing." However, the paper expressly conveyed that safeguarding U.S.–Sino relations should not come at the expense of Chen and his family. Blaming Chinese leaders for setting the debacle in motion, the *Times* claimed, "there would be no crisis if China's autocrats didn't deny their people the most basic rights." According to the newspaper, "corrupt officials and disregard for the rule of law are the true threat to China, not Mr. Chen and others who courageously defend human rights."[61] Thus adopting a "universalist" position that assumes one version of human rights is applicable in all situations, the U.S. news portrayals of Chen assumed that the United States had both the moral right and the actual means for intervening in China's domestic politics.

The United States' culpability for the outcome of Chen's saga heightened as reports emerged that the activist was compelled by U.S. officials to accept a deal with Chinese leaders. Initially, Chen wished to remain in China free from the restrictions of house arrest. U.S. officials brokered a deal that would allow Chen and his family to relocate to a different Chinese city and enable the activist to enroll in law school. However, Chen's friend claimed he was pressured by U.S. officials to accept this deal so as to not jeopardize the U.S.–China Strategic and Economic Dialogue. In response to the controversy, U.S. officials said Chen did not request asylum. Claiming Chen asked to go to the hospital, they denied allegations that the dissident was forced to leave the embassy. Amid allegations by Republican presidential nominee Mitt Romney that the Obama administration was reckless in its response to the crisis and had jeopardized Chen's safety, the administration responded that Chinese officials had already granted Chen permission to study in the United States when he left for the hospital. According to the *Post*, whether the Chinese upheld their assurances would be a "test of U.S. mettle." If Chen was granted his freedom, "the Obama administration can claim credit for a human rights breakthrough." However, the paper asserted that if Chinese officials failed to keep their promises, the United States had a responsibility to intervene "and not allow business as usual in U.S.–Chinese relations."[62] In these stories, we see the *Post* succumbing to a typical Western fixation on individual liberties, regardless of larger-picture issues, in turn backing the Obama administration into a corner while belittling China.

As U.S. officials negotiated Chen's release, the *Post* characterized Chen's case as a synecdoche for the United States' approach to the issue of human rights in U.S.–Sino relations. According to the paper, the outcome of Chen's saga provided significant lessons that should be applied to the nations' negotiation of human rights. The *Washington Post* cited U.S. negotiations with China that resulted in Chen's ability to go to the United States with his family as evidence that "the United States has the capacity to influence Beijing's human rights behavior and aggressively pressing that agenda won't necessarily damage cooperation on other bilateral issues." The *Post* urged U.S. leaders to continue this assertive approach in its dealings with Chinese officials by framing Chen as a synecdochical representation of China's handling of human rights in general. According to the newspaper, the United States' responsibility did not end once Chen and his family arrived safely in the United States. Rather, the *Post* claimed, "it will be important that the administration keep pushing if . . . Mr. Chen seeks to return to China after spending time in the United States." Linking China's treatment of Chen to the country's handling of political dissent in general, the paper explained that the United States must press Chinese officials on Chen "in order to establish the principle that human rights activists can work within the law without persecution." To bolster this point, the editorial concluded with the words of Hillary Clinton, who stated, "this is not just about well-known activists. It's about the human rights and aspirations of more than a billion people here in China . . . and it's about the future of this great nation."[63] Ignoring the unique particularities of Chen's plight, while exaggerating the United States' influence in Chinese domestic policy, the *Post*'s coverage and Clinton's response operate from the same flawed assumption: that U.S. leaders' success in securing the activist's release translated into the United States' ability to intervene and resolve other human rights violations within China. In this way, Chen was turned into a local example (a rhetorical part) justifying and extending an exceptionalist version of national imagining (a political whole) in which the United States righteously intervenes abroad in the name of justice.

For example, the *Post* repeatedly expressed frustration with both U.S. and Chinese leaders' handling of the activist's situation and urged American leaders to adopt a harder line on China's human rights practices. In April 2013, the *Post* criticized both the Chinese and U.S. governments for failing to uphold the promises made when the nations negotiated Chen's release. Recounting Chinese officials' failure to conduct an investigation into Chen's oppression as well as the continued mistreatment of the activist's family, the paper reported that Chen's nephew had been sentenced to three years in prison for defending his family against armed intruders and that his brother and sister-in-law were also threatened with criminal charges. According to Chen, "the U.S. government tended to be quiet and keep a distance" in response to the ongoing repression of his family. While noting that Secretary of State John Kerry had spoken with Chinese leaders on the matter and that the Obama administration had expressed concern about the situation, the *Post* declared that Kerry's desire to foster a "special relationship" with China would not be "possible if China does not keep the promises it makes—or if the United States does not honor its commitments to people like Mr. Chen."[64] In mid-May 2013, the *Post* again criticized U.S. officials' response to the continued mistreatment of Chen's relatives by Chinese officials and recommended that American leaders should take stronger action. Upon learning that Chen Guangfu, Chen Guangcheng's older brother, was beaten in Shandong Province and that Chinese police did not attempt to locate the assailants, the paper concluded that the assault "seems to be a defiant message that China could not care less about the promises made last year." Linking the beating to upper-level Chinese officials, the *Post* stated that the incident "suggests that China is far more determined to intimidate Mr. Chen than to honor any pledge made to Washington." The editorial criticized what it interpreted as a weak response by the United States, which issued a written protest from Kerry to Chinese Foreign Minister Wang Yi. Although noting that navigating the intricacies of U.S.–Sino relations required the balancing of "conflicting imperatives—security, economics, human rights and politics," the paper claimed some instances require the United States "to stand up and shout that something is amiss. This is one of those times."[65]

These characterizations of Chen as a synecdochical representation of human rights in China and of the United States' relationship with China bear several important rhetorical implications. According to the *Times*, the United States was responsible for the safety of Chen and his family before and during negotiations for his release from China. Likewise, the *Post* extended the United States' culpability for the safety of the activist and his family. This is illustrated by the *Post*'s repeated assertions that the United States' responsibility to protect Chen and his family continued even after negotiations secured his release and that U.S. leaders had a duty to protect Chen's extended family in China from retribution. In these ways, U.S. political leaders were portrayed as being culpable for the outcome of Chen's saga. In short, the *Post* assumed an interventionist stance in which the United States was not only able but obligated to intervene in Chinese affairs. Moreover, both the *Post*'s and, to a lesser degree, the *Times*'s coverage heightened the gravity of Chen's ordeal and U.S. leaders' responses to it. Chen was not portrayed as just one man who had suffered abuse at the hands of government officials; instead, he was held up as a symbol of China's larger disregard for human rights. Not only did he represent China's human rights violations, Chen was simultaneously representative of the United States' handling of—or desired handling of—human rights in U.S.–Sino relations. Due to this rhetorical conflation of Chen/human rights/American ideals, the papers conveyed the clear sense that the United States has the responsibility and right to intervene on Chen's behalf with the Chinese government. From this perspective, Chen's ordeal was not a domestic issue, as Chinese leaders viewed it, but rather a matter of U.S. concern, as it represented the United States' commitment to human rights on a global scale. While such arguments may have made sense to American readers conditioned to assume that U.S. exceptionalism justifies such interventions abroad—our national imagination virtually hinges on this assumed right—such assumptions strike the Chinese as arrogant at best, warrant for imperialism at worst.

These rhetorical patterns are troubling for several reasons. First, the *Washington Post*'s depiction of Chen as a synecdoche for human rights in China and in U.S.–Sino relations ignores several significant issues. By expanding U.S. responsibility to encompass not only Chen but also his extended family in China, the *Post* ignores the special circumstances surrounding the initial negotiations that led to Chen being able to come to the United States. At that time, leaders of both countries were preparing for important deliberations at the nations' Strategic and Economic Dialogue. Additionally, China was grappling with the transition of power from Hu Jintao to Xi Jinping, meaning the Obama administration was faced with trying to forge a solid working relationship with the new Chinese president. The fact that Chen sought and was given refuge in the U.S. embassy in Beijing also helped facilitate U.S. involvement in the situation. The *Post*'s assertion that the United States could protect Chen's extended family in China communicates an overly confident belief in the power of U.S. influence and ignores the contextual particularities of the nations' initial negotiations regarding the activist, to say nothing of the immense economic and military matters swirling in the background of this case.

Finally, the *Times*'s and the *Post*'s synecdochical representations of Chen ignore both the complex nature of human rights and other approaches to human rights advocacy in China. For while Chen has pursued confrontation via heroic and prophetic rhetoric, legal scholars have noted that China is now roiling with multiple approaches to activism. For example, John Wagner Givens, a researcher at the Center for Asian Democracy at the University of Louisville, points out how other activist lawyers in China have managed to win smaller cases against the state while avoiding a similar fate as Chen, in part by deploying less confrontational rhetorical strategies. Unlike these lesser-known lawyers, who use less aggressive tactics, Chen pursued a case on "a nationally sensitive issue," included over one thousand plaintiffs, and orchestrated public demonstrations. Additionally, Chen's repeated critical interviews with foreign media outlets after local courts ignored his appeal, as well as his lack of government contacts who could potentially shield him from severe repercussions, contributed to his plight and differentiated him from other activist lawyers in China. Givens claims, "these lawyers may ultimately prove more effective than Chen . . . partially because they are so much more numerous and partially because they can continue to work in China." Characterizing Chen as "an uncompromising rebel," Givens acknowledged that while "China could probably use more rebels like Chen . . . it could certainly use many more moderate figures who can advocate for change in China."[66] Although Givens applauds the work done by well-known activist lawyers, he worries that focusing solely on a small number of high-profile activists "fails to give credit to the accomplishments of many less prominent lawyers or shed light on the larger picture."[67] In short, by turning Chen into a shining hero, the newspapers eschewed reasoned discussion of the thousands of other activists working quietly to change Chinese society for the better. The synecdochical Chen overwhelms his grassroots allies, ironically leading to less, not more, coverage of human rights action in China.

Critique and Optimism: Chen's Discourse after Arriving in the United States

From his earliest contact with Western reporters, Chen repeatedly recounted the physical abuse he and his family had suffered at the hands of local officials, describing the suffering as "beyond imagination."[68] The activist described how "a furious pack of thugs" forced their way into his home after realizing he had escaped and beat his "sister-in-law and nephew with pickaxe handles."[69] In recounting the mistreatment of his family, Chen made sure to explain that his was not the only family targeted. Rather, other lawyers and their loved ones had also been beaten, prosecuted, disbarred, and even kidnapped.[70] When asked what compelled Chen to be a vocal opponent of the government, knowing that his activism would make him and his family targets for violence, Chen replied that "it was very natural" for him to speak out, explaining "I feel it's in people's nature to want to stop evil and embrace the good."[71] By sharing the pain he and his family endured, Chen gave insight into his own experience while simultaneously providing a voice to the scores of other human rights activists in China who have experienced similar abuses.

Even while his early comments were tied to factual reportage of abuses suffered in China, it is important to notice how Chen's rhetoric included absolutist notions of "good" versus "evil," thus suggesting his

leaning toward the prophetic mode and a tendency to make strong demands against the CPC. For example, in his public statements, Chen
repeatedly criticized China's legal system and outlined the steps the CPC
and the Chinese government must take to rectify the situation. Deeming his own 2006 trial a "farce," the activist asserted that China must
face and remedy the lawlessness that plagues the nation and victimizes
its people.[72] Chen declared, "the fundamental question the Chinese
government must face is lawlessness." He described how legal cases "of
any significance are controlled at every level of the judicial system by a
Communist Party political-legal committee, rather than by legal officials."
While Chen noted that China did "not lack laws," he explained the nation
was severely lacking in "the rule of law."[73]

However, Chen also conveyed optimism that Chinese officials would
abide by the agreement made before his release, investigate those who
tormented his family, and bring them to justice. In a *New York Times*
editorial published on May 29, 2012, he outlined his purpose in coming to
the United States, what he wanted to see happen in China, and how the
United States could aid in this endeavor. Claiming that he was not seeking political asylum, he explained that he was only in the United States
temporarily to study. Chen resolutely stated that he wanted both the Chinese government and the CPC to keep their promises to undertake a serious investigation into the mistreatment endured by his family. Explaining
that the Chinese government had failed to keep similar promises in the
past, Chen expressed hope that it would keep its word while calling on
"the government and people of the United States and other democratic
countries to insist that the Chinese government make timely progress in
this matter."[74] Thus, as of the summer of 2012, Chen's critiques of the
CPC were still laced with hope that trust could be built, that he would
eventually return to China, and that international diplomacy and legal
norms would be upheld.

Indeed, while Chen continually criticized the Chinese government
and the CPC in public statements throughout 2012, his tone was much
more measured in comparison to his public remarks made in 2013. Although he pointedly critiqued both the Chinese government and the
CPC, the activist also expressed gratitude and hope. During a press
conference upon his arrival in the United States, for example, he stated

he was "gratified to see that the Chinese government has been dealing with the situation with restraint and calm." Chen conveyed hope that the government will "continue to open discourse and earn the respect and trust of the people." He also expressed optimism that Chinese officials would conduct a thorough investigation into the mistreatment of activist lawyers, stating "I believe that the promise from the central government is sincere, and they're not lying to me."[75]

Although Chen provides an accurate depiction of the abuses suffered by his family and scores of other human rights activists in China, as well as a reasoned critique of China's legal system, he, like the *New York Times* and the *Washington Post*, exaggerates the extent to which the United States can and should continue to intervene on his behalf with Chinese leaders. While Chen was optimistic that Chinese officials would conduct an effective investigation into the mistreatment of his family and other lawyers, he also called upon the United States "and other democratic countries" to ensure that the Chinese government successfully completed this task.[76] Similar to the *New York Times*'s and *Washington Post*'s coverage of his plight, Chen characterizes the United States' connection to and responsibility for his dispute with the Chinese government as ongoing—the relationship did not end with his safe arrival in the United States. According to the activist, the U.S. government has a long-term responsibility that requires it to intervene, if necessary, on his behalf in matters with the Chinese government. Of course, just securing Chen and his family's departure from China was a monumental undertaking that could be considered a significant intervention in Chinese affairs. But, similar to the *Times* and the *Post*, Chen ignored the important contextual factors that helped legitimize the United States' involvement in the affair and that made Chinese officials more amenable to engage in negotiations on the matter.

Additionally, Chen's rhetoric, as well as coverage by the *Times* and the *Post*, obscured significant differences between conceptualizations of the law in China and the United States. Although both nations' constitutions include protections for assembly, speech, and the press, political stability takes precedence in China, where rule of law is secondary to the safeguarding of CPC power. After its Fourth Plenum meeting in 2014, the Central Committee of the CPC announced efforts to strengthen the rule of law.[77] Legal reform efforts in China include decreasing local governments' influence over local courts, increasing transparency in court cases that do not deal with politically sensitive issues, and increasing the judicial independence of the Supreme People's Court.[78] However, the CPC still maintains unlimited power to make and apply laws, thereby compromising rule of law.[79] For example, China's leaders use vague laws against "picking quarrels and provoking troubles" to suppress rights lawyers.[80] This discrepancy between Chinese and American perspectives regarding the rule of law is just one example of the difficulties inherent in discussing democracy and human rights.

I am arguing, then, that by engaging in this part-for-whole transference, in which Chen was represented and represented himself as a synecdoche for global human rights debates, the subtle complexity of the U.S.–China relationship was lost, as were the details of alternative forms of legal activism within China. Moreover, as we shall see below, Chen's conceptualization of the United States' obligations as long-term had significant rhetorical implications in his 2013 discourse. For as time went on, the United States' role in Chen's ordeal with the Chinese government did not shrink in the mind of the activist; rather, it expanded to encompass infeasible expectations that when not met, left the "barefoot lawyer" speaking in increasingly sharp tones against not only the CPC but what he perceived as hypocrisy within America as well.

Chen's Prophetic Turn: Imagining an Ideal Democracy

Although Chen had criticized the Chinese government, the CPC, and China's legal system in public statements and interviews given to media outlets since his arrival in the United States, his critiques turned increasingly vitriolic throughout his first year in the States. In an interview with the *Telegraph* in early April 2013, he expressed skepticism that China's new president, Xi Jinping, would bring much-needed political reform to China, stating "the new regime is just a continuation of the old regime." Rather than expecting Chinese rulers to instigate social change, he predicted "the future of China is actually in the hands of the Chinese people, not a few Emperors." Angered that Chinese officials had not pursued an investigation of the abuses suffered by his family, the activist derided the Chinese government, describing the central government to be "as evil as the local government." Chen also explained that he had begun work on a memoir to chronicle his activism and the oppressive measures endured by both himself and his family. According to the activist, the book would illustrate how "the Chinese regime had challenged the moral bottom of human beings."[81] In an interview with global media outlets at the Oslo Freedom Forum in May 2013, Chen made similar accusations, describing the Chinese government as "evil." He denied that Xi Jinping's assumption of the Chinese presidency would result in greater openness and significant political reform. Instead of making progress on human rights issues, he claimed China was "going backwards." Characterizing communism as "a scam," Chen concluded that Chinese leaders are not actual adherents of communist ideology, reasoning if they were "they wouldn't need to accept bribes and they wouldn't be so corrupt."[82] Continuing this pattern of escalation during a speech at Princeton University in October 2013, Chen espoused increasingly negative and malicious characterizations of the Chinese government, the CPC, and its leaders. Throughout his remarks, he describes Chinese government officials in unflattering terms, using words such as "cold-blooded and ruthless," "red terror," "robbers," and "kidnappers." He accused government officials of abducting the country and declaring "themselves as the leaders of China, though they are actually the robbers and kidnappers of the country." Chronicling China's human rights abuses, including flouting the International Convention on Civil and Political Rights, violently oppressing the Chinese people, and supporting dictatorial governments abroad as well as the intimidation, beatings, detainments, and harassment faced by Chinese activists, he likened contemporary China to having "nearly regressed to the days of the Cultural Revolution."[83]

Chen's use of vitriolic language mirrors the divisive quality typical of prophetic rhetoric, as it often characterizes situations as struggles between good and evil. Casting China's rulers as "emperors" and "kidnappers of the country," Chen both questions and denies the legitimacy of CPC rule. According to Chen, the Chinese government does not represent the will of the people. Rather, it is a system of repression. Additionally, the activist's description of Chinese leaders as emperors harkens back to the corrupt and decadent rulers of China's past, thereby conveying the sense that the Chinese government is only interested in safeguarding its own interests and power rather than enacting the will of the people. It is true that the Chinese government implements repressive measures against any group it perceives as a threat to the power and stability of the CPC and has developed close economic ties with dictatorial regimes. However, Chen simplifies the complexities of Chinese domestic and foreign policies, as well as the economic and military factors that undergird them, to cast CPC officials as purely evil and as the only world leaders concerned about maintaining power. In this sense, we can see that by 2013 Chen's rhetoric is veering from fact-based critiques of specific Party shortcomings to loose caricatures of the nation's history as a whole. Moreover, as he loses his focus, he seems to be raising the stakes.

For example, by denigrating the CPC and the Chinese government in the manner noted above, Chen fails to differentiate between local and national governments. When Chen's saga initially unfolded, it offered national Chinese leaders the opportunity to maintain face by blaming the activist's detainment and mistreatment on corrupt local officials, thereby safeguarding the central government from any responsibility for the debacle. However, by 2013 Chen obfuscates any attempts to distinguish between the two, declaring both evil. As a result, the activist communicates his increasing frustration with Chinese leaders, and his sense that any hope that the Party would fulfill its promise of a thorough investigation is gone. According to Chen, it is no longer possible to negotiate with local or national leaders in China; instead, he argues that much more extreme means are needed in responding to corrupt, evil officials. While some Americans may find it unsurprising to describe the CPC as "evil," Chen's words belie evidence that many Chinese people distinguish between the legitimacy of China's local governments and the national government. Scholars have found higher levels of satisfaction with and support for China's central government among Chinese people in comparison to lower levels of support and satisfaction for local levels of government.[84] Of course, this does not mean that all Chinese people unconditionally support the CPC. However, it does speak to the nuances and complexities embedded in Chinese attitudes toward the CPC's legitimacy. If national imaginings are always complex and layered, in this case shuttling between allegiances with and dissent against both local and national branches of the Chinese government, then here we see Chen flattening this complexity into strident, moralizing claims. As he veers into such prophetic moralizing, his national imaginings become more demanding.

Within this escalatory rhetoric, Chen's most potent charge was his depiction of China as having "nearly regressed to the days of the Cultural Revolution." Mao instigated the Cultural Revolution to purge the CPC of what he perceived to be debilitating capitalist influences. To complete this task, Mao encouraged the proletariat masses to identify enemies of the state; his supporters carried out this command by creating large character posters identifying specific individuals as being counterrevolutionaries.[85] Red Guards, an organization of Maoist zealots, demonstrated their commitment to the leader by inciting terror and violence. Virtual vigilante militias, the guards would obliterate anything perceived as connected to the four olds: old culture, old folklore, old customs, and old ideas.[86] Ruthless in their pursuit of rooting out enemies, they routinely detained, beat, and killed those suspected of being counterrevolutionaries. One of the bloodiest and most chaotic periods in the history of the PRC, the Cultural Revolution resulted in over one million deaths. The traumatic events, brutal public persecutions, and bombastic rhetoric have left deep psychological scars that continue to inform and influence Chinese political discourse.[87] Chen's reference to this volatile period in his description of contemporary Chinese political leaders further solidifies the polarizing nature of his rhetoric. Just as Mao's disastrous policies during the Cultural Revolution led to unimaginable death and destruction, Chen argues that the current Chinese leadership is guiding the nation on a similar destructive path. While the plight of activists such as Chen in China is certainly grave, comparing contemporary China with one of the most catastrophic periods in the nation's history creates a skewed and sensationalized view of the situation by associating the present Chinese leadership with the worst excesses of Mao's rule.[88]

In response to the inherent and long-standing evil of the CPC, Chen crafts a synecdochical representation that conflates the U.S. political system with his conceptualization of the democratic ideal, but Chen's discussion of democracy is largely limited to vague generalities. For example, in an appearance before the Council on Foreign Relations several weeks after his arrival in the United States, the dissident acknowledged critics' concerns about the feasibility of trying to emulate Western democracy in China. "It's true; we cannot just copy Western democracy," Chen replied. "Some Western countries . . . still have aristocrats and royal families. We can't do that." He noted the need for China to draw inspiration from both Western and Eastern democracies, citing South Korea, Taiwan, and Japan as examples. Instead of mimicking these democratic systems, Chen stated China should adopt favorable aspects of the institutions and leave behind the unfavorable components. "If it's good, just learn from it," explained Chen. "If it's bad, don't take it. I don't care where it comes from."[89] In Skype conversations with Chinese activist Hu Jia, Chen explained "he had no interest in siding with the Democratic or Republican Party." Instead, "he was on the side of democracy and freedom."[90]

Chen expressed a similarly vague, idealistic view of U.S. democracy when discussing his advocacy work and potential collaboration opportunities. In response to a *New York Times* article written by Daniel Chung, who warned Chen to guard against allowing himself to be exploited by others, Chen declared "if any person, organization, party—whatever— works to promote human rights and social justice, I will cooperate with them. Don't call that exploitation." If "you feel like you can't accomplish anything because someone tells you to do something," questioned Chen, "then what will you ever do?"[91] In discussing a possible employment opportunity at the Witherspoon Institute with a friend, Chen was unfazed by the organization's opposition to abortion and same sex parenting. Illustrating Chen's vague conceptualization of democratic ideals, he urged his friend, "don't call them conservative. They are principled. And if they are willing to support the struggle for freedom, then that's good enough for me."[92] Chen later accepted a fellowship with the institute after he left New York University.[93] These examples illustrate that Chen does not possess a thorough understanding of, or is even aware of, the discrepancies between the ideals of democracy and the messy realities of U.S. political life, including political polarization, faulty campaign finance reform efforts, and the domination of the political system by a small, wealthy elite.[94] Instead, he naively conflates the United States and an imagined ideal democracy while using terms like "good" and "bad." And so, while

Chen aligns the CPC with pure evil, he conflates U.S. democracy with ill-defined, lofty ideals, thus creating a false dichotomy based on prophetic idealism.

Uncompromising in his quest to align American leaders' dealings with China with his vision of the democratic ideal, Chen warns U.S. officials and the American public that its credibility and the very survival of democratic values would be endangered if the country did not take a stronger response to China's human rights violations. After his efforts to secure a meeting with President Obama failed, Chen told the *Telegraph* that if given an audience with the president, he would tell the U.S. leader "if an agreement between the United States and China can't be fulfilled, then U.S. credibility as the standard bearer of universal values, freedom and democracy will be jeopardized."[95] Chen later broadened this argument concerning the United States' duty to encompass the obliteration of authoritarian regimes such as the Chinese government. Equating these governments with barbarianism and evil, the activist resolutely claimed that "the greatest threat to human civilization" is the continued existence of totalitarian regimes such as the Chinese government. In order to defend the survival of universal human rights, he declared, "the removal of totalitarian governments needs to be the priority." Those people and nations who do not work to end authoritarian regimes will be corrupted by the "wickedness" of such institutions. "As a result of such insidious erosion," explains Chen, "your heart becomes distorted, and you start to set limits for yourself and give up your principles."[96] These examples demonstrate the progression of Chen's vitriolic rhetoric as he advocated increasingly extreme and unrealistic measures. Because the gulf separating good and evil in the activist's rhetoric became insurmountable, Chen privileged violence over discourse, sounding less like a human rights activist than a belligerent war hawk willing to use force. Drawing from faulty logic that stipulates either the United States helps depose of the CPC or it must face the extinction of its founding principles, Chen attempted to persuade listeners that there was only one solution—a traditionally imperialist one—to this conflict. Indeed, because the time for dialogue with Chinese leaders had passed, Chen argued that the only option was to topple China's political leadership. In this way, Chen's prophetic rhetoric ended up mirroring the long-standing and exceptionalist national imagination shared by many in the United States, which assumes the right to use force to change the minds and policies of others.

Predicting that a democratic revolution in China is inevitable, Chen urged Americans to support human rights activists "and stand on the side of the people." He resolutely stated "the historical trend of constitutionalism and democracy cannot be reversed by dictators."[97] Chen espoused support for the use of violence as self-defense in the face of government-sponsored oppression, likening such action to efforts undertaken during the American Revolution. Calling for support from both the American people and the U.S. government, he countered critics who point to the economic importance of U.S.–Sino relations as a critical reason to retain favorable engagement with China. According to Chen, the United States' commitment to democratic values was in jeopardy from the corrupting influence of its relationship with China. He claimed "attaching importance to economic interests alone will keep the United States further away from fundamental ideals such as freedom, democracy, [and] human rights, which are the founding principles of the nation."[98] Chen made a similar argument in a May 2013 interview in which he stated that "what needs to be done is the decoupling of trade and human rights issues" in U.S.–Sino relations.[99] Chen's call for severing the connection between trade and human rights issues ignores the fact that his own release was secured in large part due to the economic importance of U.S.–Sino relations. The realities of an increasingly globalized economy necessitate continued economic, political, and diplomatic engagement between the United States and China. Due to the importance of the nations' relationship and the interconnected and interdependent nature of their economies, neither can afford to jeopardize stable relations with the other. As one State Department official surmised with regard to the diplomatic ordeal concerning Chen, "the days of blowing up the relationship over a single guy are over."[100] This is one reason why leaders from both countries were motivated to reach a quick resolution on Chen's situation. Contrary to Chen's assertions, the significance of continued economic engagement between the nations can potentially serve as a conduit for, instead of solely an impediment to, human rights discussions.

Despite these political realities, by the summer of 2013 Chen was taking an aggressive and uncompromising rhetorical approach by characterizing the CPC and the Chinese government as evil barbarians and calling for help from the American people, the U.S. government, and other democratic nations to bring about the demise of totalitarian regimes such as the Chinese government. In so doing, Chen rhetorically forged a narrow perspective on human rights in China and how the issue should be approached in U.S.–Sino relations. He conveyed a zero-sum conceptualization of human rights, as he argued that the United States risked its credibility as a global power—as well as jeopardizing its democratic values—if it did not stand up to China and make more stringent demands. Positioning the United States as a synecdochical representation of the democratic ideal, he argued that the country had no choice but to topple China's authoritarian regime. According to Chen, there could be no relationship between the United States and China until the CPC was deposed and the will of the Chinese people reigned supreme. In summary, Chen's discourse escalated throughout his first year in the United States, as he adopted an uncompromising strategy that included elements of prophetic rhetoric.

Chen's turn to increasingly vitriolic rhetoric can also be attributed, at least in part, to his dispute with NYU officials. Not only had American and Chinese leaders fallen short in Chen's eyes, so too had NYU. In a statement released by Chen in June 2012, he described NYU as being under "unrelenting pressure" from "Chinese Communists" to end the university's relationship with his family. Nonetheless, he expressed renewed determination to stand strong in the midst of such hardships, promising to "never bow my head to evil or to lies. I will always do everything I can for my compatriots back in China who still are not free and who are now being oppressed."[101]

Chen's fiery rhetoric, increasingly intractable demands of U.S. officials, and fallout with NYU can be traced, in part, to the activist's synecdochical conceptualization of the American political system. In imagining the United States as embodying the democratic ideal, Chen conflated a dream version of democracy with the messy realities of the U.S. political system. In so doing, he underestimated the extent of compromise embedded within democracy in practice. Increasingly frustrated by American leaders' unwillingness to hold China accountable for its broken promises and for what he perceived to be NYU officials' bowing to CPC pressure, Chen demanded that the United States enact its role as a beacon for democracy. If the country failed to protect human rights and encroachments on academic freedom, he predicted that the very survival of the principles the United States was founded upon would be endangered. His national imagining, then, was unitary and uncompromising. Indeed, no longer asking U.S. officials to intervene with China on his behalf, or to ensure the completion of a criminal investigation into his mistreatment, Chen demanded that America stop privileging its economic ties to China over human rights and aid in bringing about the dissolution of the CPC. In short, Chen's naive understanding of the United States' long-term interests in China, when expressed via increasingly prophetic rhetoric, resulted in his calling upon the U.S. to support a political revolution in China.

Conclusion: The Limitations of Synecdochical Representations and the End of Human Rights?

Chen's radical rhetoric, like that of Liu Xiaobo, drew international attention to the subject of human rights abuses in China and galvanized those who were already members of the international human rights movement. While these are certainly salutary accomplishments, it is important to examine the negative implications of Chen's rhetorical approach. I have therefore argued that Chen's conflation of actual Western democratic practices with the ideals of democracy illustrates a profound naïveté regarding the complexities underlying U.S.–Sino relations. Ultimately, Chen advocates a radical approach that would jeopardize the stability of U.S.–Sino relations in the pursuit of extreme demands that could never be implemented. Although the U.S. government does provide assistance to Chinese activists—by providing computer software to help surmount China's digital firewall, in order to help facilitate public discourse and political organization—it does so covertly, not through bombastic declarations that the Chinese government must be abolished.[102]

Chen's discourse illustrates the limitations of prophetic rhetoric in discussions of human rights. While prophetic rhetoric can gain attention and bolster the convictions of those already supportive of the movement, it often serves to alienate nonsupporters and escalate tensions rather than provide a conduit for negotiation and cooperation. Thus, prophetic rhetoric is often counterproductive to advancing human rights, which entails transcending the binary of good vs. evil and engaging in meaningful dialogue. In turn, people may find nuanced and ethical arguments regarding the most tenable ways of furthering human rights in China more compelling than prophetic calls to forcibly change U.S.–Sino relations.

Indeed, Chen exhibits naïveté with regard to his potential to radically alter the economic, political, and diplomatic relationships between the United States and China. According to the activist's discourse, he believes he will be able to compel U.S. political leaders to privilege human rights over economic issues in their dealings with China. But as time went on and both U.S. and Chinese officials failed to meet his expectations, the activist became increasingly disillusioned and resorted to more radical demands, such as calling for the United States' direct involvement in toppling the CPC. In response, the *Global Times*, a publication under the direction of the *People's Daily*, criticized the activist's naïveté, claiming Chen possessed a "shallow understanding of the rules of Western politics and overestimation of his own value to the West." Comparing Chen to other Chinese activists who have sought refuge in the United States, the publication alleges they "mistakenly flatter themselves when they think they will be a 'treasure' in Washington when they get to the US." In reality, exiled Chinese activists come to realize that they are not as highly valued as they assume and that the United States' "cooperation with China is what prevails."[103]

Political responses to and U.S. news coverage of Chen's drama illustrate how increasing globalization has functioned to curtail human rights politics in U.S.–Sino relations. As the case of Chen Guangcheng demonstrates, "the days of blowing up" the United States' relationship with China "over a single guy are over" and "cooperation with China is what prevails."[104] As the world's second largest economy and the largest holder of U.S. foreign-owned debt, China has become a key player in the global economy and a critical pillar supporting the United States' economic stability. The two nations have become so vital to one another's fiscal health that they are economically intertwined. According to foreign policy scholar Jiakun Zhang, "the fates of the American and Chinese economies are so interdependent that they have become the most important stakeholders of each other's economic well-being."[105] Thus, it would be a financial impossibility for China to be eliminated as a key economic partner of the United States. While the interconnected and interdependent nature of the countries' economies has cemented China as a permanent and prominent player in U.S. economic and foreign policy, it has also stymied meaningful engagement between the nations on human rights. Although deeming China's treatment of human rights "deplorable," Secretary of State Hillary Clinton conceded that the United States does "business with a lot of countries whose economic systems or political systems are not ones we would design or choose to live under." While Clinton acknowledged U.S. efforts to encourage Chinese human rights reforms via private negotiations and public pressure, she conveyed the United States' reluctance to jeopardize economic ties with China by surmising, "We don't walk away from dealing with China because we think they have a deplorable human rights record."[106]

Due to the importance of the United States' economic relationship with China, U.S. political leaders are reluctant to take meaningful action on China's human rights violations. Instead, I contend that they rely on symbolic initiatives to create the appearance that the United States is critically engaging China on human rights issues. For example, in the midst of the twenty-fifth anniversary of the Tiananmen Square protests, a U.S. congressional committee voted to change the address of the Chinese embassy to "Liu Xiaobo Plaza." According to Republican congressman Frank Wolf, the initiative was designed "to highlight Liu's unjust imprisonment."[107] Although changing the Chinese embassy's address garnered U.S. media coverage of Liu's plight, the action was largely symbolic and accomplished no tangible gains in terms of meaningful negotiations between the United States and China on human rights or Liu's treatment. Instead, the initiative provided U.S. politicians a means to conflate themselves with the work of a persecuted Chinese human rights activist, thereby conveying the image of being "tough on China." Such political theater allows U.S. leaders to claim hollow, symbolic victories in the discursive tug of war between the United States and China, yet it impedes meaningful efforts to engage China on human rights.

There are parallels underlying U.S. politicians' changing of the Chinese embassy's address and the synecdochical representation of Chen

Guangcheng. Like the renaming of the street, Chen Guangcheng has become a hollow victory and, thus, a symbolic distraction in discussions of U.S.–Sino engagement on human rights issues. The U.S. press's construction of Chen as representative of the whole, rather than a part, of the human rights situation in China engenders the championing of Chen's flight from China to the United States as a human rights victory for U.S. political leaders. This synecdochical conflation of Chen with human rights in China obscures other human rights activists in China and, as a result, stunts our appreciation of other approaches to activism beyond prophetic appeals. Characterizing Chen as the embodiment of human rights in China promotes a prophetic view of human rights that casts the United States as the hero in a battle between good and evil. Such a mentality further exacerbates the ire of Chinese leaders who are already suspicious of Western powers' intrusions on issues they view as domestic matters. By relying on prophetic rhetoric to cast symbolic initiatives as heroic human rights victories, synecdochical representations of questions about human rights in China only fuel continued misinterpretation and distrust between U.S. and Chinese leaders. As I have shown here, this rhetorical pattern oversimplifies the complexities of political dialogue, international negotiation, and global cooperation—precisely the areas of communicative action that successful human rights activism requires.

NOTES

1. "SPIEGEL Interview with Chen Guangcheng: 'I'm Not Free,'" SPIEGEL Online International, May 7, 2012, http://www.spiegel.de.

2. "China: Activist's Imprisoned Nephew Needs Effective Care," Human Rights Watch, April 30, 2013, http://www.hrw.org.

3. Ibid.

4. Bei Ling, Peter Englund, and Per Wastberg, "This Is How China Treats a Nobel Prize Winner's Wife," *The Guardian*, January 15, 2014.

5. Chen Guangcheng, *The Barefoot Lawyer: A Blind Man's Fight for Justice and Freedom in China* (New York: Henry Holt, 2015), 121.

6. Ibid.

7. Michael Martinez, "Chinese Activist Chen Gives First In-Depth TV Interview since Escape," CNN, May 25, 2012, http://www.cnn.com.

8. "Chen Guangcheng," *New York Times*, May 1, 2012, A24.

9. "Chen Guangcheng's Uncertain Future," *New York Times*, May 5, 2012, A22.

10. "A Great Escape," *Washington Post*, April 28, 2012, A14.

11. John B. Thompson, "Chen Guangcheng: Rebel of the Year 2012," *GQ*, November 23, 2012.

12. Chen Guangcheng, "Full Text on Chen Guangcheng's Statement on Leaving NYU," *China Real Time Report* (blog), June 17, 2013, http://blogs.wsj.com/chinarealtime.

13. Andrew Jacobs, "After Epic Escape from China, Exile Is Mired in Partisan U.S.," *New York Times*, July 10, 2013.

14. Chen Guangcheng, "The Next Human Rights Revolution" (speech), Witherspoon Institute, Princeton University, trans. Jessica Zheng, October 17, 2013, http://www.thepublicdiscourse.com.

15. For one of the most detailed explanations of the pivot to Asia policy, see "Remarks by President Obama to the Australian Parliament," November 17, 2011, http://obamawhitehouse.archives.gov. For discussion of Chinese leaders' suspicion of the pivot to Asia policy, see Robert S. Ross, "The Problem with the Pivot: Obama's New Asia Policy Is Unnecessary and Counterproductive," *Foreign Affairs* 91, no. 6 (November/December 2012): 70–82; Ely Ratner, "Rebalancing to Asia with an Insecure China," *Washington Quarterly* 36, no. 2 (2013): 21–38; and Justin Logan, "China, America, and the Pivot to Asia," *Policy Analysis*, no. 717 (January 8, 2013), http://www.cato.org.

16. "Defense Ministry's Regular Press Conference in November, 2011," Ministry of National Defense of the People's Republic of China, November 30, 2011, quoted in Michael Swaine, "Chinese Leadership and Elite Responses to the US Pacific Pivot," *China Leadership Monitor* 38 (2012): 1–26.

17. As of spring 2014, only excerpts from *Document No. 9* have been leaked online and translated into English. A full copy of the document is not publicly accessible. For excerpts from the document translated into English, see Jayadeva Ranade, "China: Document No. 9 and the New Propaganda Regime," Institute of Peace and Conflict Studies, November 14, 2013, http://www.ipcs.org.

18. Wang Jisi quoted in "What's Gone Wrong with Democracy," *The Economist*, March 1, 2014.

19. For examples, see "USA: Life, Liberty, and the Pursuit of Human Rights," Amnesty International, September 16, 2013, http://www.amnestyusa.org; "Presumption of Guilt: Human Rights Abuses of Post-September 11 Detainees,"

Human Rights Watch, August 15, 2002, https://www.hrw.org; "World Report 2014: United States," Human Rights Watch, http://www.hrw.org; and "UN Human Rights Committee Issues Concluding Observations on State Reports of Chad, Kyrgyzstan, Latvia, Nepal, Sierra Leone, and the United States," International Justice Resource Center, April 3, 2014, http://www.ijrcenter.org.

20. While President Obama pushed hard for the TPP, President Donald Trump has announced the United States' withdrawal from the process, a move China has welcomed.

21. Hillary Clinton, "America's Pacific Century," *Foreign Policy*, October 11, 2011, http://www.foreignpolicy.com.

22. For a detailed analysis of China's territorial disputes, see Ratner, "Rebalancing to Asia with an Insecure China."

23. Ibid., 25.

24. "Statement by Spokesperson Qin Gang of the Ministry of Foreign Affairs of China on the U.S. State Department Issuing a So-called Press Statement on the South China Sea," Ministry of Foreign Affairs of the People's Republic of China, August 4, 2012, http://www.fmprc.gov.cn/mfa_eng.

25. "China Media Tell U.S. to 'Shut Up' over South China Sea Tensions," Reuters, August 6, 2012, http://www.reuters.com.

26. Jonathan Watts, Damian Carrington, and Suzanne Goldenberg, "China's Fears of Rich Nation 'Climate Conspiracy' at Copenhagen Revealed," *The Guardian*, February 11, 2010.

27. Associated Press, "China Suspends Military Exchanges with U.S. over Planned $6B Arms Sale to Taiwan," *New York Daily News*, January 30, 2010.

28. Stephen Hartnett, "To 'Dance with Lost Souls': Liu Xiaobo, *Charter 08*, and the Contested Rhetorics of Democracy and Human Rights in China," *Rhetoric & Public Affairs* 16 (2013): 223–74.

29. Ross, "The Problem with the Pivot," 71.

30. See ibid.; and Leon Panetta, "Shangri-La Security Dialogue," June 2, 2012, http://archive.defense.gov.

31. Logan, "China, America, and the Pivot to Asia," 5–6.

32. See Ross, "The Problem with the Pivot," 71; and Logan, "China, America, and the Pivot to Asia," 7.

33. Patrick Mendis, "How Washington's Asia Pivot and the TPP Can Benefit Sino–American Relations," East Asia Forum, March 6, 2013, http://www.eastAsiaforum.org.

34. Ratner, "Rebalancing to Asia with an Insecure China," 23.
35. See Kenneth G. Lieberthal and Wang Jisi, "Addressing U.S.–China Strategic Distrust," Brookings, March 30, 2012, http://www.brookings.edu.
36. Ibid., viii.
37. Ibid.
38. Ranade, "China: Document No. 9 and the New Propaganda Regime."
39. Hu Jintao, "Firmly Continue the Unique Chinese Socialism Development Plan, Strive to Build a Prosperous Country with Strong Socialism Culture," *Qiu Shi*, January 2012. While President Hu originally wrote this essay in October 2011, it was not published in *Qiu Shi* until January 2012.
40. Ibid.
41. Stanley Lubman, "Document No. 9: The Party Attacks Western Democratic Ideals," *China Real Time Report* (blog), August 27, 2013, http://blogs.wsj.com/chinarealtime.
42. Andrew Jacobs, "Chinese Professor Who Advocated Free Speech Is Fired," *New York Times*, December 10, 2013.
43. Wang Tingyou, "Some Thoughts on Constitutionalism" [in Chinese], *Hong Qi Wen Gao*, June 9, 2013.
44. Wang Tingyou, "Some Thoughts on Constitutionalism" [in Chinese], *Hong Qi Wen Gao*, June 9, 2013.
45. James Darsey, *The Prophetic Tradition and Radical Rhetoric in America* (New York: New York University Press, 1999), 16.
46. Ibid.
47. Ibid., 111.
48. Robert Terrill, "Protest, Prophecy, and Prudence in the Rhetoric of Malcolm X," *Rhetoric & Public Affairs* 4 (2001): 26.
49. Hartnett, "To 'Dance with Lost Souls,'" 226.
50. Ibid., 225.
51. Ibid.
52. Ibid., 226 and 230.
53. Ibid., 226.
54. Mark Tushnet, "A Critique of Rights: An Essay on Rights," *Texas Law Review* 8 (1984): 1360–406.
55. Leonard C. Hawes, "Human Rights and an Ethic of Truths: Pragmatic Dilemmas and Discursive Interventions," *Communication and Critical Cultural Studies* 7 (2010): 261–62.

56. Michael Ignatieff, *Human Rights as Politics and Idolatry* (Princeton, NJ: Princeton University Press, 2001), 21.

57. Kenneth Burke, *A Grammar of Motives* (Berkeley: University of California Press, 1969), 507–8.

58. Ibid., 508.

59. Ibid.

60. "A Great Escape."

61. "Chen Guangcheng."

62. "A Dissident in Limbo," *Washington Post*, May 3, 2012, A16.

63. "Dissidents and Diplomacy in Beijing," *Washington Post*, May 5, 2012, A14.

64. "Letting a Dissident Down," *Washington Post*, April 26, 2013, A16.

65. "China's Promise," *Washington Post*, May 13, 2013, A16.

66. John Wagner Givens, "Chen Guangcheng, Still Raising Heck," *The World Post*, July 3, 2013, http://www.huffingtonpost.com.

67. John Wagner Givens, "The Silent Majority: China's Other Lawyers," *The World Post*, July 29, 2011, http://www.huffingtonpost.com.

68. Martinez, "Chinese Activist Chen Gives First In-Depth TV Interview since Escape."

69. Chen Guangcheng, "How China Flouts Its Laws," *New York Times*, May 29, 2012.

70. Ibid.

71. Martinez, "Chinese Activist Chen Gives First In-Depth TV Interview since Escape."

72. Ibid.

73. Chen, "How China Flouts Its Laws."

74. Ibid.

75. "Chen Guangcheng's First Public Words in U.S." YouTube video, 7:15, posted by New Tang Dynasty Television, May 19, 2012, http://www.youtube.com.

76. Chen, "How China Flouts Its Laws."

77. Stanley Lubman, "As China Cracks Down on Dissidents, It Also Promises Legal Reform," *China Real Time Report* (blog), November 28, 2014, http://blogs.wsj.com/chinarealtime.

78. Stanley Lubman, "After Crackdown on Rights Lawyers, China's Legal Reform Path Uncertain," *China Real Time Report* (blog), July 31, 2015, http://blogs.wsj.com/chinarealtime.

79. Ibid.

80. Stanley Lubman, "China's Criminal Law Once Again Used as Political Tool,"

China Real Time Report (blog), December 1, 2015, http://blogs.wsj.com/chinarealtime.

81. Peter Foster, "China's New Leaders Will Not Bring Change, Says Blind Lawyer Chen Guangcheng," *The Telegraph*, April 9, 2013.

82. Olga Khazan, "Chen Guangcheng: 'Communism Has Always Been a Scam,'" *The Atlantic*, May 13, 2013.

83. Chen, "The Next Human Rights Revolution."

84. See Tony Saich, "Chinese Governance Seen through the People's Eyes," *East Asia Forum* 3, no. 2 (July 24, 2011), http://www.eastasiaforum.org; and Michael Lewis-Beck, Wenfang Tang, and Nicholas F. Martini, "A Chinese Popularity Function: Sources of Government Support," *Political Research Quarterly* 67 (2014): 16–25.

85. See Lincoln Cushing, "Revolutionary Chinese Posters and Their Impact Abroad," in *Chinese Posters: Art from the Great Proletarian Cultural Revolution*, ed. Lincoln Cushing and Ann Tompkins (San Francisco: Chronicle Books, 2007), 7–23.

86. Wen-hui Tsai, *Class Struggle and Deviant Labeling in Mao's China: Becoming Enemies of the People* (Lewiston, NY: Mellen Press, 2001), 121.

87. See Xing Lu, *Rhetoric of the Chinese Cultural Revolution: The Impact on Chinese Thought, Culture, and Communication* (Columbia: University of South Carolina Press, 2004).

88. See Daniel Vukovich, *China and Orientalism: Western Knowledge Production and the PRC* (New York: Routledge, 2013).

89. "What's Next for Chen Guangcheng?" Council on Foreign Relations, May 31, 2012, http://www.cfr.org.

90. Jacobs, "After Epic Escape from China, Exile Is Mired in Partisan U.S."

91. Chen Guangcheng quoted in Thompson, "Chen Guangcheng: Rebel of the Year."

92. Chen Guangcheng quoted in Jacobs, "After Epic Escape from China, Exile Is Mired in Partisan U.S."

93. According to the Witherspoon Institute's website, Chen's official title is Distinguished Senior Fellow in Human Rights at the William E. and Carol G. Simon Center on Religion and the Constitution. The site also lists Chen as a faculty member of the Institute for Policy Research and Catholic Studies at the Catholic University of America. He is also affiliated with the Lantos Foundation for Human Rights and Justice as a Senior Distinguished Advisor. See "Chen Guangcheng," The Witherspoon Institute, http://winst.org.

94. Pew Research Center, "Political Polarization in the American Public," June 12, 2014, http://www.people-press.org/; Dave Levinthal, "Another Massive Problem

with U.S. Democracy: The FEC Is Broken," *The Atlantic*, December 17, 2013; and Martin Gilens and Benjamin I. Page, "Testing Theories of American Politics: Elites, Interest Groups, and Average Citizens," *Perspectives on Politics* 12 (2014): 564–81.

95. Foster, "China's New Leaders Will Not Bring Change."

96. Chen, "The Next Human Rights Revolution."

97. Ibid.

98. Ibid.

99. Rosie Gray, "Chen Guangcheng: Chinese Government 'In a State of Madness,'" BuzzFeed News, May 14, 2013, www.buzzfeed.com.

100. Steven Lee Myers and Mark Landler, "Behind Twists of Diplomacy in China Case," *New York Times*, May 9, 2012, A1.

101. Chen, "Full Text on Chen Guangcheng's Statement on Leaving NYU."

102. Dominic Rushe, "US to Spend $30m Fighting Internet Censorship," *The Guardian*, May 11, 2011.

103. "Chen Misread Washington Politics," *Global Times*, June 20, 2013.

104. See Myers and Landler, "Behind Twists of Diplomacy in China Case"; and "Chen Misread Washington Politics."

105. Jiakun Jack Zhang, "American Perceptions, Chinese Realities: Roadmap for Congress in 21st Century U.S.–China Relations," paper prepared for the Center for the Study of the Presidency & Congress, 2011, http://cspc.nonprofitsoapbox.com/storage/Fellows2011/Zhang-_Final_Paper.pdf.

106. Jeffrey Goldberg, "Danger: Falling Tyrants," *The Atlantic*, April 26, 2011.

107. Tom Phillips, "Beijing Fumes at US Plan to Rename Embassy Street after Dissident Liu Xiaobo," *The Telegraph*, June 25, 2014.

Alternative Modernities, Postcolonial Colonialism, and Contested Imaginings in and of Tibet

Stephen J. Hartnett

> The angel of history. . . . sees one single catastrophe which keeps piling wreckage upon wreckage and hurls it in front of his feet. The angel would like to stay, awaken the dead, and make whole what has been smashed. But a storm is blowing from paradise. . . . it irresistibly propels him into the future to which his back is turned, while the pile of debris before him grows skyward. This storm is what we call progress.
>
> —Walter Benjamin, "Theses on the Philosophy of History"

S purred by increased shelling of the city, and worried by rumors of impending assassination attempts, the Fourteenth Dalai Lama fled Lhasa, Tibet, on March 17, 1959.[1] Within days of his escape, Chinese forces had slaughtered ten thousand Tibetans;[2] Tsering Shakya has described how "the streets were littered with corpses."[3] Over the next twenty years, as the Communist Party of China (CPC or the Party) colonized Tibet, "a staggering 15 to 20 percent of all Tibetans, perhaps half of all adult males, were thrown into prison"; the nation's population of more than 110,000 monks was reduced by starvation, murder, and forced exile to 7,000.[4] The Dalai Lama has estimated the death toll from these events, circa 1959–70, as reaching one million, or roughly "one sixth of the population."[5] China's war on Tibet was so complete—encompassing the blowing-up of hundreds of monasteries, the repression of local religious customs, the forced transition from centuries-old agricultural practices to disastrous collective farming units, the marginalization of local languages, and the obliteration of ancient kinship systems—that John Avedon has portrayed it as "an orgy of destruction."[6] Shakya reports that Tibetans were so pulverized by these events, both physically and emotionally, that they began to refer to the Chinese occupation of their land as triggering a nearly apocalyptic tragedy wherein "the sky fell to the earth."[7] While the heavens collapsed in Tibet, the People's Republic of China (PRC) embarked on an ambitious expansion of its borders: roughly half of Tibet was absorbed into China and eventually renamed as the Tibet Autonomous Region (TAR); the other half of Tibet was folded into the much-expanded Chinese provinces of Sichuan, Qinghai, Yunnan, and Gansu.[8]

Exiled to northern India, ignored by the United Nations, and largely abandoned by the United States (leaving aside for the moment the CIA's duplicitous involvement in the situation),[9] the Dalai Lama and his entourage became what John Knaus has called "orphans of the Cold War."[10] Nonetheless, the Dalai Lama sought to salvage some of Tibet's people and culture by establishing a government in exile. Based in Dharamsala, India, now often referred to as "Little Lhasa," the Tibetan government in exile (formally called the Central Tibetan Administration, CTA) amounts to one of the world's most remarkable examples of an exile community working for both a return to their occupied homeland and the construction of a new, diasporic notion of postnational global solidarity.[11] As Pico Iyer notes, this experiment with exiled imaginings asks us "to think about home in a new way, without the limitations of nationality or race," for the CTA is attempting to constitute a new Tibet "linked not by common soil but common purposes," hence establishing "a community of vision."[12] And so, while Tibet has been physically absorbed as a part of China's imperial expansion, "Little Lhasa" offers a living laboratory for exploring the possibilities of postterritorial nationality and exiled community in an age of globalization. In this sense, addressing debates about the contested imaginings of Tibet (created in China proper, in the TAR, in Dharamsala, in the United States, and elsewhere) offer insights into how the rhetorical work of imaging communities can simultaneously involve local, national, continental, and global layers—in this case, with dizzying and contentious consequences.

While this chapter frames the contested imaginings of community both of and in Tibet as compelling examples of constitutive rhetoric at work,[13] I want to try to add a new layer of conceptual complexity to that intellectual lineage by situating "Little Lhasa" within the rubric of postcolonial criticism broadly and the more recent theoretical work known as the study of alternative modernities. As argued by Raka Shome and Radha Hegde, "to think about, and resurrect, stories of other modernities is, at some level, to think through and against Western modernities." "The driving force of postcolonial work," they argue, "is to interrogate the universalizing discourse of Western modernity."[14] Working alongside this version of postcolonial scholarship, in 1999 Dilip P. Gaonkar announced the launching of a new subfield of postcolonial criticism dubbed "alternative modernities."[15] Within this area of work, scholars sought to study postcolonial situations while jettisoning the long-standing obsession with Euro-U.S. modernity as the presumed metagenerator of history. As Frederick Cooper argues, the assumption that there was (or is) a unified, hegemonic, all-conquering "West" actually "perpetuates what is being criticized. Europe remains the reference point to which everyone else has to point."[16] What makes the exile Tibetan situation so pertinent for postcolonial criticism in general, and for theories of alternative modernities in particular, is that the colonizing force decimating Tibet is not some imagined "universalizing discourse" from the "West," but the CPC, an organization that has spent the better part of the past sixty years trying to frame its national project as a heroic response to Western incursions. Indeed, given that the CPC has so relentlessly portrayed itself not only as a postcolonial state but as the model postcolonial state, even while acting in Tibet in a traditionally colonialist manner, I argue that critics could frame the CPC's actions in Tibet as a stunning example of *postcolonial colonialism*.[17]

While Tibetan resistance movements can still be approached productively via the lens of postcolonial criticism, this chapter offers an important caveat: rather than striving to destabilize some assumed Western hegemony, Little Lhasa is trying to reverse the policies of the CPC, in large part by appealing to the same Western forces—the United Nations, the United States, and a grab bag of Western-based nongovernmental organizations (NGOs)—generally criticized by postcolonial critics as little more than fronts for U.S.-driven neoliberal globalization. This study of exile Tibetan communication therefore draws upon and advances a new vein of postcolonial criticism that tackles the multifaceted rifts, cross-national ruptures, and everyday contingencies of postcolonial colonialism within the PRC's sphere of influence. Consistent with Gaonkar's and Cooper's critiques—and the similar arguments made by Ann Laura Stoler, Carole McGranahan, Peter Perdue, and others[18]—this analysis indicates how postcolonial colonialism in Tibet is being driven by an imperial China advancing its own versions of enlightenment, modernity, and nationalism. In this sense, while the rhetorical work of imagining communities has always been dauntingly complicated, this chapter shows how the constitutive work of building a sense of nation and nationalism is made even more difficult by our collective immersion in the infinite flow of goods, ideas, and bodies that mark our age of globalization.

Indeed, this chapter illustrates how *all politics are now global*. In the case addressed here, while the PRC and Tibetan supporters volley accusations back and forth, the White House is inevitably caught in the middle. It has become virtually an annual ritual, in fact, for the Dalai Lama to tour the offices of Western leaders, who, hoping not to annoy the CPC, host their meetings in tangential spaces, often without inviting the press, only to have the CPC nonetheless argue that this delicate dance is a charade that masks meddling in China's internal affairs. As these charges and counterclaims indicate, while there are many key factors at play in shaping the future of U.S.–China communication in our age of globalization, the fate of Tibet stands among the most raw, controversial, and rhetorically fraught among them. Indeed, along with questions about Hong Kong's Umbrella Revolution, rising tensions in Xinjiang, evolving relations with India, and heated debates about sovereignty in the South

China Sea, the status of Tibet haunts U.S.–China communication at both formal and informal levels.

To pursue these claims about variations of postcolonial criticism and alternative modernities, to chart the rhetorical work of imagining as illustrated in the case of exile Tibetan politics, and to demonstrate the significance of debates about Tibet to the larger U.S.–China relationship, the chapter unfolds in four steps. First, "The Storm of Progress in Occupied Lhasa" reprises Walter Benjamin's famous line, which appears here in the epigraph, to help explain how the CPC's forced modernization of Lhasa has left that city both destroyed and resurgent, both reeling with poverty yet teeming with new riches. Second, to explain how these processes in Lhasa are indicative of larger patterns within China, the section titled "China's Alternative Modernities" demonstrates how the CPC's actions in Tibet are consistent with the same forms of modernization-as-destruction being practiced on some of China's oldest neighborhoods as well.[19] I argue, however, in the third section of the essay, "Competing Nationalisms," that the CPC's project is doomed to fail because—precisely as postcolonial critics suggest—imperial state projects attempting to extend administrative control over new regions tend to be so politically ham-handed, so culturally inept, and so rhetorically crass (they are less "constitutive" than overwhelming) that rather than cultivating the consent of the colonized, they produce virulent opposition. Despite this claim, the CPC has held Tibet for sixty-plus years and shows no inclination to leave. And so the essay's fourth section, "The Dilemmas of Statelessness," ponders the prospects and paradoxes of Little Lhasa's postnational project of imagining a new sense of nation. Taken as a whole, I hope to make a contribution to the literature on alternative modernities and postcolonial criticism, to participate in ongoing debates about globalization, and, more importantly, to venture some preliminary comments on the prospects of exiled Tibetans returning home, or reinventing the notion of home for a global age, or possibly both.[20] In short, the contested imaginings of community both of and in Tibet stand as compelling case studies of the complexity of constitutive rhetoric in the age of globalization.

Throughout the chapter, to provide readers with visual supplements to my arguments, I include photographs taken in China, Tibet, Nepal,

and India during eight years of research and travel throughout the Himalayan states that straddle the "roof of the world." I offer these photographs
not as truth statements, but as suggestive visual glimpses—images of the
process of imagining—into my immersive, deeply personal, and embodied experiences, which have been crucial to helping me make sense of
the hopes and fears that haunt occupied Tibet, exiled Little Lhasa, the
sprawling avenues of Beijing, and the surrounding region. In this sense, I
aspire to be a practitioner of what Carole McGranahan calls "research as
kora"; *kora* is the Tibetan word for "a form of walking prayer," as practiced
by Buddhists when they circumambulate holy sites. McGranahan argues
that "research as *kora*" centers around the ideas of "being in motion, of
being engaged and embodied, and of circling around and through Tibetan communities."[21] As the Buddhist adventurer Ian Baker notes in his
magnificent memoir of his explorations in the Himalayas, the notion of
kora is "guided by the intuition that the sacred cannot be approached in
a straight line, still less by linear thought."[22] In keeping with the spirit of
that idea, the photographs offered herein document my own confused,
enthralled, zigzagging practice of *kora* and stand as visual fragments of
the beauty, horror, and maddening complexity of what postcolonial colonialism has wrought in occupied Tibet, Little Lhasa, and the Himalayas
more broadly.

The Storm of Progress in Occupied Lhasa

After lighting incense, bowing our heads in respect, snapping photos,
and walking for hours amid the pilgrims circumambulating the Jokhang
Temple, one of the holiest sites in all of Tibetan Buddhism and an iconic
marker of downtown Lhasa (Figure 1), my traveling companions and I
strolled east down Yuthok Street, a gorgeous boulevard graced with tow-
ering poplars.[23] The sweet Himalayan air was tinged with hints of the
juniper and rosemary burning in the giant urns back at the temple, yet
our senses were jarred by the passage of platoons of riot-gear-clad Chinese soldiers with machine guns held at the ready, black-clad security
personnel with discreet communication devices planted in their ears,
and camouflage-wearing troops who marched with fire extinguishers—to

Figure 1. The interior courtyard of Lhasa's Jokhang Temple, one of the holiest sites in Tibetan Buddhism.

douse any possible self-immolators—strapped to their backs (Figure 2).²⁴ Our heads spinning from another day of immersion in juxtaposed beauty and barbarism, myth and militarism, development and destruction, we ducked south into the stairway leading up to Namaseti, a local eatery where Nepali, Indian, and Tibetan dishes sit side by side with pizza, hamburgers and fries, and blessedly cold beer. On the second floor landing, before turning in to the restaurant on the right, we were greeted on the left, at the entrance to the Lhasa Cinema, by a wall-filling, glossy, full-color banner announcing the opening of *Battleship*, the 2012 science fiction, alien invasion, hard body, naval nostalgia war film that features giant Transformers and a menagerie of operatic battle scenes. In occupied Lhasa, there is no free press, no voting, widespread poverty, armored personnel carriers parked on the corners equipped with a half dozen tubes for launching crowd-dispersing tear gas canisters (Figure 3), and so much booming Chinese development that the Tibetans feel like a minority within their own town; still, the locals can drop their money

Figure 3. The armored troop carriers sport six-packs of launch tubes for firing crowd-dispersing tear gas. As figures 2 and 3 indicate, Lhasa exists in a de facto state of martial law.

down for a bar of chocolate and the latest Hollywood blather, which, fittingly in this case, depicts a war over the fate of human civilization. We roaming scholars move amid these layered conditions with a sense of shame, fascination, and bewilderment.

Our experience of the enmeshing of international cuisines, Chinese occupation forces, society of the spectacle dreamscapes, religious sites turned into museums, and the selling of everything triggered a conversation about *The Postmodern Condition: A Report on Knowledge*, wherein Jean François Lyotard offered this observation on the diffusion of capital and confusion into all corners of contemporary life:

Figure 2 (*opposite*). Chinese soldiers patrolling Lhasa. While the Tibetans circumambulate in a clockwise direction, the soldiers march in the opposite direction, thus serving as both an occupying military force and a rebuke to ancient Buddhist traditions. Photo courtesy of Patrick Shaou-Whea Dodge.

> Eclecticism is the degree zero of contemporary general culture: one
> listens to reggae, watches a western, eats McDonald's food for lunch
> and local cuisine for dinner, wears Paris perfume in Tokyo and "retro"
> clothes in Hong Kong; knowledge is a matter for TV games. . . . By be-
> coming kitsch, art panders to the confusion which reigns in the "taste"
> of patrons. Artists, gallery owners, critics, and public wallow together in
> the "anything goes," and the epoch is one of slackening. But this realism
> of the "anything goes" is in fact that of money.[25]

There was a period when Lyotard's portrayal of a global economy of consumer abundance, critical "slackening," and epistemological relativism
seduced his legion of followers to envision an emerging postmodern age
of cultural multiplicity and kitschy eclecticism, yet such heady talk has
been shadowed by the seemingly endless catastrophes of what Jurgen
Habermas famously described as "the project of modernity," which "has
not yet been fulfilled."[26]

   Thinking about Lyotard and Habermas's emerging-postmodernity vs.
incomplete-modernity debate points to the obvious fact that Lhasa is a
city simultaneously premodern, modern, and postmodern.[27] In premodern fashion, the villagers who stream into the city from the hinterlands
still orient their lives to a labyrinthine world of deities and dedicate their
days to preindustrial forms of artisanal and agricultural production, a
lifestyle the International Campaign for Tibet (ICT) celebrates, in a fit of
environmentally tinged nostalgia, as "one of the last examples of sustainable nomadic pastoralism."[28] In classic modern fashion, the Chinese have
rolled into Tibet in a show of colonial occupation and cultural destruction
that rivals any the world has ever seen, with the forced transformation
justified, of course, in an avalanche of museum pieces, TV shows, billboards, speeches, and other media celebrating the heroic spread of communist modernity.[29] London's *Guardian* reports, however, that because
of the Party's modernization program, Tibet's "identity is being buried
under tons of concrete and glass"[30] (compare Figures 4 and 5). Andrew
Martin Fischer has shown that this onslaught of forced modernization
has not been launched on behalf of improving the living standards of
Tibetans, but in the cause of building the infrastructure of occupation. In

Figure 4. "Old Lhasa," a dense sea of merchants, beggars, families walking home from school, monks, tourists, billboards, food sellers, rickshaws, and nests of cables above—a cacophonous crush of goods and bodies packed into tight spaces.

fact, he reports that "by far the largest [recipients of CPC funding] have been government agencies, party agencies, and social organizations"; in other words, the CPC's developmental efforts are directed overwhelmingly toward building "the administrative apparatus of the state"[31]—the infrastructure of colonial oppression. For these observers, the CPC's forced modernization of Tibet in general and Lhasa in particular stands as a gut-wrenching example of how what Benjamin called the storm of progress feels, at the ground level, like a catastrophe. These examples therefore demonstrate the remarkable complexity of the rhetorical work of imagining communities, as the same actions the CPC celebrates as examples of "progress" and "liberation" and "development" are loathed by many Tibetans as evidence of "genocide" and "occupation" and cultural "destruction."[32]

Figure 5. "New Lhasa" features multilane thoroughfares designed to facilitate the movement of troops, tourists, and goods across instrumental spaces built, as illustrated here, to maximize sightlines of the Himalayas' majestic beauty. To their credit, the CPC has lined such streets with walls of poplars and CO_2-eating evergreens

While such dire observations about what modernity has done to Lhasa illustrate how constitutive rhetorics are always enmeshed in contestation, they also miss the many ways that postmodern juxtapositions have infused the city with new life. Pizza joints pop up next to noodle shops; bike rentals stand next to troop stations; tourists representing a dizzying array of nations swarm over the key historical sites while snapping photographs that will feed exiled activist websites;[33] immense video billboards advertise the latest Mercedes Benz dream machine for sale just down the street from the Potala Palace, which is now mummified as a dirty museum; the previously chaste culture is infused with sexual innuendo and lingerie shops; angry youth strut by the temples reciting hip-hop fantasies and struggling to look hard while monks who have been tortured preach forgiveness; immigrant/settler Chinese grandmothers dance to nostalgic, Maoist revolutionary folk songs in the park while the armed police sweep Tibetans off the streets. In postmodern fashion, the daily lives of folks in Lhasa are enmeshed within an ever-expanding range of consumer choices and daily contradictions, bizarre architectural juxtapositions, media offerings both public and underground, and other lived daily sensorium that announce, in their sheer proliferation and audacity, the end of traditional Tibetan culture in favor of a swirling and smiling mess of international consumerism. Is it progress or hell? Are we witness to multiculturalism in practice or slow-motion genocide? What has the storm of progress wrought?[34] And what does this "radical coexistence of different temporal-spatio orders" foreshadow for life in Lhasa?[35] As the ultimate frontier town, the crown jewel of China's postcolonial colonialism, and yet another example of globalizing capitalism's intensities, Lhasa confounds explanation and exemplifies how what Fredric Jameson calls "late capitalism" must be understood—honoring Benjamin's "angel of history" parable—"as catastrophe and progress all together."[36]

China's Alternative Modernities

Approaching Tibet as "catastrophe and progress" is one way of asking about the status of globalizing capitalism in the hands of the CPC. For while Soviet and Chinese versions of communism once stood as counterweights to U.S.-led post–World War II capitalist modernity—think of them as offering alternative imagined communities—the monumental events of 1989 (the dismantling of the wall in Europe, the Tiananmen protests in China, the beginning of the dissolution of the U.S.S.R., the fall of the Iranian Shah, etc.) led to the opening of a post–Cold War era marked by the realignment of markets, resources, audiences, and alliances.[37] Rushing to join this post–Cold War moment of opportunity, no longer communist, proudly postcolonial, and determined to achieve superpower status, post-Mao China offers a staggering example of an alternative modernity that strives, even while renouncing the West, to reproduce its combination of modernizing capitalism, military imperialism,

racial chauvinism, and cultural destruction.[38] This post–Cold War journey has produced a winding path of rhetorical invention and, sometimes,
political confusion. Moreover, while I and others have argued that the
United States has sought for the past two decades to build a form of global
imperialism without colonialism,[39] the geographic proximity of Tibet to
China lured the CPC into pursuing a more traditional, absorptive version
of colonialism-as-occupation. As Eric Hobsbawm argues in *Nations and
Nationalism*, when large modernizing states begin to look toward their
smaller neighbors, bad things happen: "If the only historically justifiable
nationalism was that which fitted in with progress, i.e. which enlarged
rather than restricted the scale on which human economies, societies,
and cultures operated, what could the defense of small peoples, small
languages, small traditions be, in the overwhelming majority of cases,
but *an expression of conservative resistance to the inevitable advance of
history?*"[40] Seen from this perspective, as one of China's resource-rich,
strategically placed, historically backward, and militarily weaker neigh-
bor states, Tibet—like Inner Mongolia to the north and Xinjiang to the
west[41]—never stood a chance in the face of China's modernizing and
postcolonial colonizing ambitions.

Hoping to counter this sense of modernity as a form of inevitable
conquest, and contrary to the portrayal of those who resist it as conservative hold-outs against progress (a view Hobsbawm was critical of), scholars in many disciplines have produced a slew of studies arguing that upon
closer scrutiny, the assumed uniformity and universality of Eurocentric
modernity has always been contested by "alternative modernities," "multiple modernities," "varieties of modernity," "global modernities," "Asian
modernities," and, especially germane to this study, "Tibetan modernities."[42] Bill Ashcroft argues, for example, that "globalization may now be
characterized by the *multiplicity* of modernities."[43] For these scholars, the
rhetorical work of imagining communities is always deeply local, even
while striving toward a sense of something as grand as a nation. Because
these imaginings are driven by local concerns, these multiple, alternative
modernities are often understood as *oppositional* in nature, as in the following passage, where Ranajit Guha describes how subaltern studies in
particular and postcolonial criticism in general strive "to confront the supposedly universal status of the European experience—the universalizing

function of its capital, the universality of its reason, and the complicity of capital and reason in elevating the particular brand of European modernity to a universal model valid for all continents."[44] While such arguments tend to assume that a deconstructed Eurocentric modernity will be replaced by local, democratic, and nationalist forms of cultural life and political organization, I argue in this chapter that China is less interested in authoring a fractured, alternative modernity than in creating a *new master narrative* in which CPC-style state-controlled markets fuel regimes stripped of any notion of human rights or democracy.[45] The sense of hope and change implied in the theories of alternative or multiple modernities appears, at least in the case of China's actions in Tibet, to be terribly misplaced. The China/Tibet dynamic appears, in fact, to confirm Hobsbawm's worst fears while indicating the likely trajectory of the CPC's version of an alternative modernity, wherein the "China Dream" means absorbing Tibet into an expanding and heroic Chinese nationalism.

As a result of this process of absorption, it is now common, when reading through documents about Tibet, to encounter advocates deploying the trope of genocide.[46] Even while foregrounding disputed death counts at the hands of the PRC's forces in Tibet, the notion of genocide seems most often to indicate a sense of cultural destruction. While not wanting to dismiss such claims, it seems important to situate them within the larger contexts of globalization, for Tibet is not the only region of the world experiencing rapid modernization. Fredric Jameson summarizes the postmodern literature on culture in an age of globalization as dividing into two main camps: the utopian visionaries depict "an immense global urban intercultural festival without a center or even any longer a dominant cultural mode," whereas an opposite camp envisions "the rapid assimilation of hitherto autonomous national markets and productive zones into a single sphere" marked by "standardization on an unparalleled scale."[47] In short, Jameson asks, does globalizing capitalism lead to proliferating differences or relentless homogenization? Are we experiencing an age of giddy cosmopolitan decadence or market-driven cultural genocide? Jameson's answer, in good dialectical fashion, is that these patterns happen at once, together, both feeding and contradicting each other. Indeed, as Terry Eagleton has observed, postmodernity's "philosophy of difference" comes wrapped in neoliberal capitalism's "remorseless cultural homogenization,"[48] meaning that as Beijing's *hutongs* are pulled down to make room for Starbucks, McDonald's, and KFCs, so the culture itself changes. Street vendors give way to Big Macs, independent fruit stands are replaced by corporately produced frozen fruit pops, a culture of bicycling along alleyways and riverside paths is buried beneath twelve-lane freeways that cut up the city into concrete enclaves; the feel of everything transforms from local to international, from autonomous production to chain production, from a cash economy to a credit-card economy. Debates abound about the causes and consequences of these processes around the globe, yet in the pro-Tibetan sources cited herein, and when discussing how this development has been unleashed across the TAR, this process is often called genocide.

On the other hand, Beijing's and Lhasa's swanky new consumer zones pop with a carnivalesque energy fueled by what appear to be artisanal boutiques selling gear to young fashionables, who strut with as much style and hauteur as anyone in Greenwich Village or Miami Beach—but preceding it all, the storm of progress leaves the city pockmarked by neighborhoods reduced to rubble in preparation for their rebirth as tributes to globalizing capital (Figure 6). Thus, precisely as Marx argues in the *Communist Manifesto*, authoring new imaginings about emerging forms of development always entails a preliminary stage of "enforced destruction."[49]

Such remarkable and rapid-fire transformations in daily life can feel like progress or catastrophe depending on your political perspective and personal mood. Moreover, one's perspective and mood will determine whether these processes point toward the welcome production of discreet particulars—all those consumer choices flooding the world in every shape and size—or toward the relentless homogenization of daily life beneath an avalanche of mass-produced commodities. Writing about this same process in America, Don DeLillo laments in his magnum opus, *Underworld*, how "capital burns off the nuance in a culture . . . making for a certain furtive sameness, a planning away of particulars that effects everything from architecture to leisure time to the way people eat and sleep and dream."[50] China seems at times to embody this phase of capitalism gone global, where the market has become an immense machine of commodified differences, yet the picture changes the minute you enter the countryside's small towns or any city's forgotten neighborhoods, where every encroaching

Figure 6. A destroyed Beijing *hutong*, with construction cranes erecting the postmodern present in the background—a typical scene of the storm of progress in Beijing, this one from the near-east side of Beijing, a short walk from Tiananmen Square.

Western outlet is celebrated as what Peter Berger has described as an opportunity "to participate vicariously in America-style modernity."[51] This notion of "participation" is crucial, for what looks like inane commodification from one perspective feels, from another angle, like an eruption of subjectivity. Indeed, the rhetorical work of imagining community is always deeply personal and affective; in this case, the politics of development are felt, embodied, experienced as moments within the day. This explains why Jameson characterizes the "joyous intensities" driving this process as part of "the excitement of the immense, unfinished social experiment of the New China," wherein we witness "the freshness of a whole new object world produced by human beings in some new control over their collective destiny." From this view, the "Storm of Progress" in New China is a necessary prerequisite for "the signal event . . . of a collectivity that has become a new 'subject of history.'"[52] At the same time, the creative destruction required to launch this new subjectivity is so intense, as seen in figure 6, that Chinese novelist Yu Hua has observed that the "large scale demolitions" preceding development "can make Chinese cities look as though they have been targets of bombing raids."[53]

These questions come home on the streets of Lhasa with an impact that hammers your senses. The Muslim barbeque men from Xinjiang rotate their kebabs at street-side grills while talking of being treated like suspected members of Al Qaeda in the global war on terrorism; the Tibetan woman selling "authentic" silk shawls in the Barkhor Square confesses that her products are made in factories in Nepal and trucked into Tibet via the Chinese-built "Friendship Highway"; the rooftops are stuffed on one side of the square with Germans and Italians drinking beer and debating the Universal Declaration of Human Rights while the CPC's snipers smoke Russian cigarettes on the opposing roofs while checking their cell phones; we children of Google lament the blocked access to the Web while worshippers complete their circumambulations, doing a thousand prostrations before heading home to butter tea and *tsampa* dumplings; and the evening air echoes with the sounds of bulldozers, earth movers, graders, and wrecking balls as Chinese work crews tear down and then build up a new, Sinified Lhasa. And encircling it all stands the Chinese army, enforcing a communication blockade so severe that, as far as the world outside of China is concerned, the storm of progress unfolds in Lhasa as if in secret.[54] Whether or not the process amounts to genocide, it seems clear that the alternative modernity being forced onto Tibet by the CPC embodies values, hopes, and practices that mesh nicely with popular Chinese imaginings of China's rise to greatness, even while they violate popular imaginings of Tibet as a place separate from such worldly strivings.

Competing Nationalisms

I have sought in the first two sections of this chapter to describe the storm of progress in Tibet and to frame China's actions there as one example of an alternative modernity—albeit one that involves many aspects of former U.S. and Eurocentric versions of modernity, including military occupations launched in the name of national defense, forced modernization justified in the name of progress, institutionalized racism offered in the name of social improvement, and local cultural destruction pursued in the name of universalism. In this section of the chapter I argue that thinking critically about nationalism provides a useful analytic frame for making sense of the tragedy unfolding on the roof of the world. For even while China has economically, militarily, and administratively absorbed Tibet into the PRC, it is clear that for both the Chinese and the Tibetans, the land formerly known as Tibet, and now called by the Chinese the TAR, stands as a separate nation, an indigenous space, a cultural zone wherein clashing and, I believe, irreconcilable imaginaries roil beneath the surface of the occupation. From this perspective, even while the CPC strives to deploy constitutive rhetoric to reinvent Tibet in accordance with popular Chinese imaginings, the lived realities of daily life in the TAR militate against such efforts.

As a prominent Tibetan exile said in an interview in Delhi, "what the Chinese wear and what the Tibetans wear is different. The language the Tibetans speak and the Chinese speak is different—completely different. How we write and how the Chinese write is totally different. *So basically there is no commonality between the Chinese and the Tibetans*, except that we are all human beings."[55] While he was writing about postcolonial India, Partha Chatterjee's reminder in this regard is crucial: "If the nation is an imagined community, then this is where it is brought into being. In this, its true and essential domain [the imagination], the nation is already sovereign, even when the state is in the hands of the colonial power."[56] As the interviewee's comments make clear, both the lived experiences and imagined communities of most Tibetans—their sense of a local, indigenous *nation*—have "no commonality" with the state being imposed by their conquerors.

Chatterjee's *The Nation and its Fragments* is based in part on his reading of Benedict Anderson's *Imagined Communities*, where he noted that the modern nation-state was "an imagined community" wherein localized senses of place, culture, and language—the ground-level particulars of daily life—were reimagined as subsidiary elements of a larger political entity bound together by a central administrative apparatus and a homogenizing "language of power."[57] The modern state, in this regard, is the formalized political entity that enmeshes preexisting nations. Chatterjee and Anderson's writings, and the exiled Tibetan's words above, help us to remember, however, that the nation (a lived set of daily practices) and the state (a formal political entity bound by power) are by no means coterminous and can in fact, as seen in Tibet, coexist in a state of perpetual tension and rhetorical refashioning.

Anderson in particular was concerned with the roles of early communication technologies—especially the newspaper and Bible—in fueling the transition from linguistically diverse, premodern tribes, feudal kingdoms, and unaffiliated city-states to the geographically sprawling and linguistically homogeneous entities that we call nation-states. This was a process full of struggle. However, in the case of most developed Western nation-states, these transitions happened so long ago—in the decades surrounding 1776, for example, in the case of the United States—that only a handful of historians have access to the intricate dynamics at play. Thus, except for those small pockets of scholars who study the transatlantic politics of slavery and the decimation of indigenous cultures, the United States appears to most of its citizens as an ahistorical a priori, as always already complete, as a finished entity beyond anything like controversy or contestation. Hence Michael Rogin's description of contemporary Americans as committed to "motivated forgetting" and "political amnesia."[58] Still, if certain historically deep nation-states like the United States or Britain seem to contemporary observers to have an organic, intrinsic, transhistorical wholeness to them, Anderson and Chatterjee remind us that when modern nation-states attempt to spread themselves into new lands, the process of the colonizing state absorbing the colonized nation is played out as a highly visible political contest.[59] Anderson thus describes colonialism as an inherently unstable attempt to "stretch the short, tight, skin of the nation over the gigantic body of the empire." This process, he claims, is doomed to fail because of the "incompatibility" between imperial ambitions to expand a version of the state presumed to be universally desirable and the sheer factual rootedness and stubborn particularity of local cultures.[60]

Within this unstable dynamic of imperial expansion, Anderson was particularly interested in the importance of a sense of national history.

"The paradox of imperial official nationalism," he argues, "was that it inevitably brought what were increasingly thought of and written about as European 'national histories' into the consciousness of the colonized."[61] These "national histories" were attempts by supporters of new nation-states—think, for example, in the United States, of George Bancroft's efforts as a national historian, or Benjamin Franklin's role as fabulist-in-chief—to give relatively new political entities the sheen of deep historical resonance.[62] If communities could be, in this sense, imagined into being, and thus turned via print communication from many small things (fragmented and localized minor nations) into one bigger thing (a unified nation-state), then surely those being colonized could utilize the same narrative structure for their own benefit. Alternative imagined communities could be constituted to resist colonial ambitions; new national histories could be invented to counter imperial claims.

For example, in the case of Tibet/the TAR, Carole McGranahan has argued that China's initial 1950 invasion galvanized the fragmented and premodern nation of Tibet—which overlay multilayered and sprawling regions held together mostly by devotion to the Dalai Lama—to seek to become a more modern, unified, nation-state. Observing the long-standing cultural differences, economic competitions, monastic rivalries, and geographic barriers between the western U-Tsang region, the northern Amdo region, and the southeastern Kham region, McGranahan observes that in preinvasion Tibet, "political allegiances were never singular."[63] George Dreyfus states the matter bluntly: "Tibetans did not have a full-fledged nationalism before 1950."[64] As Shakya argues, preinvasion Tibet was not so much a modern-style nation-state as a loose Buddhist "civilization" united by allegiance to the Dalai Lama.[65] Worse yet, the government that existed prior to the PRC's invasion was plagued, as described by Gyalo Thondup, the Dalai Lama's brother, by "disastrous incompetence."[66] Nonetheless, the discursive logic addressed herein suggests that the Tibetans likely culled from their invaders a vocabulary and worldview that could support the consolidation of their own, resistant nationalism. Peter Hansen has thus asked "if the Chinese imported into Tibet not merely a set of reforms against which Tibetans rebelled, but also a discourse (people, class, strata, etc.) that enabled the articulation of subaltern positions crucial to Tibetan resistance?"[67] Lobsang Sangay answers that question in the affirmative;

he reports that the CPC's "rhetoric introduced into the Tibetan language such terms as *maangtso* (people's democracy), *rawang* (freedom), and *dranyam* (equality)," thus equipping the Tibetans with a new vocabulary for opposing their colonizers.[68] Elliot Sperling summarizes the dynamic this way: "systematic Marxist education and the concomitant circulation of Marxist ideas about nations inevitably raised the question of Tibetan identity . . . in a new way."[69] From this perspective, what we saw Anderson call "national history" may have begun to evolve in occupied Tibet as part of resistant, anticolonial imaginings that appropriated some of the key terms of the CPC's imperial discourse.

At the same time, and like all such national histories, Tibet's imagined community would need to be as reductive as it was empowering. Anderson argued in *Imagined Communities* that one of the chief functions of the imagined "comradeship" of the nation-state was to occlude "actual inequality and exploitation."[70] Fleshing out that claim for the Tibetan situation, McGranahan argues that by the time the exiled Dalai Lama landed in India in 1959, and even while a brutal war of resistance was being fought, largely by Khampan rebels in Tibet's vast mountains, the Dalai Lama and his inner circle sought to constitute "a homogenous and hegemonic Lhasa-centered identity" that turned the diverse nations of Tibet into a human-rights-pursuing state in exile.[71] On the one hand, this effort to create the appearance of a narratively coherent and politically occupied nation-state has helped produce a global outpouring of support for Tibet; on the other hand, building this image of a homogeneous nation-state has—as all such efforts do—entailed the virtual erasure of messy particulars from the story.[72] Flabbergasted by this process of nation-state construction via the homogenization of differences, Hansen has asked, "why is there no subaltern studies for Tibet?"[73] The dynamic of the imagined community thus cuts in multiple directions, as the Dalai Lama and his fellow Dharamsala-based elites strive to author a coherent nation-state deserving of international support against the invading Chinese, even as McGranahan, Hansen, and others strive to portray the struggles of subalterns within Tibet's vast countryside (both in the TAR and in Yunnan, Gansu, Qinghai, and Sichuan). In this case, the power of nationalism serves both as a source of resistance for Tibetans against the CPC and as a form of forced internal marginalization for those regionally based, gendered, or classed individuals who do not fit into the chosen master narrative. Much as I argued earlier that China's actions in Tibet need to be appraised as both progress and catastrophe, so the rhetorical work of imagining communities within occupied and diasporic Tibet needs to be understood as unifying and resistant but also as marginalizing and oppressive.

These fractured allegiances and overlapping imaginations need to be appraised as crucial, and potentially even crippling, contradictions within China's postcolonial version of its expanding nation-state, for as some observers argue, China cannot move forward into a role as twenty-first-century superpower while its own internal political dynamics are so obviously unstable. For example, Stefan Halper notes that "China aspires to a seat at the table of great powers," yet "here in its own backyard, the government is forced to resort to state violence and cultural genocide in order to force-draft Tibetan acceptance of the Chinese hand."[74] Because this "state violence" is so widespread, so internationally denounced, and so internally destabilizing, Robert Barnett argues that "Tibet is not merely an idiosyncratic element among China's many problems but a core issue that . . . has direct implications for the viability of the state."[75] To put Halper's and Barnett's claims in the language of this book, if the "core issue" of the nation-state is the perceived legitimacy and propulsive force of its unifying myths and dreams—the imagined community writ large—then the stain of violence, so prevalent and obvious throughout former Tibetan lands, undercuts the entire process.

Addressing this core issue may be impossible for the CPC in Tibet, however, as the theorists of nation-states and postcolonialism consistently point out that violence is not only a key aspect of the initial stages of colonialism but a necessarily repeated aspect of most colonial enterprises. Indeed, one of the many contradictions of modern nation-states with colonial ambitions is that while they strive to alter the colony in their own image, in the name of universalizing reason and market development—*progress* writ large, as Hobsbawm warned—so colonialism also creates, as demanded especially by racism, the constant reproduction of hierarchies in which the colonizer and the colonized are taught to know their unequal places. The "universal truth" of modernity—the promise of uplift, development, justice, etc.—thus stands in tension with what

Chatterjee calls the "rule of colonial difference."[76] From this perspective, the production of political ranks, military orders, social clubs, and other explicitly exclusionary hierarchies meant to institutionalize racial differences accounts for the perpetually "ambiguous image of the state in popular consciousness," for the universalizing state produces both unprecedented "progress" but also stifling on-the-ground racial and national disparities, thus appearing to the locals as both the agent of awesome historical change and a demon of awful oppression.[77] This explains why the ICT foregrounds the CPC's racism against Tibetans—the "rule of colonial difference"—as undermining the goals of the developmentalist state: Prejudice against Tibetans is so deep, the ICT argues, that even while the developmentalist state has launched an unprecedented program of modernization, "regional socio-economic disparities have worsened."[78] Rather than binding Tibetans to their new Chinese-run state, this production of disparities has, so the ICT notes, "inadvertently reinforced a broad sense of Tibetan identity that is highly distinct from the Chinese one."[79] As Bhuchung Tsering argues, "Chinese policies have led to the growth—if not outright origin—of Tibetan Buddhist nationalism."[80] Achieving the broad-based sense of justice and decency required for the CPC-imposed state to appear legitimate in the TAR may therefore be impossible. As one Tibetan diplomat said in an interview in Delhi, "the Chinese have forgotten that *you cannot impose respect*, you must earn it."[81] In short, colonizing efforts like those of China in Tibet can rely upon domination, but they cannot build assent; they can strive for power, but they cannot earn authority; they can construct the governing apparatus of the state, but they cannot constitute an attractive national imagination.

In the long run, the colonizing state will strive to make these institutional hierarchies, structural disparities, and racial hatreds appear less like the results of intentional political domination than the unintended consequences of market forces. As Chatterjee puts it, "it is the narrative of capital that can turn the violence of mercantilist trade, war, genocide, conquest and colonialism into a story of universal progress, development, modernization, and freedom."[82] From this perspective, the "New Lhasa" discussed earlier in this essay should be understood as a site of cultural contestation, for the urban development taking place there—all pursued in the hope of making a brutal colonial occupation look instead like the benign consequences of the invisible hand of capitalist modernity—points to what Lisa Rofel calls "a spatial disciplining of consciousness."[83] This "spatial disciplining" seems ill-equipped to produce assent, however, leaving in its wake subjugation. From this perspective it appears that what Chatterjee calls "the narrative of capital" cannot fulfill the political needs of the PRC in Tibet: to seduce the masses into granting allegiance to their oppressors.

These questions are made even more complicated in the case of the TAR by the fact that since the Dalai Lama and his inner circle fled Lhasa in 1959, many of Tibet's leading scholars, politicians, artists, and entrepreneurs have lived in exile. Writing about colonial India's struggle for independence from Britain, Chatterjee argued that the key ingredient for the insurgent imagined nation to take control of an indigenously driven and empowered state was "to overcome the subordination of the colonized middle class."[84] This model is problematic for Tibet, however, as the exiled middle class is now entrenched in Dharamsala, Hong Kong, New York City, and elsewhere. As one disappointed Tibetan complained to Meenakshi Ganguly, "if they [the exiled Tibetan middle class] are building houses here [in Dharamsala], how can they be planning on going back [to Tibet]?"[85] This question points to the complexities of engaging in the rhetorical work of imagining community in the age of globalization, for even while the CPC's imagined community strikes many (if not most) Tibetans as a colonial imposition, so the interviewee quoted above points to the sheer externality of the exiled community: *they are not there* (in Tibet), the speaker seems to complain, *and they appear content to stay here* (in Dharamsala), so how can their exile national imaginings align with local conditions and ambitions in occupied Tibet?

This is where the rhetorical work of imagining communities confronts one of the dilemmas of globalization: that even as we live in nation-states, the fluid flow of goods, ideas, and bodies—the accelerating sense of motion and mobility that underwrites globalization—undercuts the sanctity of national borders and cultures. This is why McGranahan argues that "as a transnational state centered within the territorial boundaries of another state (India), the exile Tibetan state departs from geographic expectations of statehood but meets other norms."[86] Arjun Appadurai is helpful here, as he argues in *Modernity at Large* that the age of globalization requires critical humanists to think more creatively about "diasporic public spheres," which might, he hopes, help to build new "non-territorial, post-national forms of allegiance."[87] Such theorizing may do nothing to assuage the hopes and fears of the common folk of Lhasa, who suffer the Chinese occupation with quiet dignity and simmering resentment, yet it may point to the exiles in Dharamsala—and the global communities of support for the Dalai Lama—as harbingers of a new, postmodern solidarity divorced from a territorially bounded place. In this sense, China's absorption of Tibet has produced a state with no nation (the TAR) and a nation (diasporic Buddhism's "community of vision") with no state. The key question, then, is can a stateless nation of exiles constitute an imagined community strong enough to sustain political momentum?

The Dilemmas of Statelessness

The muddy streets teem with the joys of life: monkeys swing from balconies above while allegedly sacred cows lumber beside you in search of the next pile of trash; the homeless Punjabi boys scramble from tourist to tourist trying to pick up a shoeshine customer while a gaggle of Australian backpackers debate whether they want New York–style pizza or Vietnamese pho for dinner; a chorus of birds sings from the treetops while cars, taxis, rickshaws, motorcycles, scooters, and small vans blast their horns in a perpetual aural onslaught; one of our team is negotiating a price for a set of gorgeous rosewood prayer beads a few stalls down the hill while another is scribbling notes from a conversation with a sunburned grandfather from Wisconsin who teaches English to refugees at one of the transition centers; monks of every shape and size and age navigate the congestion en route to their next meditation, cell phones and iPads in hand, while a strutting youth with a Yankees cap asks if I would like to purchase some "first rate Hash, man, great stuff"; we are late for an interview with a representative of the Tibetan Youth Congress a few blocks away and should be hurrying onward but are delayed yet again when a team of German college kids, a whirling blur of tie-died skirts and flowing white tops and mud-encrusted sandals, approach us asking to sign their

Figure 7. Sprawling across the foothills of the Dhauladar Range, the southern-most outcropping of the Himalayas, Dharamsala and McLeod Ganj feature waves of vertical houses, inns, and monasteries clinging to hillsides.

petition protesting China's latest crackdown on Tibetan monasteries—it is another day in McLeod Ganj, the glorious, bizarre, utterly packed hilltop town in far northern India that serves as the epicenter of exiled Tibetan life (Figure 7).[88] Like Manhattan, or Hong Kong, or Paris on hustling afternoons, it seems as if the whole world presses into McLeod Ganj, making it one of the global nodal points in what Mark Poster—echoing Lyotard's language cited earlier—calls "transculture," the phenomenon whereby "everyone appropriates and changes the culture of everyone else."[89] Tibetan victims of Chinese torture report that their CPC abusers often shout at them, "you are a stray dog of the Dalai Lama,"[90] but here, in McLeod Ganj, we are all stray dogs, happily roaming the streets, soaking up the wonders of transculture.

Like parts of Berkeley or Amsterdam, McLeod Ganj can feel like a town committed to globalizing social justice, a cosmopolitan nodal point of transnational activism, a foreshadowing of what postmodern civil society might become. Oliver Richmond argues that "a postcolonial civil society indicates a legitimacy that transcends the state and market, liberalism and cosmopolitanism," thus "rais[ing] the issue of an emancipatory form of peace without modernist (or modernizing) notions of sovereignty and the territorial state."[91] This utopian premise crashes upon the bleak realities of exiled Palestinians and Kurds, or the tens of millions of African refugees fleeing civil wars, or the millions of Iraqi, Iranian, Afghan, and Syrian refugees running from conflicts in those failed or failing states. Thinking globally, most of the world's forty-two million displaced persons are not building "an emancipatory form of peace" but struggling for clean drinking water, dependable food sources, safe shelter from the elements, and protection from marauding armies and murderous gangs.[92] In contrast to these scenarios, Little Lhasa offers rays of hope for what an exiled postcolonial civil society might accomplish by pursuing the opportunities and dilemmas of being, as Julia Hess has described the Tibetan diaspora, "stateless in a world of states."[93]

The first and most important observation in this regard is to remember that many, if not most, of the exiled Tibetans in Dharamsala are refugees who want to go home. As one of the leaders of the National Democratic Party of Tibet lamented in an interview, "we don't have a land."[94] Moreover, because the exiled Tibetan communities, and the CTA in particular, have no recourse to the traditional power instruments of states—armies, intelligence agencies, federal reserves, international treaties, access to the World Bank and International Monetary Fund, a seat at the UN, embassies in the world's capital cities, and so on—they are dependent for their standing in the global community exclusively upon their communication skills. Their only tool is mediated representation. Yet despite the best efforts of Tibetan activists, supportive NGOs, and wealthy Western backers, the CTA in particular and the Tibetan diaspora in general has not built a print, radio, TV, or Web-based communication infrastructure that can rival the massive communication apparatus managed by the CPC.[95] Moreover, the fledgling communication channels supportive of Tibetan causes are confronted by daunting representational challenges that, as described by Dibyesh Anand, include the tensions between celebrating the fluid nature of diasporic life and "the need to present an overarching stable identity," between building productive relations with their host states and "avoiding cultural assimilation," between honoring lost traditions and slipping into the global stream of postmodernity, between celebrating Tibetan "uniqueness" and "highlighting its universal features," and between drawing upon Western supporters yet emphasizing Buddhism's alternative worldview.[96] While the leaders of the exiled community are keenly aware that they "don't have a land," Anand's five tensions indicate that the rhetorical work of imagining Tibet is laced with complicated questions about identity, culture, history, and future imagined communities.

Perhaps the most daunting tension within this contested and complicated rhetorical work is the slippage between the Dalai Lama's version of infinitely patient and nonviolent Buddhism and the rising anger of younger activists, who seek other routes toward independence. For example, when Meenakshi Ganguly conducted interviews throughout the Tibetan diaspora, she concluded that "young Tibetans are growing tired of pacifism." One man in a bar in Dharamsala told her, "I want to go and blow up a few bridges"; another said "our government [the CTA] has no sense of urgency."[97] The communication infrastructure deficits and representational complexities facing the CTA in particular and diasporic Tibetans in general are therefore daunting.[98] Nonetheless, the exiled Tibetans continue to explore new means of building what Bree McEwan

and Miriam Sobre-Denton call "virtual cosmopolitanism," a wired, diasporic, postnational version of "hybridized global citizenry."[99]

When these theoretical questions hit the ground, they seem even
more complicated. In McLeod Ganj, on a typical roaring Saturday night,
the only hope for the snarled congestion of the main square is a bored
Indian traffic cop—the Indian state polices the community of exiled
Tibetans and global seekers. At New Delhi's gleaming international
airport, the Tibetans flying to meet political allies must travel either
under passports issued by India or China (which the Tibetans are loathe
to seek, for that requires formal citizenship in one of those states) or
under one of India's hard-to-obtain Identification Certificates, for there
are no Tibetan passports.[100] With no ability to collect taxes, the CTA is
powerless to repair the near-deadly roads of Dharamsala, or to build the
energy infrastructure that might spare McLeod Ganj the daily power
outages that leave the town besieged with the gnashing of a hundred
gas-powered Honda generators chugging along all afternoon. And so,
whether it is the simple act of walking across town, or driving down the
mountain, or hitting a light switch, or traveling abroad, daily life in the
epicenter of diasporic Tibetan life depends in large part on the goodwill
and begrudging tolerance of India.[101] Given the political turmoil in that
country, to say nothing of the violent insurgencies threatening to destabilize northern India in particular,[102] the Tibetans' situation in Dharamsala
is clearly precarious.

In that same vein, certain neighborhoods in Kathmandu, Nepal,
have served for the past two generations as home to large numbers of
exiled Tibetans. The densely packed streets are crisscrossed with Tibetan
prayer flags; groups of monks circumambulate the great Buddhist Stupa
in Boudhanath; global travelers and religious seekers speaking a dozen
different languages wander the streets scooping up trinkets, incense,
and cappuccinos; the square at Boudhanath vibrates with the frisson of
activism, marked by posters announcing a dizzying array of events—like
McLeod Ganj, the scene can feel exhilarating, like foreshadowing of a
coming global cosmopolitanism. Yet in January 2012 Nepal signed an
agreement with China wherein the CPC pledged to send $1.18 billion
of aid to infrastructure-starved Nepal.[103] Since then, "Tibetan refugees in
Nepal have come under intense pressure from local authorities, closely

Figure 8. The streets of McLeod Ganj offer a howling immersion in dense, urban noise and transcultural consumerism; traffic laws are nonexistent, making meditative strolls in the epicenter of global Buddhism a life-threatening adventure.

directed by officials from the Chinese embassy."[104] The "tighter Chinese security" has touched many facets of life in Kathmandu, the *New York Times* reports, including launching "a clampdown on open religious celebrations" and closing off avenues for refugees to cross the Himalayas out of occupied Tibet into Nepal.[105] While state-level political repression of Tibetans is becoming an agreed-upon component of Nepal–China relations, global diasporic Buddhism is nonetheless useful as a marketing tool fueling Nepal's emergent consumer zones (see Figures 8 and 9).[106] In this sense, being "stateless in a world of states" means exiled Tibetans live at the mercy of their host nation-states, whose foreign policies and domestic politics sail along regardless of, and, if China has any say, contrary to, their hopes and dreams. Despite these harrowing conditions, the

Figure 9. A typical afternoon in the Thamel neighborhood of Kathmandu, where diasporic Tibetan Buddhism meets global shopping: drugs are offered from every street corner, lattes beckon from the courtyards, Everest expeditions shout from the windows, and support for Tibetan independence underwrites the frantic buying and selling as a form of transgressive, worldly consumerism.

exiled Tibetans have managed to build communities that embody values described by Rona Tamiko Halualani—writing about postmodern Hawaiians—as "resilient . . . flexible, and enduring."[107]

Conclusion: "Nothing is Permanent"

While I have focused here on exiled Tibetans, it is important to remember that "more than 95% of ethnic Tibetans live within the claimed boundaries of political China."[108] This demographic fact means that as the leaders of the diaspora attempt to constitute new imaginings of postnational Tibetan identity and transnational solidarity, they and their supporters remain focused on the plight of their friends and neighbors in the TAR, Sichuan, Qinghai, Yunnan, Gansu, and elsewhere in the PRC. Some pro-Tibetan activists therefore continue to try to prod the CPC to dismantle the empire by publishing manifestoes offering checklists of the actions the CPC needs to take in order to meet their demands.[109] A different strategy involves calling for dramatic changes regarding China–Tibet relations in the name of advancing an assumed global sense of morality that might help save humanity from its darker impulses. For example, one leader of the exile Tibetan community, an employee of the CTA, said in an interview that his people's ongoing tragedy indicates how "We all need a little more strength and dignity if the world is going to survive. . . . At the end of the day, unless we have some sense of sameness, of the shared hopes of our human brothers and sisters, unless we have some sense of morality and ethics, well, we are not going to survive . . . the world will come to an end."[110] Whereas option one may seem politically naive, for empires tend not to self-dissolve at the request of their colonized peoples, option two offers a globalizing sentiment that is hard to translate into political action, for the CPC has shown little regard for appeals to supposedly universal notions of "morality" or "ethics." Indeed, as we have seen throughout this chapter, it is hard to square the rhetorical work of imagining community on local and/or national scales with the sweeping, would-be universalizing that globalization makes possible. Recognizing this tension, one of the leaders of Students for a Free Tibet said in an interview that his group wants "more of an action plan, not just speech." For this young activist, the goal is to "raise the cost of the occupation, the political cost, the economic cost, the interpersonal cost, and to do so by organizing nonviolent acts of resistance within the TAR."[111] The risk of this strategy, of course, as witnessed in previous CPC responses to nonviolent protests within the TAR, is that "raising the cost of the occupation" will be seen by the CPC as terrorism, thus leading to an overwhelming military response.[112]

Whether phrased as political demands from exiles to an occupying state, or as philosophical appeals to global morality, or as calls for Tibetans to take some hard action within occupied territories, all three positions are underwritten by an aching desire for a lost homeland. In fact, when asked about how he and his allies are building postnational global solidarities, one leader of the Tibetan Youth Congress said "well, sure, that is all fine and good, but *we want the chance to wake up in our own country.*"[3] Thus, even in our age of globalization, the rhetorical work of imagining a Tibetan national community hinges in part on an older sense of place, geography, the rooted physical sense of a home. In contrast to those who believe this "myth of return" is a pipedream, one of the leaders of the National Democratic Party of Tibet reminded me to "always remember the U.S.S.R.," for "systems change. Nothing is permanent. Even the CPC will collapse sometime."[4] In the meantime, the experiments in Dharamsala, New Delhi, Kathmandu, and elsewhere are, if nothing else, enabling the exiled Tibetans to preserve parts of their cultures while evolving the new democratic practices, wired and international solidarities, creative business ventures, and resistant communication strategies that might someday drive the renaissance of a free and independent Tibet. In this sense, the rhetorical work of imagining community serves not only as a forward-looking thought experiment, but also as a necessary stopgap defense against obliteration.

NOTES

1. These events are depicted in *Kundun*, Martin Scorsese's 1997 biopic of the Fourteenth Dalai Lama, which follows scene-by-scene the narrative as told in Dalai Lama, *Freedom in Exile* (New York: HarperPerennial, 1990).

2. John F. Avedon, *In Exile from the Land of Snows: The Definitive Account of the Dalai Lama and Tibet since the Chinese Conquest* (New York: HarperPerennial, 1979), 36.

3. Tsering Shakya, *The Dragon in the Land of Snows: A History of Modern Tibet since 1947* (New York: Penguin, 1999), 221.

4. Jung Chang and Jon Halliday, *Mao, the Unknown Story* (New York: Anchor Books, 2005), 448–49; this assault is chronicled in the sources listed in notes 1–3 and in International Campaign for Tibet, *60 Years of Chinese Misrule: Arguing Cultural Genocide in Tibet* (Washington, DC: ICT, 2012).

5. Dalai Lama, "Five Point Peace Plan; Address to the US Congressional Human Rights Caucus, September 21, 1987," http://www.dalailama.com; like all such

death counts, this figure is disputed.

6. Avedon, *In Exile from the Land of Snows*, 281.

7. Shakya, *Dragon in the Land of Snows*, 347. The Dalai Lama has argued that the CPC's actions in Tibet point toward "the total extermination of the Tibetan race"; see his September 9, 1959, "Cable to the United Nations," repr. in Roger E. McCarthy, *Tears of the Lotus: Accounts of Tibetan Resistance to the Chinese, 1950–1962* (London: McFarland, 1997), 262.

8. For cartographic evidence of this process, see Shakya, *Dragon in the Land of Snows*, xix–xxiv; also see the International Campaign for Tibet's "Map Project," January 30, 2008, http://www.savetibet.org.

9. For a Tibet-centered perspective, see Carole McGranahan, *Arrested Histories: Tibet, the CIA, and Memories of a Forgotten War* (Durham, NC: Duke University Press, 2010); for a U.S.-centered version, see Kenneth Conboy and James Morrison, *The CIA's Secret War in Tibet* (Lawrence: University of Kansas Press, 2002).

10. John Kenneth Knaus, *Orphans of the Cold War: America and the Tibetan Struggle for Survival* (New York: Praeger, 1999).

11. The CTA offers information at http://tibet.net/.

12. Pico Iyer, *The Open Road: The Global Journey of the Fourteenth Dalai Lama* (New York: Vintage, 2008), 5, 177.

13. Along these lines, see Michael C. McGee, "In Search of 'The People': A Rhetorical Alternative," *Quarterly Journal of Speech* 61 (1975): 235–49; Maurice Charland, "Constitutive Rhetoric: The Case of the *Peuple Québécois*," *Quarterly Journal of Speech* 73 (1987): 133–50; and James Jasinski, "A Constitutive Framework for Rhetorical Historiography: Toward an Understanding of the Discursive (Re)constitution of 'Constitution' in *The Federalist Papers*," in *Doing Rhetorical History: Concepts and Cases*, ed. Kathleen J. Turner (Tuscaloosa: University of Alabama Press, 1998), 72–92.

14. Raka Shome and Radha Hegde, "Postcolonial Approaches to Communication: Charting the Terrain, Engaging the Intersections," *Communication Theory* 12 (2002): 256 and 262; see the essays collected in Bill Ashcroft, Gareth Griffiths, and Helen Tiffin, eds., *The Post-Colonial Studies Reader* (London: Routledge, 1995), and, for a review of critiques of this subgenre, see Leela Gandhi, "The Pauper's Gift: Postcolonial Theory and the New Democratic Dispensation," *Public Culture* 23 (2011): 27–38.

15. Dilip Parameshwar Gaonkar, "On Alternative Modernities," *Public Culture* 11

(1999): 1–18.

16. Frederick Cooper, "Provincializing France," in *Imperial Formations*, ed. Ann Laura Stoler and Carole McGranahan (Santa Fe, NM: School for Advanced Research Press, 2007), 341–78, 343; Cooper's argument echoes Aijaz Ahmad's critique of Edward Said in *In Theory: Classes, Nations, Literatures* (London: Verso, 1992), where Ahmad argues that Said's critique of Orientalism is so totalizing, so awestruck, that "it sometimes appears that one is transfixed by the power of the very voice [Eurocentric modernity] that one debunks" (173).

17. For rhetorical analysis of the CPC's efforts in this regard, see Stephen John Hartnett, "'Tibet Is Burning': Competing Rhetorics of Liberation, Occupation, Resistance, and Paralysis on the Roof of the World," *Quarterly Journal of Speech* 99 (2013): 283–316; for evidence of the anti-imperial and postcolonial tenor of China's revolutionary rhetoric, see Mao Zedong, *Selections*, 5 vols. (New York: International Publishers, 1954–56); on changing patterns in Chinese political rhetoric, see Xing Lu, "From 'Ideological Enemies' to 'Strategic Partners': A Rhetorical Analysis of U.S.–China Relations in Intercultural Contexts," *Howard Journal of Communication* 22 (2011): 336–57.

18. See Stoler's, McGranahan's, Perdue's, and others' contributions to Stoler and McGranahan, *Imperial Formations*, a collection of essays illustrating how different political regimes implemented different versions of colonialism justified with different rhetorical claims—hence fracturing any notion of a unified West.

19. On China's human rights histories, see Rosemary Foot, *Rights beyond Borders: The Global Community and the Struggle over Human Rights in China* (Oxford: Oxford University Press, 2000) and Stephen C. Angle and Marina Svennson, eds., *The Chinese Human Rights Reader* (Armonk, NY: M. E. Sharpe, 2001); more broadly, see Leonard C. Hawes, "Human Rights and an Ethic of Truths: Pragmatic Dilemmas and Discursive Interventions," *Communication and Critical/Cultural Studies* 7 (2010): 261–79; Michael Ignatieff, *Human Rights as Politics and Idolatry* (Princeton, NJ: Princeton University Press, 2001); Samuel Moyn, *The Last Utopia: Human Rights in History* (Cambridge, MA: Harvard University Press, 2010); and Lynn Hunt, *Inventing Human Rights: A History* (New York: Norton, 2007).

20. Along these lines, see Rona Tamiko Halualani, "'Where Exactly Is the Pacific?': Global Migrations, Diasporic Movements, and Intercultural Communication," *Journal of International and Intercultural Communication* 1 (2008): 3–22; Hsin-I Cheng, "Space Making: Chinese Transnationalism on the U.S.–Mexican Borderlands," *Journal of International and Intercultural Communication* 1 (2008):

244–63; and Bree McEwan and Miriam Sobre-Denton, "Virtual Cosmopolitanism: Constructing Third Cultures and Transmitting Social and Cultural Capital through Social Media," *Journal of International and Intercultural Communication* 4 (2011): 252–58.

21. McGranahan, *Arrested Histories*, 31; for additional examples of "research as *kora*," see Robert Barnett and Ronald Schwartz, eds., *Tibetan Modernities: Notes from the Field on Cultural and Social Change* (Boston: Brill, 2008).

22. Ian Baker, *The Heart of the World: A Journey to Tibet's Lost Paradise* (New York: Penguin, 2004), 272, where Baker notes that *kora* is the transliteration of *né-kor*, the Tibetan word for pilgrimage.

23. Whenever I write in a plural voice, I am indicating an experience shared with Donovan Conley, Patrick Shaou-Whea Dodge, and Lisa Keränen, my colleagues in the Tibet Study Group. During the eight years of research/*kora* discussed herein, Conley, Dodge, and Keränen were my traveling companions in China, Tibet, Hong Kong, Macau, Nepal, Taiwan, and India.

24. Between March 16, 2011, and March 16, 2017, activists reported 146 immolations with 118 confirmed deaths in Tibet and/or regions of China with heavy Tibetan populations; see the Free Tibet website, http://www.freetibet.org; the ICT's "Self-Immolations by Tibetans," December 9, 2016, http://www.savetibet.org; and the Tibetan Youth Congress's fact sheet, http://tibetanyouthcongress.org; also see *Tibet Burning: Profiles of Self-Immolators Inside Tibet* (Dharamsala: Tibetan Youth Congress, 2013) and *Human Rights Situation in Tibet, Annual Report, 2012* (Dharamsala: Tibetan Centre for Human Rights and Democracy, 2013).

25. Jean François Lyotard, *The Postmodern Condition: A Report on Knowledge*, trans. Geoff Bennington and Brian Massumi (1979; Minneapolis: University of Minnesota Press, 1984), 76.

26. Jurgen Habermas, "Modernity—An Incomplete Project" (1981), repr. in *The Anti-Aesthetic: Essays on Postmodern Culture*, ed. Hal Foster (Port Townsend, WA: Bay Press, 1983), 3–15, 13.

27. To situate my analysis of postmodernity in Tibet in its larger context, see Arif Dirlik and Zhang Xudong, "Introduction: Postmodernism and China," *boundary 2* 24 (1997): 1–18.

28. International Campaign for Tibet, *Tracking the Steel Dragon: How China's Economic Policies and the Railway Are Transforming Tibet* (Washington, DC: ICT, 2009), 6; also see Abrahm Lustgarten, *China's Great Train: Beijing's Drive West and the Campaign to Remake Tibet* (New York: Times Books, 2008); for an

example of the Party's version of events, see "China's West: Generating Change," *China Today*, April 2011, 47–49.

29. For analysis of the CPC's rhetoric regarding Tibet, see Hartnett, "'Tibet Is Burning'"; for overviews of what modernity has wrought in Tibet, see Shakya, *Dragon in the Land of Snows*, and Melvyn C. Goldstein, *A History of Modern Tibet, 1913–1951: The Demise of the Lamaist State* (Berkeley: University of California Press, 1989); for analysis of the visual and spatial aspects of these debates, see Lisa Keränen, Patrick Shaou-Whea Dodge, and Donovan Conley, "Modernizing Traditions on the Roof of the World: Displaying 'Liberation' and 'Occupation' in Three Tibet Museums," *Journal of Curatorial Studies* 4 (2015): 78–106.

30. "Lost in Tibet," *The Guardian*, March 13, 2009.

31. Andrew M. Fischer, *State Growth and Social Exclusion in Tibet* (Copenhagen: Nordic Institute of Asian Studies, 2005), 40; and see Emily T. Yeh, "Tropes of Indolence and the Cultural Politics of Development in Lhasa, Tibet," *Annals of the Association of American Geographers* 97 (2007): 593–612.

32. For examples of these terms in use, see the sources listed above in notes 28, 29, and 31.

33. When I was last in Lhasa, in the summer of 2012, foreign tourists were still welcome; since the escalation of the immolations noted earlier, however, the CPC has closed the TAR to most if not all outsiders. As noted by Reporters Without Borders and numerous pro-Tibetan NGOs, gaining access to the TAR is now more difficult than entering even North Korea; see "Authorities Tighten Grip, Isolating Tibet Even More from the Outside World," Reporters Without Borders, March 1, 2012, http://en.rsf.org, and the stories about sealed borders posted by the groups listed in note 24.

34. For pro-Tibetan responses, see ICT, *60 Years of Chinese Misrule*; Yeh, "Tropes of Indolence"; and Ian Buruma, *Bad Elements: Chinese Rebels from Los Angeles to Beijing* (New York: Vintage, 2001), 299–315. For the CPC's perspective, see Zhang Xiaoming, ed., *Eyewitnesses to 100 Years of Tibet: Interviews with Witnesses, History Instead of Conclusion* (Beijing: China Intercontinental Press, 2005); Chenqingying, *Tibetan History: Series of Basic Information of Tibet in China* (Beijing: China Intercontinental Press, 2003); and Che Minghuai and Zhange Huachuan, *Zhang Jingwu: The Representative of the Central People's Government in Tibet*, trans. Tao Geru (Beijing: China Tibetology Publishing House, 2009).

35. This quotation refers to Beijing, but is just as apt for Lhasa; see Wang Mingxian,

"Notes on Architecture and Postmodernism in China," *boundary* 2 24 (1997): 163–75, 174.

36. Fredric Jameson, *Postmodernism, or, the Cultural Logic of Late Capitalism* (Durham, NC: Duke University Press, 1991), 47; and see David Harvey, *The Condition of Postmodernity* (Cambridge, MA: Blackwell, 1990), esp. 119–97.

37. On the post–Cold War era, see Bryan C. Taylor and Stephen J. Hartnett, "'National Security, and All That It Implies . . .': Communication and Post–Cold War Studies," *Quarterly Journal of Speech* 86 (2000): 465–91.

38. In high modern fashion, China's actions in Tibet are driven in part by a sense that the Tibetans are barbarians; see Human Rights in China, *China: Minority Exclusion, Marginalization, and Rising Tensions* (London: Human Rights in China/Minority Rights Group International, 2007), and Melvyn Goldstein, Dawei Sherap, and William R. Siebenschuh, *A Tibetan Revolutionary: The Political Life and Times of Bapa Phüntso Wangye* (Berkeley: University of California Press, 2004), where Phünwang (the Tibetan communist who opposed the Tibetan aristocracy, worked for the CPC, and then was imprisoned by the Party) recounts how China's policy toward Tibet was based in part on what the Party elite called "Great Han Chauvinism" (281).

39. This is one of the theses of my and Laura Ann Stengrim's *Globalization and Empire: The U.S. Invasion of Iraq, Free Markets, and the Twilight of Democracy* (Tuscaloosa: University of Alabama Press, 2006); also see David Harvey, *The New Imperialism* (Oxford: Oxford University Press, 2003); Chalmers Johnson, *Blowback: The Costs and Consequences of American Empire* (New York: Metropolitan, 2000); and Michael Mann, *Incoherent Empire* (London: Verso, 2003).

40. Eric Hobsbawm, *Nations and Nationalism since 1780: Programme, Myth, Reality* (London: Cambridge University Press, 1990), 41, emphasis added.

41. Human Rights in China has run a series of stories about the situation in Xinjiang, formerly known as East Turkestan: see "The Repressive Framework of Religious Regulation in Xinjiang," *China Rights Forum*, 2005, no. 2, 13–26; "A Voice for the Uyghurs, an HRC Interview with Rebiya Kadeer," *China Rights Forum*, 2006, no. 4, 58–59; and Alim Seytoff, "Letter from East Turkestan," *China Rights Forum*, 2008, no. 4, 55–57; since 9/11, the CPC has used U.S.-style war on terrorism rhetoric to label Kadeer and other supporters of the Uyghurs as "terrorists."

42. See Gaonkar, "On Alternative Modernities"; Shmuel Noah Eisenstadt, "Multiple Modernities," *Daedalus* 129 (2000): 1–29; Volker H. Schmidt, "Multiple

Modernities or Varieties of Modernity?" *Current Sociology* 54 (2006): 77–97; Mike Featherstone, Scott Lash, and Roland Robertson, eds., *Global Modernities* (London: Sage, 1995); Raka Shome, "Asian Modernities: Culture, Politics, and Media," *Global Media and Communication* 8 (2012): 199–214; and Barnett and Schwartz, *Tibetan Modernities*.

43. Bill Ashcroft, "Alternative Modernities: Globalization and the Post-Colonial," *Ariel* 40 (2009): 81–105, 81; and see Arif Dirlik, "Global Modernity? Modernity in an Age of Global Capitalism," *European Journal of Social Theory* 6 (2003): 275–92.

44. Ranajit Guha, "Introduction," in *A Subaltern Studies Reader, 1986–1995*, ed. Guha (Minneapolis: University of Minnesota Press, 1997), ix–xxii, xxi; and see Raka Shome, "Postcolonial Interventions in the Rhetorical Canon: An 'Other' View," *Communication Theory* 6 (1996): 40–59.

45. See Yunxiang Yan, "Managed Globalization: State Power and Cultural Transition in China," in *Many Globalizations: Cultural Diversity in the Contemporary World*, ed. Peter L. Berger and Samuel P. Huntington (Oxford: Oxford University Press, 2002), 19–47; also see Stefan Halper, *The Beijing Consensus: How China's Authoritarian Model Will Dominate the Twenty-First Century* (New York: Basic Books, 2010), and Martin Jacques, *When China Rules the World* (New York: Penguin, 2009).

46. For examples, see ICT, *60 Years of Chinese Misrule*; Halper, *Beijing Consensus*; the Dalai Lama, "Cable to the United Nations"; and the postings in the Tibetan websites cited herein.

47. Fredric Jameson, "Notes on Globalization as a Philosophical Issue," in *The Cultures of Globalization*, ed. Jameson and Masao Miyoshi (Durham, NC: Duke University Press, 1998), 54–77, 66, 57; and see Jan Nederveen Pieterse, "Globalization as Hybridization," in Featherstone, Lash, and Robertson, *Global Modernities*, 45–68, esp. 62 for a table that summarizes the homogenization vs. diversification debate.

48. Terry Eagleton, "The Contradictions of Postmodernism," *New Literary History* 28 (1997): 1–6, 5.

49. Karl Marx, *The Communist Manifesto*, ed. Frederick Bender, Norton Critical Edition (New York: W. W. Norton, 1988), 61.

50. Don DeLillo, *Underworld* (New York: Scribner, 1997), 785–86.

51. Peter L. Berger, "Introduction: The Cultural Dynamics of Globalization," in Berger and Huntington, *Many Globalizations*, 1–16, 7; on the destruction and re-creation of Beijing, see Michael Dutton, Hsiu-ju Stacy Lo, and Dong Wu, *Beijing*

Time (Cambridge, MA: Harvard University Press, 2008); James Fallows, *Postcards from Tomorrow Square* (New York: Vintage, 2009); and Michael Meyer, *The Last Days of Old Beijing* (New York: Walker, 2008).

52. Jameson, *Postmodernism*, 29; in his "Future City," *New Left Review* 21 (May–June 2003), Jameson celebrates this process as part of "an extraordinary expansion of desire around the planet" (8).

53. Yu Hua, *China in Ten Words*, trans. Allan H. Barr (New York: Anchor Books, 2011), 126; these processes will impact the future of urban design (see Nicolai Ouroussoff, "Instant City: China's Wild West Gets Tamed," *Harper's*, June 2013, 39–47) and urban citizenship in China (see Li Zhang, "Spatiality and Urban Citizenship in Late Socialist China," *Public Culture* 14 [2002]: 311–34).

54. The blockade on communication is so tight that it prevents news from getting out of, and information from getting into, Tibet; on the CPC's attempts to render communication impossible in Tibet, see Hartnett, "'Tibet Is Burning,'" and RWB, "Authorities Tighten Grip." Activists are trying to circumvent the CPC's communication blockade by using untraceable cell phones, as seen in "Mobile Phone Security," one of the handouts produced by the Tibet Action Institute in collaboration with Students for a Free Tibet (readers can access this document at https://www.tibetaction.net).

55. Interview with the Tibet Study Group, May 30, 2013, in Delhi, India; note that to protect them from possible reprisal, all interview subjects are quoted herein anonymously; all interviews used herein were conducted according to Colorado Multiple Institution Review Board Protocol 13-1348.

56. Partha Chatterjee, *The Nation and Its Fragments: Colonial and Postcolonial Histories* (Princeton, NJ: Princeton University Press, 1993), 6. The obvious critique of this position is that regardless of colonial or postcolonial situations, national "imaginations" are fractured along class, kinship, regional, gendered, and ethnic lines; for a bitter story of such fractures within a colonized people, see V. S. Naipul, *Magic Seeds* (New York: Vintage, 2004), wherein displaced metropolitans seek to launch a Marxist revolution amid India's peasants, who have no interest in the project.

57. Benedict Anderson, *Imagined Communities: Reflections on the Origin and Spread of Nationalism* (1983; London: Verso, 2006), 6, 45; Hobsbawm notes in *Nations and Nationalism since 1780* that such "national languages" are "almost always semi-artificial constructs. . . . They are the opposite of what national mythology supposes them to be" (54).

58. Michael Rogin, "'Make My Day!': Spectacle as Amnesia in Imperial Politics," in *Cultures of United States Imperialism*, ed. Amy Kaplan and Donald E. Pease (Durham, NC: Duke University Press, 1993), 499–534, 504, 506.

59. Regarding how Tibet and China debate history, see John Powers, *History as Propaganda: Tibetan Exiles versus the People's Republic of China* (Oxford: Oxford University Press, 2004).

60. Anderson, *Imagined Communities*, 86, 93.

61. Ibid., 118.

62. For case studies, see Jennifer R. Mercieca, *Founding Fictions* (Tuscaloosa: University of Alabama Press, 2010), and Sacvan Bercovitch, *The Rites of Assent: Transformations in the Symbolic Construction of America* (New York: Routledge, 1993).

63. McGranahan, *Arrested Histories*, 7.

64. George Dreyfus, "Are We Prisoners of Shangri-La? Orientalism, Nationalism, and the Study of Tibet," *Journal of the International Association of Tibetan Studies* 1 (2005): 1–21, 10.

65. Shakya, *Dragon in the Land of Snows*, 209; regarding preinvasion Tibet's fractured political allegiances, see Goldstein, *A History of Modern Tibet*, 1–37, which describes how the monastery-based system of manorial estates—what the CPC would later characterize as slavery and feudalism—created a "fragmenting and conflicting force" within Tibetan society (37). While Buddhism united multiple nations via shared religious commitments, the institutional bases of the main Buddhist sects also fueled intense rivalries that "played a major role in thwarting progress" toward a unified, modern nation-state (37).

66. Gyalo Thondup, with Anne F. Thurston, *The Noodle Maker of Kalimpong: The Untold Story of My Struggle for Tibet* (New York: Public Affairs, 2015), 93.

67. Peter Hansen, "Why Is There No Subaltern Studies for Tibet?" *Tibet Journal* 28 (2003): 7–22, 17.

68. Lobsang Sangay, "Tibet: Exiles' Journey," *Journal of Democracy* 14, no. 3 (2003): 119–30, 120–21.

69. Elliot Sperling, "The Rhetoric of Dissent; Tibetan Pamphleteers," in *Resistance and Reform in Tibet*, ed. Robert Barnett (Bloomington: Indiana University Press, 1994), 267–84,269.

70. Anderson, *Imagined Communities*, 7.

71. McGranahan, *Arrested Histories*, 17.

72. In the U.S. context, James Morone has noted how virtually all postrevolutionary

attempts to author a coherent nation-state were based on "wholesale denial of the entire colonial experience." *The Democratic Wish: Popular Participation and the Limits of American Government* (New York: Basic Books, 1990), 44.

73. Hansen, "Why Is There No Subaltern Studies for Tibet?"

74. Halper, *Beijing Consensus*, 229.

75. Robert Barnett, "Introduction," in Wang Lixiong and Tsering Shakya, *The Struggle for Tibet* (London: Verso, 2009), 1–34, 19.

76. Chatterjee, *The Nation and Its Fragments*, 22; see HRC, *China* for case studies of this process in the TAR.

77. Chatterjee, *The Nation and Its Fragments*, 218; for ground-level evidence of this claim, recall Frantz Fanon's outraged *The Wretched of the Earth* (1961; New York: Grove, 2004), wherein he calls for violent revolution under the banner that the colonizers *"must pay up"* (59) for their crimes.

78. ICT, *60 Years of Chinese Misrule*, 76; and see Yeh, "Tropes of Indolence."

79. ICT, *60 Years of Chinese Misrule*, 76.

80. Bhuchung Tsering, "Man on Fire," ICT, February 10, 2012, http://www.savetibet. org.

81. Interview with the Tibet Study Group, May 30, 2013, in Delhi, India.

82. Chatterjee, *The Nation and Its Fragments*, 235.

83. Lisa Rofel, *Other Modernities: Gendered Yearnings in China after Socialism* (Berkeley: University of California Press, 1999), 262.

84. Chatterjee, *The Nation and Its Fragments*, 10.

85. Meenakshi Ganguly, "Generation Exile," *Transition* 87 (2001): 13.

86. McGranahan, *Arrested Histories*, 15.

87. Arjun Appadurai, *Modernity at Large: Cultural Dimensions of Globalization* (Minneapolis: University of Minnesota Press, 1996), 4, 166, and see 41, where he calls this search for postmodern nationalism one of the age's "central paradoxes"; for a case study, see Tashi Rabgey, "newtibet.com: Citizenship as Agency in a Virtual Tibetan Public," in Barnett and Schwartz, *Tibetan Modernities*, 333–52.

88. On McLeod Ganj and Dharamsala, see Dibyesh Anand, *Geopolitical Exotica: Tibet in Western Imagination* (Minneapolis: University of Minnesota Press, 2007), 109–27; Canyon Sam, *Sky Train: Tibetan Women on the Edge of History* (Seattle: University of Washington Press, 2009), 191–242; and Keila Diehl's wonderful *Echoes from Dharamsala: Music in the Life of a Tibetan Refugee Community* (Berkeley: University of California Press, 2002), esp. 32–56.

89. Mark Poster, "Postcolonial Theory in the Age of Planetary Communications,"

Quarterly Review of Film and Video 24 (2007): 379–93, 388; note that Poster, in large part, fears this phenomenon, as these appropriations are skewed by asymmetrical access to global capital and media.

90. In an interview with Thomas Laird recounted in *The Story of Tibet: Conversations with the Dalai Lama* (New York: Grove, 2006), Chuying Kunsang, a Tibetan nun, describes how this phrase was shouted at her and other nuns when they were tortured (363).

91. Oliver P. Richmond, "Critical Agency, Resistance, and a Postcolonial Civil Society," *Cooperation and Conflict* 46 (2011): 419–40, 433.

92. Forty-two million refugees reported in "Global Trends 2011," a video/slide report posted by the United Nations High Commissioner for Refugees at http://www.unhcr.org.

93. Julia Meredith Hess, "Statelessness and the State: Tibetans, Citizenship, and Nationalist Activism in a Transnational World," *International Migration* 44 (2006): 79–101, 95; also see the essays collected in P. Christiaan Klieger, ed., *Tibet, Self, and the Tibetan Diaspora: Voices of Difference* (Boston: Brill, 2002).

94. Interview with the Tibet Study Group, June 4, 2013, in Dharamsala, India.

95. In addition to the *People's Daily*, *Global Times*, and *China Daily*, CPC-run newspapers printed in a dozen languages and in batches by the millions, CCTV is broadcast globally and reaches, *outside of China*, as many as "219 million households in 156 countries"; see Gillian Wong and Isolda Morillo, "China TV Blames Dalai Lama for Tibet Immolations," Associated Press, May 16, 2012, accessed through the *San Francisco Chronicle*, http://www.sfgate.com. Regarding the CPC's global communication strategies, see David Barboza, "China Puts Best Face Forward in New English-Language Channel," *New York Times*, July 2, 2010, A4; for a critique of the communication patterns deployed in these outlets, see Guoguang Wu, "Command Communication: The Politics of Editorial Formulation in the *People's Daily*," *China Quarterly*, no. 137 (1994): 194–211; for a more hopeful response, see Guobin Yang, *The Power of the Internet in China: Citizen Activism Online* (New York: Columbia University Press, 2009).

96. Anand, *Geopolitical Exotica*, 109; these issues are not limited to Tibetans, as seen in Aihwa Ong, *Buddha Is Hiding: Refugees, Citizenship, the New America* (Berkeley: University of California Press, 2003), which addresses Cambodian refugees living in the United States. Regarding Web-based efforts to counter the CPC's communication machine, see Meg McLagan, "Computing for Tibet: Virtual Politics in the Post–Cold War Era," in *Connected: Engagements with the*

Media, ed. George E. Marcus (Chicago: University of Chicago Press, 1996),
159–94, and Rabgey, "newtibet.com"; at the library in the Tibet House in Delhi,
readers can peruse issues of *Seeds of Peace* (Bangkok), *Tibet Journal* (Dharamsala),
Turning the Wheel (Berkeley), *Tibet House Bulletin* (New Delhi), *Tibetan Journal*
(Dharamsala), *Tibetan Review* (Delhi), *Tibet Foundation Newsletter* (London),
Mandala (Portland), *Tibet Forum* (Hamburg), *Tibet Info* (Luxembourg), *Bulletin
of Tibetology* (Sikkim), and a dozen others, thus indicating print-based efforts to
spread pro-Tibetan messages; for Web-based options, see the websites listed in
notes 11 and 24.

97. Ganguly, "Generation Exile," 18.

98. On these questions of how the culture industries of various Western nations
depict Tibet and Tibetans, see Orville Schell, *Virtual Tibet: Searching for
Shangri-La from the Himalayas to Hollywood* (New York: Henry Holt, 2000); Meg
McLagan, "Spectacles of Difference: Cultural Activism and the Mass Mediation
of Tibet," in *Media Worlds*, ed. Faye D. Ginsburg, Lila Abu-Lughod, and Brian
Larkin (Berkeley: University of California Press, 2002), 90–111; and Donald S.
Lopez Jr., *Prisoners of Shangri-La: Tibetan Buddhism and the West* (Chicago:
University of Chicago Press, 1998).

99. McEwan and Sobre-Denton, "Virtual Cosmopolitanism," 254.

100. See Julia Meredith Hess, *Immigrant Ambassadors: Citizenship and Belonging
in the Tibetan Diaspora* (Stanford: Stanford University Press, 2009), 132 on
Identification Certificates, 132–62 on the dilemmas and opportunities of exile life
in India, and 77–100 on the "stigma" (89) of seeking formal citizenship in India,
Nepal, or China.

101. For heartbreaking poems depicting how this situation leaves some exiled Tibetans
feeling lost, see Tenzin Tsundue, *Kora: Stories and Poems*, 4th ed. (Dharamsala:
TibetWrites, 2006); for evidence of the special relationship between the exile
community, the CTA, and India, see *Commemorating 50 Years in Exile: A
Commemoration to Express the Tibetan People's Appreciation to the Government
and People of India* (no publication information is printed in the book, and
no online links for this document work; I found it at a resource center in
Dharamsala).

102. See Gardner Harris and Bettina Wassener, "A Summer of Troubles Saps India's
Sense of Confidence," *New York Times*, August 18, 2013; dozens of other such
stories are hosted by "India Ink: Notes on the World's Largest Democracy,"
the blog of the *New York Times* accessible at http://india.blogs.nytimes.com/;

for coverage from India, see *The Times of India*'s website: http://timesofindia.indiatimes.com/.

103. See Banyan (blog), "Nepal and Its Neighbors: Yam Yesterday, Yam Today," *The Economist*, January 18, 2012.

104. "Calling the Shots: Chinese Influence in Nepal Grows," *The Economist*, March 17, 2012; also see "US Official Talks to Nepal about Tibetan Refugees," Associated Press, April 4, 2012, posted by the ICT, http://www.savetibet.org.

105. Edward Wong, "China Makes Inroads in Nepal, and Stanches Tibetan Influx," *New York Times*, April 13, 2013; and see "Nepal Urged to Respect Rights of Tibetan Refugees," Phayul, June 22, 2013, http://www.phayul.com.

106. See Peter Moran, *Buddhism Observed: Travelers, Exiles, and Tibetan Dharma in Kathmandu* (London: Routledge, 2004), and Ann Frechette, *Tibetans in Nepal: The Dynamics of International Assistance among a Community in Exile* (New York: Berghahn, 2002).

107. Halualani, "'Where Exactly Is the Pacific?,'" 17.

108. Toni Huber, "Shangri-La in Exile: Representations of Tibetan Identity and Transnational Culture," in *Imagining Tibet: Perceptions, Projections, and Fantasies*, ed. Thierry Dodin and Heinz Rather (Boston: Wisdom Publications, 2001), 357–71, 358.

109. For examples of this genre, see Wang Lixiong, "Twelve Suggestions for Dealing with the Tibetan Situation, by Some Chinese Intellectuals" (March 22, 2008), repr. in Wang and Shakya, *The Struggle for Tibet*, 271–75; Liu Xiaobo, "So Long as Han Chinese Have No Freedom, Tibetans Will Have No Autonomy," in *Liu Xiaobo: No Enemies, No Hatred*, ed. Perry Link, Tienchi Martin-Liao, and Liu Xia (Cambridge, MA: Harvard University Press, 2012), 262–66; and Liu Xiaobo and collaborators, "China's Charter 08," which appears in Link, Martin-Liao, and Liu, *Liu Xiaobo*, 300–12.

110. Interview with the Tibet Study Group, June 2, 2013, in Dharamsala, India.

111. Interview with the Tibet Study Group, June 3, 2013, in Dharamsala, India.

112. The severity of CPC responses to political action within Tibet is chronicled in many of the essays in Barnett, *Resistance and Reform in Tibet*; in the pro-Tibetan websites cited throughout this essay; in Avedon, *In Exile from the Land of Snows*; in McCarthy, *Tears of the Lotus*; and in ICT, *60 Years of Chinese Misrule*; for visual evidence, see the opening sequences of *Tibet: Cry of the Snow Lion*, dir. Tom Piozet (Earthworks Films, 2003).

113. Interview with the Tibet Study Group, June 4, 2013, in Dharamsala, India; this sentiment was nearly universally expressed in our interviews with Tibetan activists in Nepal and India.
114. Interview with the Tibet Study Group, June 4, 2013, in Dharamsala, India.

Imagining China
in Twelve Vignettes

Photographs by Jeremy Make
Captions by Stephen J. Hartnett

"Where I Go When Love Seeps In"

Beijing's *hutongs* stand among the world's unique living arrangements. Whereas urban development in China since the 1970s has climbed ever skyward in the form of slick skyscrapers and vertical condominiums, the brick-and-mud *hutongs* sprawl around narrow alleys, twisting lanes, and intimate squares, creating immense, single-story courtyard neighborhoods designed for communal intimacy and wandering foot traffic. In some *hutongs*, neighbors are so closely packed together that they can reach out their windows to shake hands; in this dense network, family quarrels, raucous card games, and the afternoon laundry are public events. As Beijing razes more and more *hutongs* to make way for new developments, the neighborhoods have become sites of political resistance and intense real estate jockeying. To stroll amid the *hutongs* on a gentle summer evening, with the bulldozers idling nearby, invites thoughts of generations past, friends present, and hopes dispersed through the latticework of Chinese history. These remarkable neighborhoods indicate how the rhetorical work of imaging the nation is multilayered, embodied, and lived.

"Security Monk"

For as long as anyone can remember, Buddhist monasteries have been places of spiritual reflection, philosophical training, and rhetorical debate. Throughout the provinces of Sichuan, Qinghai, Yunnan, and Gansu, and all across the Tibet Autonomous Region, anyone entering a monastery who says *namaste* (roughly translated as "may the light in me acknowledge the light in you") or *tashe delek* (roughly translated as "peaceful greetings") might be met with joyous smiles from the monks, who welcome wanderers with questions of dealings abroad. Driven by fear that Buddhism poses a political threat to communism, the Party has sought greater control over the monasteries, in part by placing Party loyalists in the monasteries, where they function less like spiritual guides than political watchdogs. At the same time, the immense popularity of Buddhist sites as tourist attractions means the Party must now simultaneously protect them from bustling crowds eager to consume a part of China's culture. In this image, taken at the Yong He Gong Lama Temple in Beijing, we see a monk wearing a communication earpiece, thus marking him as a part of his monastery's security team. In contemporary China, the work of imagining the nation is powerfully linked to questions of faith and spirituality coupled with tourism and consumption.

"Tank Woman"

In the summer of 1989, the world was transfixed by the student protests that eventually grew into what some parties called a revolution and what others called a criminal disturbance. After Chairman Deng ordered the People's Liberation Army to clear Tiananmen Square, and after the army had to fight its way from the suburbs into downtown Beijing, killing and injuring untold numbers of unarmed civilians, the heart of Beijing grew still and silent—mourning was in the air. The next day, a column of tanks tried to enter the square, but as they rolled toward Tiananmen, an unidentified man leapt in front of the tanks and became a global icon: the lone individual, shopping bags in hand, dared to defy the military, only to vanish since then into anonymity. "Tank Man" captured the Western imaginary and has come to signify the generation's lost heroes and the painful memories of what happened in June 1989. This image seems to capture China twenty-eight years later: with stylish running shoes and her arms full of shopping bags, "Tank Woman" walks home along one of Beijing's side streets, with immense housing units looming behind another wall. And then, just for a moment, she too was in front of the tanks, now celebrated in this mural.

"The North Face"

As developing countries are flooded with new consumer goods, so the daily lives of billions of people have come to embody juxtapositions in which old cultural norms and practices jostle up against the new trinkets, clothes, foods, sounds, and technologies that announce our age of globalization. This man, photographed while relaxing at the Summer Palace, in the leafy northwest corner of Beijing, sports what looks like a classic Mao jacket from the late 1960s, when such military wear was part of the mandatory uniform of the Cultural Revolution. In China today, wearing such a jacket often signals one's allegiance to and perhaps nostalgia for an old China that was still committed to communism and collectivism. The Summer Palace has in fact become a weekend gathering place for older generations of Beijingers, who come together to talk about the old days, fueling what Xing Lu calls the "Mao fever." Yet, at the same time, this man also wears a new cap sporting the logo of the North Face, a U.S.-based company specializing in the marketing of outdoor adventure as a gung-ho and high-cost lifestyle for emboldened individuals. To walk the streets of China means immersing your senses in this balancing of old and new, communist and capitalist, thus wading into embodied globalization.

"China Rising"

Among the world's great skylines, a special place is reserved for Shanghai. The Pudong neighborhood, now one of the epicenters of global capitalism, features enormous towers of every shape, many of which convert at night into massive light shows and video installations. The iconic Oriental Pearl TV Tower, the science fiction beauty at the center of this image, must certainly be among the most photographed buildings in the world. Beneath the sparkling skyscrapers of the Pudong district, and rolling past the solid, imposing imperial architecture that lines the Bund, the older neighborhood that lies on the other side of the water, the Huangpu River, is a hive of industrial energy, as coal barges laden with fuel chug upriver to factories, while cargo tankers loaded with consumer goods float back toward port, where they discharge their booty to the ocean vessels that carry China's enormous productivity through the Yellow Sea and on into the world. Zipping between the river's giant boats, tourist-booked party vessels rock along, with their decks covered by scantily clad revelers, drunken businessmen, and the incessant popping of flashes as everyone records their immersion in the carnivalesque world of China's rise.

"Young Soldiers"

The U.S.-based purveyors of war-hawk hysteria have built a cottage industry around threat construction, portraying the People's Republic of China as a rising power committed to winning regional, if not world, domination. China does indeed have a long martial history and the Web is full of Japan-bashing and anti-U.S. nationalists. But when watching the troops parading around Tiananmen Square, in the shadow of the Gate of Heavenly Peace, you catch the sense that some of the young men in uniform are using the military, as youth do in the United States and other nations as well, as an escalator out of poverty and away from boredom. Like such young men everywhere, the role-playing becomes deadly when military arms are inserted into the equation, when natural curiosity and love of country become channeled into militarized nationalism. Still, on this day, at the moment caught here, the soldiers seemed less like warriors than young men happy to march in the shadow of their forebears. As is true in America as well, it seems that soldiers in China play a powerful, synecdochical role, as they are the embodied parts representing the whole of China's pride and ambition.

"Captain of the Grand Canal"
(with translations by Patrick Shaou-Whea Dodge)

Before airplanes, cars, and trains mechanized the movement of bodies and commerce, China, like America, was a nation of canals—families, goods, and ideas all floated their way through the empire. Just north of Shanghai, cradled in the Yangtze River Valley, one of the oldest cities in China, and home to an ancient network of canals, Suzhou is often called "the Venice of the East." The Captain of the Grand Canal commands one of the boats plying these waters, which now cater mostly to the historical fascination of tourists seeking a glimmer of China's rapidly disappearing past. Even on the overcast and intermittently rainy day pictured here, the smell of "stinky tofu," a delicacy, stimulated the senses, offering a slice of local cuisine. As we glided under a bridge and into a wide opening of water, a local opened her third-floor window and dumped a pail of garbage down into the canal below, where her kitchen scraps left a circling smudge of grease. The previously polite captain barked "Wŏ cao! Naozi jin shui ma?!" (which loosely translates as "F*** me! Have you lost your mind?!")

"Visiting the Chairman"

Since 1949, the Party has sought to reclaim and rebuild the once imperial Tiananmen Square for nationalist purposes. Since 1989, this has meant infusing the space with a popular flag-raising ceremony that draws thousands of celebrants every morning, clamping down on anything that smells of protest, and supporting a burgeoning tourist industry that brings tens of thousands of visitors each day from the countryside into the historical heart of China. Surrounded by the spectacular Forbidden City to the north, the world's biggest museum to the east, the Chairman Mao Memorial on the south side, and the imposing Great Hall of the People to the west, Tiananmen Square stands as one of the world's great urban centers of history and culture—it is the epicenter of Chinese national imaginings. It is also an enormous frying pan, as the immense space has no trees, just millions of shale slabs that reflect the day's heat. In this image, we see four women, part of a tour that had just visited the mausoleum containing Chairman Mao's body—complete with the museum's trademark red bags, full of souvenirs—seeking refuge in the shade of a nearby building. The tourists dress up in colorful, playful outfits, making their pilgrimage to the chairman's body something of a party, a nationalist outing that reclaims Tiananmen for the purposes of nationalist longings and lots of shopping.

"The Blanket"

Nestled in the leafy northwest corner of Beijing, the Haidian district, home to dozens of China's top universities, is often called "the academic northwest"; this area includes the microneighborhood called Zhongguancun, often called "the Silicon Valley of the East." This part of Beijing is home to the corporate headquarters of the tech giants that are transforming China and to numerous bars, clubs, cafés, and restaurants. While walking one evening from the elegant grounds of Peking University back to the International College Beijing, thus bisecting Haidian from west to east, a group of friends stopped in one of the few remaining *hutongs* for a snack of salted peanuts, pineapple on a stick, and cold beer, with each pleasure purchased from a different vendor hawking goods from little stalls packed from floor to ceiling. Sitting on our humble seats—discarded peach cartons—we looked up from the alleyway to catch the last glimmers of the day's sun sliding off the glassy tower just a few blocks away. While the postmodern world seeks to hide labor from the commodities that fill the consumer world, the ancient square before us held mops and brooms, stacks of vegetables to be carted to market, scooters and wagons and other means of transportation, and the ubiquitous laundry line, in this case featuring a tattered old blanket woven in a floral pattern—providing quiet testimony to the hands-on labor that survives in the shadows of the towers that announce the age of Google.

"A Reflective Education"

Amid the frantic hustle and bustle of Beijing, the city's universities offer cherished spaces of quiet. One night, after seeking comfort food in the form of pizza at the Tube Station (a raucous joint where ex-pats go for a taste of home) and while walking home to the symphony of car horns, bicycle bells, and bus blasts, some of the authors in this book sought refuge on the well-manicured grounds of Peking University, which feels more like an elite botanical garden than a typical college campus. With swaying willow trees lining the shoreline and a ninety-year-old Boya pagoda (designed and funded in 1924 by an American architect) rising above the trees, a stroll around Weiminghu Lake takes visitors back to an older, quieter, slower way of life. On this beautiful evening, the lake was surrounded by older couples taking picnics, children playing in the grass, lovers snuggling up on the benches, and a few stray Rollerbladers weaving amid the otherwise mellow foot traffic. While so much of daily life in China seems committed to catching up and bypassing the West, or to getting rich, or to displaying newfound wealth in performative ways, the reflective education pictured here evokes the Confucian principles of calm, ordered, dignified learning in the cause of self-knowledge and worldly wisdom.

"Open Source Nuns"

The futures of China—both internally and internationally—hinge in part on how the Chinese people adopt new media technologies, and for what purposes. Over eight summers of doing research and interviews in China, India, Hong Kong, Tibet, Taiwan, and Nepal, virtually every time the editors entered a Buddhist monastery, we found the monks and nuns—like consumers everywhere—glued to their laptops, iPads, iPhones, and other gadgets. In one ancient monastery, nestled in the dusty foothills of the Himalayas, with goats bleating up on the scrubby rise behind a temple, one young monk surprised us with the score from the NBA finals. "You looked like you might care," he said, before returning to an online game. In this image, one nun looks at her phone while another looks directly into the camera, establishing a triangle of sight lines and multiple modes of information sharing and image production between the "open source nuns" and the viewer. While our talks with these open source nuns went undisturbed, a similar chat with a Buddhist monk and his grandmother, sitting on a bench in Chengdu on June 4, 2014, the twenty-fifth anniversary of the Tiananmen Square incident, led to our being surrounded by soldiers, policemen, and plainclothes police, who all seemed to think that our conversation required monitoring.

"The Crawling"

At the Nanjing Massacre Museum, gut-wrenching statues depicting scenes of slaughter greet patrons as they wait in long lines to enter the museum. Once inside, visitors are led underground, into a cavernous labyrinth of rooms recounting the murder of an estimated three hundred thousand Chinese citizens at the hands of the Japanese Army. As part of Japan's invasion of China, an early chapter in World War II, the Japanese decided in 1937 to turn Nanjing into a scorched-earth exemplar of what would happen to those who resisted the empire's march. The subsequent tidal wave of rapes, tortures, and mass killings stands among the worst horrors of the war and serves as a call for nationalist imaginings. Inside the museum, one plaque describes the massacre as a "fascist atrocity of bestiality strangling humanity and brutality smothering civilization." The museum seems designed to produce a sense of traumatized nationalism, the us-against-them idea that the nation can find strength in tragedy and build purpose out of the wreckage of imperial violence. Perhaps he couldn't fully comprehend the scale of his ancestors' suffering, but this little boy waved his flag nonetheless, thus fulfilling the nationalism-building purposes that fuel this cultural site.

Imagining Communities
in the Age of Risk

Preface to Part Two

Mohan J. Dutta

China offers a unique vantage point for thinking about risk, as it
negotiates both capitalism and communism, rapid development
and a widening wealth gap, and urban growth and rural reform,
revealing the interplays of power structures that construct narratives of
markets and trade, goods and labor, and hazards and opportunities. For
example, China's economic growth success story, in which the country
pulled record numbers of citizens out of poverty, was built on a heavy
industrial base, leaving China with monumental air, earth, and water
pollution, growing health needs, and continuing citizen concerns. The
chapters in this section take up questions of how various discourses
reimagine China as a nation and a global power in the face of these multiplying health risks. Moreover, these chapters address how discourses
about China originating from outside of China interpenetrate with discourses originating from within China, illustrating how local, national,
regional, and transnational arguments mutually influence each other.

Mohan J. Dutta

The triumphant narratives of growth, development, and modernization so popular in China today depict the arrival of a new Asian hegemony, even as they erase other narratives of dispossession, displacement, environmental degradation, and inequality, all while replicating national representations of neoliberal governance. The symbolic enunciations of the nation-state are thus intertwined with the material inequalities that constitute Chinese modernity, with these discourses in turn wrapped up in competing regional and international arguments. In this way, the nation-state, expressing its affinities with global capital and simultaneously seeking to enact a Chinese identity attached to the rhetoric of communism, emerges as a site of innumerable new risks to individual and community health, well-being, and the broader ecology, or what the authors in this section of the book refer to as "ecologies of risk."

Considered together, the chapters in Part Two explore how symbolic enunciations of health and risk are constituted within global networks of power, how they are tied to the materiality of bodies and global flows, and how they are rooted in specific, local cultural situations. Here, the social construction of health and risk in China occurs within depictions of nation-states, which enact imaginaries of public health and risk preparedness that seek to control the pathways of disease, even while the government espouses rhetorics that champion aspirations for open economies and minimized resistance to the free exchange of goods, labor, and capital. The rhetorics of risk addressed in this section therefore oscillate within this tension between control and flow, between clamping down on disease circulation while accelerating the international exchange of goods. Analyzing this tension helps to explain how our anxieties about contamination across global sites of production and exchange form the backdrop for global narratives of health risks, illness, healing, and curing. Ecologies of risk are thus located amid the fragmented and disrupted global ecosystems that respond to the ever-expanding quest of capital to create new markets, find new sources of cheap and exploitable labor, and extract new raw materials to feed global capitalism. As these chapters indicate, the acceleration of global capitalism across specific parts of the planet engenders the multiplication of risks, both symbolic and material.

To illustrate how ecologies of risk operate in contemporary China, these chapters address how health, capitalism, communism, materiality, symbols, and bodies converge in constituting risks and forming the politics of risky locations. In "China's Fraught Food System: Imagining Ecological Civilization in the Face of Paradoxical Modernity," Donovan S. Conley depicts the paradoxes that constitute the discourses and materialities of modernity in China, where, despite the tensions Conley addresses, the Communist Party of China (CPC or the Party) has built a celebratory narrative of communist development, historical progress, and national growth. In contrast to the Party's one-dimensional rhetoric, Conley shows how risks to health are intertwined with risks to ecology, with both health and ecological risks being generated by the structures of large-scale development and modernization championed by the Party. Via interpretation of the everyday embodiments of risks and the policy articulations of the CPC, Conley argues that the Party's support for modernization, progress, and development through large-scale industrialization and urbanization projects has led China to the brink of ecological disaster. Attending in particular to the risks to food systems that are posed by large-scale material structures of growth, Conley explores the paradoxes negotiated by Chinese civil society as it negotiates the consequences of rapid national development, depictions of harmonious relationships, and limited spaces for resistance and dissent. The theoretical appeal of Conley's chapter lies in its explorations of risks at the intersections of the pathways of Chinese modernity and global capitalism. As is true in the United States and elsewhere as well, Conley observes that questions of materiality, flow, and threats to the environment are uttered alongside multiplying buzzwords such as "sustainability," "green development," "healthy development," and "smart planning," with the inherent contradictions within this discourse magnified by the growth needs of global capitalism and the political needs of nation-states.

Zhuo Ban's chapter, titled "Her Milk Is Inferior: Breastfeeding, Risk, and Imagining Maternal Identities in Chinese Cyberspace," further unpacks this theme of risks proliferating amid the macroprocesses of urbanization and development. In this case study, symbolic articulations of modernity, attached to depictions of American formula as a source of safe and secure health care, are mobilized in the everyday practices and perceptions of mothering among urban women sharing their experiences on a forum, or what is called in China a bulletin board service

(BBS). Ban argues that the online space of the BBS emerges as a site for self-governance, where mothers internalize a narrative of healthy motherhood driven by discourses of consumption, normative gender roles, and individualized responsibility. As an example of self-governance attached to an internalized position of individual responsibility, the framing of breastfeeding as risky is negotiated amid the everyday lived experiences of the women, which are based in large part on their understanding of their urban identities and their roles as mothers, their feelings of guilt and accountability, the heavy influence of experts and in-laws, and their desires for good health for their children—which all swirl together amid the global forces that are commodifying health in general and motherhood in particular. Moreover, while both the CPC and the World Health Organization (WHO) advocate for breastfeeding as a healthy practice, the BBS studied here featured posts mostly focusing on anxieties regarding the risks to child health posed by breast milk. The dangers of breast milk, portrayed in discourses of toxicity, nutritional deficiency, and developmental threats, are also juxtaposed against the unregulated sale of contaminated milk by the powerful brand Sanlu and the marketing of formula milk, which appears here as medically safe, nutritionally superior, and emotionally preferable for both mother and child. In short, breast milk becomes a synecdoche for the larger social and material problems challenging China, indicating both a discourse of risk and a powerfully embodied form of agency, which serves as a contested harbinger of China's national health.

Yet, even as risk discourses voice broader, national concerns, a cross-cultural comparative approach can reveal unique cultural constructions. For example, in "Imagining Health Risks: Fear, Fate, Death, and Family in Chinese and American HIV/AIDS Online Discussion Forums," Huiling Ding and Jingwen Zhang explore the discourses of online communication in HIV/AIDS-related discussion forums in China and the United States. Drawing on their analysis of the content and organizing structure of forum posts, these authors point to the similarities and differences between the U.S. and Chinese discourses of HIV/AIDS amid the familial and sociocultural contexts of health risks. Whereas the U.S. forums are professionalized in the paid structure of moderators, the Chinese forums are run by volunteers. Discourses of HIV/AIDS in the context of the U.S.

forums highlight the negotiations of living with HIV/AIDS, whereas the discourses on the Chinese forums revolve mostly around high-risk sexual behavior and anxieties related to contamination. Particular to the cultural context of familial care and filial piety, Chinese discourses of HIV/AIDS discuss responsibility toward parents and family members. In both the U.S. and Chinese forums, discourses of uncertainty are prevalent and contributors employ sociocultural scripts, depicting the interplay of cultural metaphors and the governing structures of risk and risk management. The contribution of this chapter is its depiction of the interplays between the embodied narratives of HIV/AIDS, the cultural contexts of the disease, and the everyday negotiations amid familial, social, and cultural understandings and expectations. Even while local contexts and national differences emerge from the study, the authors note how the discourses of risk regarding HIV/AIDS in both China and the United States are connected with global narratives of fear, concern, and, in some cases, hope.

Emphasizing this theme of global versus local disease narratives in "Imagining the People's Risk: Projecting National Strength in China's English-Language News about Avian Influenza," Lisa B. Keränen, Kirsten N. Lindholm, and Jared Woolly analyze English-language Chinese media coverage of the 2013 avian influenza outbreak, depicting how the national imaginaries of risk are voiced in conversation with global imaginaries of risk mobilities, porous borders, security, and disease management. Comparisons of coverage in Chinese newspapers run by the state (*People's Daily* and *China Daily*) with a semi-independent Hong Kong newspaper (*South China Morning Post*) reveal the competing discursive frames through which the outbreak is narrated. The Party's depictions of its response to the health crisis focused on its effective and transparent management of the situation, using the outbreak to portray a Chinese government evolving away from its former, secretive habits. Still, within the state-controlled media, the Party's two newspapers, *People's Daily* and *China Daily*, written both for internal publics and also with an externally situated global audience, diverge in their framing of the risk and in their depiction of the roles of the state. Editorial responses to the outbreak in the *South China Morning Post* sometimes reinforce an articulation of the mainlander as Other, staking out the realms of threat that are tied to the porous boundaries between China and Hong Kong, which facilitate the movement of mainlanders—who are coded in some vernacular discourses in Hong Kong as embodying filth, bad manners, and possibly disease—in and out of Hong Kong. Moreover, as the authors show, the CPC's responses to the avian influenza outbreak were shaped largely by globally circulating discourses about the gaps and failures in China's earlier, and much-criticized, response to the SARS crisis and by a drive to display the power and competence of the present day nation-state. In this way, news coverage of outbreaks reveals broader articulations of responsibility, accountability, cooperation, and transparency, even as it reiterates the anxieties of flow that are intrinsically tied to the global appeal of market capitalism and the discourses governing risks in our age of globalization.

Taken as a whole, the four chapters in this section outline the paradoxes that are constituted in the global imaginaries of progress and development and particularized in the enunciations of risk in various contexts of health, illness, food, ecology, disease, and care in China. In each of the chapters, these enunciations are brought about by sweeping transitions in urbanization and industrialization. As Conley eloquently elucidates, more modernization is narrated as the solution to problems brought about by modernization in contemporary China. Development is understood through the language of materiality, foisting the story of hyperconsumption and consumerism on formerly communist citizens. At the same time, consumer discourses mute the voices of those who call attention to the inequalities, environmental degradation, and displacement brought about by the rapid industrialization and urbanization of China. Attending to the specifics of everyday interactions, health seeking, and personal relationships, while situated in the macro context of enormous economic, political, and social changes in China, which in turn are nested within global movements in capital, labor, goods, and resources, suggests the interplay of the symbolic and the material in global constructions of risk and health. These discourses of risk and health are materially linked to the threats to human health catalyzed by high-speed industrialization and urbanization, yet these discourses are also intertwined with long-standing discourses of and about China. Thus, even as China negotiates its transactions on a global platform, colonial tropes portraying China as "not yet arrived" continue to occupy the global discursive space, as demonstrated in Keränen and her coauthors' analysis of Hong Kong's news coverage of avian flu risks. Furthermore, the portrayals of threats to human health posed by Chinese dietary practices depict the spectacle of the bizarre configured into global discourses of Chinese communism, authoritarian governance, and lack of transparency. This means that the layering of the local, national, regional, and global discourses of risk addressed here are all deeply influenced by long-standing historical narratives, many with roots in the era of colonialism.

Thus, across the chapters in this section of the book, we witness the mobilization of risks at the intersections of culture and structure, depicting the cultural specificity of discourse that is locally emergent in everyday lived experiences yet simultaneously punctuated by global narratives of risks amid hypercapitalism, modernization, urbanization, and development. The local representations of risks in various contexts are contingent, then, upon the anxieties and desires resulting from China's rapid modernization, weaved into pathways of development through economic growth that are dependent upon industrialization and urbanization. The chapters thus raise vital questions: What is this version of China's modernity and how does it relate to its broader risk ecology? Is it distinctly different from Eurocentric and neoliberal notions of modernity? How are the tropes of culture (such as Confucianism) marshaled to explain, justify, and celebrate the arrival of Chinese modernity? To what extent is this Chinese version of modernity an invitation to an alternative pathway of being (what Hartnett calls an "alternative modernity") that challenges the global status quo rooted in Eurocentric articulations of freedom, liberty, and individualism? To what extent are health risks understood as national or global problems?

While answers to these questions are still forthcoming, these chapters illustrate how the enunciation of risks to the body and to the broader ecological body, mostly brought about by the large scale and rapid speed of modernization in China, call for the theorizing of communication in and about China as a series of overlapping possibilities, contradictions, and imaginations. Given the large-scale changes that China is undergoing and the specific communicative constraints associated with surveillance and censorship in China, the essays invite us to consider the discourses and ecologies of risk as spaces for working out a politics of transformation.

China's Fraught Food System: Imagining Ecological Civilization in the Face of Paradoxical Modernity

Donovan Conley

On March 15, 2014, the Central Committee of the Communist Party of China (CPC or the Party) and the State Council launched something called the "National New-Type Urbanization Plan." A colossal, $6.8 trillion undertaking, this initiative aims to migrate one hundred million rural Chinese farmers into the nation's urban centers by 2020, reaching the staggering number of 250 million relocated by 2025.[1] The prevailing belief of the CPC equates urbanization with modernization, and modernization with progress, so this massive social-engineering project—the thirty-chapter report covers everything from roads, hospitals, schools, and residential buildings to social security, water cleanliness and basic health conditions, public services for entrepreneurship, and so on—is touted to increase the quality of life for approximately 60 percent of the overall population.[2] The plan will also dramatically increase domestic consumption, since urban residents spend far more than their rural counterparts, thus reducing China's reliance on export markets while addressing its worrisome housing bubble.[3] Already the modern world's most expansive and dynamic example of sociohistorical transformation, China's National New-Type Urbanization Plan will carry a seismic ecological toll. Indeed, the plan amounts to the single largest engineered human migration in the history of the world.[4] The unintended consequences of this undertaking are therefore unimaginable, yet we can be certain that the ecological impact will be unprecedented.

What makes China's National New-Type Urbanization Plan all the more consequential is the 2014 report by the UN International Panel on Climate Change (IPCC), which confirms the existence of a global ecological emergency brought on by human factors. The report is the boldest statement to date by the world's leading body studying climate change and the result of a more than two-decade-long collaboration involving thousands of scientists from almost two hundred countries. The unequivocal message of the report is that "changes in climate have caused impacts on natural and human systems on all continents and across the oceans."[5] Glaciers are shrinking, disrupting water resources in both quantity and quality; negative impacts on crop yields have become more prevalent than positive ones (with the price of grain being linked to social unrest);[6] and extreme weather events are increasing. Further, the report asserts,

> People who are socially, economically, culturally, politically, institutionally, or otherwise marginalized are especially vulnerable to climate change and also to some adaptation and mitigation responses (*medium evidence, high agreement*). This heightened vulnerability is rarely due to a single cause. Rather, it is the product of intersecting social processes that result in inequalities in socioeconomic status and income, as well as in exposure. Such social processes include, for example, discrimination on the basis of gender, class, ethnicity, age, and (dis)ability.[7]

The implicit conclusion of the IPCC report is that advanced global capitalism has wrought and continues to wreak havoc on the planet and its populations, with ever greater risks posed to those increasingly cut out of the winnings. As Jeff Goodell puts it, "Climate change is, at its base, an environmental justice issue in which the rich nations of the world are inflicting damage on the poor ones."[8] The 2010 earthquake devastation in

Haiti offers a stark illustration of how sufferings are multiplied when eco-logical upheaval and global inequality collide.[9] As the UN report makes clear, this interfacing of environmental catastrophes and political turmoil is going to increase over the coming decades, plunging large swathes of the planet into turmoil. Even the U.S. Department of Defense recently acknowledged that climate change is now among the United States' top national security concerns.[10]

China's urbanization plan is of grave importance, then, for it will be-come the primary theater where the dynamics of global capital and eco-logical turbulence collide during the coming decade. Despite the plan's erstwhile commitment to such public virtues as "people-oriented urban-ization" and being "ecologically friendly" and "sustainable," to "agricul-tural modernization" feeding "green cities and smart cities" designed with "smart planning" to create "healthy development," there is every reason to expect a portentous decade.[11] At present, China stands at the global apex of both socioeconomic growth and ecological upheaval, a tenuous situa-tion I describe throughout this chapter as *paradoxical modernity*: unprec-edented progress borne out of unprecedented environmental calamity. No nation on earth has achieved such colossal expansion with such speed while wreaking such ecological destruction. I argue that this paradox will place increasing levels of pressure on civil society in mainland China, for as Goodell puts it, "The blunt truth is that what China decides to do in the next decade will likely determine whether or not mankind can halt—or at least ameliorate—global warming."[12] While civil society exists in China today, it is cloaked by censorship, repression, and the apathy of a growing leisure class. My conclusion is that something will have to give: ecologically speaking, the paradox of Chinese modernity cannot endure, and the burden will inevitably fall on civil society to address the dilemmas caused by unchecked growth and, thus, unchecked destruction.

My analysis unfolds in two main sections, representing each dimen-sion of China's paradoxical modernity; the first examines China's sociohis-torical and material expansion, and the second focuses on its discursive and political imaginaries. First I explore the ecological dimensions of China's modernizing miracle, tracking the seismic growth and calamity of a thirty-year socioeconomic boom. This section discloses a number of ecological realities, from air pollution to water wars to food scares, thus identifying the stark empirical relations between state and citizenry. Second, I turn to what I describe as the "fraught rhetorical space" that exists between citizens and the state in China today. This section examines the crowding of social space by CPC official discourse, which eclipses the rhetorical work of citizens converting local experiences into shared narratives and, ultimately, political demands.

My contribution to the phenomenon of social imaginaries is to raise the question of where the virtual lines of public trust are drawn between the state and its citizens. The case of China is unique, for the CPC endeavors to manufacture universalizing rhetorics, like "ecological civilization," that often fail to align—spectacularly so, in some cases—with ground-level conditions and lived experiences. I argue here that public trust cannot simply be mandated by the state; functional and binding social imaginaries cannot be imposed upon citizens but must be collectively shared. From this perspective, I argue that China's civil society, currently frozen in political stasis, with ecological urgency on one side, repression on the other, and consumerism in the middle, is fated to confront demands for substantial political reform in the coming generation. This means the Chinese people will soon need to conjure their own social imaginaries, out of which new political demands will be born. The wager here is that the burdens of ecology will eventually upend the official discourse of "harmony" that organizes so much of Chinese society today.[13] In short, the reigning imaginary of contemporary China is on a path to be upended by the unavoidable crises produced by paradoxical modernity.

The Predatory Grandeur of Chinese Modernity

Ecology—that is, food, water, and energy—forms the core of the paradox of modern China. Until as late as the 1970s, one third of the country's population was undernourished.[14] As Brian Palmer notes, "For most of China's history, famine was just an extreme version of the normal state of affairs."[15] Although significant famines claimed millions of lives in 1876–79 (thirteen million), 1927–30 (six million), and 1942–43 (six million), the dubious honor of world's deadliest famine dates to Mao's China, beginning in 1958, claiming between thirty and forty-five million lives (the great Irish famine, by comparison, carried a toll of around one million). Each calamity was brought on by a combination of ecological and human factors, but the broader point is the normality of scarcity in China's history.[16]

Fast forward mere decades to the 1990s when a relatively slight 11 percent of the population—roughly 140 million—was undernourished. Compare this to the 30 percent figure from the 1970s, which would have accounted for about 350 million individuals. While still an enormous figure, it astonishes how dramatically the CPC has managed to lift so many of its people out of poverty with such rapidity. "Whatever China has done it has done in a hurry. A decade's time at Chinese speed creates as much change as occurs in other countries over one or two generations," note Ma and Adams.[17] All told, the economic reforms of modern China have improved the lives of some five hundred million citizens, thus leading some observers to refer to the "China miracle."[18]

Within this narrative of development, 1978 was a decisive year.[19] Chairman Mao died two years prior, Deng Xiaoping was the new leader, and reform was in the air. Meanwhile, in the village of Xiaogang, north of Nanjing, a group of impoverished and desperate farmers decided in a secret meeting to break the law and harvest their own surpluses to hold in reserve for their families.[20] They signed a secret document, swearing to care for the children of anyone who might be imprisoned for breaking the law. They divided up their land, worked feverishly on their own plots, quietly competed with one another, and ultimately produced a bigger harvest the first year than the previous five combined. Word of this unprecedented yield quickly floated up the ranks of the CPC, and instead of being punished, the group's innovation was held up as a new model of economic progress. That year, the Third Plenum of the CPC Central Committee announced an abrupt departure in the Party's developmental purpose and ushered in a new era of market liberalization. Mao's stodgy collectivist agricultural model was replaced with one built on competition, ownership, and incentives called the Household Responsibility System. According to Yang Yao, "since China began undertaking economic reforms in 1978, its economy has grown at a rate of nearly ten percent a year, and its per-capita GDP is now twelve times greater than it was three decades ago."[21] This is a miraculous achievement for a nation of such magnitude, and it is to a considerable extent a story about how the alleviation of hunger rapidly gave way to the production of abundance.

There is a twist, however, as Dexter Roberts asserts: "In the first half of 2010, per capita income rose 13 percent in the countryside, to $935 a year, and 10 percent in the cities, to $2,965 a year. Nevertheless, swelling slums in the suburbs of Beijing, Shanghai, and Guangzhou attest to a yawning wealth discrepancy between thousands of newly minted rich and millions of poor."[22] Further, according to the Gini coefficient—a measure of economic inequality in which zero equals perfect equality and 1 absolute inequality—income distribution worsened from below 0.3 thirty years ago to near 0.5 today. That is roughly the same level as the United States (compared with Norway at 0.25 on the low end). Roberts adds, "Poverty researchers recognize anything above 0.4 as potentially socially destabilizing."[23] Incomes are higher in the city than the country, it is true, but vast disparities remain between incomes *within* cities as well. China's New-Type Urbanization Plan may raise the income floor overall, but the issue of skyrocketing wealth and deepening inequality haunts the country's fastest growing urban and industrial sectors. Mike Davis warns, "'Overurbanization'. . . is driven by the reproduction of poverty, not by the supply of jobs. This is one of the unexpected tracks down which a neoliberal world order is shunting the future."[24] Metropolitan growth, in other words, does not equal economic growth and is closer to the opposite. Davis's findings are rooted in a 2003 report by the UN's Human Settlements Programme, titled *The Challenge of the Slums*, which bluntly asserts, "The primary direction of both national and international interventions during the last twenty years has actually increased urban poverty and slums, increased exclusion and inequality, and weakened urban elites in their efforts to use cities as engines of growth."[25] Through these findings we glimpse around the corner of China's grand modernizing aspirations. Davis adds a warning: "Instead of cities of light soaring toward heaven, much of the twenty-first urban world squats in squalor, surrounded by pollution, excrement, and decay."[26] Shiny promises of "opportunity" and "growth" aside, the insistent rhetorical assurances of urbanization cannot be counted on to improve the living conditions within cities.

THE NUCLEAR WINTER OF PROGRESS

Wealth of China's magnitude, generated at such a breakneck pace, does not occur in a vacuum. There is another dimension to the predatory grandeur of Chinese modernity, a supplementary history of usurpation, corruption, suppression, and environmental mayhem. In lifting half a billion of its citizens out of hunger and tripling the GDP in less than three decades, the CPC has left a path of ecological destruction that haunts its modernizing imaginaries. Not simply ghosts lost to the past, the unintended consequences of Chinese modernization are real, even if repressed. I am referring to the disappeared multitudes that will not go away, the toxic air and polluted waterways, the leveled villages and old *hutong* neighborhoods, the artists and intellectuals and dissidents, and the Tibetan and Uyghur ethnic populations the CPC is allegedly liberating. Indeed, the most extreme illustration of China's predatory modernization, as I detail in the next section, is to be found in Tibet. The culture and resources of this nominally autonomous region are undergoing erasure, usurpation, displacement, and utter transformation by the CPC's modernizing machinery. Today one may purchase Adidas sports gear and high-end Hermès scarves in the glittering new commercial district of Lhasa, yet Tibetans have to fight for the right to learn and study their native language in CPC-run schools. This is how a culture is disappeared, by being transformed into an object of tourist fascination and generic consumerism under the banner of what the CPC imagines to be progress.[27]

For mainland Chinese, the most apparent unintended ecological consequence of the country's staggering growth is the air pollution, a toxic consequence of coal-burning factories and vehicle emissions that has reached lethal levels. In January 2013, the concentration of particulate matter with a diameter of 2.5 microns or less—small enough to penetrate deep into the lungs and enter the bloodstream—hit nine hundred parts per million, which is forty times the level the World Health Organization accepts as safe.[28] No less a figure than Chen Zhu, China's recent health minister, coauthored a startling "Comment" piece in the December 2013 issue of *The Lancet*. Some of the arresting statistics he and his coauthors cite include the following:

- China was the world's biggest energy consumer in 2009.
- In 2012, 50 percent of the world's coal was consumed in China.
- The number of civilian road vehicles in China jumped from sixteen million in 2000 to almost ninety-four million in 2011.
- China now produces the largest number of major pollutants in the world.
- Particulate matter has become the fourth biggest threat to the health of the Chinese people (behind heart disease, dietary risk, and smoking).
- The death rate from lung cancer has soared since 1970 and is now the leading cause of death from malignant tumors in the country.
- Between 350,000 and 500,000 people die prematurely each year as a result of outdoor air pollution in China.
- Roughly 1.2 million people in China died prematurely and 25 million disability-adjusted life years (DALY) were lost in 2010 as a result of air pollution.[29]

The authors acknowledge that the timeline of China's pollution crisis directly parallels that of its thirty-year economic expansion. What they do not address, however, are the secondary channels of contamination: the country's water and soil, and hence its food supply.

Jonathan Kaiman confronts this issue in *The Guardian*, citing professor He Dongxian from China Agricultural University in Beijing. Kaiman writes, "[Dongxian] said new research suggested that if the smog persists, Chinese agriculture will suffer conditions 'somewhat similar to a nuclear winter.' She has demonstrated that air pollutants adhere to greenhouse surfaces, cutting the amount of light inside by about 50 percent and severely impeding photosynthesis, the process by which plants convert light into life-sustaining chemical energy." Kaiman continues: "She warned that if smoggy conditions persist, the country's agricultural production could be seriously affected. 'Now almost every farm is caught in a smog panic,' she said."[30] Indeed, the situation is already tense. According to Wang Shiyuan, the vice minister of land and resources, about 3.33 million hectares of China's farmland is too polluted to grow crops. This is a contaminated area roughly the size of Belgium.[31] In a *New York Times* article titled "Rural Water, Not City Smog, May Be China's Pollution

Nightmare," professor Dabo Guan is cited declaring, "From my point of view . . . water is the biggest environmental issue in China," adding, "People in the cities, they see air pollution every day, so it creates huge pressure from the public. But in the cities, people don't see how bad the water pollution is . . . they don't have the same sense."[32] China thus finds itself in a domestic agricultural squeeze: increasing pollution decreases farming capacity, while increasingly urban appetites grow geometrically. The result is a gathering storm of plummeting supply and skyrocketing demand.[33] The squeeze has given way to a massive shift toward imports. In a historic reversal, China has moved from a position of self-sufficiency in grain production only a few years ago to being very close to the world's leading grain importer today.[34] Additionally, headlines in the United States made much of China's recent purchase of Smithfield Foods, the world's biggest producer of pork. This acquisition was the largest-ever takeover of a U.S.-owned company by a Chinese firm (the Hong Kong based Shuanghui International).[35] The transaction was valued at $7.1 billion, including debt, and the transaction had everything to do with the squeeze of China's declining resources and its expanding middle-class appetite for luxury animal protein. This portrait of China's growth reveals the depth and breadth of its ecological impact. Thirty years of meteoric expansion has polluted, destroyed, and/or eradicated entire atmospheres, communities, farmlands, water systems, and human histories. Yet even grander imaginations are playing out in the south, where China's increasingly urgent need for clean water is giving rise to the world's largest—and most dangerous—engineering projects.

THE DAM RUSH

As noted by professor Guan above, China's pollution emergency has the dubious honor of being the most salient fact of daily life in the country's eastern industrial corridor. The gathering "nuclear winter" is simply inescapable, and so the government is compelled to make responding to it a priority. Considerably less visible is the "dam rush" taking place in the southwestern part of the country, where at the moment some ninety large-scale hydroengineering projects are in the works.[36] Indeed, rivers have become the key to China's modernizing aspirations, and yet, paradoxically, the country is the world's worst offender when it comes to water pollution. In 2011 more than half of China's largest lakes and reservoirs were so contaminated they were unusable for human consumption.[37] Industrial spillage has contaminated a fifth of China's land, stunting its agricultural output. As Tom Philpott writes, "Fully 40 percent of China's arable land has been degraded by some combination of erosion, salinization, or acidification—and nearly 20 percent is polluted, whether by industrial effluent, sewage, excessive farm chemicals, or mining runoff."[38] Per capita, China possesses merely one-sixth the agricultural capacity of the United States. For these reasons, the vast Tibetan plateau has become a largely unseen battleground, where the CPC has been aggressively pursuing hydroengineering projects to control water flows in this expansive resource-rich terrain. The plateau's immense glaciers, huge underground springs, and high altitude make Tibet the world's largest freshwater repository after the polar icecaps, earning this region the nickname of the "third pole."[39]

The CPC's river projects have provoked tensions with neighboring countries, however, most notably India. A particularly sensitive issue between the two nations concerns the river known in Tibet as Yarlung Tsangpo—the highest river with the deepest gorges on earth—which crashes through the Himalayas before flowing into Arunachal Pradesh, in northeastern India, where it becomes known as the Brahmaputra. Because of its enormous cache of both fresh water and hydropower reserves, China is in the midst of rerouting the river northward where it twists around the mountain Namcha Barwa (known as the Great Bend). This is a monumental enterprise, part of the Great South–North Water Transfer, with an estimated cost of 62 billion U.S. dollars. Lily Kuo puts the matter into perspective:

> The project's eventual goal is to move 44.8 billion cubic meters of water across the country every year, more than there is in the river Thames. The infrastructure includes some of the longest canals in the world; pipelines that weave underneath riverbeds; a giant aqueduct; and pumping stations powerful enough to fill Olympic-sized pools in minutes. It is the world's largest water-transfer project, unprecedented both in the volume of water to be transferred and the distance to be traveled—a

total of 4,350 kilometers (2,700 miles), about the distance between the two coasts of America.[40]

Brahma Chellaney adds, "the Chinese desire to divert the Brahmaputra by employing 'peaceful nuclear explosions' to build an underground tunnel through the Himalayas."[41] Three dams have already been constructed upstream in the Tibetan section of the river, with the Great Bend project currently in the works. Eleven total hydropower stations are planned.

This hydrorevolution is a gargantuan undertaking. When finished, China will control the river's upstream flow, which will have obvious implications downstream in Bangladesh and India—hence fueling India's anxiety over China's ongoing construction. (Similar tensions exist in Vietnam over China's handling of the upstream resources that feed the Mekong River.) In a time of increasing scarcity and growing political tensions, control of water is control of life's most valuable resource. The key ecological question—which becomes the key political question—is: What are the unintended consequences to be expected of a geomorphic undertaking of this magnitude? As Wines notes, "critics say the sheer weight of water backed up in the 410-mile-long reservoir behind the dam has increased the danger of earthquakes and landslides. The government has acknowledged that risk, but denied that the project played any role in China's powerful May 2008 quake in Sichuan Province, in which at least 87,000 people died."[42] Whether the dam was indeed responsible for the 2008 earthquake, the project's total human and environmental cost has already been immense. Policy director of International Rivers, Peter Bosshard, takes the point further: "Chinese dams have displaced and often impoverished an estimated 23 million people. Dam breaks in the country with the world's worst safety record have killed approximately 300,000 people since the 1950s."[43] Although the human population will not be affected in the same way by the remote location of the Yarlung Tsangpo Great Bend project, at three times the scale of the Three Gorges Dam, the ecological impact is almost impossible to fathom.

THE LETHAL CONVENIENCE OF CONTAMINATED FOOD

While rivers are the key to unlocking China's urbanizing agenda, providing elemental portraits of a paradoxical modernity in which national progress is built on a foundation of ecological havoc and cultural upheaval, the country's industrial food system is also fraught with the same unintended consequences. This explains why food scares, some of which are detailed below, have become a ubiquitous part of daily life in China as, for example, in the complicated social terrain where ecology and cultural politics collide over the issue of breastfeeding. Milk—where it comes from, how it is handled, the ways it affects bodies, how it shapes understandings of motherhood and gender and corporeal visibility, how cultural perceptions of breastfeeding intersect with attitudes about nationalism and public health—is both utterly banal and deeply consequential. Expanding from milk to a broader social context, I argue that food is where the CPC's vast machinery of modernization intersects with every member of the country on a daily basis (or, as importantly, does not). Indeed, food stands as the most immediate triangulation between the citizen, the state, and the larger ecology of resources, information, and practices that fuel conflicting national imaginaries. If the national imaginary is always embodied in the lived, felt ways that structure our daily lives, then surely food serves not only as our daily energy but as that which prods our imaginings.

The wave of modern food scandals in China began in 2008 when six babies died and upwards of a quarter million others fell critically ill from consuming infant formula that had been tainted with melamine, a harsh industrial chemical used in plastics and fertilizers.[44] The outbreak occurred during the Beijing Olympics, at the exact moment when the CPC was performing the face of a new modern China to the global community, so the news stayed under wraps for months. The poisoning was kept secret in order to maintain a positive Olympic facade, and the lack of shared information naturally compounded the severity of the situation. In an excellent analysis of the episode, Vivien Lim explains: "China's 2008 tainted milk scandal laid bare some of the harsher realities behind the country's economic miracle—exposing the high price that can be exacted for entrenched, institutionalized corruption and inadequate oversight during times of rapid growth."[45] This was the story: The government encouraged milk's nutritional benefits to families with rising incomes; milk demand skyrocketed; dairy firms placed huge pressure on small farmers to increase supply; poorly regulated and unprepared small farmers, unable to handle demand, cut corners and sent shoddy product through countless independent and unregulated middlemen; tainted milk found its way through the system; Sanlu—at the time the world's second largest milk producer—learned of its contaminated product through customer complaints in late 2007; Sanlu did nothing, having been awarded the national inspection exemption label by China's top safety body (a reward for large market share and established reputation); Sanlu continued to sell its toxic product through late 2008 by silencing consumers through an advertising deal with Baidu.com, which filtered negative news about Sanlu from its user's searches; public outcry eventually ensued; Sanlu ultimately collapsed; two men were executed and the former chairwoman of the company was sentenced to life in prison.[46] This scandal revealed a disastrously complex food supply chain, an inadequate and complacent system of oversight, corporate whitewashing, and government-suppressed airwaves. To date, Sanlu's melamine contamination remains the most infamous and emotionally charged of China's many food scandals, a perfect storm of public innocence and corporate-state malfeasance.

The scandal sent shockwaves through the nation, prompting a series of aggressive reforms.[47] Yet subsequent food scares continued unabated. As a full accounting of these scares is not possible, what follows is an abbreviated list of some of the more egregious cases in recent years.

- Known as the "gutter oil scandal," food regulators have been unsuccessful in eradicating the covert practice of recycling used cooking oil. Rogue capitalists "recover" discarded sludge from gutters, reheat it with other fats and harsh additives, barrel it up, and sell it back to food vendors. The reused oil contains toxins and carcinogens and is thought to account for 10 percent of the cooking oil in China. The State Food and Drug Administration issued a nationwide emergency notice back in 2010, but the trade continues.[48]
- In May 2013, some 16,000 dead pigs were pulled out of the Huangpu River, north of Shanghai, having been discarded upstream in the pig-raising district surrounding Shaoxing. In 2011, 7.7 million pigs

were raised there, with an average death rate of 2–4 percent. This means between 150,000 and 300,000 dead pigs must be processed each year. With inadequate numbers of disposal pits, currently capable of handling less than twenty thousand per year, discarding carcasses in fields and rivers has become commonplace. Before this, illegal butcher shops purchased the diseased corpses on the cheap.[49]

- In May 2013, authorities announced that they had detained over nine hundred people in recent months for "meat-related offenses."[50] One alleged gang was suspected of using illegal chemicals to transform rat, mink, and fox meat into fake mutton slices that are used in the culturally popular hot pot restaurants. In response, police in Zhejiang province posted a guide on how to tell the difference between real and fake mutton.

- In April 2014, 120 tons of frozen spoiled meat, including chicken feet and pig feet and ears—some of it produced four years ago and smuggled across the border from Vietnam through cities like Dongxing and Pingxiang—was seized by authorities in the southern province of Guangxi. According to freight orders, this mountain of rancid product was destined for Beijing, Shanghai, Chengdu, and Guangdong. As with the rat scandal, this case represents a victory for local inspectors; yet these catches raise further alarms about the question of origins in a system containing hundreds of millions of tiny suppliers and countless gaps for them to slip through.[51]

Additional scares abound, including rice laced with the metal cadmium, ginger containing the toxic pesticide shennongdan, exploding watermelons pumped with the growth accelerator forchlorfenuron, pork containing the growth steroid clenbuterol, beef and pork injected with dirty water to increase weight, shrimp injected with a jellylike substance to increase weight, cabbages sprayed with formaldehyde to preserve them during transportation, fake pig ears made from gelatin and sodium oleate, and so on.[52] The situation has grown dire enough that the State General Administration of Sports forbids its athletes from consuming meat outside of official training facilities. As far back as 2008, the government began establishing Special Food Supply centers to make sure the country's elite—Party members, athletes, and the wealthy—eats organic.[53] It is uncertain whether this ultraprivileged network of organic farms has fallen under the scrutiny of President Xi Jingping's anticorruption campaign.[54]

The point of offering this list of scandals is not to humiliate an advancing nation for its industrial transgressions; rather, my goal is to underscore a fact that is less about China and more about modernization itself: that such food scares are a reality of daily life in large-scale, for-profit industrialized economies where accelerating rates of consumption trump concerns about the safety or health of the means of production. The situation is hugely magnified in China because of its vast size and population, its adolescence as a modern nation-state, its lack of political accountability, its unreliable justice system, and the inherently conservative nature of a culture increasingly shaped by the values of consumerism. In terms of the food system there are in effect two Chinas: one hypermodern and centralized, one premodern and fragmented. The food system *is* the disjointed clash of them both. Ted Agres puts it well:

> In China, several thousand modern, large-scale multinational joint-venture companies and farms employ modern equipment and follow best food safety practices. Alongside them are 280 million small, independent farms, each less than two acres in size, raising animals and crops. There are also 10 million registered food-related businesses, including 480,000 licensed food processing enterprises, 80 percent of which employ 10 or fewer workers. These small growers, processors, and merchants rely on crude equipment and techniques and often ignore basic standards and proper practices.[55]

The editors of *The Economist* add: "In the Chinese system, the center proposes; provinces and counties dispose."[56] The New-Type Urbanization Plan is meant to address the messy coexistence of these two Chinas, merging them through urban in-migration and its corresponding grid of roads and railways and airports. The solution to the ecological calamities of hurried modernization is, it would seem, even more hurried modernization. In its continual pursuit of ease, comfort, access, and most of all convenience—the master trope of modern urban life—China has erected a food system that multiplies damages and sufferings just as it seeks to ease the strains of daily life. Indeed, it is the mutually entwined fates of the trope of progress and the hard particulars of daily life that are at issue in the paradox of modernity and that occasion a discussion of the social imaginary and the prospects of civil society in China.

Social Imaginaries, Contested Spaces

The foregoing analysis describes some of the empirical consequences of China's paradoxical modernity. I am particularly interested in the constellation of tensions and disconnections, accidents and crises, and hypocrisies and corruptions that lie between the CPC's official narrative of urbanizing progress on the one hand and the concrete history of ecological wreckage on the other. The gaps between these two realities, as has been shown, are often severe. We thus see the paradox of Chinese modernity playing out in fraught rhetorical spaces that both connect and separate official/nationalist discourses from vernacular/counterpublic discourses, creating a cat-and-mouse dynamic. These contested rhetorical spaces are the terrain of the social imaginary, an inventional zone the CPC attempts to control through totalizing rhetorics that seek to enclose social spaces in the firm embrace of Party rule. But the social imaginary is a dynamic rhetorical phenomenon, an open virtual network of symbolic and affective investments that eludes state control while linking strangers in creative ways. As Castoriadis puts it,

> Society must define its "identity," its articulation, the world, its relations to the world and to the objects it contains, its needs and desires. Without the "answer" to these "questions," without these "definitions," there can be no human world, no society, no culture—for everything would be an undifferentiated chaos. The role of imaginary significations is to provide an answer to these questions, an answer that, obviously, neither "reality," nor "rationality" can provide.[57]

Castoriadis stresses the pragmatic function of these imaginary significations, how what works is precisely that which is felt to satisfy. The imaginary is the rhetorical work of conversion between parts and wholes, wherein local practices are sutured to collective fantasies and vice versa.

The imaginary shuttles back and forth between empirical realities and collective longings, ever seeking to reconcile and satisfy. The additional twist I would offer is to suggest that while nationalistic longings underpin and overlap this process, the social imaginary is not simply a substitute term for nationalism. Indeed, my concluding argument is that this schism between the citizens' daily imaginings and the CPC's overarching national narratives is becoming unbridgeable in China today. To pursue this argument, in the remaining pages I juxtapose the emerging capacity for social actors in China to imagine, or reimagine, the terms of collective life against the Party's nationalizing master trope of modernization, which I argue is encapsulated in the Party's all-consuming image of "ecological civilization."

As one example of the latter, consider the two-hundred-page *China National Human Development Report 2013: Sustainable and Liveable Cities: Toward Ecological Civilization*, jointly authored by the UN's Development Program in China (UNDP) and the Institute for Urban and Environmental Studies wing of the Chinese Academy of Social Sciences (CASS). Although not directly sponsored and published by the CPC, this collaborative publication falls under the auspices of China's central government and, excepting some notes of caution and alternative viewpoints, generally reiterates its core modernizing values. The key rhetorical link between the report and the CPC's recently revised constitution is the notion of "ecological civilization"—a term coined by Hu Jintao in his report to Seventeenth National Congress—to which is devoted its fifth and culminating chapter: "Urbanisation: Toward a Future of Balanced Development and an Ecological Civilization." Notably, in its Eighteenth National Congress (November 2012), the CPC revised its constitution to, in part, embrace a progressive ecological vision. In outgoing General Secretary Jintao's report to the new congress, he declared, "We must give high priority to making ecological progress and incorporate it into all aspects and the whole process of advancing economic, political, cultural, and social progress, work hard to build a beautiful country, and achieve lasting and sustainable development of the Chinese nation."[58] The key—and totalizing—terms here are "all aspects," "whole process," and "lasting and sustainable," for they suggest how the Party's imagination tends toward epic, grand gestures meant to unify the nation. Oblivious to dissent or possible counternarratives, the image of a "beautiful country" fuses the aspirations of modernization and environmental friendliness into a picture of forthcoming national greatness.

The report thus offers a beautiful vision of scientific wisdom guiding industrial capitalism toward a future that is both socioeconomically transformative and ecologically gentle. As the UNDP/CASS report frames it: "Under this concept [ecological civilization], 'respect' for nature instead of 'conquest' of nature forms the ethical basis for man and nature in harmony. Industrial production, for example, needs to give greater importance to a circular process from materials to products and recyclable materials, instead of a linear process of raw materials to products to waste."[59] This shift of emphasis from a "linear" model of extraction and waste to a "circular" model of reusability taps into preferred sentiments of how to reconcile "sustainable" with "expansion." The paradox of growth and destruction lingers in this updated rhetorical formulation, however. "Sustainability," as commonly understood, refers more to the preservation of existing economic practices than to the physical systems upon which they depend. Ke Jinhua perfectly captures this rhetorical tension in his introduction to a special issue of *Social Sciences in China*, "Ecological Civilization and Beautiful China," when he writes,

> "Beautiful China" as a concept has two-fold meanings. On one hand, it contains new eco-civilization ideas such as respecting nature, complying with nature and protecting nature, which demonstrate new value orientations and ecological ethical concepts. And on the other hand, the concept also implies that attaining such a goal will be a long-term and arduous task with no quick and easy short cuts, requiring the unremitting efforts of generations of Chinese.[60]

In other words: growth now, harmony later. "Sustainability" in these formulations means reckoning with the ecological effects of modernization when the nation's socioeconomic goals are satisfied. This is precisely the sort of gap—between trope and lived conditions—that the CPC's totalizing rhetoric is obliged to ignore.

The problem with this particular gap, however, is that socioeconomic growth and ecological stability do not share the same timeline. As

Magdoff and Foster put it, "Given the growth juggernaut that character-izes capitalism, the system is most destructive toward the environment when it is working well and economic growth rates are high. It is least environmentally destructive when the system is in economic crisis and growth is faltering."[61] The catch, then, is that pure economic expansion and pure ecological conservation are not just difficult concepts to recon-cile; they are squarely at odds. Naomi Klein goes even further, declaring that "our economic system and our planetary system are now at war."[62] This realization has begun to take hold among the Chinese populace, but as detailed next, the rhetorical spaces linking citizens to the state are so riddled with the kinds of contradictions and gaps noted above that robust social imaginaries cannot form. The parts of daily life (experienced as environmental wreckage) cannot align with the Party's totalizing imagi-nation (and its dream of "ecological civilization"), thus preventing the conversion of local experiences into a reimagined whole.

Public Trust and Social Imaginaries

The question of Chinese citizenship in a context of paradoxical mod-ernization and ecological emergency is a consequential one, and the question ultimately boils down to the prospects of civil society. A basic syllogism frames the issue: the planet confronts ecological devastation; China is fast becoming the world leader in environmental offenses; the greatest challenge of proportional alleviation (whether anyone likes it or not) therefore falls to the people of China. In other words, new social imaginaries are needed if the Chinese hope to avoid total environmental collapse. But governments do not reform themselves; change only hap-pens when social movements, as mediated through the public sphere and civil society, begin to produce new legitimacy-bearing social imaginaries.[63] A new sense of Chinese political citizenship could, then, intersect with the CPC's notion of ecological citizenship, but only if given the space to grow and mature without retribution. Given the environmental stakes discussed herein, to wonder about the possible futures of political life in China in any meaningful way means, simultaneously, confronting the question of how its citizens negotiate their relations to the state, on the one hand, and how the nation's paradoxical modernity is impacting the planet, on the other. The space where these relations overlap—where notions of patriotic duty ("harmony") collide with daily experiences of poisoned water, burning lungs, and risky food—is precisely where the hard work of building new social imaginaries could take hold, but this inventional space is cloaked by the Party's interdictions against free thought.

A particularly stark illustration of this fraught rhetorical space today is China's new "social credit" initiative, or S.C.S. The goal of this sweeping program is to compile a massive, comprehensive national database of citizens' fiscal, governmental, and even personal information. As Jiayang Fan writes,

> First publicized last year [2015], in a planning document published by the State Council, S.C.S. was billed as "an important component part of the Socialist market-economy system," underwriting a "harmonious Socialist society." Its intended goals are "establishing the idea of a sincerity culture, and carrying forward sincerity and traditional values," and its primary objectives are to raise "the honest mentality and credit levels of the entire society" as well as "the over-all competitiveness of the country," and "stimulating the development of society and the progress of civilization."[64]

The CPC's goal here is to totalize social space, linking every citizen's economic, political, social, and private behaviors to a single credit score that summarizes their moral standing as a member of the nation. Judgments would be rendered about an individual's civic integrity by whether they regularly purchased, say, diapers (hard working, family-oriented, responsible) versus video games (lazy, selfish, irresponsible). The purported goal of the S.C.S. is to nourish a totalizing bond of harmonious social trust: trust between citizens and the state, trust between citizens and one another, trust and sincerity overall. Yet little effort is required to spot the gaps in this fantasy of social cohesion. Trust on a level of this magnitude, housed in an official database, cannot be manufactured through complex algorithms and reduced to a single number. The very notion seems monstrous, but this is the way totalizing rhetorics of progress and harmony eclipse the possibilities of new social imaginaries taking hold. In order for that process to unfold, civil society must find expression through the vibrancy of public sphere activity.

Civil society, driven by the public sphere, involves what Jurgen Habermas has called the "criticism and control" of state activities.[65] John Dewey, writing almost a century prior, said as much when he asserted that "the Great Community" must become an object of desire pursued through relentless inquiry and the artful dissemination of findings.[66] Civil society is thus predicated on the dogged pursuit of at least two essential political commodities: transparency and accountability, or exposure and consequence. What unites these is what Warner calls "autotelic circulation," the self-organized linking of utterances through social space. Transparency involves making state processes visible, whereas accountability involves creating effective disincentives. Both require Dewey's notion of relentless inquiry and Warner's notion of rapid circulation; critical investigation on the one hand, and broad dissemination on the other. Whistleblowing, culture jamming, public shaming, artful subversion, boycotting, pamphleteering, and simply getting the word out through any and all available channels—these are the rhetorical expressions of civil society. The social imaginary arises from this framework of inquiry and alignment.

The encouraging news is that an increasingly restless civil society already exists in China. According to Lagerkvist, "in just 2011 alone, the country saw a staggering 180,000 protests."[67] Guobin Yang and Craig Calhoun also acknowledge the emergence of a "green public sphere," citing the case of a halted dam project on the Nu River due to civic opposition. They attribute the rise of a green public to "the proliferation of environmentalist discourse—a green-speak. Contrary to an earlier Maoist and Marxist view of the human conquest of nature, this new discourse warns about the dangers of irresponsible human behavior toward nature and calls for public action to protect the environment."[68] It is difficult to ignore the environmental calamities wrought by China's breakneck modernization, and the people are bending toward this dimension of their political lives. Additionally, much excitement surrounds the power of "netizenship," the artful use of social media for political purposes. Indeed, much discussion about the public sphere in China today focuses on Sina Weibo (China's Twitter), which has become the people's largest online discussion parlor.[69]

However, while this evolving online civil society is bringing new political life to China, it too is cloaked by a rhetorical landscape full of the Party's master tropes ("harmony," "progress," "ecological civilization," "China Dream," and so on), which are in turn propped up by governmental censorship, surveillance, and spasms of martial rule. Indeed, according to Evan Osnos, "One known fact about China's censored world is that it is growing."[70] And Lagerkvist adds,

> Last year . . . Beijing tightened the noose around microbloggers with large followings on the Twitter-like Sina Weibo platform. Well-known bloggers such as Kai-Fu Lee (a venture capitalist) and Pan Shiyi (a business magnate) have recently had their accounts suspended or rebuked for irresponsible comments about air pollution, corruption, and government censorship. And this year, the trials of civil rights lawyer Xu Zhiyong and members of his New Citizens Movement also indicated that, although the party is intent on liberating the economy, it envisages no such liberalization for China's restless civil society.[71]

Recent reports of a "vigorous new campaign to clean up the Internet, to purge it of everything from pornography to 'rumors' that might undermine Communist Party rule," only exacerbate the problem.[72] The airwaves are managed by the state, the streets are blocked from public protest, and the court system offers little recourse; so China's civil society is less of a public than a sporadically emergent collection of enclaves.[73] The real question is one of threshold and scale: When and how do these scattered "micro imaginaries" coalesce into a set of collective demands? What event or rhetorical performance becomes the tipping point?

This is the legacy of China's paradoxical modernity: as its ecological binge continues, pressure mounts for citizens to demand reform, in turn requiring a change in the country's intractable political culture. Civic life finds itself trapped in an impasse between ecological urgency and political repression, and what holds this impasse in place is the grip of materialist social values. The rising tide of free-market opportunity maintains a veneer of the harmony of things as they are. Economic growth, rising incomes, consumer spending, and social mobility keep the paradox at bay. As Yang Yao puts it in *Foreign Affairs*, "Since the Chinese Communist

Party (CPC) lacks legitimacy in the classic democratic sense, it has been forced to seek performance-based legitimacy instead, by continuously improving the living standards of Chinese citizens. So far, this strategy has succeeded, but there are signs that it will not last because of the growing inequality and the internal and external imbalances it has created."[74] China's much vaunted principle of harmony is glued together with the nationwide aspiration for more and better material conditions, which create the facade of social stability. Yanghong Huang puts the matter into sharp focus when he writes, in an opinion piece for the *New York Times*,

> Historically, two state ideologies—Confucianism and communism— acted as restraints on commercial dealings. Traditional Chinese society acknowledged the human desire for wealth, but it also warned that, "A man of noble character acquires his wealth by just and ethical means." Later, the Maoist regime's emphasis on sacrificing the individual self to the collective also served as a moral check on people's behavior. The destruction of Confucianism during the cultural revolution and the hollowing out of communism during the recent reform era left behind a vacuum of belief. This was quickly filled in by materialism. . . . In China, the revival of capitalism has been driven almost entirely by the pursuit of wealth. In the words of Deng Xiaopeng, "To get rich is glorious."[75]

The CPC is unlikely to deliver near double-digit growth indefinitely, however, and with resources choked and inequality growing, a political reckoning would seem to loom. The imagination that holds the facade of harmony together could conceivably disintegrate when opportunity favors only the already favored or material conditions hit their limit. At that point, the myriad grassroots forces that constitute civil society—even the constrained versions allowed by the Party—would be compelled to throw off the cloak of CPC rule and demand substantial political reforms. This development in turn would require a new social imaginary, a new sense of felt togetherness produced through the rhetorical work of converting local experiences into collective demands.

Conclusion: Moving through Crisis to Kairos

All nations are riddled with paradoxes to their very core. The United States holds itself aloft as a beacon of freedom and inclusion, yet continues to reckon with a history of slavery and prejudice of every stripe; it makes grand proclamations about openness and opportunity, yet has some of the worst rates of inequality and incarceration of any advanced nation. China is certainly not alone in its contradictions, although its internal tensions are uniquely fresh and acute. As Osnos emphasizes,

> The defining fact of China in our time is its contradictions: The world's largest buyer of BMW, Jaguar and Land Rover vehicles is ruled by a Communist Party that has tried to banish the word "luxury" from advertisements. It is home to two of the world's most highly valued Internet companies (Tencent and Baidu), as well as history's most sophisticated effort to censor human expression. China is both the world's newest superpower and its largest authoritarian state.[76]

We might add the shocking disconnect between a communist state that provides basic services to more people than any other nation on earth, yet also routinely imprisons and tortures these same people without regard to due process—and so on, as the contradictions multiply.[77] What makes China's paradoxes especially significant, however, is the sheer scale and immediacy of what's at stake. Rhetorical scholars write often of the ancient Greek concept *kairos*, which refers to the notion of timeliness. Saying the proper thing at the proper moment is how this concept is most commonly understood, and so timeliness goes hand in hand with "appropriateness." John Poulakos offers an insightful emendation to this basic concept, adding that to the timely and the appropriate should be included the notion of risk. Two comments of his are worth noting:

> In short, the right thing must be said at the right time; inversely, the right time becomes apparent precisely because the right thing has been spoken. . . . But the rhetorician is not confined to a single movement. After he captures the appropriate and places it temporally, he moves toward the suggestion of the possible. The starting point for the

articulation of the possible is the ontological assumption that the main driving force in man's life are his desires, especially the desire to be other and to be elsewhere.[78]

This is an enticing insight, this notion that at its core humanity desires to be other and elsewhere. If so, it might be worthwhile to frame the question of Chinese citizenship today, caught in an impasse between ecological urgency and political repression and possibility, as one of kairotic timeliness on a global scale. The rhetorical action that we call citizenship operates on a chronological spectrum, and the ecological clock is ticking. China's civil society will find itself pressed to disseminate new desires than the ones they are only just beginning to crave. Out of these conditions a new social imaginary may take hold, as the shared expression of evolving longings.

NOTES

1. Dexter Roberts, "A 6.8 Trillion Dollar Price Tag for China's Urbanization," *Businessweek*, March 25, 2014.

2. Ian Johnson, "China Releases Plan to Incorporate Farmers into Cities," *New York Times*, March 17, 2014.

3. "Double Bubble Trouble," *The Economist*, March 22, 2014; see also Gordon G. Chang, "China Property Collapse Has Begun," *Forbes*, April 13, 2014; and Dexter Roberts, "China's Urban Economic Might to Dominate in 2030, Report Says," *Businessweek*, May 8, 2014.

4. Jon R. Taylor, "The China Dream Is an Urban Dream: Assessing the CPC's National New-Type Urbanization Plan," *Journal of Chinese Political Science* 20, no. 2 (2015): 107–20.

5. Christopher B. Field, Vicente R. Barros, David Jon Dokken, Katherine J. Mach, Michael D. Mastrandrea, T. Eren Bilir, Monalisa Chatterjee, Kristie L. Ebi, Yuka Otsuki Estrada, Robert C. Genova, Betelhem Girma, Eric S. Kissel, Andrew N. Levy, Sandy MacCracken, Patricia R. Mastrandrea, and Leslie L. White, *IPCC, 2014: Climate Change 2014: Impacts, Adaptation, and Vulnerability. Part A: Global and Sectorial Aspects. Contribution of Working Group II to the Fifth Assessment Report of the Intergovernmental Panel on Climate Change* (New York: Cambridge University Press, 2014), 40.

6. Joshua Keating, "A Revolution Marches on Its Stomach," *Slate*, April 8, 2014, http://www.slate.com.

7. Field et al., *"IPCC, 2014,"* 6.

8. Jeff Goodell, "China, the Climate and the Fate of the Planet," *Rolling Stone*, September 15, 2014.

9. On this issue, see Adetayo Alabi, "Introduction: The Caribbean and Globalization," *The Global South* 4, no. 2 (Fall 2010): 1–8, and Nicholas St. Fleur, "The Dangerous Underestimation of Climate Change's Cost," *The Atlantic*, January 14, 2015.

10. See the CNA Military Advisory Board report, *National Security and the Accelerating Risks of Climate Change* (Alexandria, VA: CNA Corporation, 2014).

11. No English translation of the plan exists. These quotes are taken from the CPC's press conference, held upon the report's unveiling. See "Transcript: Press Conference on New Urbanization Plan," March 19, 2014, http://china.org.cn.

12. Goodell, "China, the Climate and the Fate of the Planet."

13. The literature on "harmony" is vast. For a compelling sample, see Stephen C. Angle, "Human Rights and Harmony," *Human Rights Quarterly* 30 (2008): 76–94.

14. Brian Palmer, "Why Does China Not Have Famines Anymore?" *Slate*, April 2, 2014, http://www.slate.com.

15. Ibid.

16. For a stunning account of China's great famine, see Tom Standage, *An Edible History of Humanity* (New York: Walker Publishing, 2009), 171–98.

17. Damien Ma and William Adams, *In Line Behind a Billion People: How Scarcity Will Define China's Ascent in the Next Decade* (Upper Saddle River, NJ: FT Press, 2014), 10.

18. See Justin Yifu Lin, Fang Cai, and Zhou Li, *The China Miracle: Development Strategy and Economic Reform* (Beijing: Chinese University Press, 2003); an enormous debate has followed, with some commentators referring not to the "miracle" but the "nightmare."

19. For the history of China's market reforms, see Immanuel C. Y. Hsü, *The Rise of Modern China*, 6th ed. (Oxford: Oxford University Press, 2000), and Doug Guthrie, *China and Globalization: The Social, Economic, and Political Transformation of Chinese Society* (New York: Routledge, 2006).

20. Palmer, "Why Does China Not Have Famines Anymore?"

21. Yang Yao, "The End of the Beijing Consensus," *Foreign Affairs*, February 2, 2010, 1.

22. Dexter Roberts, "China's Growing Income Gap," *Businessweek*, January 27, 2011.

23. Ibid.

24. Mike Davis, *Planet of Slums* (New York: Verso, 2006), 17.

25. UN-Habitat, *The Challenge of the Slums: Global Report on Human Settlements 2003* (London: UN-Habitat, 2003), 6.

26. Mike Davis, "Planet of Slums: Urban Involution and the Informal Proletariat," *New Left Review* 26 (March–April 2004), 19.

27. The tale of resource extraction and cultural eradication in Tibet is too involved for a proper recounting here; for overviews, see Stephen John Hartnett, "'Tibet Is Burning': Competing Rhetorics of Liberation, Occupation, Resistance and Paralysis on the Roof of the World," *Quarterly Journal of Speech* 99 (2013): 283–316, and International Campaign for Tibet, *60 Years of Chinese Misrule: Arguing Cultural Genocide in Tibet* (Washington, DC: International Campaign for Tibet, 2012).

28. "The East Is Grey," *The Economist*, August 10, 2013.

29. Zhu Chen, Jin-Nan Wang, Guo-Xia Ma, and Yan-Sheng Zhang, "China Tackles the Health Effects of Air Pollution," *The Lancet* 382, no. 9909 (December 14, 2013): 1959–60.

30. Jonathan Kaiman, "China's Toxic Air Pollution Resembles Nuclear Winter, Says Scientists," *The Guardian*, February 25, 2014; see also Tom Philpott, "Why China's Farms Are Failing," *The Atlantic*, August 21, 2013.

31. Wang Yue, "Polluted Farmland Leads to Chinese Food Security Fears," *Chinadialogue*, January 7, 2014, https://www.chinadialogue.net.

32. Chris Buckley and Vanessa Piao, "Rural Water, Not City Smog, May Be China's Pollution Nightmare," *New York Times*, April 11, 2016.

33. Urban lifestyles centered on processed convenience food (high in sugar, salt, and fat) and a growing appetite for meat (especially pork and increasingly chicken and beef) have already led to national health alarms. See Sun Kiaochen and Lei, "Obesity Rate on the Increase," *China Daily*, August 6, 2013; and Tom Levitt, "China Facing Bigger Dietary Health Crisis Than the US," *Chinadialogue*, April 7, 2014, https://www.chinadialogue.net.

34. Yue, "Polluted Farmland."

35. Doug Palmer, "US Approves Purchase of Smithfield," *Politico*, September 6, 2013, http://www.politico.com.

36. Christina Larson, "China's Rush to Build Dams Leaves Resettled Communities in Limbo," *Businessweek*, March 24, 2014; the article also notes that at least seventy dam sites are located in areas classified as "biodiversity hotspots" by the nonprofit

Conservation International.

37. Damien Ma and William Adams, "If You Think China's Air Is Bad . . .," *New York Times*, November 7, 2013.

38. Philpott, "Why China's Farms Are Failing."

39. Brahma Chellaney, "Coming Water Wars: Beware the Future," *International Economy*, Fall 2009, 38–39.

40. Lily Kuo, "China Has Launched the Largest Water-Pipeline Project in History," *The Atlantic*, March 7, 2014.

41. Chellaney, "Coming Water Wars," 39.

42. Michael Wines, "China Admits Problems with Three Gorges Dam," *New York Times*, May 19, 2011, https://www.nytimes.com.

43. Peter Bosshard, "Sacrificing the Planet's Arteries to Save Her Lungs?" *China Environment Series*, 12: *Special Water and Energy Issue*, Wilson Center, November 4, 2013, https://www.wilsoncenter.org, 110–11.

44. See Xu Nan, "The Battle for China's Milk," in *Food Safety in China*, ed. Zhou Wei, special issue, *Chinadialogue*, November 23, 2012, https://www.chinadialogue.net.

45. Vivien Lim, "Tainted Milk: Unraveling China's Melamine Scandal," *Think Business*, March 1, 2013.

46. Lim, "Tainted Milk"; and Ma and Adams, "If You Think China's Air Is Bad . . .," 68.

47. The Food Safety Law, enacted in 2009, was meant to prohibit the use of unauthorized additives and strengthen oversight from "farm to fork." In 2010, a national commission of three vice premiers and a dozen minister-level officials was set up and tasked with increasing punishment for food crimes. Three new regulatory bodies were formed, the State Council Food Safety Commission, the Food Safety Risk Evaluation Expert Committee, and the Food Safety Standard Examination Committee. See Xu Nan, "A Decade of Food Safety in China," *Chinadialogue*, June 8, 2012, https://www.chinadialogue.net.

48. David Barboza, "Recycled Cooking Oil Found to be Latest Hazard in China," *New York Times*, March 31, 2010.

49. Lü Minghe, "Shanghai's Dead Pig Story Stretches Back Upstream," *Chinadialogue*, March 25, 2013, https://www.chinadialogue.net.

50. Jonathan Kaiman, "China Fake Meat Scandal: Telling Your Rat from Your Mutton," *The Guardian*, May 3, 2013.

51. Mandy Zuo, "120 Tonnes of Spoiled Food Seized from Smugglers in Nanning,

Guangxi," *South China Morning Post*, April 13, 2014.

52. These and other food troubles are documented in *Food Safety in China*, a special issue of *Chinadialogue*, November 23, 2012, https://www.chinadialogue.net.

53. Yanzhong Huang, "China's Corrupt Food Chain," *New York Times*, August 17, 2012; and see Barbara Demick, "In China, What You Eat Tells You Who You Are," *Los Angeles Times*, September 16, 2011.

54. On Xi Jinping's anticorruption efforts, see Andrew Jacobs, "In China's Antigraft Campaign, Small Victories and Bigger Doubts," *New York Times*, January 15, 2015.

55. Ted Agres, "Despite Regulatory Reform, China's Food Safety Remains Problematic," *Food Quality and Safety*, February 15, 2013, http://www.foodqualityandsafety.com.

56. "The East Is Grey."

57. Cornelius Castoriadis, *The Imaginary Institution of Society*, trans. Kathleen Blamey (Cambridge, MA: MIT Press, 1987), 147.

58. Hu Jintao, "Report of Hu Jintao to the 18th CPC National Congress," November 16, 2012, http://www.china.org.cn.

59. Luis Gomez-Echeverri, "Urbanisation: Toward a Future of Balanced Development and an Ecological Civilization," in *China National Human Development Report 2013: Sustainable and Liveable Cities: Toward Ecological Civilization* (Beijing: China Publishing Group, 2013), 100.

60. Ke Jinhua, "Introduction," in *Ecological Civilization and Beautiful China*, special issue, *Social Sciences in China* 34 (2013): 139.

61. Fred Magdoff and John Bellamy Foster, *What Every Environmentalist Needs to Know About Capitalism: A Citizen's Guide to Capitalism and the Environment* (New York: Monthly Review Press, 2011), 61.

62. Naomi Klein, *This Changes Everything: Capitalism vs. the Climate* (New York: Simon and Schuster, 2014), 21.

63. Although closely related, the public sphere and civil society are not interchangeable terms. The public sphere is the social space of discourse's autotelic circulation, whereas civil society is the realm of semiformal association (nongovernmental organizations). On the former, see Michael Warner, *Publics and Counterpublics* (Brooklyn: Zone Books, 2002); on the latter, see Jean L. Cohen and Andrew Arato, *Civil Society and Political Theory* (Cambridge, MA: MIT Press, 1992).

64. Jiayang Fan, "How China Wants to Rate Its Citizens," *The New Yorker*, November 3, 2015.

65. Jurgen Habermas, "The Public Sphere: An Encyclopedia Article," *New German Critique* 3 (Autumn 1974): 49–55, 49.

66. John Dewey, *The Public and Its Problems* (Athens: Ohio University Press, 1954), 151.

67. Johan Lagerkvist, "China's Risky Reforms," *Foreign Affairs*, February 19, 2014.

68. Guobin Yang and Craig Calhoun, "Media, Civil Society, and the Rise of a Green Public Sphere in China," *China Information* 21, no. 2 (2007): 211–36, 212.

69. Guobin Yang is the leading voice here; see his *The Power of the Internet in China: Citizen Activism Online* (New York: Columbia University Press, 2011).

70. Evan Osnos, "China's Censored World," *New York Times*, May 2, 2014.

71. Lagerkvist, "China's Risky Reforms."

72. Simon Denyer, "China Launches Campaign to Purge Internet of Porn, Rumors and, Critics Say, Dissent," *Washington Post*, April 17, 2014.

73. Nancy Fraser describes enclaves as spaces of withdrawal and retreat, cut off from the larger arena of public affairs, in "Rethinking The Public Sphere: A Contribution to the Critique of Actually Existing Democracy," *Social Text* 25 (1990): 56–80.

74. Yao, "The End of the Beijing Consensus."

75. Huang, "China's Corrupt Food Chain."

76. Osnos, "China's Censored World."

77. See Stephen John Hartnett, "To 'Dance with Lost Souls': Liu Xiaobo, *Charter 08*, and the Contested Rhetorics of Democracy and Human Rights in China," *Rhetoric & Public Affairs* 16 (2013): 223–74.

78. John Poulakos, "Toward a Sophistic Definition of Rhetoric," *Philosophy and Rhetoric* 16 (1983): 35–48.

Her Milk Is Inferior: Breastfeeding, Risk, and Imagining Maternal Identities in Chinese Cyberspace

Zhuo Ban

In May 2008, an anonymous entry on Tianya-BBS, a popular online discussion forum in China, struck anger and anxiety among many parents around the country.[1] Detailing what the World Health Organization (WHO) called "one of the largest food safety events the UN health agency has had to deal with in recent years," the post revealed that the well-known milk product brand Sanlu had been selling baby formula containing dangerous levels of melamine, a toxic industrial compound.[2] This news arrived after a raft of publicity detailing numerous food safety violations in China. But even among China's plentiful food scandals, the Sanlu case seemed especially shocking, because the contaminated food was targeted at one of the most vulnerable groups of consumers: infants. Although the original post soon disappeared from the forum, news of the tainted product triggered an avalanche of on- and offline discussions about infant formula safety.[3] These virtual discussions about infant health risks prompted parents in China to find alternative sources of nutrition for their children; in fact, according to the China Ministry of Agriculture, milk formula imports increased by more than 100 percent in the first two months of 2009.[4] As this example demonstrates, the Chinese "public screen" has become a vital part of how Chinese citizens make everyday decisions about risk, safety, health, and identity.[5] Here, even a disappeared online post significantly amplified the already-frenetic tone of Chinese public discourse around risks to infant and child health, a vestige of China's controversial one-child policy, to include the risks inherent to breast milk (and formula-fed) diets.

In China, as in other countries, the decision to breastfeed occurs within a complex matrix of individual preferences, personal and familial experiences, and structural factors like employment expectations, available free time, parenting strategies, and more.[6] In addition, the changing sociological landscape around childbirth and childrearing in China in light of the one-child policy has rendered infant nutrition decisions more salient and therefore has positioned breastfeeding as a topic of significant concern in the Chinese public sphere.[7] Within this context, discussions about breastfeeding reveal emerging—and conflicting—imaginaries about both individual maternal identities and the relationships between these new mothers and larger issues about national health, cultural norms, and global networks of food production and consumption. To support this claim, I examine the rhetorical construction of breastfeeding as a risky practice for infant health and address how such rhetoric affords new social imaginaries around motherhood in China. I locate the formation of these maternal identities through the articulation of three "risks"—pathological and toxicological, nutritional, and developmental—prevalent in the discourse around breastfeeding on the Tianya-BBS. While these articulations of risk are themselves rich and detailed, I argue that they are further complicated by their relationship to certain national imaginaries that shape the contours of what are "acceptable" and "unacceptable" maternal formations. In a nutshell, the practice of breastfeeding among certain segments of the population in China is both yoked to the problematics of the Chinese nation-state and also construed in opposition to the benefits of (American) formula-based diets. These conflicting rhetorical gestures extend the particular, localized practice of breast- or bottle-feeding into the realm of the national imaginary.[8] I thus argue that the everyday discourses around infant health serve, synecdochically, to represent emerging social imaginaries about the health of China as a nation. To use a different metaphor, if national identities are constituted through the warp and weft of intersecting narrative threads, then public discourse around breastfeeding represents a particular knot in the fabric—a moment in the national Chinese social imaginary that I believe is worthy of reflection.

To make my case, I draw from Michel Foucault and Deborah Lupton to argue that the construction of breastfeeding as "risk" exemplifies and extends the self-surveillance of the childbearing (female) body as a form of "governmentality," or a series of power relations between the self and state that are based on disciplining the conduct of the self.[9] Before making this argument, and in order to provide a context for this chapter, I begin with a review of existing research on breastfeeding in China. I then discuss risk discourses and the self-regulation of the pregnant body. Ultimately, I excavate the discursive and embodied interrelationships between the state and the self, showing how these entwined imaginaries shape localized meanings of health and risk and draw from larger debates about the health of contemporary China.

A Short History of Breastfeeding in Modern China

A vast body of research documents breastfeeding practices within the highly heterogeneous Chinese context.[10] The significant geographic, linguistic, cultural, and economic diversity of China has meant that breastfeeding practices are more productively studied locally and regionally, even though some large-scale reviews of breastfeeding practices and determinants in China depict national trends.[11] Breastfeeding rates in China have historically been lower than international recommendations, such as the one established by the WHO, which urges that infants should be "exclusively breastfed" for the first six months and that breastfeeding be continued along with "appropriate nutritious complementary foods" for two years of age or longer.[12] However, as Amy Koerber has noted, the decision to breastfeed is situated within a matrix of medical discourses that often challenge official guidelines—such as WHO recommendations—in favor of more locally situated norms.[13]

Published research on breastfeeding in China shows that while the number of infants that were "ever breastfed" was comparable in urban and rural populations until the 1970s, that decade experienced a marked drop in breastfeeding rates in large urban centers, owing perhaps to the increased availability of substitutes.[14] Although regional efforts to promote breastfeeding continued through the 1980s, it was not until the early 1990s that breastfeeding promotion became a national priority in China.[15] For instance, cross-sectional data from the 1990s shows that the rates of four-month-old infants receiving "any breastfeeding" deteriorated every consecutive year, from nearly 63 percent in 1989 to 55 percent in 1992.[16] Only 31 percent of infants in the same period were "exclusively breastfed" at four months of age.[17] As is consistent with many rapidly modernizing nations, China's rates of breastfeeding were impacted by the comingling of local, regional, national, and emerging global trends that felt to some mothers like modern, scientific liberations from the past, even as other mothers clung to more traditional practices. Nonetheless, under the National Program of Action for Child Development, the Communist Party of China (CPC or the Party) targeted an "exclusive breastfeeding rate at four months of 80% by 2000."[18] As these preliminary notes indicate, evolving practices around breastfeeding in China are immersed—like so many other aspects of daily life—in both globalizing networks of power and Party-led national programs.

Indeed, the 1990s witnessed the development of a series of local, regional, national, and global initiatives to support breastfeeding,[19] including the WHO's "Baby-Friendly Hospital Initiative," which aimed to "protect, promote and support breastfeeding" globally.[20] While the national emphasis on breastfeeding promotion as a public health priority in China has led to moderate increases in overall breastfeeding rates, we do not know whether this increase can be attributed solely to these promotional efforts. For instance, the recent public health emergencies regarding the presence of melamine in animal milk and the domestic formula scandal mentioned above have led to sudden but temporary spikes in breastfeeding rates.[21] The National Program of Action for Child

Development, which ran from 2001 to 2010, increased the targeted rate to 85 percent "exclusive breastfeeding" at four months. However, it was only in 2007 that China's national breastfeeding promotion strategy reached the WHO target recommendations.[22]

Despite the efforts of both the WHO and the Party, the differences between rural and urban health behaviors in China reveal declining rates of urban breastfeeding. While a study conducted in the 1980s found minimal differences between urban and rural rates of exclusive breastfeeding, the decline in exclusive breastfeeding has been much steeper in the urban centers than in the rural provinces.[23] For instance, by 2005, 79 percent of rural infants were breastfed between four and five months, compared to 72 percent of urban infants of the same age.[24] The comparative lack of access to formula and medical services typical of China's rural provinces in the 1980s and 1990s conferred an interesting protective effect from malnourishment and infectious diseases to rural breastfed infants below the age of one. The importance of breastfeeding promotion efforts in China is made especially relevant given that the highest rate of malnutrition has been found to be among one-year-old infants.[25] The recent histories of breastfeeding in China, then, and the constitutive rhetorics driving these histories, are entwined with debates about accelerating urbanization, lingering rural poverty, and the pace and consequences of rapid economic development.

A study conducted among urban mothers in Beijing reported that while most infant feeding practices generally followed the WHO recommendations for the first three months of life, exclusive breastfeeding rates at three months fell below recommendations.[26] Moreover, researchers found that "non-optimal" feeding practices, such as early weaning and the introduction of solid and semisolid foods, appeared quite common and were associated with mothers' education level and employment.[27] Not surprisingly, decisions to continue or cease breastfeeding among women in China were closely related to maternal and child illness, the mother's employment status and pressures to return to work, and the perceived insufficiency of breast milk. A cross-sectional study showed that mothers from large metropolitan areas reported their return to work as an especially prominent reason for stopping breastfeeding.[28] Relatedly, Ping Liu, Lijuan Qiao, Fenglian Xu, and their coauthors also report that high maternal education and employment are important "risk factors" for the introduction of semisolid foods.[29]

As I have outlined in this section, breastfeeding rates among urban Chinese women fall below the WHO guidelines, even when the recommendations present breastfeeding as being the most "natural," "maternalistic" thing a woman can do for her child.[30] These policies advocate a "breast is best" philosophy that tends to ignore the structural situations within which mothers make nonoptimal infant feeding decisions.[31] The WHO's recommendations therefore exemplify the notion of "medicalization," wherein complicated and localized everyday life situations are recast in universalizing medical terms that often fly in the face of local cultural practices.[32] Moreover, as I show below, the medicalization of pregnancy and child-rearing practices is manifested through discourses of breastfeeding, especially in the conception of infant feeding choices as a risk.[33] Indeed, I demonstrate below how the linkage of risk to breastfeeding amounts to a new discursive paradigm, part of an emerging social imaginary in which the burdens of motherhood extend beyond caring for your baby's health and out into the very health of the nation-state.

Imagining Risk: Breastfeeding and the Self-Surveilling Body

Critical health communication scholarship emphasizes the social and cultural discourses that inform notions of health, disease, and the body.[34] For example, a complex dynamic exists between media coverage, political stereotypes, and public discourses about health risk issues in China and Hong Kong. In the context of the HIV/AIDS epidemic, perceptions of high-risk behaviors are shaped by the structure and power dynamics of online discussion forums.[35] Similarly, this chapter problematizes the tension between overarching health discourses and daily health decisions in the context of breastfeeding. In all three case studies, risk is understood as one of the consequences of postmodern media technologies, expanding networks of consumerism, and rapid modernization, which, when combined, offer individuals a new world of everyday choices that are also laced with inherent risks and frequently cast in nationalistic terms.

While breastfeeding is often construed as a "natural," "healthy," and "normal" choice of infant feeding within the discourse of global public health institutions such as the WHO, women's breastfeeding experiences are heterogeneous, complex, and often contradictory, shaped as they are by the cultural, economic, and political contexts within which women choose—or choose not—to breastfeed.[36] Previous communication scholarship on women's experiences with breastfeeding has explored the dialectical tensions between medical and social views on breastfeeding,[37] the discursive construction of the breastfeeding mother as "ideal,"[38] the practical challenges of working mothers to continue breastfeeding,[39] and women's experiences with breastfeeding failure.[40] As these studies demonstrate, breastfeeding practices are interwoven with an almost innumerable number of local and personal everyday factors that are, simultaneously, influenced by national laws and norms and emerging global expectations.

Within this body of literature, a wealth of research documents women's challenges to breastfeed vis-à-vis workplace requirements. For instance, L. M. Rose points to the mixed messages that contemporary working mothers receive about breastfeeding, wherein they are bombarded with information that supports the ideology of "breast is best," while at the same time facing institutional structures of work, including the gendered division of labor and societal attitudes toward breastfeeding in public, all of which challenge the possibilities of breastfeeding successfully.[41] Rose therefore documents how the "medicalization" of breastfeeding blurs the lines between breastfeeding being considered a "public concern" and a "private activity."[42] Addressing this thin line between public and private in turn raises questions about the dialectic between agent and society, self and culture, and empowerment and surveillance. Thus, the commentators cited above point to how the rhetorical work of imagining communities—in this case, emerging communities of breastfeeding mothers—is both liberating and empowering but also constraining and disciplinary.

For example, the notion of women's bodies as loci of risk typifies a renewed attention to (pregnant) embodiment within other societal and medical discourses at the end of the twentieth century.[43] From this perspective, risk is not a simple calculation of benefit vs. harm, but rather, as Claudia Aradau and Rens van Muster argue, a systemic, "heterogeneous assemblage of discursive, administrative, legal, technical, institutional and material elements."[44] Drawing from Lupton's, Rose's, and Aradau and Muster's work, I argue that the self-regulating impulses engendered from the centrality of risk discourses during pregnancy are also extended to the postpartum period, when women make infant feeding decisions.[45] In other words, breastfeeding decisions are now subject to the same appara- tuses of governmentality as the pregnant woman's body, thus revealing a disciplinary process that synecdochically positions women's bodies (their individual, daily enactments) in relation to broader notions of culture and society, to the imagined community of the nation.

Indeed, both lay and expert discussions around the pregnant woman in modern society invoke a gendered subject constructed by a series of assumptions about the woman's central role in the health of the family.[46] For instance, in an influential essay, Foucault details the broad societal developments in medicine and politics in nineteenth-century Europe that shifted the responsibility for individual health from the public realm of the state to the private sphere of the "family."[47] This strategy of govern- ing saw health, Foucault argues, as the "duty of each and the objective of all."[48] This kind of "biopolitics" hinges upon the production of a docile, self-regulating private subject, the "mother," whose realm of expertise is the "home," albeit without the right of taking that domestic expertise into the public realm. Mothers were thus charged with regulating their health, as well as that of their children, while their relationship to the state, as citizens, became mediated through their responsibilities in the domestic sphere.[49] For Foucault, such apparatuses of "biopower" were not coercive acts imposed upon women by the state, but rather reflected the "produc- tive" nature of power.[50] The idea that the mother is the sole repository of children's health allowed for productive relationships and hierarchies to form within the family, producing relationships that were characterized by self-regulation and self-disciplining.[51]

Decisions made by women during and after pregnancy in contempo- rary society can be viewed as an ossification of this modern, self-surveil- ling gaze, which focuses on the female body. Discourses on the female body paint it as fragile, needing preparation and practice for pregnancy, and requiring extra care and attention inasmuch as it now "harbor[s] the potentiality of another human."[52] The increased attention to women's embodiment is carried out through the language of "risk," wherein a pregnant woman who does not closely scrutinize and examine her bodily processes—the most direct vehicle of a potential child's health—is necessarily engaging in risky behaviors that threaten the self, the child, and society. Within this framework of what critics are now calling "the risk society," risk becomes the overriding metaphor to understand pregnancy and postpartum care.[53] This construction in turn means that avoiding any risks to one's own body and any potential risks to the fetus (and eventual infant) become a woman's self-responsibility. Indeed, Lupton notes that both medical and social discourses on pregnancy emphasize self-responsibility as a risk-mitigating strategy. Witness, for instance, how in the medical realm, the increasing popularity of invasive screening technologies and the development of specialty disciplines (like fertility counseling) coincide with broader social discourses found in pregnancy care books, online resources, and media depictions. Together, these discourses frame pregnancy as a time of risk management. Moreover, within this emerging regime of biopower, women are expected to imagine breastfeeding not only as a deeply personal and private act but also, simultaneously, as part of their many other obligations to the health of the nation.

Indeed, this discourse of risky motherhood has been further compounded in China by the unique sociological challenges caused by the one-child policy.[54] Given the fact that, until recently, most women in China were prohibited by the CPC from having more than one childbirth experience, pregnancy has become an even more pressure-packed, once-in-a-lifetime experience. The one-child policy therefore created unique subjectivities between women, care providers, and broader social institutions, wherein the self-regulation of the body has exceeded the norms typical in Western contexts. The pressure of having "only one chance to get it right" produces a specific kind of biopower that extends the self-surveillance of the pregnant body beyond the physical process of childbirth and carries into infancy and toddlerhood. Within this context, restrictions on diet, activities, and exposure to environmental hazards during pregnancy are seldom lifted upon childbirth, especially for breastfeeding mothers in China. After all, if "you are what you eat," then your milk becomes subject to great scrutiny, as do the external environments that determine the perceived quality or safety of the milk.

Imagining Breastfeeding as Risk
in the Online Public Sphere in China

The online public sphere includes a range of discourses on pregnancy and infant nutrition in the urban Chinese context. Discussion forums are a popular mode of online public participation in China, with some forums receiving nearly three hundred thousand visitors a day.[55] These forums—colloquially referred to as BBS, owing to the technical nomenclature "bulletin board system" have become crucial sites for the formation of public opinion within Chinese cyberspace. Some of the largest forums, including the one used for gathering this study's data, are organized topically, starting from general discussions to specific ones on issues such as product reviews, health, family, entertainment, and current events. As I demonstrate below, China's BBS forums provide new opportunities and challenges to the study of civic engagement in the digital age, for China's heavily monitored "public screen" decouples the link between online public participation and democratic governance, thus producing interesting conditions for the study of rhetoric and publics.[56] While the role of state-ownership and censorship of online participation lies outside of the scope of this paper, it is important to consider participation in BBS forums as an enactment of a particular kind of mediated citizenship. For instance, Li has discussed the role of BBS forums as crucial to the construction of online discourses of nationalism within the body politic.[57] Likewise, Huiling Ding and Jingwen Zhang also stress using online posts as a way to get "first-hand data" about lived experiences and social understandings from people encountering specific health scenarios.[58]

In terms of discussions about breastfeeding, I argue that users' contributions reproduce a *discourse of governmentality*, a networked thread about women's lifestyle choices and their impact on the collective health of infants. Given the heavy urban skew of China's online population, it is safe to assume that this discourse is of particular relevance to working mothers—by which I mean women who are engaged in paid work outside of the home—and encapsulates the challenges of breastfeeding within the structural context of employment. Contributors to the forum, exclusively women, discuss and share stories, experiences, and challenges that are involved in making nutritional decisions for their children. In this way, this public sphere of open and often passionate discussion also acts as a site of self-disciplining wherein the regulation of women's bodies is cocooned within legitimate concerns for infant health, emerging notions of consumerism, and long-standing notions about the roles of mothers in Chinese society. Thus, the online communities made possible by the BBS amount to living laboratories for imagining new Chinas, albeit ones laced with cultural norms, family assumptions, and political practices held over from earlier, pre-Internet times.

In order to analyze the construction of risk in Chinese online discussion forums about breastfeeding, I conducted a discourse analysis of a sample of entries from 2013 from China's most popular BBS service, Tianya-BBS.[59] I selected the sample by visiting the section titled "Mother and Baby Center" (*Qinzi Zhongxin*) and entered the search terms "breast milk" (*muru*), "breastfeeding" (*wei nai*), and "milk" (*nai*). I restricted my search to these terms because the Chinese expression for formula contains the root ideogram *nai*, which refers to milk in its standard usage. The resulting more than five hundred posts formed the primary data corpus for this study.[60] I then conducted a close reading of all the posts, marking out snippets, paragraphs, and articulations that seemed relevant and/or interesting. Having read the entire corpus, I then proceeded to translate these initial codes or discursive fragments. As I am a native Chinese speaker who learned English in high school and earned an undergraduate degree in English, the translation process was systematic. My analysis took on an iterative approach, which allowed me to travel back and forth between the data and the theoretical lens that informs my analysis.[61] Such an abductive approach, neither purely inductive nor deductive, is an established mode of conducting discourse analysis.[62] To further crystallize the operation of risk discourses in my corpus, I guided my analysis through the question "How does this articulation construct infant nutrition as risk?"

When reviewing posts in this breastfeeding forum, it quickly became evident that risk plays a key role in discourses about breastfeeding among contemporary Chinese participants. While many moms, citing sources such as La Leche League International and the Chinese Ministry of Health, demonstrate health literacy about the many benefits of breastfeeding to infant health and development, they often dismiss these benefits in their decision making, instead focusing on what they consider to be more concrete, immediate risks that breastfeeding poses to their infant's well-being. Moms compared breast milk to formula and lamented breast milk's lack of standards, consistency, and predictability. They further magnified the risk of choosing breast milk over formula by emphasizing its exclusiveness; that is, whereas breastfeeding supplements often reduce breast milk supply, formula seems to work well with other infant diets. Across my sample, the articulated risks of breastfeeding on infants fell into three categories: pathological and toxicological, nutritional, and developmental.

PATHOLOGICAL AND TOXICOLOGICAL RISKS

Many mothers conversing in this forum believed that their milk contains substances that harm their babies. Although true allergies to a mother's milk are uncommon, some moms related stories about allergic reactions to breast milk. The symptoms of these rare and pathological reactions, such as diarrhea and rash, are actually quite common in young infants, but mothers in the forums cited these symptoms as evidence that their babies were allergic to breast milk. In one thread of conversation, for example, the mother of a four-month-old told the story of her child having diarrhea for two weeks. The baby's condition improved when she switched to another formula brand and stopped breastfeeding per her pediatrician's instructions. After reading her post, several other moms claimed that similar reactions must have been the reason for their children's conditions as well. Noting that she was already using the same "hypo-allergenic formula" recommended by the writer of the first post, one mom reasoned that "breast milk seems to be the only thing left to question." As these examples demonstrate, the Tianya-BBS discourse often reveals a marked divergence between individual decisions about breast feeding and what professional medical experts recommended.

Consider the fact that while some mothers expressed concern about immediate and visible reactions to breast milk, other mothers shared concerns about slow or "invisible" manifestations. Because mothers are exposed to toxic chemicals in their food, air, and water, they described themselves as conduits passing toxins to infants through breastfeeding.

This risk is silent but threatening because there is no easy way to assess the levels of toxicity in breast milk or to measure its long-term impact on infant health. As one forum contributor wrote, "[Humans are] at the top of the food chain, therefore breast milk has concentrated levels of dioxins, heavy metal, and antibiotics. Dioxin content in breast milk in Japan contains dioxin twenty-six times higher than the safety level. Imagine what it would be like in China." According to the WHO, 90 percent of human exposure to dioxins, which are carcinogens found in the environment, occurs through food, including dairy products.[63] In this case, China's highly polluted cities serve as a backdrop for fears about the risks that environmental pollution potentially spreads to breastfed children: in these popular imaginations, mother's bodies are vectors for conveying pollutants to innocent children.

Such claims about the toxicological risks of breast milk resonated with many mothers who experienced similar anxieties about exposure to the toxic environment. This concern about the environment emerged as a salient factor shaping maternal discourses—and the identity of Chinese mothers—who breastfed. The following excerpt, for example, offers a vivid description of the worrisome dinner table in China today:

> There is no statistical proof that breast milk in China is better than cow milk. Just have a look around us. I find it difficult to believe that mothers whose diet contains illegally recycled cooking oil, vegetables with excessive pesticides, pork that is pumped with antibiotics, and fast-grown chicken can produce high-quality breast milk. . . . My second child is now three months old, and suffers from frequent diarrhea. I've been thinking about stopping breastfeeding and giving her cow milk.

While agreeing with these issues of food safety, one poster pointed out that there is no guarantee that the living conditions and diet of the cow, the primary source for formula, is any better; "cows in China cannot be trusted either," she observed, so "the best thing to do is to ask someone to mail formula directly from abroad." These kinds of comments point toward a popular belief in China: that the nation is now so hopelessly polluted, its food chain so corrupt, that only products from abroad can guarantee safety.

As a corollary to this emerging narrative, many contributors contended that it is irrational to insist on breastfeeding as superior to imported formula milk, which provides a ready (and trusted) alternative to breastfeeding. For example, consider this excerpt: "The uneasy truth is: formula-fed babies are healthier and taller. . . . In the U.S., preterm babies after the twenty-second week have a good survival rate, all thanks to Similac's premier liquid formula. They would certainly die if they were breastfed. In China, babies born before the twenty-eighth week are considered miscarriages." In these posts, foreign-made formula offers a cleaner, safer, risk-free alternative to any products—be they mother's breast milk, cow's milk, or locally made supplements—that bear the taint of China's hyperpollution. Consider the juxtaposition here: the United States is imagined as a safe space where infants can survive early-term deliveries to be fed unquestionably superior formula, while China is marked by pollution, uncertain relations, and a lack of care for premature infants. This rhetorical work of imagining China, the United States, and the mothers caught between the two powers not only positions Chinese urban mothers within the realities of Chinese pollutants, but also presents them as working to transcend that position through the practice of "importing American formula."

It comes as no surprise to find that many posts on the forum offered information about how to access superior American products. Such posts often started with the statement that "we know someone who is living in the US/Europe where the air is clean and the sky is blue." Throughout these discussions, breastfeeding is constructed as the option for people who do not want to spend the money or effort to access safer international products. One mom, for example, contended that lack of access is not an excuse for not providing infants with imported formula: "Nowadays, everybody knows at least someone overseas." This discourse about risk thus indicates how the notion of motherhood within the urban Chinese body politic requires referencing connections—personal and familial—to the United States or Europe. Perhaps more worrisome for the CPC, this discourse offers grassroots evidence of how the social imaginary in contemporary China recognizes that modernity is, literally, polluting the nation's future, forcing mothers to turn abroad for safe, healthy milk.

NUTRITIONAL RISK

Throughout the posts I studied, many mothers believed that by putting the infant on an exclusively breastfed diet, they were keeping the baby hungry, or at least providing an inadequate supply of necessary nutrients. Within this thread, women used weight gain as an indicator of nutritional adequacy in new moms, although the benchmarks used for evaluating weight gain were often arbitrary and intuitive. Consider the following excerpts:

> I fed on demand during the postpartum month and supplemented with formula only occasionally. Neither the baby nor I had any good sleep, and my supply didn't seem to be increasing either. I was in a super lousy mood. The baby gained only 0.6 kilo by day thirty-eight. So I started to add formula to her diet. The baby is fed to full and sleeps well, and my mood is improving. The baby gained 1.5 kilos in a month. I regret that I let the baby go hungry for a month!
>
> My supply has always been low. My baby is five months old now. Even with thick winter clothes, she is not yet 8 kilos, thinner than babies of her age. I have always been worried that low milk supply will hinder her growth and want to wean her at six months and start her on formula.

In both accounts, faster weight gain appears as a normative health standard. Alternatively, moms cited only the risk of being underweight, not overweight. Similarly, mothers cited characteristics such as "chubby," "baby fat," "round cheeks," and "creases on the belly" as normative standards for evaluating the physical development of their infants, which drove their desire for increasing their baby's dietary intake. As Lupton points out, accounts of risk often play a role "not only in drawing audiences' attention to risks but in constructing what is considered a 'risk.'"[64] In this case, the health risk of breastfeeding is constructed using the language of statistical rationality, as seen when the mom in the second excerpt compared her child with the norm estimated from an imaginary comparison group. She thus drew the conclusion that her child is "thinner than babies of her age," which she attributed to her self-reported low milk supply.

The obsession with intake drives the rhetoric of risk related to breast-feeding because, unlike formula, there is no way of measuring how much an infant takes from the breasts, leaving room for doubt about whether the supply is sufficient for the nutritional need of the baby. As a result, when the infant appears to be upset and no observable cause can be found, such distress is often explained as an indication that the child is underfed. The following excerpt from a young mom with an infant less than one month old made the point: "The first half month I had to supplement with formula for almost every feed, and I leaked all the time. Now I can barely manage day feeds and still do not have enough supply at night. I tried to breastfeed exclusively at night, but my baby is always whining at night, so I had to supplement with formula twice at night." Here, typical infant behavior, such as fussing, is unquestioningly linked with the complications of breastfeeding.

Such negative associations are not only self-assigned, but are also often imposed on the breastfeeding mother by family members and other care-takers. Indeed, many contributors to the forum claimed that their mothers-in-laws exert powerful influence over breastfeeding risks and actively push formula feeding. For example, one woman described how her mother-in-law "closely monitors [her] every day when [she] breastfeeds, and waits with a bottle in her hand." The following excerpt illuminates this point:

> I'm a new mom. My breast milk started slow because I didn't have the chance to let the baby suck on my breast immediately after birth. My mother-in-law told me directly that I don't have milk. She wouldn't allow me to feed the baby in the postpartum month, saying that I would keep the baby hungry. Without the baby sucking, obviously my supply was minimum. Mothers-in-law are magic weaning machines.

Similarly, another mom explained that her mother-in-law insisted that she did not have enough milk and wanted her to supplement with formula. While she persisted through breastfeeding, she commented on the feelings of guilt and vulnerability involved in the process:

> The first week after the baby was born . . . my mother-in-law insisted that I didn't have enough milk and wanted to supplement with formula.

She put the blame for the baby crying or not sleeping all on my milk supply. If I were not as insistent, my baby would be drinking formula now . . . the new moms are very vulnerable. When the supply is low, they are more concerned about the baby than anybody. But people around her will only question her ability to have enough milk, instead of reassuring or encouraging her. I still feel bad for myself when I look back at those days.

Here, the discourse of risk, unlike that of chance or fate, is associated not only with palpable guilt but the guilt that stems from family dynamics, with mothers-in-law playing prominent roles in disciplining the bodies and practices of new mothers.

As these examples illustrate, a risk is thus an unrealized potentiality where the foreseeable harm only manifests when someone takes the risk.[65] In essence, the discourse of risk is linked with the construction of breastfeeding as irrational and irresponsible, as seen in this excerpt from a mom ridden with guilt for breastfeeding her daughter:

The baby was found to have moderate calcium deficiency when she was three months old, but she wouldn't take any medicine or formula. We were all very concerned. My sister told me, "We can't go on like this. Your baby does not take anything but your milk and now she is deficient in calcium. I think you should make up your mind and wean her from breast milk. She does not take formula because she is addicted to your breast. You should formula feed her exclusively. That's the only way to give her enough nutrition." I've never thought about weaning her at such a young age and felt very bad when my sister said this. But I talked to my husband about it, and he said, "Let's do it. Don't hesitate any more. We have to do what's best for the baby, no matter how painful it is." I was not ready for it, really unprepared. I sat on the bed, and my tears started to fall on my daughter's face.

In this post, the mother claimed that breast milk hindered her daughter's calcium intake from other sources. Here, the risk involved in breastfeeding was its exclusivity; that is, an exclusively breastfed baby may refuse to take a bottle. This mom, like many other users of the online forum, considered the baby's preference of breast milk over formula as a risk factor, since nutrition is often discussed in the language of "inclusion" and "comprehensiveness." Value-laden terms such as "addicted" and "hesitate" point toward her sense of being a compassionate (read: weak) mother who yielded to the irrational choice of breastfeeding, thereby putting her baby's health at risk. Meanwhile, the voices of reason came from her sister and husband, who asked her to wean the baby, "no matter how painful it is."

As the examples cited above indicate, discussions of the nutritional risk of breast milk are often couched within the rhetoric of uncertainty, hedging specifically with reference to the fluctuations in and individual differences of supply. Mothers offered numerous reasons as causes for dips in their milk supply: housework, their emotional state, the resumption of their menstrual cycle, consumption of certain foods and beverages, and so on. Many believed that breast milk supply would inevitably drop by about six months after the child was born, when adding supplements or switching to other food sources becomes mandatory. One contributor, for example, pointed out that her milk turned "clear, water-like" by the six-month mark and that her mother-in-law told her that her milk conveyed "no more nutritional value than water." The dynamic between breastfeeding mothers and their mothers-in-law provides an interesting set of exchanges that demonstrate how imagined communities exert material ramifications on social practices. In the backdrop of China's transient society, where women's professional identities compete with filial expectations of family life, breastfeeding emerges as a particular point of conflict. If successful, long-term breastfeeding is related to the gendered division of labor in families and how much time women can get away from their jobs, then bottle feeding "allows" women to return to the workforce. In so doing, foregoing breastfeeding for the bottle often has the consequence of conferring the responsibility of infant care and infant nutrition to the mother-in-law, who cares for the infant while the mother is at work.

In another interesting argument against breast milk, the quantity and quality of breast milk is seen as determined by the elusive concept of the mother's physique. In essence, many commentators argued that dainty, sedentary, urban women are unfit for breastfeeding. For example, the following excerpts offer contrasting descriptions of the urban and rural mothers:

> [The] mother's physique and diet can have direct impact on the nutritional content of the milk, regardless of the supply. I have a friend [the contributor later revealed that she is a working, urban woman] who is a picky eater, and her milk was as clear as thin rice congee.
>
> In real life, there's only one case in which an exclusively breastfed baby is nice and chubby. She's my friend's neighbor. However, that mom is from the countryside and has been working in the field since when she was a little girl. She's very strong and healthy. That's why her milk is nutritious. Nowadays, young mothers often work in offices. Their health cannot compare to manual laborers', and their milk is inferior too.

Here, the stated difference between urban and rural mothers in terms of breastfeeding ability resonates with the discursive construction of rural women as having animalistic reproductive abilities.[66] While the rural mothers are depicted as younger, stronger, and sturdier—supposedly embodying the qualities deemed important for milk production—the inference made here against a typical urban woman is that she is older, less robust, and caught in the motherhood-limiting life patterns of urban life, thus leading to "inferior" milk. The online discourses about breastfeeding therefore reflect ongoing tensions in contemporary China about urbanrural differences and their impacts on gender roles.

DEVELOPMENTAL RISK

While the posts analyzed from the Tianya-BBS depict formula feeding as instrumental and straightforward, breastfeeding, like many other aspects of infant care, appeared as emotional and ambiguous. While formula offers nutrition, breastfeeding is bound up in attachment, comfort, motherhood, and inevitably, because it manifests from the breasts of the mother, female sexuality. As a consequence of these complex gendering processes, breastfeeding often appeared in the BBS as a "guilty pleasure" that discouraged a child's development into an independent and well-adjusted adult. When breastfeeding is understood in this way, as a transitional phase toward both modernity in general and healthy toddler development in particular, it becomes problematic when the infant refuses to move on to other forms of feeding.[67] For example, this comment reveals some of these fears about development:

> You have to let her be hungry and stop breastfeeding. My baby is nine months old. When we visited the pediatrician last month, we were told again that we had to give the baby some formula. Otherwise, she will suffer when she weans from the breast. We started her on formula when we returned home. She wouldn't take formula at first. So we let her be hungry [without breastfeeding] for one day, and she took it [formula] the next day. Have to toughen up. Even the doctor said that we should let her go hungry if she won't take formula.

Here, and in the many other posts along these same lines, breastfeeding is portrayed as an obstacle to the development of the infant. This pattern of casting breastfeeding as a kind of emotional blockage is further complicated by the fact that many moms seem to agree that weaning from the breast is a traumatic experience, largely due to the "addictive" nature of breastfeeding. While it is uncommon for language describing adult substance abuse and addiction to be used regarding "breast milk addiction" in the West, in this forum, many moms believed that a child could easily become fixated on breastfeeding and refuse to move out of this phase until reaching an advanced age. Stories of children continuing to breastfeed until three or four, even age six in one case, abounded in the forum discussions. One woman, explaining her rationale for choosing formula feeding over breastfeeding, wrote that this "will save the child the pain of letting the breasts go when he grows older." The discourse of risk in this thread hinges on the fear that mothers who become addicted to breastfeeding can doom their child to a lifetime of emotional trauma and that children who become addicted can experience negative outcomes and pain.[68]

Another developmental risk of breastfeeding is articulated in terms of the "maternal sexuality" involved in feeding the baby from the breast.[69] Rosalia Rodriguez-Garcia and Lara Frazier found that notions of the female breast as a primarily sexual object are found to be one of the most influential factors in a woman's decision not to breastfeed in the United

States.[70] Among Chinese mothers using the forum, maternal sexuality is inferred through discussions about the role breastfeeding plays in sexual development of the child. One woman stated that the idea of breastfeeding into toddlerhood was abhorrent to her: "Those women in La Leche League are really obsessed and lunatic. They all talk about breastfeeding until the baby is several years old. Is that really good for the baby? Do babies really have no sense about sex and sexuality? I immediately got myself out of the mailing list [of La Leche League]." Here, the forum user appeared to project her own implicit unease with the unavoidable exposure of the sexualized female breast to the infant during breastfeeding onto the child herself.

Following the logic of maternal sexuality spurring on childhood sexuality, children of different sexes were cast as being at risk from breastfeeding in different ways, according to some forum users. One woman, for example, stated that her family insisted that she wean her baby daughter from the breast at one year of age, although both her daughter and she preferred to continue breastfeeding: "They told me that breastfeeding for too long will lead to sexual precocity among girls. For a baby girl, one year is the maximum duration [that breastfeeding can continue]." When it came to infant boys, however, articulations of developmental risks of breastfeeding often accompanied innuendos of the Oedipus complex. One contributor, who self-identified as a developmental psychologist, made the following comment about breastfeeding beyond one year of age:

> Breastfeeding for too long is not good for the psychological development of the child. Breast milk carries the message that the baby and the mother are together. "You are safe in mommy's arms." Children one year or older want to break this tie and explore their independent selves. Children who are weaned late have less courage to explore the world and are less independent. Some boys may develop sexual-psychological problems. This will have a negative impact on his ability to function in the society alone later in his life or his ability to build intimate relationships with the opposite sex.

Here, the developmental risks of breastfeeding are constructed at two levels: first, breastfeeding reinforces an attachment to the mother and thus delays the development of the "independent self"; and second, breastfeeding triggers abnormal "sexual-psychological" development in some boys, thus inhibiting healthy relationship forming later in life. These risks can be averted, according to the contributors, by stopping breastfeeding when the child is one, or a maximum of two, years of age.

Claims like the ones above, which all promulgate earlier weaning, sound unscientific and challenge WHO recommendations, but they are consistent with the overall discursive construction about breastfeeding risks in this forum. As my analysis of online Chinese discussions indicates, breast milk is depicted as not only allergenic, toxic, and nutritionally depleted, but also as addictive to child and mother, and thus as posing a serious threat to a child's physical and mental health. Moreover, such depictions were synecdochically linked to broader understandings of expected family relations, the needs of the nation-state, global networks of health information and commodities, and long-standing gender stereotypes, which place a series of complicated and conflicting expectations on new mothers.

Conclusion: Breastfeeding, Controlling the Female Body, and Imagining Alternatives

Breastfeeding is intensely personal, yet is shaped through social, political, medical, and gendered discourses. My response to these overlapping lattices of power and possibility is also personal, for the initial foment that led to my writing this chapter was my journey of breastfeeding my first child. Moreover, my unique identity position as a diasporic Chinese academic living in the United States, who had several middle-aged Chinese women, arranged through familial and professional ties, participate in caring for my infant, meant that while I was conducting this research, I was also living it. By the time I completed this chapter, I was breastfeeding my second child. I have steered away from conjoining my narrative with the discourse emerging from my data—I find that my voice seeps through often enough anyway—but feel it necessary, in order to be authentic, to flag how my own experiences have evolved in tandem with the voices that have emerged from the data, so to speak. In the end, my experiences with the issues discussed herein have helped me to sort out the connections between the rhetorical work of imagining communities ("healthy American babies," "polluted Chinese landscapes") and specific health practices, like breastfeeding, that impinge on, and recast, identity formations at individual, national, and global levels.

Through my analysis of online discourses around the issue of breast-feeding and infant health risk among Chinese women, I identified the construction of three types of infant health risks: pathological and toxico-logical, nutritional, and developmental. I found that the Tianya-BBS, as a site for women to exchange personal experiences with breastfeeding and other forms of infant nutritional practices, provided a window into a series of exchanges through which women define and grapple with risk in ways that connect to broader social, political, and scientific narratives. The narratives shared online about breastfeeding support the construction of the very idea of risk by providing personal and embodied manifestations to what might otherwise remain an unrealized potentiality.[71] But perhaps the most significant contribution of this essay is in its exposition of how the language of risk is used to police the realms of acceptable and unac-ceptable maternal identities, and the conflation of these identities with broader social imaginaries around the Chinese nation-state.

Contributors to the discussion forum thus created what seems to be a collaborative story when they exchanged details about the symptoms of dairy allergy, malnutrition, and insufficient milk supply.[72] Moreover, the forum provided a platform for exchanging expert voices from medical professionals and experienced elders on the issue of infant health risk. These expert and elder voices (mostly mothers-in-law) not only identi-fied various risk phenomena, but also offered concrete suggestions as to how such risks can be avoided. This combination of voices creates a powerful narrative depicting formula as superior to breast milk for urban mothers in China. More pointedly, the many potential risks—toxic pollu-tion, inadequate nutrition, and developmental problems—eventually boil down to a criticism of the contemporary Chinese urban woman's inability to manage her own body. Moreover, this criticism is leveled despite the fact that the shattered environment, obsessive work habits, and evolving lifestyles in China's cities are fundamentally incompatible with many of the assumed responsibilities of motherhood.

Admittedly, complaints about the urban environment and its effects on health are not unfounded. Other authors in this section provide extensive discussions on how the many aspects of modernity—industrialization, urbanization, and pollution—are exposing people in China to new risks in close, personal, and sometimes devastating ways. These risks loom large in people's everyday lives, often with alarming visuals, like the image of "16,000 bloated pig carcasses floating in the Huangpu River" or that of fake mutton slices transformed from "rat, mink, and fox meat" and served to diners in popular restaurants.[73] If the chapters in this section are taken as a whole, they demonstrate the complex links among culture, nation, environment, and the enactment of specific bodily practices, with each category shot through with new and multiple forms of material, symbolic, and imagined risks. Indeed, in the context of these grave risks to health and well-being, the discussion about breastfeeding is further predicated upon portrayals of an infant who is not only extremely vulnerable, but also prone to suffering irreversible damage. Mothers are directed to judge their own lactation performance by closely monitoring every meal of the infant, by gauging whether the infant is gaining weight at a certain speed, or by assessing whether she is appearing happy and content. Normative standards for infant health are also established for mothers so that they can compare themselves to their peers. The image of a perfectly healthy baby appears as chubby-cheeked, rotund, and full of good cheer. To secure this state in their infant, many mothers are willing to go to any lengths: they not only closely monitor their own body in order to achieve the optimal milk supply, but they also stay vigilant in examining the quantity and quality of breast milk. As seen here, these passions are so strong that many mothers choose alternatives to breastfeeding in order to avoid the risks perceived to be involved in breastfeeding.

When breastfeeding is interpreted as an extension of pregnancy in the broader risk assemblages that constitute motherhood for these forum posters in China, mothers are repeatedly construed as conduits through which risk factors flow to the child. Anecdotal and statistical data shared in cyberspace claim that the risks involved in the life of an urban woman—pollution, food safety, and substance abuse—pass through her mammary glands to the infant. Thus, it is important for her to self-police her behaviors around these risk factors: the breastfeeding mother is directed by various experts to critique her own diet, lifestyle, and environment in the same way that she is expected to monitor her body during pregnancy. In these ways, surveillance and empowerment are entwined in a complex gendering dynamic. Indeed, as is the case with pregnancy, mothers are led to feel individually responsible for the well-being of their infant. As Lupton posits, individual responsibility is central to the idea of risk.[74] This means that the governmentality constructed in risk discourse is configured around self-discipline, where citizens are meant to actively participate in risk avoidance exercises, even while many of the risks they are meant to avoid are the direct product of the Chinese government's irresponsibility. Still, in the case of the urban breastfeeding risks addressed here, self-governance is realized through a culture of prudence, where any form of risk taking is constructed as irrational and essentially irresponsible. One of the tragedies of contemporary China, then, is that women are imagining their own bodies as contaminated purveyors of risk. But as my own breastfeeding experiences suggest, alternative imaginations are possible.

NOTES

1. The discussion post originally appeared online at https://bbs.tianya.cn. The author conducted translations of the discussion posts from Chinese to English.
2. Lisa Schlein, "China's Melamine Milk Crisis Creates Crisis of Confidence," Voice of America, September 26, 2008, http://www.voanews.com.
3. Ibid.
4. For detailed information and statistics, see Wang Jun et al., "China—People's Republic of: China Food Manufacturing Annual Report," U.S. Department of Agriculture, Global Agricultural Information Network, February 4, 2013, http://gain.fas.usda.gov.
5. Kevin Michael DeLuca and Jennifer Peeples, "From Public Sphere to Public Screen: Democracy, Activism, and the 'Violence' of Seattle," *Critical Studies in Media Communication* 19 (2002): 125–51.
6. Subas Neupane, Bright I. Nwaru, Zhuochun Wu, and Elina Hemminki, "Work Behaviour during Pregnancy in Rural China in 2009," *European Journal of Public Health* 24 (2014): 170–75.
7. Ping Tu, "The Effects of Breastfeeding and Birth Spacing on Child Survival in

China," *Studies in Family Planning* 20 (1989): 332–42.

8. Richard Lanham, *A Handlist of Rhetorical Terms: A Guide for Students of English Literature*, 2nd ed. (Berkeley: University of California Press, 1999), 189.

9. Michel Foucault, "Governmentality," in *The Foucault Effect: Studies in Governmentality*, ed. Graham Burchell, Colin Gordon, and Peter Miller (Chicago: University of Chicago Press, 1991), 87–104; Deborah Lupton, *Risk and Sociocultural Theory: New Directions and Perspectives* (New York: Cambridge University Press, 1999); and Deborah Lupton, *Risk* (New York: Routledge, 2013).

10. Liubai Li, Sujun Li, Moazzam Ali, and Hiroshi Ushijima, "Feeding Practice of Infants and Their Correlates in Urban Areas of Beijing, China," *Pediatrics International* 45 (2003): 400–6; Ping Liu et al., "Factors Associated with Breastfeeding Duration: A 30-Month Cohort Study in Northwest China," *Journal of Human Lactation* 29 (2013): 253–59; Neupane et al., "Work Behaviour during Pregnancy"; Ya-qin Zhang, Hui Li, and Xiu-lan Xia, "Complementary Feeding Practice in Nine Cities of China," *Chinese Journal of Child Health Care* 4 (2008): 397–402.

11. Fenglian Xu, Liqian Qiu, Colin W. Binns, and Xiaoxian Liu, "Breastfeeding in China: A Review," *International Breastfeeding Journal* 4 (2009): 1–15.

12. Commission on Macroeconomics and Health, *Macroeconomics and Health: Investing in Health for Economic Development* (Geneva: World Health Organization, 2001).

13. Amy Koerber, "Rhetorical Agency, Resistance, and the Disciplinary Rhetorics of Breastfeeding," *Technical Communication Quarterly* 15 (2006): 87–101.

14. Xu et al., "Breastfeeding in China."

15. Liu et al., "Factors Associated with Breastfeeding Duration," 254.

16. Xu et al., "Breastfeeding in China." Note that this definition is for "any breastfeeding," which includes infants who were only breastfed once in the period.

17. Ibid.

18. Ibid.

19. Li et al., "Feeding Practice of Infants"; Xu et al., "Breastfeeding in China."

20. World Health Organization and UNICEF, "Protecting, Promoting and Supporting Breast-Feeding: The Special Role of Maternity Services," http://www.who.int.

21. Ted Greiner, "Beyond Melamine: More Reasons Not to Use Animal Milk in Infant Feeding," *Journal of Human Lactation* 25 (2009): 397–99; and Changbai Xiu and K. K. Klein, "Melamine in Milk Products in China: Examining the Factors

That Led to Deliberate Use of the Contaminant," *Food Policy* 35 (2010): 463–70.

22. Liu et al., "Factors Associated with Breastfeeding Duration," 254.

23. Tu, "Effects of Breastfeeding."

24. Zhang, Li, and Xia, "Complementary Feeding Practice," 397.

25. Li et al., "Feeding Practice of Infants," 400.

26. Ibid.

27. Ibid.

28. Xu et al., "Breastfeeding in China."

29. Liu et al., "Factors Associated with Breastfeeding Duration," 255.

30. WHO and UNICEF, "Protecting, Promoting and Supporting Breast-Feeding."

31. Amy Koerber, *Breast or Bottle? Contemporary Controversies in Infant-Feeding Policy and Practice* (Columbia: University of South Carolina Press, 2013).

32. Michel Foucault, *The Birth of the Clinic: An Archaeology of Medical Perception*, trans. Alan Sheridan (New York: Routledge, 1989).

33. Emily T. Cripe, "Supporting Breastfeeding? Nursing Mothers' Resistance to and Accommodation of Medical and Social Discourses," in *Emerging Perspectives in Health Communication: Meaning, Culture, and Power*, ed. Heather Zoller and Mohan Dutta (New York: Routledge, 2009), 63–84.

34. Deborah Lupton, *Medicine as Culture: Illness, Disease and the Body in Western Societies*, 2nd ed. (Thousand Oaks, CA: Sage Publications, 2003).

35. Huiling Ding and Jingwen Zhang, "Imagining Health Risks: Fear, Fate, Death, and Family in Chinese and American HIV/AIDS Online Discussion Forums," this volume.

36. Cripe, "Supporting Breastfeeding?" 64–65.

37. Ibid.

38. Lindsey M. Rose, "Legally Public but Privately Practiced: Segregating the Lactating Body," *Health Communication* 27 (2012): 49.

39. Patrice M. Buzzanell and Laura L. Ellingson, "Contesting Narratives of Workplace Maternity," in *Narratives, Health and Healing: Communication Theory, Research and Practice*, ed. Lynn M. Harter, Phyllis M. Japp, and Christina S. Beck (Mahwah, NJ: Lawrence Erlbaum, 2005), 277–94.

40. Amy Koerber, Linda Brice, and Elizabeth Tombs, "Breastfeeding and Problematic Integration: Results of a Focus-Group Study," *Health Communication* 27 (2012): 124–44.

41. Rose, "Legally Public but Privately Practiced," 50.

42. Ibid.

43. Lupton, *Risk*, 77; Lupton, *Medicine as Culture*, 139–40.

44. As cited in Lupton, *Risk*, 118.

45. Ibid., 89.

46. Marika Siegel, *The Rhetoric of Pregnancy* (Chicago: University of Chicago Press, 2013).

47. Michel Foucault, "The Politics of Health in the Eighteenth Century," in *The Foucault Reader*, ed. Paul Rabinow (New York: Vintage/Random House, 1984), 273–89. Readers sometimes ask about the appropriateness of adopting Foucauldian analysis to a non-Western culture such as China's. One justification provided by Ruth Rogaski was that it is not as much the similarity of Chinese and Western medical culture, but the fact that the system of modern Chinese medicine was modeled after Western biomedicine. Rogaski also points out that there was a clear move toward the Western biomedical system by citing early Chinese policy makers who mandated that "the health of the nation is not the responsibility of the government, but the responsibility of the citizen as he eats, drinks and orders his daily life." See Ruth Rogaski, *Hygienic Modernity: Meanings of Health and Disease in Treaty-Port China* (Berkeley: University of California Press, 2004), 126.

48. Foucault, "The Politics of Health in the Eighteenth Century," 277.

49. Lupton, *Risk*, 62.

50. On "biopolitics," see Lisa Keränen, "Biopolitics, Contagion, and Digital Health Narratives: Pathways for the Rhetoric of Health and Medicine," *Communication Quarterly* 65 (2015): 504–9; and "Addressing the Epidemic of Epidemics: Germs, Security, and a Call for Biocriticism," *Quarterly Journal of Speech* 97 (2011): 224–44.

51. Foucault, "The Politics of Health in the Eighteenth Century," 282–84.

52. Lupton, *Risks*, 60.

53. Ibid.

54. The term "one-child policy" is a misnomer. Although one essential element of China's family-planning policy involved discouraging and strictly controlling pregnancy and childbirth after the first child, the policy has substantial room for negotiation and flexibility among the agricultural population, and it was not applied to ethnic minorities. Moreover, there are recent trends toward further relaxing the birth restrictions. For an early review of this area, see Susan Greenhalgh, "Science, Modernity, and the Making of China's One-Child Policy," *Population and Development Review* 29 (2003): 163–96; also see Guan Xiaofeng,

"Most People Free to Have More Child," *China Daily*, July 11, 2007.

55. Shubo Li, "The Online Public Space and Popular Ethos in China," *Media, Culture & Society* 32 (2010): 63–83.

56. DeLuca and Peeples, "From Public Sphere to Public Screen."

57. Li, "The Online Public Space and Popular Ethos in China," 73–74.

58. Ding and Zhang, "Imagining Health Risks," this volume.

59. For the discussion posts, see https://bbs.tianya.cn.

60. While the term "discourse" is contested, I am interested in how discursive constructions create "opaque as well as transparent structural relationships of dominance, discrimination, power and control as manifested in language," as discussed in Ruth Wodak and Michael Meyer, "Critical Discourse Analysis: History, Agenda, Theory, and Methodology," in *Methods for Critical Discourse Analysis*, 2nd ed., ed. Wodak and Meyer (Los Angeles: Sage, 2009), 10. While there are several strands of discourse analysis, my approach resembles standard practice in media/cultural studies, where it is important to go beyond the "textual" construction of risk to consider the "contextual" environment in which such discourse is produced; see Sarah Tracy, *Qualitative Research Methods: Collecting Evidence, Crafting Analysis, Communicating Impact* (Chichester: Wiley-Blackwell, 2013).

61. Tracy, *Qualitative Research Methods*, 184.

62. Ruth Wodak, "Critical Discourse Analysis at the End of the 20th Century," *Research on Language and Social Interaction* 32 (1999): 185–93; abductive approaches to data analysis emphasize an iterative mode of reasoning, allowing both data and theory to inform each other, as seen in Zhuo Ban, Shaunak Sastry, and Mohan Jyoti Dutta, "'Shoppers' Republic of China': Orientalism in Neoliberal U.S. News Discourse," *Journal of International and Intercultural Communication* 6 (2013): 280–97.

63. World Health Organization, "Dioxins and Their Effects on Human Health: Fact Sheet," October 2016, http://www.who.int.

64. Lupton, *Risk*, 20.

65. George S. Rigakos and Alexandra Law, "Risk, Realism and the Politics of Resistance," *Critical Sociology* 35 (2009): 79–103.

66. On this trope, see Tiantian Zheng, "Political Struggle of Rural Migrant Hostesses for First-Class Citizenship in Postsocialist China," in *Diversity, Social Justice, and Inclusive Excellence: Transdisciplinary and Global Perspectives*, ed. Seth N. Asumah and Mechthild Nagel (Albany: SUNY Press, 2014), 89–120.

67. Examining the discursive construction of breastfeeding in *Parents' Magazine*, Foss and Southwell argue that infant formula is closely connected to consumption and modernity; see Katherine A. Foss and Brian G. Southwell, "Infant Feeding and the Media: The Relationship between Parents' Magazine Content and Breastfeeding, 1972–2000," *International Breastfeeding Journal* 1 (2006): 1–9.

68. Ibid.

69. Alison Bartlett, "Maternal Sexuality and Breastfeeding," *Sex Education* 5 (2005): 67–77.

70. Rosalia Rodriguez-Garcia and Lara Frazier, "Cultural Paradoxes Relating to Sexuality and Breastfeeding," *Journal of Human Lactation* 11 (1995): 111–15.

71. Lupton, *Risk*, 18.

72. Sunwolf, Lawrence R. Frey, and Lisa Keränen, "Rx Story-Prescription: The Healing Effects of Storytelling and Storylistening in the Practice of Medicine," in Harter, Japp, and Beck, *Narrative, Health, and Healing*, 237–57.

73. See, respectively, Lisa Keränen, Kirsten Lindholm, and Jared Woolly, "Imagining the People's Risk: Projecting National Strength in China's English-Language News about Avian Influenza Outbreak," and Donovan S. Conley, "China's Fraught Food System: Imagining Ecological Civilization in the Face of Paradoxical Modernity," this volume.

74. Lupton, *Risk*, 93.

Imagining Health Risks: Fear, Fate, Death, and Family in Chinese and American HIV/AIDS Online Discussion Forums

Huiling Ding and Jingwen Zhang

In August 2015, a story titled "Nanjing, AIDS Patient Escaped from the Hospital? Do Not Panic" circulated virally on Chinese social media.[1] Some readers leaped to extreme conclusions, with one person commenting online, "this is horrible and I am afraid to go out!" Lacking verified sources, and running counter to the preferred, evolving health communication practices of the Communist Party of China (CPC or the Party), the story nonetheless attracted the public's attention, thus revealing an inconvenient truth: although China has worked on HIV/AIDS prevention for three decades, ignorance, stigma, and ungrounded fear about HIV/AIDS remain entrenched among large sections of the public. While we caution against the spread of this kind of misinformation and fear, concern about how online commentators communicate about HIV/AIDS is a crucial question within China, for in 2009 the Chinese Ministry of Health announced that HIV/AIDS had surpassed tuberculosis and rabies to become the nation's leading cause of death and noted a fivefold increase in the number of HIV/AIDS deaths from three years earlier.[2] Responding to the continued spread of HIV, Chinese President Xi Jinping, in conjunction with the 2013 World AIDS Day, called for legal and scientific prevention and control of HIV/AIDS as well as various social support platforms for carriers and patients.[3] Meanwhile, U.S. President Barack Obama launched the HIV Cure Initiative and redirected $100 million into research efforts aimed at curing HIV.[4] Together, Presidents Xi and Obama's policies demonstrate how diseases transcend lived, everyday experiences to acquire sociopolitical force.[5]

Indeed, as Paula Treichler has shown, the HIV/AIDS epidemic is "simultaneously an epidemic of a transmissible lethal disease and an epidemic of meanings or signification."[6] Public communication about HIV/AIDS, then, points to both medical and health issues and also to larger cultural questions of how different communities imagine the health of the nation. As we demonstrate below, the discourse communities in the United States and China are so different regarding their conceptions of HIV/AIDS that it is reasonable to argue that China and the United States face different HIV/AIDS epidemics.[7] Behind each country's formal HIV/AIDS policies we find disparate cultural and linguistic histories, meaning the millions of people living with HIV/AIDS, along with their families, friends, and local communities, experience the epidemic differently in China and the United States. We offer this comparative framework, in part, because existing communication studies on HIV/AIDS have been predominantly contextualized in Western cultures; similar approaches for understanding the disease in China have received much less attention.[8] Moreover, because of the stigmatization of HIV/AIDS in many parts of both China and the United States, online communities form a vital space for discussion and social support in both nations. To date, the few relevant works addressing the communicative dimensions of HIV/AIDS largely focus on media representations and the stigmatization of HIV/AIDS patients.[9] A lack of critical discussion of the online discourses may breed ignorance and misunderstanding, leading to greater difficulties in both local and global public health responses. By examining online discourses testifying to the life experiences of people living with HIV/AIDS (and at-risk populations) in both China and the United States, we aim to provide a comparative perspective for understanding the epidemic in two sociopolitical systems, health risk ecologies, and complex cultures.

To pursue this comparative and cross-cultural analysis, we ask a series of nested questions: How do people living with HIV/AIDS (and at-risk populations) view and cope with the illness and its related risks in online discussion forums? How does culture influence the way HIV/AIDS health and risk discourses are constructed? And what synecdochical implications may we draw from these online forums about how the participants constitute themselves, their respective governments, and the health of their respective nations? This chapter takes a grassroots approach to these questions by analyzing online posts written by people who are experiencing HIV/AIDS or who are worried they have contracted HIV; these posts provide firsthand, vernacular data about the constructed meanings of HIV/AIDS in specific cultural contexts.[10] Our chapter also investigates the roles played by an emerging, participatory public engaging in risk communication and meaning making via the Chinese Internet.[11] Here, we see Chinese citizens participating in online sense-making activities that interpret their lived experiences of illness through long-standing social, familial, and cultural terms. In summary, our analysis of the most-viewed posts published in top AIDS forums provides an opportunity to examine how high-risk populations and people living with HIV/AIDS talk about their experiences by constituting imagined communities of people living through similar experiences.

By focusing on how online communities interpret and negotiate their high-risk behaviors and/or their experiences of living with HIV/AIDS, our chapter reveals the complicated social and cultural factors that drive the rhetorical work of imagining such communities. We begin with a brief review of the epidemic in the two countries; then we explain our research methods; then we examine how participants use online forums to discuss HIV/AIDS. Our critical reading of the content contributed by online participants leads, in synecdochical fashion, to debates about normative sexuality, communal responsibility, and entrenched notions of morality and fate.

Online HIV/AIDS Discourses and
Imagined Communities

Although the established national narratives on the HIV/AIDS epidemic can provide us with a brief overview of the history and development of the epidemic, they cannot reveal the nuanced and complex cultural and sociopolitical meanings of HIV/AIDS as constructed, practiced, and negotiated in everyday lived experience. Particularly in China, where the CPC has been slow to respond to the crisis, people have come to learn about HIV/AIDS, understand its consequences, and construct their own beliefs and attitudes largely through reading and reflecting on other people's stories as shared in online sites.[12] In order to shed light on different cultural understandings of HIV/AIDS in the United States and in China, we adopt Arjun Appadurai's approach to culture, which stresses the "dimensionality" rather than "substantiality" of culture and the "context-sensitive, contrast-centered" approach to examining cultures.[13] We assume the local cultures of online HIV/AIDS communities are influenced not only by national cultures, values, and HIV/AIDS-related policies, but also by local structures such as hierarchies within the online discussion forums, the interface and information architecture of the sites, and the power dynamics between forum staff, volunteers, and participants. Furthermore, the creation and circulation of online HIV/AIDS discourses are rhetorical practices, requiring research attention to "all parts of the rhetorical triangle—the speaker, the subject matter, and the audience."[14] From this perspective, Internet users are both the authors and audience members who produce and transform online HIV/AIDS discourses, meaning these online health communication discussion forums help to create imagined communities that coalesce around shared problems, beliefs, values, and hopes.

Here we turn to Anderson's concept of imagined communities, which is often used to explore how geographically distributed groups of people view their connections with a nation or a society.[15] Seeing nationality and nationalism as "cultural artefacts of a particular kind," Anderson emphasized, "all communities larger than primordial villages of face-to-face contact (and perhaps even these) are imagined."[16] We are particularly interested in investigating how the high-risk and/or infected individuals view their relationships with the larger communities and the nation by imagining not only individual identities but also a "productive place of their bodies within ideas of the social and the nation."[17] Thus, we seek to understand how the health of individual bodies is converted synecdochically into harbingers of the health of the nation.

IMAGINING OTHERS: "GAY CANCER," "LOVING CAPITALISM DISEASE," AND *KONG AI*

From its earliest known appearances in the two countries considered herein, HIV/AIDS has acquired divergent cultural understandings. In the United States, HIV/AIDS is now believed to have entered the country in 1969, when HIV likely spread through a single infected immigrant from Haiti, although it was not until years later, in the early 1980s, that doctors in Los Angeles, New York City, and San Francisco began seeing young men with rarely occurring cancers and lung infections.[18] Soon after, various names including "gay compromise syndrome," "gay-related immune deficiency" (GRID), "acquired immunodeficiency disease," "gay cancer," or "community-acquired immune dysfunction" referred to the disease.[19] In its early days, HIV/AIDS was thus portrayed in the United States as a gay disease and framed in terms of the familiar boundary between the healthy us and the diseased other.[20] During the latter half of the 1980s, and due largely to the brave work of activists and concerned health professionals, the framing of HIV/AIDS shifted away from its depiction as a morality-driven gay plague to a health-driven chronic disease. In 2010, men who have sex with men were the most severely affected group in the United States, accounting for more than half (52 percent) of those living with HIV and 63 percent of all new HIV infections.[21]

What makes the epidemic in China different from the one in the United States is that the epidemic was first seen in China as a consequence of contact with the West. In China, which was closed off for much of the mid-twentieth century, the first HIV infection is believed to have been introduced in 1985 by a foreign traveler.[22] One interpretation of AIDS's Chinese name, *ai zi bing* (in Pinyin) translates to "loving capitalism disease."[23] HIV/AIDS was thus configured as a product of the "corrupt Western life" and was associated in much Chinese public discourse with sex work, drug use, and promiscuity. Indeed, by the end of the 1980s, the first outbreak of HIV infection in China appeared among intravenous drug users (IDUs) and their partners.[24] Since then (and as of 2011), 76 percent of HIV infections were acquired through sexual contact, of which about 14 percent occurred through homosexual contact.[25] As a result of these patterns, in the past three years, the term *kong ai* has frequently appeared on national news in association with HIV/AIDS; *kong ai* is the Chinese equivalent of AIDS phobia, which refers to the fears that people with high-risk behaviors have about the possibility of contracting HIV/AIDS.[26] In fact, in an example of what Elaine Showalter might call a *hystory*, an infectiously spreading communication about an imagined illness, one group of people in China claimed they were infected with HIV-negative AIDS despite repeated negative HIV test results.[27] This phenomenon reveals a widespread lack of public education on HIV/AIDS in today's China. Given the social stigma and confusion attached to HIV/AIDS, many turn to online discussion boards to discuss their fears and experiences. In this way, the online forums discussed here offer powerful insights into how both Chinese and U.S. citizens struggle to make sense of HIV/AIDS and, in the process, engage in the rhetorical work of making sense of themselves, their nations, and the roles health risk plays in our communities.

Methods: CADS and Metaphorical Analyses

In order to understand the contours and meanings of online health discourses, we used both corpus-assisted discourse studies (CADS) and metaphorical analysis to examine the selected online posts.[28] Both researchers are fluent in English and Chinese, which aided our comparative analysis. While metaphorical analysis focuses on meanings, computer- and hand-tagged keyword extraction from CADS helps to analyze meanings, frequency, and distribution of keywords; aids in the generation of coding schemes for text analysis; and ultimately helps to isolate the various meanings of individual keywords by displaying the occurrences of the word with its surrounding context. In short, CADS analysis brings new and additional insights that complement the findings of our metaphorical analysis. In our analysis of the English corpus, we read all posts repeatedly to find recurring themes and important issues. Meanwhile, we employed a concordancing software package, Concordance, to create a computer-generated word frequency count and to produce passages containing keywords related to recurring themes for further analysis. After examining the list of keywords and comparing them with preliminary findings from our readings, we selected those concerning high-risk behaviors and self-reflection, testing, experiences learning about HIV/AIDS and its accompanying issues, emotional expressions, and coping strategies. For the Chinese corpus, because of the lack of specialized concordance software for Chinese characters, we used holistic reading and inductive analysis to identify salient patterns and recurring themes. We then conducted semiautomated scanning and coding in Microsoft Word, using computer- and hand-tagged analysis to examine the use of key terms and concepts in the text. While one author (Ding) performed CADS analysis, the other author (Zhang) isolated metaphors from the posts, sorted identified metaphors into groups, and then looked for patterns in metaphor uses in the two forums. We each coded 10 percent of the corpus using the methods employed by the other author, and the inter-rater agreement rate was 85 percent. While metaphor analysis provides access to cultural framings at the conceptual level, careful corpus-assisted discourse studies (CADS) analysis of collocational, or co-occurring, words in original passages allows us to examine individuals' views of their belongings in and against larger cultural contexts.

Because studying controversial online communities' participation on the Internet requires ethical considerations, we collected only archived, publicly available data from the Internet discussion forums. To protect the privacy of forum participants, we paraphrased all site and board names and deleted identifying information of the participants. Furthermore, while the original posts were used in the analytical processes, we paraphrase all texts from forum posts whenever they are cited here so as to eliminate the possibility of tracing the language of the post back to the online identity of the participants.

To understand how people communicate online about HIV/AIDS with one another, we include in the units of analysis not only the discourses themselves but also the interfaces that create such discursive possibilities

TABLE 1. DISCUSSION FORUMS SELECTED IN CHINA
AND IN THE UNITED STATES

	CHINESE FORUM	U.S. FORUM
Members	> 44,200	> 13,900
Posts	> 536,000	> 487,000
Average Post Length	813 words	403 words

in the first place. We selected two online HIV/AIDS discussion forums, one from China and one from the United States, using three criteria, namely, open public access, function, and popularity among HIV/AIDS patients and at-risk populations (as reflected by statistics of members and total posts in 2013, see Table 1). We selected the most popular open forums with broad sets of functions (including both medical discussions and social interactions) in each country for this study.

Differences in Forum Infrastructures, Functions, and Participants' HIV Status

As a first step, we examined the respective structures and main boards of the two forums. The Chinese forum contains five categories of boards, with three for all types of users and two that are specifically devoted to homosexuals, *tong zhi*, and people with concerns about sexually transmitted disease. The three boards with the most participation cover counseling, HIV/AIDS knowledge, and testing procedures and results. Only one board is devoted to the discussion and sharing of illness experiences for people already tested positive for HIV. Most posts on these boards are individual narratives about high-risk behaviors and questions surrounding testing and diagnosis, which reveal the prevailing fear of contracting HIV—*kong ai*—among high-risk populations. By contrast, the U.S. forum includes four categories of boards covering issues in HIV transmission and testing, living with HIV, treatment information, and research news. The three boards with the most participation cover infection and diagnosis, living with HIV, and offline social gatherings. Two thirds of the boards are devoted to discussions about health issues and life conditions of people already infected with HIV. Moreover, forum moderators impose restricted participation on two boards to protect the privacy of those participants who are AIDS survivors and women living with HIV. Our comparison of the structures of the two discussion forums reveals the differences in topic composition and emphasis between them, which in turn condition their respective HIV/AIDS discourses and the social imaginaries of which they are a part. Both discussion forums share a similar mixed community of people living with HIV and people fearing that they may have contracted HIV/AIDS. While the Chinese forum attracted people suffering from AIDS-phobia panic attacks after high-risk behaviors, the U.S. forum often involved AIDS patients and their family members.

After identifying and categorizing dominant topics in the two online forums, we chose five boards from each forum based on their similarity in topics and purposes. We then identified the most-viewed/commented ten posts from each board. Thus, we compiled fifty posts for each forum, or one hundred posts total into two corpora. The complete set of data consists of 60,824 words both in Chinese (40,728) and in English (20,096). As we shall see in more detail below, our analysis points toward the Chinese online forums fulfilling deeply emotional and culturally influenced roles reflecting Confucian notions of shame and duty, while the U.S.-based forum tended toward discourses that were about managing HIV/AIDS within professional health rhetorics.

Another salient infrastructural difference between the two forums is the composition of their moderators and supporting staff. The Chinese discussion forum relies on volunteers, particularly three volunteering physicians specializing in HIV/AIDS diagnosis and treatment. The three physician volunteers not only moderate twelve of the seventeen actively moderated boards but also provide ongoing medical consultation and psychological counseling to many participants who write with worries about contracting HIV after high-risk behaviors. Other than the three physicians, the forum relies on volunteers who have recovered from their anxiety about contracting HIV and who hope to help similarly situated others. The three physicians ask all volunteers to demonstrate HIV/AIDS knowledge by taking tests in order to establish them as semiexperts in

HIV/AIDS symptoms and/or treatments before the volunteers are allowed to begin their service.

In contrast, the U.S. forum includes two paid staff, one volunteer, nine advisory board members, and nine contributing writers. It functions both to provide supporting platforms for subscribers of its print and digital AIDS magazines and to reach out to a wider audience. The U.S. forum views its target users as people living with HIV/AIDS, their friends, family, and caregivers, as well as others concerned about HIV/AIDS. The forum's welcome message stipulates that any licensed medical providers must clearly define themselves as such if they want to use the forum. In other words, the U.S. forum closely demarcates the line between people with HIV/AIDS and medical experts treating AIDS patients, and it seeks to provide community for the former via assistance from the latter. The interface structure of this U.S.-based online forum thus imagines a community of HIV/AIDS patients and caregivers united around a shared discourse of health professionalism and community empowerment.

Whereas only ten of the Chinese forum participants reported a positive HIV test result, forty-five out of the fifty U.S. forum participants had HIV/AIDS or reported recently testing positive (see Table 2). Twenty in the Chinese forum reported negative test results and another twenty awaited results. In contrast, only four in the U.S. forum had negative test results, and one participant did not reveal his or her HIV status. This finding suggests differences in the primary audiences each forum serves: the majority of the Chinese forum participants had recently engaged in high-risk behaviors and were concerned they might have contracted HIV; in contrast to this widespread AIDS phobia in China, only some participants in the board of infection questions in the U.S. forum shared such fears.

Fear of HIV/AIDS, High-Risk Behavior, and Kong Ai

One prominent difference between the Chinese and U.S. forums concerns participants' references to high-risk behaviors and fear in their discussions about HIV/AIDS. The keyword of *high risk* (*gao wei*) appeared thirty-seven and two times respectively in the Chinese and U.S. corpora, even though the word *risk* appeared forty-six and twenty-eight times

**TABLE 2. HIV STATUSES OF FORUM PARTICIPANTS
IN THE CORPORA**

HIV TEST RESULTS	CHINESE FORUM	U.S. FORUM
Positive	10	45
Negative	20	4
Still waiting, unreported, or unknown	20	1

respectively in the two corpora. Our analysis of the collocational passages of the keywords reveals that the U.S. posters used terms such as *low risk* (5) and *no risk* (7) more frequently. In comparison, most Chinese posters identified the exact dates and settings of their one-time high-risk encounters before scheduling testing and interpreting testing results ranging from six weeks, three months, six months, to one year. Many posts also offered extensive details about the perceived high-risk encounters and a wide range of AIDS-related symptoms the writers experienced after the encounter. One poster wrote "I had a high-risk, one-night affair with a stranger four weeks ago and suffered from AIDS phobia for over three weeks. This is my first post here since I will get my life-or-death sentence tomorrow." Another observed that "I had high-risk sex on September 28, 2008, when I had a business trip in Yunnan." These and other posters reported committing high-risk behaviors without prior knowledge about the forum. Indeed, they suffered from prolonged panic attacks about possibly contracting HIV/AIDS before searching online for more information about the disease and finding the forum. Many also spent months surfing the forum and observing others' posts before publishing anything about their own situations, perhaps after feeling comfortable enough with the forum to talk about their situations in public.

Kong ai is another common theme in the Chinese corpus. While the lexical item for fear in Chinese (*kong*) appeared 141 times in the Chinese forum, the concept of fear appeared 18 times in the U.S. forum. The Chinese participants used the term *kong* in five different ways:

1. Fear related to HIV/AIDS (*kong ju*, 45).
2. Fear of contracting HIV/AIDS (*kong ai*, 26).

3. Fear experienced by participants' friends who also worried about contracting HIV/AIDS (*kong you*, or in literal translation, *fear friend*, 23).
4. References to stopping worrying about contracting HIV/AIDS, often because of repeated negative testing results (*tuo kong*, 4).
5. Recurring fears of contracting AIDS because of high-risk behaviors (*fu kong*, 2).

An example of each of these themes appears below.

> After my high-risk sex, like most fear friends (*kong you*), my life was worse than death. I looked for rashes all over my body and for hairy leukoplakia inside my mouth, skimmed through websites and documents about AIDS like crazy, and lived like a highly depressed zombie.
>
> I incidentally became someone who worried repeatedly about contracting AIDS (*old kong you*). I had my last high-risk sex last October, experienced a wide range of AIDS-like symptoms, and got my third negative testing result after four months. Four months after my negative testing result, I had unprotected sex with my wife, who started having random symptoms such as dizziness, headache, and rashes in two weeks. I was almost scared to death by my recurring fear of contracting AIDS (*fu kong*).
>
> I had negative results from eighth-week home testing after a negative result on a four-week home testing. I now completely stop worrying about contracting AIDS (*tuo kong*). I hope all brothers in this forum will stop worrying about their risks (*kong ai*) in scientific ways. If you reply to my post, you will get negative results!

Each of these posts reveals the multiple fears forum participants faced as they negotiated their health identities online. To unpack these fears in more detail, we turn now to a series of thematically organized subsections of analysis.

IMAGINING (AND TESTING FOR) THE WORST:
SYMPTOMS AS INDICATION OF INFECTION

Testing is one of the most discussed topics in both forums. Participants ponder the need to get tested after high-risk sex, raise questions about their testing methods and results, and describe the ways they cope with stress and fear while waiting for testing results. Participants in the Chinese forum publish posts about testing far more frequently than their U.S. counterparts (191 vs. 85). In addition, the sampled data from the Chinese forum contain far more words about negative results (120 vs. 27). Two factors contribute to this drastic difference: the actual number of negative testing reports from AIDS-phobic forum participants and the ritualistic gestures of praying for negative results in the Chinese forum. Such ritualistic messages also promise virtuous conduct in the future— which is closely associated with the rebirth metaphor—and urge others to do the same: "Six-month AIDS phobia experience teaches me love and responsibility. Reject high-risk behavior! Those who reply will all get negative results!!!!" In that same vein, another commentator wrote "One sentence! Never repeat high-risk behaviors! I wish all brothers good luck! Wish everyone negative results!!!!" One of the problems with analyzing these kinds of conversion narratives is that we have no way of knowing if the posters actually followed through on their promises to change their behaviors.

We observed a marked difference in the use of words related to symptoms (such as "symptoms" and "signs") across the two forums, which reveals the preoccupation with HIV testing and diagnosis in the Chinese context. The keywords related to symptoms are used ninety-five times in the Chinese forum, as compared to eleven in the U.S. discussions. A scan of posts containing those keywords shows the tendency for Chinese AIDS-phobic participants to list all symptoms perceived as similar to common HIV/AIDS symptoms, sometimes along with photos of results using home testing kits. Those who tested negative often share their entire high-risk behaviors and testing experiences with fellow participants and volunteers, sometimes seeking confirmation that negative results do indeed mean "no HIV infection." Those still waiting to get tested or to learn of test results dwelled a lot on their HIV/AIDS-like symptoms and suffered from panic attacks and self-blame. Because of the rumors of an

unknown virus causing HIV/AIDS-like symptoms in those who test negative in China, many forum participants take a skeptical attitude toward
their testing results and have difficulties overcoming their fears about
HIV/AIDS.

**PREOCCUPATION WITH UNSAFE SEXUAL CONTACT
AND CONDOM USE**

Posts from both forums also discuss sexual behaviors that are often perceived to be high-risk, including both protected and unprotected intercourse and oral sex with sex workers, strangers, and at-risk partners. It is
interesting to observe that the Chinese corpus contains 159 sex-related
terms, while the U.S. corpus has 59 (see Table 3). In addition, the Chinese corpus contains three times as many references to sex workers than
its U.S. counterpart (37 vs. 12). Posters tended to take a pathologized
approach in their discussions about their perceived high-risk sex contact
by focusing on only parts of their intercourse that would make them
vulnerable to HIV/AIDS. Participants from both forums offered great
details about suspicious things that might have suggested a sexual worker
living with HIV/AIDS and worrisome signals that they might have used
condoms in the wrong way or exposed themselves to possible infection.
Compare the first excerpt, from the U.S. forum, with the one from China
that appears below it:

> After a very drunken night I ended up in a brothel in South Africa. I
> vaguely remember having brief oral sex and perhaps vaginal sex (ALL UN-
> PROTECTED). . . . My doctor said my chances of HIV infection were less
> than 1 percent even if there was brief vaginal sex and the lady was HIV+.
>
> I went for a prostitute for the first time in my life. . . . Unfortunately
> there is no way back. . . . My behavior was unprotected oral sex for three
> minutes and protected vaginal sex for five minutes. The condom did
> not fall out and I found some semen in it after taking it off. Did I get
> infected because of the oral part?

Both forums question the role that oral sex plays in transmitting HIV/
AIDS. One U.S. discussant emphatically claimed that he contracted AIDS

TABLE 3. FREQUENCY STATISTICS FOR SEXUAL BEHAVIORS AND CONDOMS

KEYWORD	CHINESE	U.S.
Sexual behaviors	159	59
Intercourse	48	20
Oral sex	28	21
Sex workers	37	12
Condoms	102	23
Sex with condom	19	13
Unprotected sex	28	9

because of excessive unprotected oral sex with homosexual men. He also warned fellow forum participants of the potential danger of contracting HIV/AIDS orally, despite scientific evidence supporting the extremely low risk of such behaviors. Similarly, the volunteer physicians running the Chinese forum insisted that oral sex poses virtually no risk of contracting HIV/AIDS, perhaps because of the existing difficulties they face in alleviating heightened fears among their discussants about the possible risks posed by a single incident of unprotected vaginal or anal sex.

The prevalence and valence of discussions about condoms also differed across the two forums. The Chinese corpus contains far more references to condoms: 102 vs. 23. Twenty-eight of those 102 references discuss unprotected sex as compared with nine mentions in the U.S. posts. Moreover, discussions of condom use in Chinese posts echo lay distrust of scientific claims and focus on the quality of the condom, appropriate ways to use it, and the risks of contracting HIV after oral sex without a condom or after sex with a condom. One post asked: "I wore two condoms before having sex with the sex worker. . . . Will I get infected if she has AIDS?" In contrast, one U.S. discussant complained about the media's preoccupation with social stigmatization of people with HIV/AIDS instead of prevention education. She pointed out that media reports about people contracting HIV from sexual encounters with AIDS patients put too much emphasis on the need for HIV-positive people to reveal their infected status and missed numerous opportunities to educate the public about condom use as effective protection against HIV/AIDS.

FAMILY AND FILIAL PIETY

We also searched for keywords related to family, such as *family, families, parent, mother, father, spouse, wife, husband, partner, child, son,* and *daughter.* We then examined concordances with each keyword to learn how participants talked about such relations regarding their testing and treatment processes. Family-related keywords are used respectively 178 versus 40 times in the Chinese and the U.S. forums. While Chinese participants focused more on family love and their desire to or inability to fulfill their familial responsibilities, the U.S. participants mostly talked factually about their conversations with and visits to and from family members. Similarly, the word *love* is used sixty-eight and twelve times respectively and the keyword *parents* is used thirty-two and five times respectively in the Chinese and the U.S. forum. One Chinese poster wrote about his parents' response after hearing about his high-risk encounter and fear of contracting HIV/AIDS:

> SON: I left home because I may have contracted HIV [and] I don't want to be your burden.
> FATHER: You can talk about anything with us. Why did you run away instead? You will never be our burden because you are our son. If possible, I would die in place of you so that you can live. We will pick you up and take you to the best hospital.

Consider the fact that most Chinese forum participants are young men who are the only son of their parents, and consider that their contraction of HIV/AIDS will often mean their premature death due to the high costs of treatments and medication; this in turn means their deaths will result in their inability to provide any support to their aging parents, thus violating cultural expectations. In fact, among the thirty-two references to parents, twenty-five instances identified contracting HIV/AIDS as being unfilial to parents because of the perceived inability—caused by the disease—to financially and emotionally support aging parents. One commentator wrote: "I got positive testing results. . . . I felt that the sky collapsed on me. What should I do? I am only twenty-four. What can I do with my parents? I feel terribly sorry for them." Another commented, "I urge you all to reject high-risk behaviors. Indeed, you should not take any risks. Treat your parents well. Be faithful to them so that you won't regret when they pass away." Another addressed his parents directly, saying "Mom and Dad, your son is unfilial since he cannot take care of you when you get old." Such sentiments reveal how Chinese forum participants understand their diagnosis as impacting both their parents and their family's multigenerational lineage.

LITERAL AND FIGURATIVE SENSES OF DEATH

Death is another concept that appears frequently in both the Chinese and the U.S. corpora (58 vs. 51 occurrences). HIV/AIDS is often associated with death because it shortens life expectancy and hastens death. Upon close examination, we found that participants in the two fora employ different approaches in their discussions of AIDS and death, and that they associate death with different concepts. Because the Chinese forum attracts mostly AIDS-phobic people who have committed high-risk behaviors, the Chinese corpus tends to approach death as an abstract and metaphorical concept (as we demonstrated above). Within this discourse, two idiomatic terms, "life-or-death trial" and "my life [is] worse than death," appear ten and five times respectively in the Chinese corpus; in these passages, participants describe their emotional distresses, panic, guilt, and despair while waiting for testing results. With most participants being the only son of their parents, and sometimes husbands and fathers, another topic raised nine times in the corpus was the fear of the social stigma and emotional wreckage that a possible death would inflict on their families: "I don't fear death, but I fear that my death will humiliate my parents/family/kids and break their hearts. How can they live on without me?" Posters considered themselves a betrayer of loving family members because of the tremendous shame, humiliation, and discrimination they would bring to their entire family if they tested positive. One participant wrote "I fear death. I do tremendously. But what I fear the most is that dying from AIDS will bring stigma to my parents." Another wondered "how I can die secretly with AIDS to avoid imposing humiliation on my family. I often hope for accidents so that I can die with a good reputation. My kid will not live in the dark shadow caused by my death." Yet another suggested that "If the hospital does not allow me to die without revealing my HIV status, I will save enough sleeping pills so that no one will have the chance to condemn me." These are heart-breaking commentaries, wherein the sense of the posters' social shame associated with an HIV-related cause of death is palpable.

In contrast, the U.S. forum participants focus more on the literal sense of death as the cessation of life, along with intolerable physical and emotional pains and the economic and cultural hardships caused by HIV/AIDS. One participant wondered whether he was "already dying internally" because of excessive weight loss and side effects. Others wrote about repeated job losses as well as difficulties paying medical bills, coping with failing treatments and side effects, and dealing with constant taunting and threats, which drove them so far that they did not see the point of continuing to struggle. One poster said "All my salary has been used to pay for meds, tests, and doctors. My debt keeps growing and I can no longer pay my living expenses. I would rather die than continue this miserable life." Another shared how "I was told that I would die a miserable death and I should end my life now." While these commentators ponder self-harm in response to HIV/AIDS, it is noteworthy that their causes all point back to a sense of an aggrieved self, not to the Chinese sense of having shamed their families.

Some in the U.S. forum suffering from severe depression wrote about possible suicide as a quick solution to end their physical and emotional pains and economic and social pressures. One commentator asked "Why should I keep fighting? If we will all eventually die, would it help to have it come sooner? It would save me so much pain." Another wrote how "I want to give up and to end all this pain. . . . I don't care whether I will go to heaven or hell." Yet another confessed how "All I've been thinking about is committing suicide, as a lot of people on these forums feel." Thus, even while it is important to celebrate groundbreaking developments in medical treatment, these U.S.-based posts indicate how HIV-positive commentators can be flooded with painful, gnawing thoughts of self-harm.

Despite the Chinese and American evidence of how contracting HIV/AIDS can hammer the individual's emotions, leading to thoughts of imminent death and possible self-harm, it would be fair to say that participants in both discussion boards also generally agree that contracting HIV/AIDS is not a death sentence. For instance, one Chinese participant wrote, "Although AIDS does not kill, it brings a fatal psychological blow. I feel that I have been sentenced to death without a date of execution, and all I can do is to wait for the arrival of the god in charge of death." Similarly, a participant in the U.S. forum ruminated: "Now that HIV is medically treatable, our experiences will be more shaped by social factors than medical ones." Here, regardless of the fact that death is delayed, participants know their lives are curtailed and subject to ongoing medical management. In addition to their structural and content differences, the two corpora utilized divergent metaphorical clusters.

Metaphors Used in the U.S. Forum: Living with HIV/AIDS as War and Possible Allies

The war metaphor has been widely studied in different contexts, which may inspire false hopes of the rapid "conquest" of this condition and/or cement paralyzing fears of imminent surrender. We speak of our battle with AIDS and vow to fight it. A war, as Sontag notes, involves an enemy, soldiers on both sides, weapons, and a struggle to win.[29] Also, it suggests an outcome: the idea that the war will end in victory or defeat. On the one hand, the war metaphor promotes fantasies of complete victory; on the other hand, it encourages the equally problematic image of unconditional defeat. In the following examples, people use war metaphors such as "fight" and "battle" to describe their experiences:

> Go out. We will fight against everything and you will have our support. Please smile.
>
> Unfortunately, my fear and paranoia are, for the moment, winning this battle.
>
> I have given up all the things I wanted from life: career, money, love. In addition, I have lots of problems in my recent jobs, medical

coverage, and bankruptcy. . . . Why should I keep fighting if we are all going to die some day and when death would stop all my pains?

All instances of the war metaphor referred to the posters' lonely battles against their enemies including HIV/AIDS, the financial burdens it brings, and its side effects, such as physical pains and depression. Due to advances in medicine, people living with HIV/AIDS can now fight a long battle. For example, Hasina Samji and coauthors reported that an otherwise healthy twenty-year-old who begins antiretroviral therapy (ART) shortly after HIV infection can live into the seventh decade of life by strictly conforming to medical prescriptions.[30] While this is welcome medical news, the financial costs of ART can be staggering, as the CDC estimates $379,668 in lifetime treatment costs (in 2010 dollars) for people living with HIV/AIDS.[31] One long-time survivor wrote about his battle: "I strongly feel as if I am done with my life, mentally feeling like a seventy-five-year-old even though I am only fifty. Is this caused by the constant fight, the struggle to stay alive after losing your job and health at a relatively young age?" Several posters reported suffering from depression because they had experienced great difficulties paying the medical bills and supporting themselves financially despite their hard work.

Several possible supports, such as decent jobs, Medicaid, disability benefits from social security, Medicare, families, and partners, were discussed in the forum, particularly by people living with HIV/AIDS. Moreover, as the landscape of treatments, health insurance plans, and social security changed in the last few decades, the younger generation of people living with HIV/AIDS may have to resort to different coping strategies to respond to such changes, as one poster asked:

Should I plan to resort to disability, which requires lots of work and time, by giving all my savings and equity in the house to my partner so that I can live on disability and get the programs I will need for the rest of my life? Or should I work till I die? I know those of you who have been around for twenty years had to go immediately on disability and get things in order, but what about those who got this in the 2000s?

Another poster described his experience of having to skip treatment for two years when waiting to be qualified for Medicare:

> I have spent the last two years preparing to die. . . . I lost my health care when the meds were failing and the side effects became intolerable. Medicaid was useless with the high deductibles. . . . Being a dad kept me going, and I had this one little glimmer of hope that I could make it to the date when Medicare starts to kick in, which would give me some tolerable health care. I got qualified last week.

While the kinds of concerns quoted above were prominent, most U.S. posters saw the forum as a welcoming and inclusive community that provides emotional support and information guidance in their long battle against HIV/AIDS. For many participants, their online community would be a primary ally for a long time, as explained by one poster, who confessed that "I have no support system other than my treatment team. This forum will provide me with the encouragement and understanding I need until I feel comfortable enough to get family and friends involved." Another long-time survivor discussed the tremendous support he gained from the forum: "As veterans living with the virus, we share experiences, information and points of view here. Those who have lived through the earlier years of the epidemic share amazing perspective and knowledge about everything from meds to politics to coping strategies."

As these examples make clear, the contributors to the U.S. forum are making active efforts to navigate through the increasingly complicated landscape of work, healthcare, social security, and family responsibilities by resorting to the forum as an imagined community of support. While some posters talk about the guilt they experienced for losing stable incomes, inflecting pain and economic burden upon family members and partners, or outliving friends who had contracted HIV/AIDS, most posts deal with navigating the complicated day-to-day struggles of people living with HIV/AIDS. Within this imagined community of support, many commentators observed how the support provided by federal programs, such as Social Security benefits and disability insurance, often serves as a crucial resource for handling some of the financial burdens faced by people living with HIV/AIDS. Their counterparts in China, however,

TABLE 4. THE USE OF METAPHORS IN THE TWO FORUMS

METAPHORS	CHINESE	U.S.
War	0	13
Mistakes	24	4
Punishment	20	0
Fate	13	1
Family betrayal	11	0
Negative test result as rebirth	10	0

did not have access to such national benefits programs and had either to shoulder the economic burden themselves or pass it on to their families and parents. This is not the place for an analysis of the different federal responses to HIV/AIDS in China and the United States, yet our analysis of the online forums demonstrates how the U.S. government's support for people with HIV/AIDS is recognized and appreciated by the posters. This is just one of the many ways individuals grappling with health risks constitute themselves as part of (or apart from) the nation.

Metaphors in the Chinese Forum: Mistakes, Punishment, Fate, Family and Family Death, and Rebirth

A different set of metaphors populated the Chinese forum; we have grouped them into five overarching metaphors: mistakes, punishment, fate, family betrayal and family death, and rebirth. Interestingly, these metaphors mostly deal with different aspects of *kong ai* experienced by the posters, which include condemning oneself for immoral behaviors, infidelity, and lack of filial piety; expecting possible punishment for moral laxity; worrying about betraying one's family, causing financial burdens, and possibly being unable to continue the family line; and seeing HIV/AIDS as a death sentence because of the lack of cure for the disease.

METAPHORS 1 AND 2: MISTAKES AND PUNISHMENT

To make a mistake is to do something that is deemed wrong in a given society. The mistake metaphor assumes that there is a right way of life, that one mistake could cause disaster, and that mistakes might be avoided and corrected. The mistake metaphor therefore suggests guilt and regret as well as the possibility of fixing such mistakes. Confucianism emphasizes that marriage is the appropriate place for sex, which should culminate in childbirth and thus the continuation of the family line.[32] As most posters, single or married men, had intercourse with female commercial sex workers before panicking about possibly contracting HIV/AIDS, they both lamented the mistakes they made and feared they might become infected because of such risk exposure.

> We all have happy families and loving parents. But we may destroy all these because of one single mistake.
>
> I drank some alcohol because of issues at work that day, went to a bath center, and made the fatal mistake without realizing what I was doing.
>
> Why did I have such bad luck and suffer from such fatal punishment after making one single mistake [of having sex with a prostitute once]? Maybe that's my fate.
>
> Please help us [to have a baby], please! After all, it is my fault, not my wife's or my parents'.

The use of punishment-for-mistake metaphors carries two entailments. First, those who tested negative often expressed feeling lucky about their narrow escape from ill fate and often promised—now given a miraculous second chance—to lead a virtuous life. Second, those who tested positive often felt that they had no opportunity to recover from their mistakes and so were forced to confront HIV/AIDS infection as the ultimate punishment. In a study of 209 market workers in an eastern coastal city in China, Lee and colleagues found that half of the participants believed that punishment was an appropriate response to people living with HIV/AIDS, because they believed certain sex behaviors were morally unacceptable.[33] Because of stigmatization, people who become infected because of sexual contact in China often feel culpable and accept their infection as punishment. Meanwhile, the punishment metaphor potentially reproduces the self-blame and self-isolation of people living with HIV/AIDS, since they may feel they deserve the disease and its consequences. In contrast to the innocent people infected through blood transfusion or donation, our data set suggests that the so-called culpable people encounter greater social and cultural impediments when communicating about their illness, even with families and friends. In such a situation, the Internet becomes a primary place where some participants feel safe disclosing possible or actual infection channels. Therefore, it is important here to distinguish the mistake part of the metaphor, which focuses on the carelessness of one's choices, from the punishment metaphor, which emphasizes possible social disapproval, moral condemnation, and discrimination.

Many Chinese homosexuals (*tong zhi*) stress that homosexuality is only one part of their life and note that they are also heterosexually married. The punishment metaphor is widely used by this group because of their failure to conform to men's expected cultural roles, as reflected in the following statement: "As a gay infected with HIV, I cannot give what my parents want (grandchildren and social support) whether I survive it or not." The punishment metaphor here puts more emphasis on the failure to fulfill social and filial responsibility than on their sexual orientation. In this way, metaphors depicting HIV/AIDS as punishment for mistakes also point to a powerful and long-standing social imaginary wherein the Confucian value of rendering honorable duty to family overrides the individual's desires or wishes.

METAPHOR 3: CONTRACTING HIV/AIDS AS FATE

Along with the Confucian sense of duty noted above, online discourse about HIV/AIDS in the China forum also circled back, time and time again, to the notion of fate, another deeply rooted belief in Chinese culture. For many Chinese, fate is a given, not an achievement; fate is what life does to you, regardless of your choices or actions. Historically, the Chinese people often attribute problems to fate, also often referred to as destiny, thus positing an external locus of control to explain events. The fate metaphor indicates that if it is one's destined time to die, then changes in sexual behaviors would not help; if it were not, then one could take risks. Our analysis of the posts demonstrates that as an external locus of control, fate often appears to force the impacted individual into difficult choices. For example, one participant wrote, "I have nothing now. I could just accept the arrangement of my fate. My future plan is to work harder and earn more money and give it to my baby." Fate also connects with supernatural forces and bad luck: "Why did I have such bad luck? I made one mistake and destructive punishment arrived. Perhaps that is my fate." Our CADS analysis identifies two terms closely associated with fate, namely, *Laotian* (lord, eleven times) and *shangtian* (heaven, nine times). These two terms suggest eternal control over an individual's fate, as indicated in one post saying "Please, heaven, forgive this kid who made mistakes and give me another chance so that I can provide for my aging parents." Another poster wrote "I am a sinner and I did wrong to my parents and my wife. I hope the lord will give me another chance to reform."

The fate metaphor therefore mingles a sense of compromised free will with some overarching external control, whether in the form of supernatural forces, political powers, or long-standing social and cultural constraints. The metaphor suggests a fundamental conflict between individual desire and cultural values, suggesting that individuals must submit to external forces and constraints. From the perspective of the United States, where liberalism celebrates the freely acting individual above all else, these metaphors of fate and punishment must feel like synecdochical evidence of a culture where the self is often crushed, but for the Chinese commentators whose posts we studied, these same metaphors pointed to the unchanging power of Confucian values, where family, duty, and honor trump the needs of the individual. In fact, these traditional cultural values are so powerful in China that, as we show below, commentators who contracted HIV/AIDS were often ashamed of having betrayed their families.

METAPHOR 4: IMAGINING HIV/AIDS AS FAMILY BETRAYAL

Another commonly used metaphor views HIV/AIDS as family death because of the inability of those living with HIV/AIDS to fulfill their filial duty to procreate, to pass on the family line, and to take care of their elderly parents or their nuclear families. Even in rip-roaring postmodern China, the world's fastest growing economy, the traditional value of family-kinship systems exerts great pressure upon both young women and men to marry, reproduce, and carry on the family line. As one of the most influential Chinese philosophers, Mencius, said, "There are three ways of being unfilial. The worst is to have no heir."[34] Chenyang Li suspects that this belief appears incomprehensible to many Westerners, due to the fundamental difference between Confucianism and Christianity.[35] He explains: "In Confucianism there is no Heaven to ensure an eternal life as is the case in Christianity. The Confucians have to look elsewhere for the meaning of life, and to satisfy the almost universal desire for immortality. The place to find it, for the Confucians, is human-relatedness, which has many dimensions. One primary dimension involves continuing the family line."[36] From this traditional, Confucian perspective, the inability to produce an heir means the death of the whole family. Here are two more examples of this theme:

> Children, my wife cries because of children. I can't have any child. But what can I do about it? Heaven, why do you punish my family when it is me who did something wrong? Why can't they have any child/grandchild? Why wouldn't any hospital help my wife to get pregnant using donors' sperm?
>
> My wife is three months pregnant. I feel so much pain about my one-night stand with a sex worker. What terrible wrong did I do to my parents, my wife, and my unborn baby?

As the first commenter intimated, people with HIV/AIDS are often denied medical surgery in rural areas of China. Safe birth thus becomes impossible for many families living with HIV/AIDS. This stigmatization may be part of the reason why the poster cited above could not find any hospitals that would help his wife conceive with donated sperm. This inability to fulfill one's family responsibility further complicates the meaning of death for people living with HIV in China; now not only health patients in their own right, these HIV-positive Chinese are also seen as metaphorically killing their families.

In addition to family death, HIV/AIDS is also connected with an inability to take care of one's elderly parents, suggesting another layer of family betrayal. Confucian values place great emphasis on fidelity and on respecting and caring for parents, and the one-child policy exacerbated the pressures on lone children to financially and emotionally support their aging parents. This pressure is illustrated by a frequently repeated claim that "my biggest wish now is to take care of my parents [until they die]." Many participants described the pain and guilt they felt after being tested positive:

> My heart breaks into tears whenever I see my father's back and my mother's exhausted face. I cry by myself every night, not because of my fear of death, but because of my fear of breaking my parents' hearts and leaving them behind. I know I erred terribly and too many times.
>
> Mother and father, please forgive your unfilial son who will not be able to take care of you in your old age.
>
> Death is not the worst. What's the worst is to die slowly in suffering. We all have happy families and loving parents, but we may betray all these because of one mistake.

Our concordance analysis confirms the presence of this metaphor by identifying a recurrent theme reflecting guilt intermixed with family concern, which is reflected in the repeated use (thirteen instances) of apologies (*dui bu qi, dui bu zhu*). Posters apologized to their parents, partners, spouses, or children for letting them down by committing high-risk behaviors, as reflected in the following passage: "I panicked for six months and found myself HIV positive. I have a newborn baby. I did terrible wrong to them, to my family!" Here, HIV/AIDS is not experienced as a condition affecting an individual, but as a burden to an entire set of interested familial relations. Indeed, our analysis of instances discussing family members reveals that though parents, partners, and spouses were reported to be devastated when hearing the testing results, they all turned out to be extremely supportive emotionally and financially and tried their best to help the posters to continue living with HIV/AIDS. This latter evidence is crucial, for it suggests a schism between how the online commentators anticipated being treated and how they were actually treated by their family and friends. Locating this schism suggests that the social imaginary in China may be shifting as regards how families respond to HIV/AIDS.

METAPHOR 5: IMAGINING NEGATIVE HIV/AIDS TEST RESULTS AS REBIRTH

Closely related to the death-as-penalty theme, rebirth is another commonly used metaphor in the forum. The rebirth metaphor refers to the ability to learn from one's past mistakes in order to better regulate and discipline oneself, or in the words of the official discourse, to "preserve moral integrity" by avoiding risky sexual behaviors.[37] Because people can unknowingly contract AIDS from high-risk encounters, "the precautions take on a life of their own [and] become part of social mores, not a practice adopted for a brief period of emergency, then discarded."[38] As a result, the posters vowed to reform and refrain from committing the high-risk behaviors that had brought them tremendous anxiety and pain. Many forum participants employed this rebirth metaphor when waiting for or writing about their negative testing results: "After this near-death experience, we will better cherish our new life, our families. Sex workers serve as the catalyst for our long-lasting pain and death. So brother, reject high-risk behaviors, act responsibly for ourselves and for our families." Closely related is the theme of rethinking one's life choices during the waiting period: "For those still waiting for the testing results, please think hard about the value of your life during this challenging period. I wish you all a pass on the test and a successful sail through dangerous waters." These examples demonstrate how promises of self-change and celebrations of rebirth can feel like classic conversion narratives, wherein some near-death or life-changing crisis prods the individual toward radical transformation.

Arthur Frank discusses three modes of rhetoric about these self-change narratives. He identified phrases of "who I always have been," "who I might become," and "reluctant phoenix without a turning point" to delineate how and to what extent people re-create identities through writing.[39] Frank explains, "The means to change your life may be rhetorical technologies of the self, but these technologies are as much resources enabling change as they are restrictions on change."[40] Chinese posts seem to suggest the existence of a dominant answer to the question of "who I might become": by cherishing life and refusing to engage in future high-risk behaviors, the reborn individual can return to honoring his family. This rebirth narrative conforms to Confucian-infused socio-cultural values, wherein honoring family responsibilities is a paramount concern.

Conclusion: Kong ai *and the Social Imaginary of Being Chinese*

The similarities and differences across the two forums reveal the imprints that the traditional Confucian values of filial honor and morality have on high-risk and AIDS-phobic individuals in China. Indeed, the metaphor clusters of contracting HIV/AIDS as punishment for immoral mistakes, fate, and family betrayal and death suggest a fuller *kong ai* narrative that many posters employed to make sense of their experiences: Their mistake of engaging in high-risk sex will bring HIV/AIDS as the punishment—for self and family—for their moral laxity. Whether it is part of their destiny or not, they betrayed their families because of their infidelity and their unfilial relation to their parents, which inevitably results in the demise of the family line. These metaphoric clusters clearly evidence the emotional turmoil and ambivalence that posters experienced when inflicting moral judgment on themselves. More importantly, these metaphors revealed posters' collective attempts to try to fit HIV/AIDS identities into the social imaginary of being Chinese, as defined by the long-standing Confucian values of filial duty to their parents, spouses, and children. In summary, the Chinese online commentators would seem to indicate how the *kong ai* narrative reveals the ongoing power of Confucian values in contemporary China.

The rebirth metaphor offers an interesting twist on the *kong ai* narrative by offering moral behaviors and conformation to sex norms as the only strategies for escaping the constant threat of HIV/AIDS infection. In fact, from the "loving capitalism disease" to the disease of deviance and infidelity, the discourse of HIV/AIDS in China has always placed its ethical burden on the individual instead of the public health efforts of the nation. Fueled by traditional Chinese cultural values, individuals often used fate as an external locus for rationalizing and internalizing the consequences of HIV/AIDS infection; this focus on prearranged fate further diminishes the roles played by prevention and treatment efforts. Indeed, it would seem that the constellation of metaphors and narratives addressed here has the clear cumulative effect of granting the CPC a free pass on the HIV/AIDS epidemic in China. This may reflect communication structures in China more broadly, where criticizing the Party is dangerous, or it may reflect the fact that, at least for these commentators, their fate transcends the Party, pointing instead to the older, deeper, more traditional Confucian norms we have discussed above.

The U.S. forum did not share this intense concern with family responsibility and moral criticism. Rather, U.S. forum participants seemed more preoccupied with issues related to testing, treatments, depression, job losses, insurance coverage, welfare programs, and, in rare instances, overt threats and stigmatization. That is, U.S. posters focused more on the daily management of HIV/AIDS as a medical condition. One reason contributing to this difference may be the large number of participants actually living with AIDS, suggesting that people who have gone through the emotionally turbulent period of testing and accepting their HIV-positive status are likely more-informed posters. Another reason might be relatively less stigma about high-risk sexual behaviors and the coding of sexuality as a private decision in the United States compared to China.

The presence—or absence—of medical experts in the forums certainly influenced how participants view themselves and communicate about their behaviors. Even though the three physician moderators in the Chinese forum tried to adopt a supportive and understanding approach in their consultation and counseling, their very presence in the forum as altruist volunteers suggests a moral hierarchy. Forum participants all demonstrate great respect for and submission to their altruism and authority. In contrast, the U.S. forum consists of people living with AIDS and people wondering whether they have contracted AIDS, without a regulating presence. Participants adopted a more matter-of-fact approach toward their situations. They were less apologetic and more focused on coping with the disease on a daily basis.

Two things may have contributed to the relative absence of people living with HIV/AIDS in the Chinese discussion forum. First, AIDS phobia is still prevalent in China, and in some posts the medical experts openly urged those claiming to be tested positive not to reveal any personal information online to avoid negative consequences, such as privacy intrusion, job loss, and social avoidance. Indeed, one poster explained why he stopped responding to comments on his post describing how he and his family had coped with HIV/AIDS by citing fear of discrimination. Second, people living with HIV/AIDS often choose to use more private technologies such as social networking tools to form smaller online and offline communities for mutual support. The same poster mentioned above resorted to a small local community of AIDS patients that he came across in Tencent QQ, a popular instant messaging application developed in China, which supports anonymous group and voice chat, and started building a local support network with offline gatherings. While Facebook and Twitter remain two of the most popular social networking tools in the United States, Chinese users rely on Tencent QQ and its mobile social networking tool, WeChat, which offers options to form more selective and not openly searchable groups based on personal interests and preferences. We do not have the space here to pursue the implications of these patterns, but it would be fascinating, in future research, to wonder whether the proliferation of these private networking sites, by not contributing to more open and public sites, have the unintended consequence of impoverishing the rhetorical work of imagining future health communities in China.

Admittedly, our comparative study of the two discussion forums produces only limited understanding about HIV/AIDS illness discourses in the United States and in China. Both forums have more men than women, and most participants in the Chinese forum were young, heterosexual men. Absent from the picture are sex workers, IDUs, and patients infected by blood transfusion. These groups of people may not need to discuss their HIV/AIDS concerns online with unknown others because members of each group face unique transmission risks and have close-knit offline communities for informational and emotional support. Another factor may be differing access to the online environment. For instance, the majority of patients infected through blood transfusion during the 1990s in China are clustered in poor rural villages. Their information sources and communications are mostly constrained in offline face-to-face encounters with village members and health workers. Ideally, an expanded study can use both forum analysis and other qualitative methods such as case studies and ethnographies to gain access to different populations and to further explore their HIV/AIDS discourses. We expect that other groups' HIV/AIDS discourses would still reveal the strong cultural beliefs in family fidelity, social death, fate, and rebirth.

Our analysis thus shows how illness experiences are shaped by personal, social, familial, and cultural overtones as citizens negotiate the meanings of stigmatized conditions via online discussions. The two online forums studied in this chapter provide insights in understanding how Chinese and American citizens construct their HIV/AIDS communities and employ unique cultural references in their discourses. Our data suggests that China and the United States are indeed experiencing different responses to the HIV/AIDS epidemic. As both nations continue to grapple with the epidemic, their citizens will no doubt continue to evolve in their everyday, online social meaning-making about the risk of HIV/AIDS. As these responses evolve, so too will our collective imaginings of how bodies entwine with nations; in this way, the HIV/AIDS epidemic, and deeply personal, embodied responses to it, will continue to exert a powerful pull on varied senses of "corporeal nationalism."[41]

NOTES

This chapter is based on Jingwen Zhang's MA thesis, conducted under the direction of Huiling Ding at Clemson University; see Jingwen Zhang, "The Rhetorics of Constructing HIV/AIDS in the United States and China: A Comparative Analysis of Two Online Discussion Forums" (Clemson University, 2011).

1. "Nanjing, AIDS Patient Escaped from the Hospital? Do Not Panic," *Xian Dai Kuai Bao*, August 28, 2015.
2. Jill McGivering, "AIDS Takes Deadly Toll in China," *BBC News*, February 18, 2009.
3. Xinhua, "President Xi Stresses Fight Against HIV/AIDS," *China Daily*, November 30, 2013.

4. Richard Knox, "Obama Launches HIV Cure Initiative, Ups Pledge for Global Health," National Public Radio, December 2, 2013, http://www.npr.org.

5. Steven Epstein, *Impure Science: AIDS, Activism, and the Politics of Knowledge* (Berkeley: University of California Press, 1996).

6. Paula Treichler, *How to Have Theory in an Epidemic: Cultural Chronicles of AIDS* (Durham, NC: Duke University Press, 1999), 11.

7. Annemarie Mol calls for a "praxeology of disease" wherein scholars view disease in terms of ontology. In her example, there is not one disease called *atherosclerosis*, but multiple *atheroscleroses*, defined by different communities of practice. In this way, we can say there are different HIV/AIDS epidemics. See Annemarie Mol, *The Body Multiple: Ontology in Medical Practice* (Durham, NC: Duke University Press, 2002).

8. Susan Sontag, *Illness as Metaphor and AIDS and Its Metaphors* (New York: Farrar, Straus, Giroux, 1989); Gilbert H. Herdt and Shirley Lindenbaum, *The Time of AIDS: Social Analysis, Theory, and Method* (Newbury Park: Sage Publications, 1992); Michael Polgar, "Social Construction of HIV/AIDS: Theory and Policy Implications," *Health Sociology Review* 6 (1996): 81–111.

9. Min Wu, "Framing AIDS in China: A Comparative Analysis of US and Chinese Wire News Coverage of HIV/AIDS in China," *Asian Journal of Communication* 16 (2006): 251–72; Jinhua Guo, "Stigma: Social Suffering for Social Exclusion and Social Insecurity, from the Ethnography of Mental Illness to the Ethnography of HIV/AIDS in China" (PhD diss., Harvard University, 2008); Yanqiu Zhou, "'If You Get AIDS . . . You Have to Endure It Alone': Understanding the Social Constructions of HIV/AIDS in China," *Social Science & Medicine* 65 (2007): 284–95.

10. Cf. Lisa Keränen, Kirsten Lindholm, and Jared Woolly, "Imagining the People's Risk: Projecting National Strength in China's English-Language News about Avian Influenza," this volume, who ask similar questions about the constitutive discourse surrounding "bird flu" narratives in Hong Kong and China; their analysis relies on formal, Party-controlled outlets, thus providing insight into the Party's thinking on these issues.

11. See also Donovan Conley, "China's Fraught Food System: Imagining Ecological Civilization in the Face of Paradoxical Modernity," and Zhuo Ban, "Her Milk Is Inferior: Breastfeeding, Risk, and Imagining Maternal Identities in Chinese Cyberspace," this volume.

12. See Leslie J. Hinyard and Matthew W. Kreuter, "Using Narrative Communication

as a Tool for Health Behavior Change: A Conceptual, Theoretical, and Empirical Overview," *Health Education & Behavior* 34 (2006): 777–92; Sally Dunlop, Melanie Wakefield, and Yoshi Kashima, "Can You Feel It? Negative Emotion, Risk, and Narrative in Health Communication," *Media Psychology* 11 (2008): 52–75.

13. Arjun Appadurai, *Modernity at Large: Cultural Dimensions of Globalization* (Minneapolis: University of Minnesota Press, 1996), 12–13.

14. Judy Z. Segal, "Internet Health and the 21st-Century Patient, a Rhetorical View," *Written Communication* 26 (2009): 351.

15. Benedict Anderson, *Imagined Communities: Reflections on the Origin and Spread of Nationalism* (London: Verso, 1983).

16. Ibid., 4, 6.

17. Emily Grabham, "'Flagging' the Skin: Corporeal Nationalism and the Properties of Belonging," *Body & Society* 15 (2009): 63–82, 64.

18. M. Thomas P. Gilbert et al., "The Emergence of HIV/AIDS in the Americas and Beyond," *Proceedings of the National Academy of Science of the United States of America* 104 (2007): 18566–70.

19. See Lawrence K. Altman, "Rare Cancer Seen in 41 Homosexuals," *New York Times*, July 3, 1981; Lawrence K. Altman, "New Homosexual Disorder Worries Officials," *New York Times*, May 11, 1982.

20. Sander L. Gilman, *Disease and Representation: Images of Illnesses from Madness to AIDS* (Ithaca, NY: Cornell University Press, 1988).

21. Centers for Disease Control and Prevention (CDC), "Monitoring Selected National HIV Prevention and Care Objectives by Using HIV Surveillance Data—United States and 6 U.S. Dependent Areas—2010," *HIV Surveillance Supplemental Report*, 17, no. 3, part A, http://www.cdc.gov; CDC, "Estimated HIV Incidence in the United States, 2007–2010," *HIV Surveillance Supplemental Report*, 17, no. 4, http://www.cdc.gov.

22. Y. Zeng, "Serological Screening of HIV Antibody in China" [in Chinese], *Zhonghua Liu Xing Bing Xue Za Zhi* 9 (1998): 138–40.

23. Bureau of Hygiene & Tropical Diseases, *AIDS Newsletter*, News item 213, 1990. Copy on file with first author. Please note that Pinyin is being used throughout this chapter, because this book is printed in English, where the characters may not render accurately.

24. Y. Ma et al., "HIV Was First Discovered among IDUs in China" [in Chinese], *Chinese Journal of Epidemiology* 11 (1990): 184–85.

25. Ministry of Health of the People's Republic of China, 2012 *China AIDS Response Progress Report*, March 31, 2012, http://www.unaids.org.

26. Judith Landau-Stanton and Colleen D. Clements draw from Hans Jager to state that "AIDS phobia is most clearly defined as a wholly unfounded fear of becoming infected with HIV despite repeatedly negative HIV test results," in *AIDS, Health, and Mental Health: A Primary Sourcebook*, vol. 1 (New York: Brunner/Mazel, 1993), 91. Also see Hans Jager, ed., *AIDS Phobia: Disease Pattern and Possibilities of Treatment* (New York: John Wiley and Sons, 1988). As Jingwen Zhang wrote in her MA thesis, "AIDS phobia is also associated with deep-seated fears of human sexuality, death and/or stigma," in Zhang, "The Rhetorics of Constructing HIV/ AIDS in the United States and China, 30. See also Robert T. Begg, "Legal Ethics and AIDS: An Analysis of Selected Issues," *Georgetown Journal of Legal Ethics* 3 (1988): 1–56.

27. Elaine Showalter, *Hystories: Hysterical Epidemics and Modern Media* (New York: Columbia University Press, 1997); Wenfang Li and Juan Shan, "Studies Solve Mystery of 'HIV-Negative AIDS,'" *China Daily*, May 7, 2011; "'Negative AIDS' Just a Phobia: Ministry," *Global Times*, April 6, 2011.

28. Alan Partington, Alison Duguid, and Charlotte Taylor, *Patterns and Meanings in Discourse: Theory and Practice in Corpus-Assisted Discourse Studies (CADS)* (Philadelphia: John Benjamins Publishing, 2013).

29. Sontag, *Illness as Metaphor*.

30. Hasina Samji et al., "Closing the Gap: Increases in Life Expectancy among Treated HIV-positive Individuals in the United States and Canada," *PLoS ONE* 8 (2013): e81355.

31. Bruce R. Schackman et al., "The Lifetime Cost of Current Human Immunodeficiency Virus Care in the United States," *Medical Care* 44 (2006): 990–97.

32. Ersheng Gao et al., "How Does Traditional Confucian Culture Influence Adolescents' Sexual Behavior in Three Asian Cities?," Journal of Adolescent Health 50 (2012): S12–S17.

33. Matha B. Lee et al., "HIV-Related Stigma among Market Workers in China," *Health Psychology* 24 (2005): 435.

34. Daniel K. Gardner, *Confucianism: A Very Short Introduction* (New York: Oxford University Press, 2014), 101.

35. Chenyang Li, "Shifting Perspectives: Filial Morality Revisited," *Philosophy East & West* 47 (1997): 211–22.

36. Ibid., 220.

37. See Rodney H. Jones, "Mediated Action and Sexual Risk: Searching for 'Culture' in Discourses of Homosexuality and AIDS Prevention in China," *Culture, Health & Sexuality* 2 (1999): 161–80; Jingwen Zhang and Huiling Ding, "Constructing HIV/AIDS on the Internet: A Comparative Rhetorical Analysis of Online Narratives in the United States and in China," *International Journal of Communication* 8 (2014): 1415–36.

38. Sontag, *Illness as Metaphor*, 162.

39. Arthur W. Frank, "The Rhetoric of Self-Change: Illness Experience as Narrative," *Sociological Quarterly* 34 (1993): 39–52.

40. Ibid., 39.

41. Grabham, "'Flagging' the Skin."

Imagining the People's Risk: Projecting National Strength in China's English-Language News about Avian Influenza

Lisa B. Keränen, Kirsten N. Lindholm, and Jared Woolly

In the spring of 2013, a World Health Organization (WHO) official's pronouncement that the outbreak of avian influenza A (H7N9) in China represented "one of the most lethal influenza viruses that we have seen so far" spread through global networks faster than the virus itself.[1] As the Chinese government hastened to identify and contain the pathogen, international headlines highlighted the challenges posed not only by the emergence of the disease threat, but also by China's record-breaking "airpocalypse," when pollution had peaked at alarming levels just months before the outbreak.[2] "On Scale of 0 to 500, Beijing's Air Quality Tops 'Crazy Bad' at 755," wrote Edward Wong in the *New York Times*.[3] Meanwhile, the unexplained presence of more than sixteen thousand bloated pig carcasses floating in the Huangpu River, the drinking water source for Shanghai's twenty-two million souls, raised international speculation about the possible environmental-germ connections.[4] "China's mysterious pig, duck and people deaths could be connected," opined the Pulitzer Prize–winning health journalist Laurie Garrett in *Foreign Policy*.[5] And thus, the specter of "bird flu," flanked by noxious smog and buoyant porcine hulls, refocused global attention on the growing health risks posed by China's rapid industrial and urban development.[6]

The 2013 avian influenza outbreak provides a useful entrée into the media-saturated landscape that sociologists call the "world risk society," signaling an era when manufactured local or regional risks to bodies, the body politic, and the environment are experienced, configured, and understood on a mediated, global scale.[7] We position the outbreak as an opportunity to examine discourses concerning germs and national identity during a time of global interconnection and change. Following scholars of epidemic discourses, we begin with the presumption that outbreaks—whether real, threatened, and/or imagined—are occasions in which national identities are constituted, invoked, reworked, and mediated with symbolic and material consequences.[8] As Ann Robertson explains, the ways "we conceptualize and speak and write about health are never just about health," but rather serve as "repositories and mirrors of our ideas and beliefs about human nature and the nature of reality."[9] These health-based narratives tell us "about the kind of society we can imagine creating."[10] Analysis of how official discourses about outbreaks envision China—its government and character—can shed insight into the nation-state as an imagined community constituted in response to perceived threats. If one of the greatest global perils beyond climate change and pollution is an infectious, mutating virus, then paying atten- tion to how Communist Party of China (CPC or the Party)–run media outlets in China portray the nation in relation to germs offers compelling insight into how the state is imagined in the face of perceived threats to health and safety.[11]

Although scholars of rhetoric have historically privileged analysis of the public discourses of predominately Western orators, genres, move- ments, artifacts, and occasions, the challenges of the twenty-first century require renewed attention to broader transnational discourses about germs, identity, and belonging.[12] Accordingly, this essay takes up the focus on "contamination, national identity, and Otherness" that first author Lisa Keränen called for in a 2012 *Quarterly Journal of Speech* essay, wherein she urged investigation of the "artifacts, texts, discursive formations, visual representations, and material practices positioned at the nexus of disease and culture."[3] This chapter examines how notions of nation, health, and the body intermingle in the face of external health risks. As all the chapters in this section contend, the rhetorical work of imagining communities is always embodied, with the health of individuals serving as synecdochal proxies for the health of the nation.

In order to understand how China's government constructed notions of nationhood in its mediated public responses to the 2013 avian flu outbreak, we pose two primary questions. First, how were the risks associated with the 2013 outbreak framed in official, state-sanctioned English-language news sources? That is, how were state-sponsored news outlets framing the outbreak for the rest of the world and for China's English-speaking residents? Second, how were concepts of the local, national, and global presented in China's state-sanctioned English-language risk discourses concerning avian flu? In other words, what visions of nationhood and citizenry were mobilized? In short, we focus on how the Party used the avian influenza outbreak of 2013 to marshal a particular imagined community—in this case, a nation of strength and competence bravely fighting against contagion.

Because mass-mediated news is a commonly employed messaging tool of the CPC, we focused on official discourse in three primary sources of English-language news: *China Daily*, *People's Daily*, and the *South China Morning Post*. Whereas the multilingual *People's Daily* tends to function as the mouthpiece of the government and reflects what Guoguang Wu has termed a "command control" communication pattern, in which government messages are rehearsed for the citizenry, *China Daily* seeks a global audience, publishing both online and in print in forms that mimic Western papers in order to reach visitors, expatriates, and English-speaking Chinese citizens.[14] Despite its less obviously progovernment public relations stance, *China Daily*'s news, like most news in China, is nonetheless heavily censored and bears a pro-Party, pro-Beijing bias.[15] In order to provide a point of comparison, we also examine the major English-language paper in Hong Kong, the *South China Morning Post*, which boasts a circulation above one hundred thousand.[16] Although Hong Kong currently enjoys more (albeit diminishing) press freedom than mainland China, the more than one-hundred-year-old *Post*, which is not technically a state-supported paper, was at the time of the 2013 flu outbreak run by a family with Beijing ties. The *South China Morning Post* has also been criticized for its increasingly Beijing, pro-Party slant.[17] Nonetheless, because the *South China Morning Post* retains a fading semblance of being a Chinese free press paper, it presents a significant countervailing set of news frames for our inductive, thematic analysis.[18]

Given widespread criticism of the Chinese government's handling of the SARS epidemic, and in light of worldwide initiatives to involve the citizenry in planning for public health emergencies, China's reports concerning the 2013 avian influenza outbreak furnish an intriguing case for analysis. Operating in a historically collectivist, communist society, the Party has generally issued risk messages via top-down, command-and-control efforts, requiring citizen participation in mandated quarantine and vaccination programs. Many commentators have observed the Chinese government's stunning capacity to accomplish its goals while forcing citizen compliance with its directives, and yet the SARS outbreak painfully revealed the costs of the Party's secrecy, hierarchy, and control.[19] Analysis of the mediated official and public framings of the outbreak reveals the roles that Chinese leaders envision the government can assume in the face of threats to public health and the ways that national identity can be enfolded into the goals of security and public health governance.[20] Therefore, tracking how the CPC framed the H7N9 outbreak in its official English-language media can illuminate how China's government wishes the world to perceive both its post-SARS response to emerging viruses and how it views future health planning and response. More broadly, understanding how the CPC portrayed the outbreak—including its own responses to the outbreak—to global audiences offers clues about potential places of rhetorical invention for citizens, officials, and risk planners alike.

In order to deepen our understanding of how the Party reimagined and reconfigured China in the face of a germ threat and against a backdrop of intensifying global interdependence, our chapter begins by outlining how the concepts of *global risk society* and *imagined community* offer frameworks for analyzing the official discourses of the 2013 avian flu outbreak. We then offer a comparative analysis of initial thematic framings of China's English-language coverage of the outbreak before discussing the implications of these cases for understanding how Chinese discourses envision the relationship between risks, the people, and national identity. Ultimately, we show that English-language news risk communication in mainland China in the earliest weeks of the influenza outbreak tended to adopt a public relations frame that praised the government's strong national response, emphasized national identity, and personalized citizen responses to the outbreak.[21] Hong Kong's dominant English-language content, by contrast, revealed anxiety about the mainland's government, with editorial content focusing on the threats posed by mainland practices. Despite this divergence, however, *China Daily* coverage shows the potential for China's newspapers to be critical of the government's past health responses in ways that encourage more transparent future governance about health risks. By investigating the interlinked imaginaries of self and other, nation and inter-nation, and threat and security as they pertain to borders and bodies, pathogens and the circulation of risk, we excavate "the 'co-evolving relations'" among imagined communities, risk, health, security, media, citizens, and states.[22]

Manufacturing and Mediating Risk in China and Beyond

A growing number of social critics, led by German sociologists Anthony Giddens and Ulrich Beck, have observed the crisis-oriented nature of what they term the contemporary "global risk society."[23] In *World at Risk*, Beck observes that "incalculable risks and manufactured uncertainties resulting from the triumphs of modernity mark the *conditio humana* at the beginning of the twenty-first century."[24] Similarly, Giddens explains that it is "a society increasingly preoccupied with the future (and also with safety), which generates the notion of risk."[25] As these statements illustrate, both Giddens and Beck have argued that modern societies are increasingly structured toward anticipating future risks that are brought about by what Beck terms *second modernity*, a time of high technological and economic interdependence that generates unprecedented scientific and technological wonders that produce unintended and often harmful consequences. As Beck clarifies, "modern society has become a risk society in the sense that it is increasingly occupied with debating, preventing and managing risks that it itself has produced."[26]

By way of illustration, consider the classic example of nuclear power, a triumph of modernity that solves energy problems yet exposes humanity to radiation leaks, fearsome weapons, "normal accidents," and the tragic dilemma of long-term radioactive waste storage, which has created centuries of hazards for human and environmental health.[27] Similar to nuclear power, both avian influenza and pollution result from ameliorative human interventions intended, in the first case, to increase food supply by keeping high volumes of poultry confined in crowded conditions and, in the second, to raise living standards and promote economic development through heavy industry and manufacturing.[28] In both cases, the norm of ever greater productivity generates greater risk. And because pollution and germs spread beyond national borders, such local risks can quickly become causes of international concern. If we think in terms of Conley's notion of "paradoxical modernity," wherein progress and destruction are entwined, then risk become the inevitable consequence of rapid economic development—risk thus becomes a key form of how we imagine our relationships to modernity, national development, and globalization.[29]

It makes sense, then, that given the People's Republic of China's (PRC) breakneck development, scholars have begun to conceive of China in terms of the risk society thesis, even though China lacks some of the civil sphere characteristics associated with Western risk societies.[30] While early risk society research from the 1980s and 1990s featured Western nations that had reached second modernity, scholars have cited China's rapid and compressed industrial and technological growth as a catalyst for the byproducts of second modernity.[31] Although China remains underdeveloped in many of its rural areas, the PRC's rapid urbanization has spurred incalculable risks.[32] As a result of these intertwined developments, the well-being of China's 1.35 billion citizens is under assault: the air in major Chinese cities teems with pollutants, the water is often too contaminated to drink, the average life span is declining, and more children head to hospitals with breathing disorders than in any other nation in the world.[33] Thus, China's push to modernize at once benefits the millions it has lifted out of poverty even as it creates costly environmental, animal, and human health burdens for millions more.

Because risks are framed within a global media environment, Beck and Levy maintain we must appreciate the "apprehension of global risks as the anticipation of (local) risks."[34] They explain:

> Unlike earlier manifestations of risk characterized by daring actions or predictability models, global risks cannot be calculated or predicted anymore. Consequently, more influence accrues to the perception of risk, largely constructed through media representations of disasters. Disasters conventionally signify interruptions. In contrast, in the context of an increasingly interconnected world, they have become limiting cases, challenging the taken-for-granted spatial assumptions of nationhood and its attendant methodological nationalism.[35]

This relation between the global and the local means that "cosmopolitan nations are reimagined through the anticipation of endangered futures."[36] What Beck calls a *catastrophe*—the actualization of the event feared by risk planners—we examine in the form of an outbreak of emerging infectious disease; the result is an occasion wherein Anderson's notion of *imagined community* and Beck's notion of *global risk society* come crashing together.[37]

The Bird Flu and Imagining Infected Others

Against the backdrop of increasingly suffocating pollution, in March 2013, the Chinese government began addressing what became known colloquially as "the bird flu." Official concerns about an outbreak had started in mid-February, when doctors first alerted China's National Ministry of Health (MOH) that two citizens had died from unexplained pneumonia in Shanghai.[38] It would take several weeks to determine that the pair had perished from a new form of influenza, an interval that led some observers to later criticize the government's delayed information sharing.[39] On March 31, China's MOH alerted the WHO of three confirmed cases of H7N9; Xinhua and *China Daily* ran brief notices that "2 Chinese Die From H7N9 Bird Flu." International news outlets soon picked up the story.[40] Early Chinese news reports provided situation updates that increasingly turned to speculation about economic impacts as the weeks passed. By late April, WHO leaders had acknowledged a "dramatic slowdown" in human cases of H7N9 following the closure of Shanghai's wet markets.[41] At that time, China's National Health and Family Planning Commission had documented a total of 109 cases, which produced twenty-three deaths in mainland China.[42] Although additional cases were confirmed through June, infections tapered down seasonally, only to reappear in the fall and spring of subsequent years, so far without evidence of human-to-human infection.[43]

Although avian influenza had been isolated in birds more than a hundred years earlier, the virus did not receive much press until journalists began to report large-scale animal deaths from the flu in the 1980s. Mika Aaltola reviewed the *New York Times* and the Finnish *Helsingin Sanomat* coverage of avian flu from 1983 to 2005 and found that early *Times* coverage, which preceded the first avian flu pandemic scare, focused on outlining containment and quarantine practices in case of a predicted future outbreak.[44] Such early avian flu coverage did not feature concerns about trans-species crossing into human populations. But in the 1990s, newspaper reportage evolved in tandem with the virus itself. Whereas coverage previously focused on potential mutation, 1990s-era news stories raised the possibility of human pandemic, thus transforming avian influenza into a global issue with China configured as a primary driver of health risk. Aaltola describes the framing of one pivotal 1997 *New York Times* article that crystallized this association: "China was turned into a new danger because of its teeming cities and different ideological system, and its veil of secrecy could be seen as being conducive for the emergence of pandemic threats. The story claimed that the disease jumped from animals to humans for the first time in China."[45] China was thus portrayed as a breeding ground of health risks; its health responses were cast as negatively influenced by government information control in a configuration that Aaltola associated with "much older orientalist images of China."[46] Notions of secrecy and lack of transparency cued readers to concerns about the Chinese government's containment of information, which were later demonstrated when the CPC withheld information during SARS. Note, too, that this framing of China-as-contagion predated the 2003 SARS outbreak, which would once again configure China as ground zero for information secrecy, outright denials, misinformation, and hence, disease spread.

While Western papers imagined China as a contagious threat, Chinese newspapers presented a different avian influenza framing altogether. Claire Hefferen, Federica Misturelli, and Kim Thompson's study of 160 articles about avian influenza in four Chinese newspapers from 2001 to 2008 found that headlines minimized the risk of the disease through "the depiction of a strong and efficient 'China' that was a leader in the fight against the disease."[47] Like Aaltola, Hefferen and her coauthors found that questions about human transmission increased in more recent years, specifically from 2006–7 onward. Pertinent to the present study is that other authors have found stark framing differences between Western coverage and Hong Kong's coverage. An empirical study by Timothy Fung and coauthors, for instance, found that the *New York Times*'s coverage of avian flu between 2003 and 2007 included more content associated with "dreadfulness, catastrophic potential, uncertainty, and unfamiliarity" than in Hong Kong's *South China Morning Post*.[48] In contrast to Fung's findings, our analysis suggests that the most recent H7N9 bird flu coverage in the *South China Morning Post* promoted its own brand of dread: fear of mutation and the mainland government's methods, as well as anxiety about the mainland as a vector of disease.

Risky Coverage: Real Time Flu Updates in the Shadow of SARS

The day after China's MOH alerted the WHO about its confirmation that two citizens had died of avian influenza, when international headlines were buzzing with the story, *China Daily* offered informational updates, while *People's Daily* remained circumspect about the outbreak.[49] Hong Kong's *South China Morning Post* featured a brief article about economic concerns in the wake of the H7N9 news. As the situation evolved, all three outlets interpreted the avian influenza in terms of SARS, which we maintain serves as a master referent in which present and future outbreaks in southeast Asia are understood. In keeping with the reassuring public relations mode, *China Daily* presented China's responses to H7N9 favorably, noting that "the government's response to the disease is completely different from 10 years ago, when information disclosure systems were not established."[50] In other words, *China Daily* praised current conditions in China as open and transparent, especially in light of earlier government missteps.

Elsewhere, *China Daily* appealed to the lessons of SARS to stress prevention during the current outbreak. For example, in an April 2 editorial calling for additional research and public disclosure, unnamed *China Daily* authors explicitly linked the H7N9 outbreak to SARS: "This year is the 10th anniversary of the Severe Acute Respiratory Syndrome outbreak, which killed more than 300 people in the whole of China. We need to remember that many lives might have been saved if the outbreak had been properly handled from the start."[51] Here, *China Daily* openly censured the government for its 2003 SARS response, even while praising it for its swift handling of H7N9 a decade later. In this same vein, *China Daily* later provided excerpts of a *Guangzhou Daily* news article calling for transparency, while simultaneously commending China for its surveillance and monitoring. "All provinces and regions in China are closely monitoring bird flu epidemic situations and the reporting system has proved timely and efficient," the article maintained, even as it requested more information about how citizens could protect themselves.[52] And thus, from the initial confirmation of the virus through its decline toward the end of spring (and even in subsequent reports the next year), *China Daily* trumpeted China's "swift," "open," and "effective" response. "China Gains International Recognition for Immediate, Effective Responses to H7N9," declared *China Daily* as infections slowed in late May.[53] Here, the tension between openness and surveillance, between a China that is at once becoming more transparent yet remaining ever watchful, reveals one of the many paradoxes of contemporary China.

While mainland news outlets stressed the government's swift and transparent action, the Hong Kong paper included editorial content that admonished China about a perceived delay in reporting to the WHO, "The impression given by China to the outside world is not always positive nowadays. If China wants to change this image, the government has to take steps to be considerate and act more ethically, for example to think more carefully about the needs and rights of others in a health alert."[54] Another article expressed concerns about China's handling of the H7N9 news, stating that "the National Health and Family Planning Commission's statements give only the age and surnames of the H7N9 patients and the date they became feverish. No further information was available because local media and hospitals were ordered to present a united front in their public responses to the outbreak—no front-page stories, just reports with a positive angle."[55] This framing of unlearned SARS health lessons appeared across editorials, citizen correspondence, and feature articles, as seen in this letter to the editor: "With the experience of severe acute respiratory syndrome, China did not learn from her mistakes. In 2003, SARS broke out on the mainland, which was not reported to the World Health Organisation immediately. Many countries blamed China for its selfishness. Some even said the mainland bore responsibility for the serious threat of the spread of SARS." The letter writer continued, "Now, not having learnt the lesson, China makes the same mistake again. While people were dying from H7N9 infection, China procrastinated for three weeks before revealing the outbreak."[56] In other words, the very same response that *China Daily* deemed swift, efficient, transparent, and praised by the WHO was cause for suspicion in Hong Kong's paper, revealing stark differences between the two sets of news reports.

What is striking upon comparing *South China Morning Post* coverage with *People's Daily* and *China Daily* is the degree of concern in the *South China Morning Post* over the mainland government's risks to Hong Kong, whereas mainland papers focused on reassuring public relations and containment rhetoric. The construction of the mainland as a health threat was readily apparent with numerous references to mainland poultry, people, and health practices as disease carriers, often appearing in editorial content: "SARS was spread to Hong Kong by a mainland university professor who came here to attend a wedding banquet. It took just one man to quickly spread the virus," observed one editorial.[57] "Moreover, there have been serious pneumonia cases of unknown origin surfacing in Shanghai hospitals recently, which have not been clearly explained. Are the mainland authorities allowing history to repeat itself by refusing to report the real situation to the outside world?" the writer wondered. He continued:

A decade ago, our doors were not yet open to individual mainland travelers. We did not have so many mainland tourists coming to the city. Now we have an average of 300,000 mainland tourists crossing the border every day. If one man could do so much damage in 2003, it's not hard to imagine the extent of damage that could be caused by so many mainland tourists.[58]

Here, mainland visitors—tourists—were imagined as disease carriers descending on an otherwise healthy population. Ignoring both the cosmopolitan ethos of Hong Kong with its steady stream of international visitors and the fact that Hong Kong suffered an outbreak of bird flu years earlier, this editorial, like a number of similarly themed *South China Morning Post* articles, editorials, and letters to the editors, portrayed the mainland as the threatening, disease-ridden Other. "Stop Mainland China Chicken Imports Says Hong Kong Vet," reported the *South China Morning Post*.[59] "Hongkongers need to keep a watchful eye on the H7N9 avian flu cases on the mainland," declared one article that noted the cases appearing "on the mainland, including Shanghai, Nanjing and Suzhou."[60] The identity rift between Hong Kong and the mainland that appeared in this 2013 coverage presaged the 2014 Umbrella Revolution, in which Hong Kong citizens identified not as Chinese but as "Hong Kongers" who deserved democratic forms of governance. Far from "one country, two systems," the coverage revealed how some Hong Kongers feared contamination by the mainland and its form of governance, both pathogenically and politically.[61]

Within this broader emplacement of H7N9 into the dominant cultural narrative about SARS, we identified three main overlapping themes, which recurred across the coverage: informational reassurance versus mutation/contagion concern, economic impacts, and citizen and national government preventive measures. In mainland news, each of these, in turn, presented a picture of the CPC as an able and strong national responder to emerging disease, while in Hong Kong, the image of the potential risk remained intact.

REASSURING SITUATION UPDATES VS. MUTATION/CONTAGION CONCERN

Predictably, informational situation updates comprised the bulk of early news coverage in both Hong Kong and mainland news outlets, which detailed the numbers of casualties, current theories about spread, and government and WHO responses. For instance, an April 3, 2013, *China Daily* headline declared, "Four More Confirmed with Rare Bird Flu," while the *South China Morning Post* headline similarly reported "Four New Cases of Bird Flu Confirmed."[62] A day before, *China Daily* announced in "China Steps Up H7N9 Monitoring," that "on Sunday, three H7N9 bird flu cases were reported, two in Shanghai and one in Anhui, the first human infections of the bird flu strain." The article further detailed: "The two [patients] in Shanghai died and the one from Anhui is in critical condition and under treatment in Nanjing."[63] By April 4, *China Daily* reported eleven cases with four deaths and stressed China's transparency and openness with the WHO, including quotations attributed to WHO appreciating China's cooperation. For instance, according to *China Daily*'s "China Briefs WHO on New Bird Flu," WHO "appreciates China's cooperation and offered technical support."[64] That this report appropriated a quotation made by the Chinese National Health and Family Planning Commission to the WHO might be unclear to many readers. Instead, this recycling of government press releases worked to bolster the image of the CPC as an efficient and effective responder.

While initial coverage in both *China Daily* and the *South China Morning Post* provided informational updates and reassurance that the disease had a low transmission rate, subtle framing differences appear. When we compared the initial two reports of substance, *China Daily*'s April 1 "Two Dead from Rare Avian Flu" and *South China Morning Post*'s April 3 "Four New Cases of Bird Flu Confirmed," we noted a framing difference between a "rare avian flu" (a term that admittedly also appears in the *South China Morning Post*) and a "deadly H7N9 strain," even though both articles comment on the deaths and flu symptoms.[65] The word *rare* worked to contain the virus, reassuring readers of a low risk, while *deadly* functioned to stress the seriousness of the outbreak. Note, too, that while both outlets reassured readers that the risk of transmission was low, the *South China Morning Post* framed the matter in riskier terms regarding possible mutation. "If highly pathogenic avian viral DNA mixes with human influenza viral DNA," one expert testified, "a serious situation of human-to-human transmission may happen. This is what we're most worried about."[66] These slight but consequential framing differences recurred in varying degrees through the bulk of the coverage, as we shall see below.

While *China Daily* sought to reassure readers that the Chinese government had the virus firmly under control, risk frames in Hong Kong's *South China Morning Post* both reassured readers that the virus did not appear contagious and that Hong Kong was stepping up surveillance, while rehearsing potential future harms, marking what Sheldon Ungar has called the contagion/mutation dialectic package.[67] In Ungar's study of global media reports about an earlier outbreak of Ebola Zaire, the author found that media reports tended to adopt a mutation/contagion frame that stressed the potential for the virus to evolve and kill large numbers of people until the potential threat became a local reality. At that point, the discourse tended to shift into a "reassurance/containment" package, stressing that leaders were controlling the situation and containing the virus.[68] This difference in media frames can be seen between mainland papers and the *South China Morning Post*. While *South China Morning Post* reporter Jeanny Yu acknowledged on April 2 that "experts say the virus does not seem to be highly contagious," she nonetheless explained that the virus "appears more deadly than other strains of the H7 virus that have previously infected humans."[69] Moreover, "controlling its spread would be more difficult than other avian flu outbreaks because it has only a relatively mild effect on birds."[70] In this framing, the *South China Morning Post* draws on hypothetical, imagined futures that speculatively make H7N9 appear more dangerous.

Similarly, in the *Post* editorial "An Outbreak We Dare Not Ignore," comparisons to the Middle East Respiratory Syndrome (MERS), an emerging infectious disease with a high lethality rate, worked to make the threat seem stronger:

> Health officials have held an emergency meeting and the city is now on high alert for two potential threats—H7N9, and a deadly new SARS-like infection, novel coronavirus. The latter has killed 11 of 17 known victims since emerging recently in the Middle East. Researchers at the University of Hong Kong have found that it is potentially more deadly than SARS and able to infect more animal species that can pass it on

to humans. It does not appear as infectious, but mutation could soon make it so.[71]

Here, the *Post* again enrolls the mutation package through simile to stress vulnerability to threats from outside. Elsewhere, the *Post* similarly emphasized the potential for mutation when it reported that "the [H7N9] outbreak is less serious than the H1N1 swine flu crisis of 2009, experts say, although there is concern among health authorities that it could evolve into a pandemic strain in the future."[72] Such a framing of the potential future harms presaged further amplification of the virus in broader global biosecurity efforts, as we shall see in the conclusion of this chapter.

ECONOMIC IMPACTS, FOR BETTER AND WORSE

In coverage in both the mainland and Hong Kong, potential and already realized economic impacts loomed large, depicting both positive and negative effects. Positively, concerns about the virus were presented as boosting pharmaceutical companies, vaccine suppliers, mask makers, and car sales. On April 2, 2013, the *South China Morning Post* business headline, "Bird Flu Fears Spark Stock Stampede," announced pharmaceutical stock surges in light of vaccine. "Domestic drug makers surged on mainland stock exchanges yesterday as investors rushed into the sector on speculation a new strain of bird flu could spread further and create a spike in demand for related medicines," the article explained. Rising food prices were presented as similarly slowing, a positive development in light of concerns about inflation.[73] On April 10, the *South China Morning Post* reported carmakers benefiting as citizens sought to avoid public transit, even as masks and hand sanitizers were "flying off the shelf."[74] Conversely, poultry and pork shares were down, as reported on April 10, with a note that the cost of pork was rising because of Huangpu River corpses, while Hong Kong's Hang Seng Index plunged about six hundred points after the news of H7N9.[75] Here, media reports situated the flu within broader monetary systems, positioning the outbreak as threatening not only to human health but also to market security. Moreover, the *South China Morning Post* ran content from Elizabeth Wong Chien Chi-lien, former secretary for health and welfare, who admonished Hong Kong's leaders about the fragility of trust in government.[76]

Although People's Daily and China Daily raised potential economic impacts, they also initially minimized them. For instance, on April 2, the People's Daily stressed "little or no impact on China's economy, regardless of what 'experts' say."[77] Days later, however, the government blamed economic impacts on hysterical media coverage. Poultry markets were affected, and the chairman and CEO of Yum! Brands, the owner of the ubiquitous Kentucky Fried Chicken, was quoted in one China Daily article: "KFC's sales and profits in China were significantly impacted by the intense media (coverage) surrounding Avian flu."[78] Meanwhile, China's Animal Agriculture Association reported that the industry lost "more than 40 billion yuan ($6.52 billion)" from March to May 2013.[79] In "Duck Farm," China Daily reported the mass culling of ten thousand ducklings in Fujian: "Hundreds of the ducklings, which were less than a day old, were thrown into plastic bags and suffocated within a few minutes" to the chagrin of a farmer who reported no one had purchased ducklings from him since news spread of the outbreak.[80] The tight interlacing of the flu with economic concerns reveals the dominance of the global health security paradigm in which the economy, disease, and national security are concatenated. In this configuration, a nation is strong not only because of the resilience of its citizens but also because of the health of its markets. Yet despite the fact that catastrophes are experienced globally, because they transcend artificial national borders, the idea of a powerful and competent nation-state remained a recurrent trope in H7N9 news reports. In short, the Party-generated "bird flu" responses we studied indicate how the Party used the outbreak as yet another occasion for projecting a vision of its steady leadership of a strong and unified nation-state.

A CAPABLE GOVERNMENT, PANICKED PUBLICS, AND INDIVIDUAL HEALTH RESPONSIBILITY

The dominant theme across China Daily and People's Daily was the strength of the national response. Both outlets tended to frame the epidemic as a national event that provided the opportunity for international bodies like the WHO to praise China's swift action. Readers were reassured that the Chinese government had the situation well under hand.[81] The able government response was echoed in the *Global Times*, another state-sponsored English news outlet, which reported on April 7 that "international opinion seems to have acknowledged 'significant changes' in China's response to disease outbreaks." The article quoted a WHO spokesman as "praising" China's response to H7N9 as "excellent," and noting that since SARS, "China has reformed its epidemic handling system, especially infection reporting and tracking mechanisms."[82] Within this national frame, the CPC appeared as an adept national leader that acted swiftly to protect its citizens in the face of potential epidemic. By contrast, the *South China Morning Post*, as noted earlier in this chapter, questioned the mainland government's response and at times appeared to adopt a more international focus. Yet both mainland and Hong Kong coverage were quick to point out the many actions Beijing's government took to survey, monitor, protect, and contain viral spread, and Hong Kong coverage stressed its government's surveillance efforts as well. In fact, surveillance was the primary metaphor for both mainland China's and Hong Kong's responses to the flu in both *China Daily* and the *South China Morning Post*, while transparency, speed, and competence were qualities the government demonstrated in response to the outbreak.

If mainland papers cast China's government as a strong and transparent national leader, what roles were envisioned for citizens, what imagined community was at risk for disease? Disaster sociologists have long noted that constructions of panic and mass hysteria often accompany descriptions of public response to catastrophe, even though the myth of the panicked public might more profitably be understood as a rational, protective response.[83] For instance, fleeing a scene or even stealing food or supplies can be seen as a logical human response to profound disruptions to normal order. In reports regarding the 2013 avian flu, the trope of the panicked public appeared more in Hong Kong than the mainland. "Public panic mounts," claimed the *South China Morning Post* on April 2, which noted there is "no vaccine."[84] Concerns about panic leading to economic impacts appear across a swath of articles: "There has been panic," Tsui Ming-tuen, of the Poultry Wholesalers Association shared with the *South China Morning Post*: "The sale [of live chickens] has been greatly affected. We're losing a lot of money."[85] Here, panic among business sectors results not from the fear of contagion but from worries about lost revenue.

Even as news outlets riffed on the trope of the panicked public, health officials urged citizens to enact personalized preventive health behaviors. Because exposure to contaminated poultry or cages was believed to cause the spread of H7N9, citizens were encouraged to avoid wet markets; the government eventually shuttered live poultry stands in Shanghai. On April 4, in anticipation of Tomb Sweeping Day, a *China Daily* headline announced, "Public Advised against Poultry Slaughtering," citing Chinese CDC representatives as telling citizens "not to contact birds or chickens during worship rituals so as to reduce the risk of contracting the H7N9."[86] By May 2013, the government had begun to promote cold-processed birds to replace live poultry, although, according to the *China Daily,* "Most Chinese believe live poultry tastes better and is more nutritious."[87] In this and other ways, citizens adapted to the perceived risks of H7N9 by making small changes in everyday life, food, hygiene, and consumer choices.

While the WHO responded favorably to the government's handling of the crisis, responsibility for health emergencies, as outlined in press reports, entailed citizen enactment of individual health responses. For instance, citizens were charged with the responsibility of voluntarily engaging in protective measures and self-quarantine, choosing pork instead of chicken, and purchasing masks and herbal remedies.[88] Beck observes that the global risk society can produce a kind of "tragic individualization," placing responsibility on the individual for responding to potential catastrophe.[89] For instance, citizens configured as consumers are asked to become "responsible" for monitoring and securing their own food and for safeguarding their and their loved ones' health. Echoing the notion of tragic individualism, Tiffany Veinot similarly explains that the "empowerment-based health discourses conceal policy agendas of health resource rationing that shift the burden of care and transform self-care practices into civic [and we would note consumer] obligations."[90] Even in a collectivist society with an authoritarian government, risk discourses are individualized as consumer choice, although some local citizens and bloggers were skeptical of certain solutions proposed in the press such as wearing face masks and drinking an herb called *ban lan gen.*[91]

On April 5, the *South China Morning Post* offered a commentary on traditional Chinese medicine (TCM) and its efficacy for stopping bird flu. "Mainland health officials have been criticised by some doctors for suggesting traditional Chinese medicine and other alternative treatments to help ward off bird flu as the months-long process of creating a new vaccine gets under way," reported the *Post*.[92] The article noted that Gansu's health commission "encouraged residents to go outdoors, preferably into wooded areas, for fresh air and sunshine" and to listen to music. The article also reviewed mainland TCM beliefs such as the idea that "massaging the side of one's nose was also said to help, as was exposing parts of one's legs and stomach to incense once a day."[93] By highlighting health beliefs that ran counter to dominant scientific advice, the *Post* article positioned Hong Kongers' knowledge and health practices as more advanced. Although the article acknowledged that some mainlanders questioned these traditional methods, it by and large focused on the damage to TCM that could be incurred by bad medical advice. A table outlining various regional recommendations, reproduced below, is interesting both in terms of the varied responses suggested by different official agencies but also because of the *Post*'s implicit framing of the superiority of Hong Kongers' medical knowledge and response compared to mainland bumpkins. Titled "Preventive measures advocated by health organisations in China and elsewhere," the chart outlined radically divergent health advice ranging from avoidance of potentially infectious material to scientific approaches to cooking meat, as reformatted and presented in figure 1.

This dramatic horizon of contradictory health advice spans from cooking practices through massage and trash disposal. Hong Kong's Centre for Health Protection focused on general hygiene and behaviors aimed at minimizing the spread of respiratory droplets in contrast to WHO's concentration on eliminating sources of infection in poultry. Note, here, too, that WHO's advice presumes a level of technological and scientific sophistication (measuring the temperature of meat, for example) that may not be widespread in many rural communities. The gap between the WHO's implied audience and the one assumed by Gansu is wide. But in both cases, personal prevention behaviors ruled the recommendations and seemed to have an effect on the individual health behaviors of a

**FIGURE I. PREVENTATIVE HEALTH RECOMMENDATIONS
FROM DIFFERENT AGENCIES**

National Health and Family Planning Commission	Avoid eating raw or half-cooked eggs and birds.
Beijing Centre for Disease Control and Prevention and Centre for Preventive Medical Research	Avoid contact with dead animals and wash hands frequently.
Jiangsu Health Bureau	Consume Chinese medicines ban lan gen (woad root) in granules and radix astragali oral liquid.
Guangxi Centre for Disease Prevention and Control	Avoid consumption of raw chicken and cook animal foodstuffs thoroughly.
Gansu Health Bureau	Massage facial acupuncture points and consume traditional Chinese medicine.
Hong Kong's Centre for Health Protection	Cover the nose and mouth while sneezing or coughing, hold the spit with tissue and put it into covered dustbins.
World Health Organization	Cook food so that it reaches 70 degree [*sic*] Celsius in all parts (with no pink parts).*

*Chen and Wei, "Doctors Worried about Traditional Medicine Advice," 3.

number of citizens. According to a survey administered by the National Health and Family Planning Commission, "fifty percent of respondents said they changed their hygiene habits in order to prevent [H7N9] infections."[94] Increased or improved personal cleanliness thus constituted one of the many roles citizens were expected to play in mitigating risk, and across the coverage, citizens were encouraged to take personal precautions to reduce their exposure to the H7N9 threat.[95]

Overall, evidence suggests that many Chinese citizens appreciated what they perceived as transparent information sharing about H7N9. In Goodwin and Sun's telephone survey of more than one thousand citizens of South China two weeks following the announcement of the first H7N9 case, the authors concluded:

> Comparatively high levels of trust in Chinese government advice about H7N9 contrast positively with previous pandemic communications in China. Anxiety helped drive both recommended and non-recommended behaviours, with potentially important economic and social implications. This included evidence of "othering" of those associated with the threat (e.g. migrants).[96]

Moreover, the authors found that the emergent virus "was associated with hygiene levels, temperature change, floating pigs in the Huangpu River and migration to the city."[97] Clearly, citizens polled in this survey were concerned about environmental-pathogen connections, regardless of whether H7N9 was linked to any of these causes.

Despite the relatively small number of cases—a mere 133 in a country of close to 1.4 billion people—and the fact that H7N9 appeared not to spread from person to person, the H7N9 virus became quickly enfolded into broader global narratives and actions regarding biosecurity. By August 2013, just months after the virus was first identified, researchers announced their plans to deliberately engineer more virulent forms of H7N9 to study potential medical countermeasures. As Kate Kelland reported to Reuter's, "the genetic modification work will result in highly transmissible and deadly forms of H7N9 being made in several high security laboratories around the world, but it is vital to prepare for the threat, the scientists say."[98] Said one leading virologist during a Reuter's phone interview, "It's clear this H7N9 virus has some hallmarks of pandemic viruses, and it's also clear it is still missing at least one or two of the hallmarks we've seen in the pandemic viruses of the last century."[99] The subsequent modification of H7N9 in 2013 triggered a global debate about the wisdom and ethics of amplifying the properties of virulence.[100] At the same time, seasonal cases of H7N9 were waning along with headlines addressing the topic, only to reappear the following spring, when they could once again be set within broader cultural narratives about SARS and secrecy, trust and transparency, and China's national competence on the global stage. In other words, the outbreak provided the occasion to reinforce narratives of national strength within which citizens were asked to play personalized consumer roles, even as the government appeared as a capable protector of the people.

Imagining Communities in a Global Risk Society

Reports of Ebola, Zika, Dengue, and avian influenza continue to circulate in our media landscape, amounting to a kind of "epidemic of signification" in which global citizens are put into contact with one another via social and mass media and encouraged to feel fearful of "contaminated" and often far-flung Others.[101] In the global risk society, such viral media encounters may be expected to become increasingly routine, as China, the United States, and other nations will continue to coevolve with pathogens. In such times, media representations commingle with cultural discourses to create narratives of contamination and cleanliness, borders and connections, and us and them.[102] These narratives project imagined communities in which rhetors reconfigure individuals and groups, nations and internations, and bodies and germs. Cynthia J. Davis explains that "culture and contagion are not just metaphorically related but in certain contexts considered synonymous, used interchangeably to connote interchange, communication, contact."[103] Yet because "this interchange never occurs in a vacuum," she suggests, "in practice it proves hard to divest culture of contagion's lingering association with disease."[104]

This chapter has examined how China's leading English-language news services imagined China during the 2013 avian flu case. In particular, we found that mainland coverage in the early days of the outbreak oscillated between offering reassurances that the government was responding appropriately and distributing health information that—perhaps counter to WHO advice—sought to minimize the potential health risks. When combined, these narratives created a Party-confirming containment strategy that clearly flew in the face of many citizen's everyday lived anxieties about China's mounting health risks. Moreover, and like Davis suggests, our analysis of the H7N9 case reveals the role of Othering in disease coverage both on the mainland and in Hong Kong. Moreover, the association between the mainland government's secrecy and disease appeared more often in Hong Kong's coverage. Perhaps surprising to some readers is that *China Daily* adopted a critical stance toward the CPC's prior handlings of previous epidemics, even as it praised the Party for its swift response to the H7N9 outbreak. We observe, following Davis, that sometimes "the healthiest thing we can do as interpreters of maladies is to recognize their symbolic potential and, where damaging, disarm it via careful, historical analysis."[105] By exploring how Chinese news outlets configured the H7N9 flu and China's national identity in the primary state-sponsored English-language sources, we were able to track how the outbreak served as a chance for China to show the world its growing strength through its demonstration of an efficient and timely response to an emerging infectious disease. Seizing the kairotic moment of infection and death, the Party projected itself as a capable national leader on an international stage.

Of course, the perception of risk, in China as in other places, is subject to social definition and human foibles. With health officials and the citizenry cued to pathogenic viruses with limited human-to-human transmission in 2013, others might have looked to health risks a little closer to home. As Nan Yu reports, China's 350 million smokers—one-third the total number of smokers in the world—pose a rising disease burden, with the WHO projecting that "tobacco-use-related death might reach 2.2 million annually by 2030 if smoking rates remain unchanged in China."[106] Moreover, lung cancer remains the top killer for China's men and women alike.[107] Yet, in our global risk society, our interconnected web of contagion, it is sometimes easier—both in China and beyond—to look to exotic and emerging threats than to focus on the mundane but deadlier ones much closer to home. In this, the time of novel and resurging infectious disease, the way we narrate our stories of health and disease projects powerful stories of identity and nationhood, Othering and belonging. As this analysis suggests, perhaps it is time we consider varying our stories and thus imagining different communities, ones where the health of bodies and states is pegged to systematic responses rather than to episodic media amplification of contagion.

NOTES

1. The quotation is attributed to Keiji Fukuda in Peter Shadbolt, "WHO: H7N9 Virus 'One of the Most Lethal So Far,'" CNN, April 25, 2013, http://www.cnn.com; Andrew Jacobs details China's response in "China Escalates Its Response to Outbreak of Avian Flu, *New York Times*, April 5, 2013; influenza viruses are categorized according to three main types: A, B, and C. A-type viruses have 16 H- and 9 N- subtypes. H5 and H7 viruses are considered to be the most pathogenic of the subtypes.

2. "Chinese Struggle through Airpocalypse Smog," *The Guardian*, February 16, 2013.

3. Edward Wong, "On Scale of 0 to 500, Beijing's Air Quality Tops 'Crazy Bad'" at 755," *New York Times*, January 12, 2013.

4. Laurie Garrett, "China's Bird Flu Mystery," Special to CNN, April 6, 2013, http://globalpublicsquare.blogs.cnn.com; "Chinese Struggle through Airpocalypse Smog." See also Nicola Davison, "Rivers of Blood: The Dead Pigs Rotting in China's Water Supply," *The Guardian*, March 29, 2013.

5. Laurie Garrett, "Is This a Pandemic Being Born?" *Foreign Policy*, April 1, 2013, http://foreignpolicy.com.

6. "Bird flu" is a colloquial name for avian influenza A. The naming of disease, illnesses, and viruses is not a neutral affair. Place names, for instance, such as West Nile or Japanese Encephalitis, which index the presumed point of origin, mislead audiences into associating groups of people with particular diseases and can promote stereotyping and culturally based fears. We prefer the scientific name, avian influenza A, subtype H7N9, even as we recognize that this term carries different connotative baggage than "bird flu." See Rick Gladstone, "WHO Urges More Care in Naming Diseases," *New York Times*, May 8, 2015.

7. Ulrich Beck, *World at Risk* (New York: Polity Press, 2009). See also Ulrich Beck, *Risk Society* (London: Sage, 1992); and Anthony Giddens, *The Consequences of Modernity* (New York: Polity Press, 1990).

8. Priscilla Wald, *Contagious: Cultures, Carriers, and the Outbreak Narrative* (Durham, NC: Duke University Press, 2008). On the constitutive role of rhetoric in calling "a people" into being, see Maurice Charland, "Constitutive Rhetoric: The Case of the *Peuple Québécois*," *Quarterly Journal of Speech* 73 (1987): 133–50; Benedict Anderson, *Imagined Communities: Reflections on the Origin and Spread of Nationalism* (London: Verso, 1991); and Michael Billig, *Banal Nationalism* (London: Sage Publications, 1995).

9. This quotation, from Ann Robertson ("Shifting Discourses on Health in Canada:

From Health Promotion to Population Health," *Health Promotion International* 13 [1988]: 155), appears in Sally Wyatt, Roma Harris, and Nadine Wathen, "Configuring Health(y) Citizenship: Technology, Work and Narratives of Responsibility," in *Health Consumers: Health Work and the Imperative of Personal Responsibility*, ed. Harris, Wathen, and Wyatt (London: Palgrave Macmillan, 2010), 1.

10. Robertson as cited in Wyatt, Harris, and Wathen, "Configuring Health(y) Citizenship," 1.

11. Laurie Garrett makes this case in *The Coming Plague: Newly Emerging Diseases in a World Out of Balance* (New York: Penguin, 1995).

12. There are, of course, a number of notable exceptions, including analyses of health and medical speeches and rhetorical forms. For an overview of representative works of rhetorical criticism, see Carl Burgchardt, *Readings in Rhetorical Criticism*, 4th ed. (State College, PA: Strata, 2010). Important for this essay is Huiling Ding, *Rhetoric of a Global Epidemic: Transcultural Communication about SARS* (Carbondale: Southern Illinois University Press, 2014), which examined global SARS discourses. Also see Huiling Ding, "Transcultural Risk Communication and Viral Discourses: Grassroots Movements to Manage Global Risks of H1N1 Flu Pandemic," *Technical Communication Quarterly* 22 (2013): 126–49; L. H. Chan et al., "China Engages Global Health Governance: Processes and Dilemmas," *Global Public Health: An International Journal for Research, Policy and Practice* 4 (2009): 1–30; Kavita Sivaramakrishnan, "The Return of Epidemics and the Politics of Global-Local Health," *American Journal of Public Health* 101 (2011): 1032–41; and Brigitte Nerlich and Christopher Halliday, "Avian Flu: The Creation of Expectations in the Interplay between Science and the Media," *Sociology of Health & Illness* 29 (2007): 46–65.

13. Lisa Keränen, "Addressing the Epidemic of Epidemics: Germs, Security, and a Call for Biocriticism," *Quarterly Journal of Speech* 97 (2011): 224–44, 225.

14. Guoguang Wu, "Command Communication: The Politics of Editorial Formulation in the *People's Daily*," *China Quarterly*, no. 137 (1994): 194–211.

15. Samuel Partridge, "The End of the *South China Morning Post* and Legitimate Investigative Journalism in South Asia," *Freedom Observatory*, September 17, 2012, http://www.freedomobservatory.org.

16. Ibid.

17. Ibid.

18. Ibid.

19. C. Fred Bergsten et al., *China's Rise: Challenges and Opportunities* (New York: Peterson Institute, 2008).

20. Monica Schoch-Spana, "The People's Role in U.S. National Health Security: Past, Present, and Future," *Biosecurity and Bioterrorism: Biodefense Strategy, Practice, and Science* 10 (2012): 77–88; Monica Schoch-Spana et al., "Disease, Disaster, and Democracy: The Public's Stake in Health Emergency Planning," *Biosecurity and Bioterrorism: Biodefense Strategy, Practice, and Science* 4 (2006): 313–19; and D. B. Reissman et al., "Pandemic Influenza Preparedness: Adaptive Responses to an Evolving Challenge," *Journal of Homeland Security and Emergency Management* 3, no. 2 (2006): Article 13.

21. We chose to focus on the early days of reportage because Gu et al.'s study of citizen infoveillance during H7N9 maintained that "the first 3 days could be a 'golden 3 days' for the government and public health authorities to release information in time and make the information transparent and open. The high public attention would last for a week; thus, this week could be a critical period for health education." See Hua Gu et al., "Importance of Internet Surveillance in Public Health Emergency Control and Prevention: Evidence from a Digital Epidemiologic Study during Avian Influenza A H7N9 Outbreaks," *Journal of Medical Internet Research* 16 (2014), http://www.jmir.org; this quotation appears in the "Conclusions" section of the online article.

22. Lisa Keränen, "Public Engagements with Health and Medicine: Guest Editor's Introduction to the Special Issue on 'Medicine, Health, and Publics,'" *Journal of Medical Humanities* 35 (2014): 1–9. Also see J. Blake Scott, "Afterword: Elaborating Health and Medicine's Publics," *Journal of Medical Humanities* 35 (2014): 229–35.

23. Beck, *World at Risk*, 191.

24. Ibid.

25. Anthony Giddens, "Risk and Responsibility," *Modern Law Review* 62 (1999): 1–10, 3.

26. Ulrich Beck, "Living in the World Risk Society," *Economy and Society* 35 (2006): 329–45, 332.

27. Charles Perrow, *Normal Accidents: Living with High-Risk Technologies* (New York: Basic Books, 1984).

28. Laura Entis, "Bird Flu Devastation Highlight Unsustainability of Commercial Chicken Farming," *The Guardian*, July 14, 2015.

29. Donovan S. Conley, "China's Fraught Food System: Imagining Ecological Civilization in the Face of Paradoxical Modernity," this volume.

30. Guizhen He, Arthur P. J. Mol, and Yonglong Lu, "Trust and Credibility in

Governing China's Risk Society," *Environmental Science & Technology* 46 (2012): 7442–43.

31. Ibid.

32. Ibid.

33. Edward Wong, "Air Pollution Linked to 1.2 Million Deaths in China," *New York Times*, April 1, 2013.

34. Ulrich Beck and Daniel Levy, "Cosmopolitanized Nations: Re-imagining Collectivity in World Risk Society," *Theory, Culture, & Society* 30 (2013): 3–31, 6.

35. Ibid.

36. Ibid.

37. Beck, "Living in the World Risk Society," 332.

38. Sirenda Vong, Michael O'Learya, and Zijian Feng, "Early Response to the Emergence of Influenza A (H7N9) Virus in Humans in China: The Central Role of Prompt Information Sharing and Public Communication," *Bulletin of the World Health Organization* 292 (2014): 303–8.

39. Rachel Wong Wing To, "Letter to the Editor: Mainland Selfishness Risks Disaster," *South China Morning Post*, April 16, 2013, 12; for contrast, see "China Deserves Credit for Rapid Response to Bird Flu," *China Daily*, April 25, 2013.

40. David Barboza, "2 Men in China Die of Lesser-Known Strain of Bird Flu," *New York Times*, March 31, 2013.

41. WHO's Anne Kelso made the "dramatic slowdown" comment in a CNN article: Shadbolt, "WHO: H7N9 Virus."

42. National Health and Family Planning Commission as cited in Shadbolt, "WHO: H7N9 Virus."

43. Centers for Disease Control and Prevention (CDC), "Avian Influenza A (H7N9) Virus," February 22, 2017, http://www.cdc.gov. As of 2017, China was undergoing its fifth H7N9 epidemic.

44. Mika Aaltola, "Avian Flu and Embodied Global Imagery: A Study of Pandemic Geopolitics in the Media," *Globalizations* 9 (2012): 667–80.

45. Ibid.," 673.

46. Ibid.

47. Claire Hefferen, Federica Misturelli, and Kim Thompson, "The Representation of Highly Pathogenic Influenza in the Chinese Media," *Health, Risk, and Society* 13 (2011): 603–20, 615.

48. Timothy K. F. Fung, Kang Namkoong, and Dominique Brossard, "Media, Social Proximity, and Risk: A Comparative Analysis of Newspaper Coverage of Avian Flu

in Hong Kong and in the United States," *Journal of Health Communication* 16, no. 8 (2001): 889.

49. Barboza, "2 Men in China Die."

50. "China 'More Transparent' in Handling Epidemics," *China Daily*, April 6, 2013.

51. "Prevention Better than Cure," *China Daily*, April 2, 2013.

52. "More Transparency Needed to Fight Bird Flu," *China Daily*, April 11, 2013.

53. "China Gains International Recognition for Immediate, Effective Responses to H7N9," *China Daily*, May 22, 2013.

54. To, "Letter to the Editor," 12; by contrast, see "WHO Says Notified by H7N9 Bird Flu Infections in China," *People's Daily*, April 2, 2013.

55. He Heifeng, "Echoes of SARS in Bird Flu Panic," *South China Morning Post*, April 16, 2013.

56. To, "Letter to the Editor," 12.

57. Albert Cheng, "Lack of Preparedness Leaves Us Exposed to Risk of Another Nightmare Like SARS," *South China Morning Post*, April 5, 2013.

58. Ibid.

59. Emily Tsang and Lo Wei, "Stop Mainland China Chicken Exports Says Hong Kong Vet," *South China Morning Post*, April 22, 2013.

60. Chris Lau, "Warning over Avian Flu," *South China Morning Post*, April 10, 2013, 5.

61. Tim Hume and Madison Park, "Understanding the Symbols of Hong Kong's 'Umbrella Revolution,'" CNN, September 30, 2014, http://www.cnn.com.

62. Zhenghua Wang, "Four More Confirmed with Rare Bird Flu," *China Daily*, April 3, 2013; and Zhuang Pinghui and Lo Wei, "Four New Cases of Bird Flu Confirmed; Hong Kong Steps Up Screening at Hospitals and Sampling at Poultry Farms as the Deadly H7N9 Strain Infects Humans in Jiangsu Province," *South China Morning Post*, April 3, 2013, 1.

63. "China Steps Up H7N9 Updating," *China Daily*, April 2, 2013.

64. "China Briefs WHO on New Bird Flu," *China Daily*, April 4, 2013.

65. Wang, "Four More Confirmed with Rare Bird Flu"; and Pinghui and Wei, "Four New Cases of Bird Flu Confirmed," 1.

66. Pinghui and Wei, "Four New Cases of Bird Flu Confirmed," 1.

67. Sheldon Ungar, "Hot Crisis and Media Reassurance: A Comparison of Emerging Diseases and Ebola Zaire," *British Journal of Sociology* 49 (1998): 36–56.

68. Ibid.

69. Jeanny Yu, "Bird Flu Fears Spark Stock Stampede," *South China Morning Post*, April 2, 2013, 1.

70. Zhuang Pinghui, "H7N9 Virus Claims Its Seventh Victim," *South China Morning Post*, April 9, 2013, 6.

71. Editorial, "An Outbreak We Dare Not Ignore," *South China Morning Post*, April 3, 2013, 12.

72. Julian Ryall, "Japan Ramps Up Defences as H7N9 Concerns Mount; Introduction of Emergency Legislation Brought Forward Amid Raft of Public Health Measures," *South China Morning Post*, April 10, 2013, 9.

73. Yu, "Bird Flu Fears Spark Stock Stampede," 1.

74. Emily Tsang and Lo Wei, "Live Bird Sales Down as Masks Fly Off Shelves," *South China Morning Post*, April 10, 2013, 3.

75. Elizabeth Wong, "Calls for Trust in These Tough Times," *South China Morning Post*, April 12, 2013, 2; Tsang and Wei, "Live Bird Sales Down," 3.

76. Wong, "Calls for Trust in These Tough Times," 2.

77. Ungar, "Hot Crisis and Media Reassurance"; "H7N9 Not Expected to Exert Significant Influence on China's Economy," *People's Daily*, April 2, 2013.

78. Wang Wen, "Bird Flu, Slowdown Hit Sales at Fast-Food Chains," *China Daily*, August 14, 2013.

79. Ibid.

80. Jin Zhu, "Duck Farm," *China Daily*, April 12, 2013.

81. Hefferen, Misturelli, and Thompson, "Representation of Highly Pathogenic Influenza in the Chinese Media," found this approach in earlier reports of avian flu.

82. Chen Chenchen, "Virus Shows China's Progress and Limitations," *Global Times*, April 7, 2013.

83. Monica Schoch-Spana, "Public Responses to Extreme Events: Top 5 Disaster Myths," paper presented at the Resources for the Future: First Wednesday Seminar Series, Washington, DC, October 5, 2005.

84. Yu, "Bird Flu Fears Spark Stock Stampede," 1.

85. Tsang and Wei, "Live Bird Sales Down," 3.

86. "Public Advised against Poultry Slaughtering," *China Daily*, April 4, 2013, 1.

87. "Shanghai to Allow Chicken Again," *China Daily*, May 22, 2013; the second and third authors were refused chicken in a restaurant in Beijing and, perhaps problematically in light of the corpses in the Huangpu, instead received pork.

88. John Artman, "Bird Flu? Take Some Ban Lan Gen and You'll Be, Ahem, Just Fine," *Beijing Cream*, April 11, 2013, http://beijingcream.com.

89. Beck, "Living in the World Risk Society," 336.

90. Tiffany Veinot, "Power to the Patient?: A Critical Examination of Patient Empowerment Discourses," in *Health Consumers: Health Work and the Imperative of Personal Responsibility*, ed. Harris, Wathen, and Wyatt (London: Palgrave Macmillan, 2010), 30–44.

91. Artman, "Bird Flu?"

92. Stephen Chen and Lo Wei, "Doctors Worried about Traditional Medicine Advice," *South China Morning Post*, April 5, 2013, 3.

93. Ibid.

94. "Most Satisfied with H7N9 Response," *China Daily*, May 24, 2013.

95. Tasha Dubriwny, *The Vulnerable Empowered Woman* (New Brunswick, NJ: Rutgers University Press, 2012).

96. Robin Goodwin and Shaojing Sun, "Early Responses to H7N9 in Southern Mainland China," *BMC Infectious Diseases* 14 (2014), http://www.biomedcentral.com.

97. Ibid.

98. Kate Kelland, "Scientists to Make Mutant Forms of New Bird Flu to Assess Risk," Reuters, August 7, 2013, http://www.reuters.com.

99. Ibid.

100. For an overview of the arguments for and against this "gain of function" research, see "Scientists Air Topics for H7N9 Gain-of-Function Research," Center for Infectious Disease Research and Policy, http://www.cidrap.umn.edu. See also Laurie Zoloth and Stephen Zoloth, "Don't Be Chicken: Bioethics and Avian Flu," *American Journal of Bioethics* 6 (2006): 5–8.

101. Elaine Showalter, *Hystories: Hysterical Epidemics and Modern Media* (New York: Columbia University Press, 1997), 5; see also Paula Treichler, *How to Have Theory in an Epidemic: Cultural Chronicles of AIDS* (Durham, NC: Duke University Press, 1999); Reed Johnson and Rogerio Jelmayer, "Dengue Outpaces Zika in Brazil," *Wall Street Journal*, March 31, 2016.

102. Wald, *Contagious.*

103. Cynthia J. Davis, "Contagion as Metaphor," *American Literary History* 14 (2002): 828–36, 829.

104. Ibid.

105. Ibid, 832.

106. Nan Yu, "China," in *Encyclopedia of Health Communication*, ed. Teresa L. Thompson (Thousand Oaks, CA: Sage, 2014), 175–79, 175.

107. Ibid, 175.

Representations, Imaginations, and the Politics of Culture

Preface to Part Three

Kent A. Ono

The West's understanding of the East for far too long has been based on the fundamental notion that there is an incontrovertible difference between the two. Whether this is configured as an us/them, modern/backward, dove/hawk, or free/censoring dialectic, part of the aim of media in sensational contemporary (and sensational historical) times is to suggest the absolute alienness of people whose differences lie beyond comprehension. Such differences have been constructed as racial (hence biological), ordained (hence religious), endowed (hence political), and willed (hence cultural). The following chapters by Dodge, Brunner, and Gruber challenge such dichotomous assertions of absolute and uncrossable differences, to instead gesture toward what we might call the "shared imaginaries" in and between the West and China. This search for shared rhetorical ground between national cultures is a necessary precursor to understanding, appreciating, and cooperating across long-standing barriers. Most intriguing about these essays is how they productively complicate a single or simple image of China. Like all good critical-communication research, they dive below the surface of the social, seeking out complexities and subtleties while theorizing the meanings of what they find. Also, like all good critical-communication research, they address objects, performances, texts, identities, histories, products, and culture writ large; in so doing, they situate their analyses within constellations of meaningful objects and spaces of memory, thus providing profoundly material and meaningful ways to reconsider China and to contemplate its possible futures.

For example, Patrick Shaou-Whea Dodge considers the ways ordinary Chinese people and artists participate in quotidian resistances through the Internet. He depicts a dialectical process, where "netizen" resistance creeps up as soon as the Communist Party of China (CPC or the Party) cracks down on political speech. Both appear in the space of the Internet, suggesting the Internet's ability to be a site both of freedom and of repression, simultaneously. His essay suggests that hegemony is not simply forced on the citizens by the government, end of story, but is constantly renegotiated in a perpetually shifting game of "cat and mouse." Dodge suggests that through this dialectic we spy the emergence of new imaginaries. He looks specifically at art on the Internet for the ways it creatively resists what he calls "the facade of harmony," focusing on Ai Weiwei and Liu Bolin for the subtle but powerful critiques embedded in their work. Dodge begins by examining the concept of harmony within China, which prescribes a social ethic of acquiescent coexistence. Within that framework, however, he suggests that harmony is an ill-fitted abstraction that actually obscures underlying tensions. He illustrates the complexity of harmony—the give-and-take, the both/and dimension that contains elements of consent and resistance, accommodation and agency, and acceptance and rejection—as a series of rhetorical postures, moves, and counter-gestures. As his analysis unfolds it becomes clear that "harmony" is a delicate performance full of countervailing forces and submerged meanings.

Similarly, Dodge studies how ordinary citizens using the Internet in China negotiate complex appearances, in which expressions of freedom may be subtly masked as conformity and compliance. The mythical creature "grass mud horse" is a perfect example of resistance that looks like harmonious discourse. This Chinese saying, taken up as a rallying point for freedom of expression, literally suggests an alpaca, but in spoken Chinese, by playing with the language's complicated tones, it can be rendered as offensive speech or a swear word, meaning roughly that someone is being censored or harmonized by the Party. The grass mud horse has, thus, become a meme in China, circulating far and wide throughout the country. It has been incorporated into a song that is part of a larger campaign geared at drawing attention to and resisting censorship. The expression contains satirical and humorous qualities, suggesting a form of resistance that is enjoyable and not merely antagonistic—the wordplay offers an invitation to make fun of censorship in a winking way. This new digital style of resistance has predigital historical roots, but whereas previous incarnations had an epic quality, Dodge argues that contemporary satire can be by turns mocking, parodic, and/or cleverly ironic in its effort to register disagreement or dissent.

To understand this use of satirical discourse, Dodge looks closely at the cases of Ai Weiwei and Liu Bolin. Ai Weiwei, well known globally as an activist artist who has challenged the Chinese government's human rights violations, corruption, greed, and censorship, has used the grass mud horse meme in nudes of himself to suggest an overt, expletive-ridden, yet humorous and satirical challenge to the government. As a result, Ai has been detained and his images have been censored. Yet his performance artwork has nonetheless become a rallying point for massive numbers of netizens and resistors both in China and globally. On the other hand, Liu Bolin creatively invokes the theme of invisibility in his performance artwork. In these pieces, Liu insinuates himself into surroundings and settings in which he might not at first be noticed, but then upon realizing where he is, his visage is clearly there, embedded within the scene. This invisible-visible dialectic synecdochically stands for the enfolding of individuals within the massive apparatus of modernity—an issue Donovan Conley tackles head on—and the overwhelming force of the nation. By seeming to emerge from the image, Liu's work illustrates an almost magical process of transformation, indicating how China is in the ever-continuing process of becoming something new and unexpected. Leaving reductive thinking far behind, Dodge's analysis illustrates how new social imaginaries are driving this becoming something new and unexpected through virtual networks of creative expression. His is an optimistic reading of what these inventional efforts portend for China's emerging political culture.

Like Dodge, Elizabeth Brunner turns to the study of art in China. While Western media continue to beat the drum of "censorship in China," as though it were a perpetually rediscovered phenomenon, Brunner eschews the censorship/free-speech dialectic by focusing instead on Beijing's bustling art district, known as "798." Through a study of visitors and local artists at 798, Brunner finds that the artists are less interested in addressing censorship than in challenging the social issues of the day: pollution, overpopulation, water safety, and the untold costs of the country's plunge into consumerism. Originally built as a network of electronics and weapons factories meant to illustrate China's Cold War–era strength as a communist nation, the locale fell for a while into disuse only to be reclaimed in the 1990s by artists who leased the space from the government and turned it into a thriving arts neighborhood. Since then, it has morphed yet again into a high-end shopping district, albeit still full of art. As China's third most visited tourist destination, 798 has become a major attraction, a site of commercial interest, and a place where globalizing cultures coexist under the banner of postmodern art and politics. In other words, 798 has evolved into a major site of artistic production and commercial profit, amounting to a laboratory for imagining multiple Chinas. Brunner accordingly situates 798 as a synecdoche for the myriad cultural, social, and political changes that constantly redefine China.

In her study of Western visitors, Brunner finds that despite the potential for the space to disrupt well-worn Western stereotypes of China, they, for the most part, were reproduced. The Westerners interviewed expected to see unhappy Chinese people trapped in a stagnant world, not cosmopolitan hipsters contributing bold ideas to a rapidly changing society. When asked whether freedom of speech was more prominent at 798 than in other parts of China, at least one replied that it assuredly was, whereas others had more complicated views of what they saw. Brunner found that many viewers saw the art through their own cultural lenses, for instance seeing the Chinese art as "copies" of western works; as such, these art viewers were unable to see the distinctly local inflections and meanings within the Chinese art, thus, in their own ways, reproducing the stereotypes they brought to China. In this sense, Brunner's chapter stands as a plea to try, literally, to see China on its own terms and thus to imagine China anew.

As a counter to these casual observers' perspective of the space, Brunner also interviewed people living in China, and their responses to questions about 798 differed dramatically from those offered by Western tourists. For instance, some suggested that Chinese artists were pandering to the interests of Western consumers. Indeed, while artists originally founded 798, encroaching commercial interests have changed the neighborhood so much that artists find they can no longer compete with the capitalized art vendors who have moved into the space. Now, while fancy stores dominate the area, the artists live on the outskirts of 798. Still, Brunner argues that the very nature of 798 as a space that both synecdochically represents and mediates the complexities of China's rapid cultural changes is never finished. The 798 district reveals China as a nation in the throes and spasms of "becoming"—but the what that it (and China) is becoming is, as yet, undecided.

Following Brunner's analysis of 798 and China's culture of change, David Gruber closes the section with an analysis of the emergence, in Hong Kong, of an iconic stuffed animal wolf named Lufsig. A doll purchased at IKEA, Lufsig has shape-shifted into a meme and an expression of contemporary Hong Kongers' dissatisfactions with encroaching mainland power, culture, and language. In December 2013, Leung Chun-Ying (aka "CY"), who was widely known to have been placed in power by officials in Beijing, was at a town hall event when a protestor threw a Lufsig doll toward him. Like the grass mud horse, Lufsig's political work was made possible by the complexities of language, for when shouted in Cantonese the doll's name sounds like a vulgar expression of anger. Thus a thrown doll becomes an act of both physical and symbolic outrage. Following the initial incident, Gruber shows how Lufsig was catapulted into popular culture, becoming a pet image expressive of Hong Kongers, Hong Kong, and the underlying tensions and disturbances cutting across many social, political, economic, and cultural vectors. For instance, the stuffed animal symbolized Hong Kongers' perception that Beijing was a wolf threatening to take over Hong Kong. Moreover, a big part of Lufsig's political power was its symbolic malleability and adaptability. For example,

Lufsig was incorporated into a dissident-themed Pac-Man video game platform; fans took photos with Lufsig and then posted them on their personal online sites; the doll proliferated in videos, songs, marches, and online postings, thus seeming at times to be everywhere. Indeed, Gruber explores how images of Lufsig were coupled with slogans such as "We are Hong Kongers," suggesting the reflective way Lufsig both mirrored and amplified a sense of identity vis-à-vis Hong Kong's evolving and contested relationship with China. Yet even as the doll helped solidify an array of identities that ultimately helped to unite protestors (both Hong Kongers and casual consumers of Lufsig and his images), it was also used in a number of online spaces where its banal appropriations arguably watered down the larger political possibilities that first launched Lufsig into the popular imagination.

If Dodge looks at the sly rhetorical protests multiplying across the Internet in China, and if Brunner sees inventional possibilities in the arts spaces of 798, then Gruber shows a political scene so volatile that even a stuffed doll can evolve into a potent symbol of unrest and a rallying point for Hong Kongers who see their magnificent city as a living rebuke to the CPC. In each case we see new forms of cultural expression pushing the limits of "harmony" in search of new social imaginaries and hence new political worlds. Taken together, these three chapters illustrate the incredible complexity of China's continuing struggles over political, economic, social, and cultural relations, particularly when played out across the country's massive virtual communication networks. By digging down into particular case studies, these chapters also provide ground-level insights into the incredibly fast-changing experiences people in China are undergoing in their daily lives. Each chapter thereby performs the critical work of "conversion" discussed in the introduction, where local practices are linked to nation-state priorities through the disruptive medium of social reimaginings. In each of the three analyses we see how everyday citizens rework and expand political norms through inventive rhetorical performances. Indeed, whether addressing media representations, the control of channels of information dissemination, the differing interpretations and assessments of audiences, or the change of place reflected in artwork and in media more generally, these chapters suggest many of the complicated ways China can be understood, has the potential to be understood, and can never be fully understood in essentialist terms. This book, as suggested by these essays, helps those in and outside of the field of communication to understand how China is barreling ahead in a remarkable process of becoming—a becoming driven by new social imaginaries, and with the whole world becoming something new along with it.

Imagining Dissent: Contesting the Facade of Harmony through Art and the Internet in China

Patrick Shaou-Whea Dodge

Living in China is like watching a play in a giant theater. The plots are absurd and the scenarios are unbelievable—so absurd, so unbelievable, that they are beyond any writer's imagination.

This claim was made by Murong Xuecun, one of China's most prominent and bawdy novelists, during his "Caging a Monster" speech, delivered at the Oslo Literary Festival in November 2011. In the speech, as in many of his novels, Murong depicts China's "rotting" system as the people's problem, with Chinese citizens bearing the responsibility for improving the country, in part by "breaking the silence" and "speaking the truth." In doing so, he calls on everyday Chinese people to "criticize the government if it does not do the right thing" and to "keep an eye on the government even if it is already doing the right thing."[1] In 2010, when he won the People's Literature Prize, Murong planned to deliver a speech "calling for a more relaxed literary censorship," but on taking the stage he was "abruptly barred from speaking" and notoriously zipped his lips closed.[2] As reported by the *New York Times*, "his speech on censorship had itself been censored," thus providing yet another example of the ongoing restraints placed on free expression in Beijing and greater China.[3] In scathing self-condemnation, Murong later called himself a "coward" and "word criminal," describing his own complicity in China's long-standing practices of censorship.[4] Murong soon recovered from this self-described "cowardice," however, and later released the banned 2010 speech—along with other speeches, essays, and books of his that have been censored in China, with the releases all taking place via online forums—in a bold move that has gained him international renown and increased scrutiny at home.[5]

Murong's initial silencing and subsequent use of the Internet to reclaim his voice are indicative of an ongoing struggle between restrictions on expression in China, on the one hand, and the citizenry's artful use of the Internet as a medium of resistance, on the other. For while the Chinese Communist Party (CPC or the Party) has ramped up efforts to repress messages of dissent, so have netizens increased their efforts to counter with indirect, and increasingly direct, messages of defiance in the face of censorship.[6] Consider further the summer of 2014, when Murong wrote a *New York Times* opinion column announcing that he would surrender himself over to officials on his return to Beijing.[7] At the time, Murong was in Australia for an academic residency, so he gave one of his works to a friend to be read at a meeting in Beijing commemorating the twenty-fifth anniversary of Tiananmen.[8] Upon hearing that several of his friends had been detained and questioned for stirring up the old ghosts of Tiananmen right before the twenty-fifth anniversary—a deeply taboo subject in China—Murong surrendered himself over to officials and was interrogated for seven hours. In his own words, "the Chinese government has evolved to appear friendly, but in its heart of hearts it is still a dictatorial regime that will never accommodate someone like me who disagrees with it."[9] As Murong's words and actions make clear, contemporary China is undergoing a wrenching process of reimagining the boundaries of dissent.

Indeed, Murong's experiences illustrate how an ongoing political game of cat and mouse plays out: whenever academics, lawyers, activists, or artists are suppressed by the CPC, netizens counter by inventing new forms of resistance. At stake in this rhetorical battle is the very platform of communication—what legitimately can and cannot be said, and how and where—in the evolving social landscape of contemporary China. As a contribution to this key question, I argue herein that to realize President Xi Jinping's "great revival of the Chinese nation," China will have to revise its national story to incorporate a diversity of perspectives and a plurality of voices.[10] Such perspectives and voices are already proliferating, as netizens continue to push the boundaries of the sayable. This struggle to forge a legitimate platform of communication is also an effort by citizens to reimagine China's national culture. By critically examining the censorship-expression dialectic playing out on the Internet in China, we glimpse the fate of civic expression and hence the very contours of China's political imaginary. Despite the CPC's censorship efforts and increased pressure on state media, change continues apace throughout China.[11] Closely examining the censorship-expression dialectic helps us better understand the ways communication is reimagining, and thus reconstituting, China's political playing field.

To pursue this thesis, my chapter analyzes specific examples of art on the Internet, noting how their direct, hidden, or camouflaged messages highlight the interplay of censorship and its contestation. Specifically, I consider different strategic approaches employed by netizens to shed light on the various challenges facing the freedom of expression movement on the Chinese Internet. These analyses are framed by what I call the facade of harmony, where presumably acceptable surface meanings belie subtextual political critiques that are hidden within. To illustrate how this process works, I address the recent appropriation of the mythical grass mud horse, which has become a raucous rallying point for netizens.[12] Here I discuss the artist and provocateur Ai Weiwei, who has waged a sly yet brash assault on both the Party's rule and Chinese sensibilities regarding protest and decorum. Then, in contrast to Ai's ribald provocations, I turn to Liu Bolin—often called China's "Invisible Man"—who subtly insinuates himself into iconic scenes and places, thus offering quiet reflections on how meaning is made in different political contexts. I argue that both artists, and the online debates circulating around their work, establish the north and south of an emerging communication platform built on rhetorical subterfuge, artistic creativity, and the political daring of engaged netizens in China. Through comparing these artists and their representative styles, it becomes clear that less aggressive modes of contention are more effective right now precisely because they operate through coyness and indirection. Ultimately, however, I contend that China's national imaginary must evolve from playing along with the facade of harmony to embracing cacophony. As we shall see, many Chinese are already moving quickly along this path, as various corners of the Web are filled with dissident voices imagining a new, and very different, China.

The Facade of Harmony and Imagining a "Conflict-Free" World

Combining the Chinese characters *he* (together, union, peace) and *xie* (harmony), the term *hexie* represents the idea of together being in harmony and peace. With hopes of transcultural understanding in peaceful interactions, Guo-Ming Chen has developed a "Harmony Theory of Chinese Communication."[3] He explains, "to Chinese, communication competence is an individual's ability to develop and keep a harmonious relationship between interactants."[4] In his theorization, harmony is "the core value of Chinese culture that guides Chinese communication behaviors," and "the most important element Chinese people use to regulate the transforming, cyclic, and never ending process of human communication. As a result, the ultimate goal of Chinese communication," he argues, "is to pursue a conflict-free interpersonal and social relationship."[5] This notion of conflict-free relationships is deeply embedded in the Chinese practice of "face," where notions of discord and inappropriateness are pacified for the sake of keeping the peace. In a similar vein, Hui-Ching Chang tells us "one must co-exist peacefully with others so as to participate in the rhythm of the universe."[6] However, Chang complicates this notion of social harmony by conceptualizing it as an "external display" that is "constructed, enacted, and negotiated," where communicators can conceal alternative and "ulterior motives."[7] In this approach to harmony, things look to be in synchronization and agreement. When probing beneath the surface, however, we find disagreement with and resistance to both authoritative mandates from the Party and long-standing Chinese cultural norms regarding obedience and deference. For instance, netizens have coined the process of being censored as "being harmonized," thus mocking the CPC's attempt to silence dissidence in the name of "harmonious" relations and a "harmonious" society.[18]

Going a step further and pointing out the limitations of past Chinese communication literature, Chang notes that studies "tend to treat social harmony as an overarching, abstract principle . . . [and to] focus only on the cooperative elements implied by social harmony," meaning that "insufficient attention has been paid to the question of how social harmony may also be conducted only at a surface level."[19] She questions the "turbulence and manipulation concealed beneath superficial politeness" in Chinese communication practices and "how social harmony as cultural performance is engaged in and conducted by interactants in specific encounters."[20] Extending Chang's argument, I suggest here that "harmony" is a master trope designed to cloak political contestation, cultural transformation, and rhetorical invention. This critical notion of harmony examines the dynamic processes of contestation and negotiation in which "harmony" is constructed, deconstructed, and reconstructed, thus showing how the meanings of the term are made, broken, and remade. In telling ways, this process of rhetorical invention illuminates an evolving alternative to the Party's facade of harmony, as netizens, dissidents, scholars, and artists join the ongoing effort to build new communicative practices, forge a new sense of community, and reinvent the national imaginary.

Within this larger sense of Chinese political rhetoric as a cat-and-mouse game—Murong's "giant theater" of the absurd—I build upon Chang's notion of *harmony as a social performance* by seeking out acts of resistance and defiance that are masked under the guise of harmony. In doing so, I honor Dwight Conquergood's call to turn our attention to "messages that are coded and encrypted; to indirect, nonverbal, and extra-linguistic modes of communication where subversive meanings and utopian yearnings can be sheltered and shielded from surveillance."[21] Such messages are "masked, camouflaged, indirect, embedded, or hidden in context."[22] In this sense, unpacking surface-level messages, which may look like the Party's mandated harmony, we can focus on the critical meanings that, even when hiding in plain sight, illustrate the tension and disharmony in contemporary Chinese communication. Within this conceptualization of the facade of harmony in China, it is important to note that its practitioners may very well be engaging in acts of self-preservation—a long-standing strategy of survival under authoritarian rule. And so, to comprehend the notion of harmony's facade, I address representative texts to unpack the details of what Goffman has called "outside" or off-stage performances, and what Scott has termed the "hidden transcript."[23] As we shall see, these "hidden" and "outside" meanings can serve to shield the artist or critic even while expressing forbidden thoughts under the ever-present gaze of an authoritarian state. Indeed, the classic Chinese notion of *xiao li cang dao* can be translated as "holding a knife behind one's smile." This Chinese phrase captures nicely the sense that contentious messages may lurk beneath the guise of harmony.[24]

Xiao Qiang explains a similar dynamic using Chinese concepts.[25] He starts from the point of resistance to censorship in China or *shai* (revealing). *Shai* occurs, in a manner similar to what I describe as the "breaking" of the facade of harmony, when censored or sensitive information is revealed. *Huo* (spreading like fire/going viral) comes next, when the message behind the facade is revealed, gains popularity, and goes viral, spreading like wildfire. In contemporary China, when such sensitive information circulates on the Web, the government quickly censors—*harmonizes*—it. This takes us back to *feng* (censorship), where the facade of a harmonious society is once again "remade." The same pattern unfolds on the Internet: netizens reveal censored information; censored information spreads like wildfire; wildfire is summarily censored by the authorities; and then netizens use the process of censorship as the raw material for authoring new cycles of rhetorical imaginings. An ongoing process that drives the evolving national imaginary of China today, this emerging communication dynamic is ever changing in the ebb and flow, cat and mouse, breaking and remaking process of "harmony." Within this dynamic process, I argue, the reconstruction of harmony by artists, dissidents, and netizens offers exciting occasions for imagining the transformation of Chinese social relations and communication patterns. To watch how this process plays out in Chinese cyberspace, I next offer two case studies of dissident artists at work.

Harmony, Harmonization, and Subterfuge on the Chinese Internet

In laying out "the battle for the Chinese Internet," Xiao Qiang, founder and chief editor at *China Digital Times,* has questioned "the capacity of the Internet to advance free speech, political participation, and social change" in China.[26] Positing that "new online freedoms have developed in spite of stringent government efforts at control and containment," Qiang argues that "the CPC and the government can no longer maintain absolute control over the spread of information."[27] An illuminating example of this contest between the Party's efforts at control and containment and the creative resistance of Chinese netizens can be found in the battle between two mythic creatures.[28] In early 2009, an animal named *Cao Ni Ma,* the grass mud horse, breached the Internet in a Baidu Baike entry.[29] A "homophone of a profane Chinese expression," the grass mud horse became the "*de facto* mascot of Chinese netizens fighting for free expression."[30] The grass mud horse, a cute and cuddly creature in all its glory, represents "the average Internet users' anger and frustration at censorship," which has boiled over "into a collective attempt at resistance."[31] The turning of this cuddly critter into a political weapon hinges on the ambiguities of Chinese, wherein even the slightest alteration in pronunciation can make significant changes in the meaning of words and phrases. In this case, slightly tweaking the characters and tones of the grass mud horse (*Cao Ni Ma*) transforms the iteration into a vulgar expletive roughly equivalent to "F*** your mother!" As deployed by artists and activists, the insult is clearly meant to be hurled at the Party and its army of Internet censors.

Within the Chinese Internet, the enemy of the grass mud horse is the evil river crab, or *hexie*. In yet another clever play on words and tones, "the word 'to harmonize' in Chinese (*hexie*) is a homonym of the word for 'river crab.'"[32] When Ai Weiwei built art installations in New York, Ontario, Tokyo, and elsewhere that contained thousands and thousands of river crabs, he was explicitly mocking the Party's attempts to censor free speech.[33] And so *hexie* quickly made its way into the vernacular of Chinese dissidents, where it served as a critique of the Party's attempts to censor and "harmonize" the Internet (*bei hexie le*). Thus, within the facade of a harmonious society, artists, dissidents, and netizens flocked to the two figures, the grass mud horse and the river crab, as sly symbols of protest.

The political storm surrounding these odd artifacts demonstrates how the rhetorical work of imagining the nation can hinge on remarkably subtle twists of phrasing, pronunciation, and attitude. Moreover, the communicative dynamics detailed above were fueled in large part by the Internet. In this case, debates about expression and censorship gained notoriety following a YouTube video that went viral in 2009. Even more telling, the popularity of the video was triggered in part by the government's crude attempts to clamp down on the grass mud horse's hidden vulgarity, as six different government agencies, in conjunction with the much-feared Ministry of Public Security, launched a campaign against "low and vulgar practices on the Internet."[34] As Meng explains, "nobody would have anticipated that a campaign that was supposed to clean up 'low and vulgar' content on the Internet would end up giving birth to a foul-named animal that symbolizes discontent with censorship."[35] Contrary to Meng's surprise, however, I argue that the dialectic of repression and dissent affirms that every Party attempt at "harmonization" actually yields new forms of dissidence. Sure enough, once the Party launched its antivulgarity campaigns, "cynical but discerning Internet users held the general view that this was essentially the suppression of freedom of expression committed under the convenient guise of protecting children," and that "the real intention behind the 'clean-up' was to silence political dissent."[36] By making "the authorities' intention ridiculous by swearing at it," the grass mud horse "provides a creative vent for people to express their suppressed sentiment."[37] Furthermore, "it is triumphant because it bypasses control and voices prohibited expressions successfully and in an innovative way. Like a political satire, the song [that accompanied the viral YouTube video] challenges and ridicules the authorities. It entertains and, at the same time, empowers ordinary people."[38] Thus, with the grass mud horse functioning via coded communication, and with the dreaded river crab standing as a symbol of what ails China, ordinary Chinese citizens invented a shared voice rooted in sly humor, playful linguistic revision, and barbed political protest.

Indeed, using coded language, double meanings, and humorous spoofing, the grass mud horse–river crab battle has given collective voice to a growing population of netizens seeking to resist the constraints placed on speech and expression in China. In a manner strikingly similar to the Hong Kong–based story of Lufsig, the politically charged stuffed wolf, I conceptualize the grass mud horse phenomenon as an example of *e gao*, or what Meng calls the Chinese genre of Web-based online spoofs. According to Meng, *e gao* represents "a new mode of communication" that "shares an artistic tradition with parody and satire, as well as an anti-establishment spirit with medieval carnivals."[39] As one of the first overwhelmingly successful, large-scale examples of netizens using creative means to contest the facade of harmony on the Internet, the grass mud horse has shown us how Chinese netizens are becoming savvy political critics with a cunning sense of humor. Indeed, the grass mud horse has served as a rallying point against Internet control and as a key symbol "for articulating social critique and fostering societal dialogue in a heavily controlled speech environment."[40] As Meng tells us, "the Internet is more than an instrument for disseminating information, it plays the key role of mediating the connection among Chinese Internet users so as to maintain the shared concern of a public issue and the dispersed participation of a public debate."[41] In short, *Cao Ni Ma* has become one of the most important examples of how debates about free speech in contemporary China are being played out on the Internet.

Following the wake of the grass mud horse phenomenon, *China Digital Times* created a "translation" section on their website dedicated to what they term the "Grass Mud Horse Lexicon."[42] The Lexicon takes the format of a Wiki-based online encyclopedia, with entries dedicated to "translating the resistance discourse of Chinese netizens." As explained on their website,

> In recent years, Chinese netizens have shown they possess boundless creativity and ingenuity in finding ways to express themselves despite stifling government restriction on online speech. Without understanding this coded but widespread "grass-mud horse discourse" through the lens of censorship and resistance, one cannot fully understand the contradictions in Chinese society today, nor the possibilities for tomorrow.[43]

The site is a large-scale attempt to document the ways netizens have circumvented the Chinese Internet. Qiang explains, "the terms in our lexicon are all created by netizens and circulated widely on websites inside China, not just by prominent bloggers or opinion leaders."[44] Clever homophones and homonyms surface daily on Chinese blogs and, when silenced or removed by the Party, the Lexicon is there to document the process. As the grass mud horse and Lexicon indicate, whenever the Party marshals new regulations and restrictions, new acts of resistance proliferate: the facade of harmony is built, broken, remade, and broken once again in an ongoing cycle of repression and invention. As the turmoil continues, each entry in the Lexicon provides testimony to the growth of new, creative, and subversive discourses on the Chinese Internet. To add detail to this theory of rhetorical reinvention, I turn below to some examples of the shifting styles of contestation that make up the work of reimagining China's civic life.

Contesting the Facade of Harmony

Resistance enacted under the guise of harmony is not new. Chang has found that "throughout Chinese history, ministers in government have been known to use clever language, involving metaphor, analogy, irony and so on, to criticize higher officials (even the emperor) while protecting themselves from punishment or death."[45] Turning to online activism and the transformation of contemporary China, Guobin Yang has found that "popular protest in modern China has an epic style."[46] He explains that this style of protest has persisted both in online and offline contexts while the "prosaic and playful styles have gained salience" in "online activism."[47] According to Yang, as argued above by Murong and as my case studies indicate, a new style of contention is evolving from the traditional, epic style of contention—the protests, sit-ins, and collective mobilization witnessed in 1989 at Tiananmen Square—toward a digital, shrewd style of online activism that privileges mockery, parody, satire, and *e gao*. Yang explains that this transition is made possible with the power of the Internet and by diverse collective actions akin to a Bakhtinian notion of heteroglossia, where plurality and creativity are directed at power and authority.[48]

The key to this stylistic transformation, Yang argues, is moving beyond calls for revolutionary change to, instead, use the Web to engage in collective problem solving while initiating movements to raise awareness among Chinese Web-users.[49] Thus, rather than framing contention on an "us vs. them platform," Yang suggests that efforts should focus on improving society, solving immediate problems, and bettering the country. Perhaps most importantly, Yang tells us that creativity will evolve through practice. For instance, blogs have sprung up to teach netizens how to use new media technology for creative purposes, as in the shift from Weibo to Weixin, which has been driven in part by the user-friendly versatility of the latter's communicative platform.[50] Still, it takes time for everyday citizens to learn both new styles of communication and the technologies for spreading them; so political change will evolve slowly in contemporary China. At the same time, it is clear that such changes are already taking place. The nature of this change is less about overthrowing state power and more about defending citizen rights while constructing new cultural norms that nourish free speech.[51] To illustrate how these transformations are playing out in contemporary China, I turn to Ai Weiwei and Liu Bolin, whose works provide insight into how different styles of contention provide distinctive ways to contest the facade of harmony and to imagine a new, different China.

IMAGING CONFRONTATION: AI WEIWEI AND THE CAO NI MA STYLE

Ai Weiwei is a globally recognized Chinese artist and activist. His bold charge for human rights and freedom of expression gained momentum in 2009, when he searched for the names of the thousands of children who were killed during the 2008 Wenchuan earthquake. Ai made a poignant argument about a politically sensitive subject, pointing out the political corruption—the Party's insiders cutting corners on construction costs while enriching themselves—that resulted in the shoddy construction of the Sichuan schools that collapsed in the quake, killing the students trapped inside. For his open criticism of government policy, corruption, and rights violations, Ai was detained for eighty-one days in 2011. Upon release, his movement at first was heavily restricted and remains heavily monitored. Despite the Party's attempts to silence him, Ai's controversial art has received much attention from netizens in China and around the world. Indeed, Ai has become a global celebrity, based in part on his tireless claim that political repression in China is a collective phenomenon, one for which citizens are as responsible as the Party. For example, in one interview, Ai argued that "we're actually a part of the reality, and if we don't realize that, we are totally irresponsible. We are a productive reality. We are the reality, but that part of reality means that we need to produce another reality."[52] In his approach to art, then, Ai creates images and spaces where audiences can reimagine civic culture and "produce another reality," frequently by tweaking existing communicative norms.

To watch how Ai pursues this goal, consider his performance art "Grass Mud Horse Covering the Middle," which was released on the Internet shortly after the grass mud horse song/video went viral in 2009 and in direct response to the government's campaign against "low and vulgar practices on the Internet."[53] As Goldman explains, "a near-nude self portrait of him titled ('grass mud horse covering the middle' [*cao ni ma dang zhong yang*]) sounds almost the same in Chinese as 'F*** your mother, the Communist Party Central Committee.'"[54] Quickly "harmonized" by Chinese censors, Ai's piece was deemed pornographic, possessing vulgar language and bad taste. Likewise, Ai's blog was harmonized in May 2009. Whereas the original, mythical animal version of *Cao Ni Ma* was a coded, sly critique, Ai's play upon the image adds a more overt challenge, literally shouting "F*** the Party!"

Standing up defiantly to the Party's Internet censors, Ai's rendition of the grass mud horse is both epic and playfully prosaic. His performance art represents a style of contention that directly challenges government censorship and the facade of harmony in China. The harmonious facework that is otherwise performed in such Chinese satire—parody, irony, and other camouflaged forms of communication—is clearly absent in Ai's pose. His legs are wide open with an arm in the air displaying a resilient jubilation, while the grass mud horse stands as the only thing between our gaze and Ai's genitals. His style of contention breaks the complacency of harmony by directly jumping into the face of those restrictions mandated in the campaign against "low and vulgar practices." His leap of delight, while completely naked except for the grass mud horse, signifies Ai's great "leap of faith," at once epic and playful. His performance conveys the message of unfettered freedom, effectively shouting, "I can do anything I want!" It is worth noting, in passing, that Ai's leap mimics the ubiquitous tourist shot, where a group leaps together in front of a famed cultural monument. By piggybacking on this trope of globetrotting celebration, Ai sneaks his political message into the casual gaze of outsiders and thereby extends his critique of the Party's censors to a global audience. To make sure his political critique was rooted in local conditions, however, Ai accompanied the image with a bitter, written testimony cataloging the many wrongs in contemporary Chinese society. That testimony argues, in part:

> There isn't education for everyone, there isn't medical insurance, there's no freedom of the press, there's no freedom of speech, there's no freedom of information, there's no freedom to live and move where you choose, there's no independent judiciary, there's no one supervising public opinion, there are no independent trade unions, there's no armed forces that belongs to the nation, there's no protection of the constitution. All that's left is a Grass Mud Horse.[55]

By combining this written catalog of wrongs with the playful image, Ai's version of "F*** your mother!" or "F*** the Party!" becomes both radical and playful, epic and deadly serious—and deliriously funny.

In another of his playful challenges to censors, we find a mischievous Ai riding a grass mud horse with the words "go home" hanging above the image, thus challenging the government and its censors to reverse course.[56] Again, Ai is naked, this time straddling the mythic creature, looking like a goofy cowboy riding for freedom of expression. Ai's critical and resistive pieces are examples of *e gao*, the emerging communicative genre of online spoofs and hoaxes meant to show the absurdity of Internet censorship in China.[57] Moreover, while poking fun at the Party's censorship, Ai's commitment to play and humor stands in stark contradiction to the long-standing tradition of Maoist seriousness. His critique, then, is both political and cultural, challenging the politics of censorship while reworking Chinese norms of communication. Along the way he is helping to forge the contours of a new social imaginary for those who "get it." To "get it" is to become stitched within this new imaginary and thereby enter the ranks of a crafty dissident.

On the other hand, we find two examples of Ai taking a direct and epic style of contention in defiance to authoritarian power in Tiananmen Square. In one image, Ai appears with the word "FUCK" written on his chest, hands confidently on hips, face clenched in a scowl, with the iconic Gate of Heavenly Peace of the Forbidden City in the background. In another image, Ai stands in the middle of Tiananmen Square while giving the middle finger to the enormous Chairman Mao picture that hangs on the front of the Gate of Heavenly Peace across the street.[58] The images convey no sense of playfulness or subtlety. Ai is directly confronting authoritative power, thus shattering the pretense of harmony. Combined, the message is unmistakably antiauthority. More to the point, Ai's stance is directed at authority as constructed in the historical symbols of the CPC and Chairman Mao. His reimaging of Chinese norms of communication and nationalism seem not merely political but even heretical; perhaps treasonous. Engaging this space and turning it into his canvas of critique, Ai's political disgust invokes collective memories of student occupation in 1989 at the "world's largest square." At the same time, such bold, in-your-face messages against the Party have propelled Ai into the spotlight of international art circles and placed him on the radar of China watchers around the globe. This stature comes in part from Ai's epic style of contention, which pits freedom of expression against censorship, resistance against domination, in a battle between good and evil. Unsurprisingly, the Party has responded to Ai's images and rising global fame by ramping up their monitoring and censorship efforts. Ai remains resilient and has continued to create art that attacks the forced facade of the Party's constructed harmony—and so the facade of harmony is built, broken, and re-created, on and on, in a cat-and-mouse game with real consequences.

It is important, however, to consider the audiences that Ai's performance art reaches, the shared imaginary his work helps constitute. For while his videos, performance art, and images can be found on YouTube, Google, and other Western Internet outlets, they are virtually impossible to access in China (unless you have the technological tools to scale over the Great Firewall). As China blogger Anthony Tao explains:

One might be tempted to argue that Ai Weiwei, meta genius that he is, is giving the middle finger to Chinese authorities who desperately want to push soft power. By not creating substance, even though he is in a prime position to do so, he is telling viewers that creativity cannot be forced, and certainly cannot be pushed by the government. But it's only on YouTube, broadcast to everyone except those in China. No, Ai Weiwei is not saying F-U to Chinese authorities, or censors, or anyone here. He's merely refilling his cache of cool with the Western world, reminding his Western fans and Western journalists that he's a good guy who "gets it." He gets it because he knows how to dance on an invisible horse, and hey, that's something you like, right?[59]

Art and the Internet are mediums that provide Chinese citizens creative ways to interpret the facade of harmony and the restrictions placed on communication in China. But while Ai's epic and playfully prosaic style has created key rallying points, as the glue of the social imaginary, each new work he releases is quickly harmonized. The core question, then, as raised by Tao, is whether Ai can remain rhetorically effective now that the Chinese authorities have focused their efforts on censoring him. What roles can he play in China, when his images are now seen almost exclusively in the West? Moreover, how are Ai's messages properly contextualized when reduced to synecdoches of the free expression and universal human rights agenda characteristic of pressures coming from the West?

LIU BOLIN: MAKING THE INVISIBLE VISIBLE

In 2007, Liu Bolin's artwork was on exhibition in the 798 Art Zone at the Klein Sun Gallery.[60] Liu is known as the "Invisible Man" for a series of performance art he presented called *Hiding in the City*.[61] Liu has gone on to create/perform similar *Hiding* exhibitions in different countries around the world. In a TED Talk Liu delivered in 2013 he explains, "by making myself invisible, I try to question the inter-cancelling relationship between our civilization and its development."[62] His art engages viewers to consider our environment in contemporary times and to consider "our relationship to our surroundings" by using "his own body as a canvas, painting himself into the background."[63] Liu seemingly blends into the background in his

Figure 1 (*above and opposite*). Liu Bolin, *The Invisible Man*. Used courtesy of Klein Sun Gallery © Liu Bolin.

work and is only visible after careful scrutiny (see Figure 1). The power in Liu's *Hiding in the City* series is that he makes that which is seemingly invisible and hidden by the facade of harmony—the independent self, the acting agent—the muted subject of his art. By painting himself into the background (as seen with the flag images below), Liu demonstrates how even amid the immense power of the nation-state the supposed-subject retains his individual form, unsilenced and uncoerced into obedience.

Liu's style differs markedly from Ai's in that his invisibility positions the message less aggressively, less directly, less in-your-face. Instead, by using quiet suggestion Liu invites the viewer to pause and contemplate whether a person has been painted into the scene or whether the image has been photoshopped. Following our initial fascination with discovering the hidden artist, we are left to ponder what message is being communicated in the image. In contrast to the didactic messages in some of Ai's more aggressive pieces, Liu's subtle work generates various possible messages and interpretations meant to complicate the dominant and taken-for-granted meaning of a given image. Liu's work draws attention to our relations with our surroundings, calls out complacency in modern China, and thus creates space for critical reflection through a visible performance of the invisible. In some cases, Liu does this while calling attention to pressing social issues. A prominent example is when Liu painted himself into the ubiquitous propaganda signs that were used in preparation for the 2008 Beijing Olympics, which the Party trumpeted as tributes to China's harmonious society (see Figure 2). Inserting himself into these propaganda posters, Liu prompts viewers to reflect on the hidden cost of the games. In doing so he challenges the Party's triumphant rhetoric with a hidden plea for civic inquiry and interrogation. Liu's work redraws the contours of the sayable and thinkable, and thus reimagines the very terrain of legitimate civic communication in China today.

As we see, then, Ai and Liu each critique censorship, human rights, and state power in different ways. In *People's Policeman* (see Figure 3), Liu is presented phantomlike, front and center, eyes covered, and his

Figure 2 (*opposite*). Liu Bolin, *Beautify Beijing to Build a Harmonious Society*. Used courtesy of Klein Sun Gallery © Liu Bolin.

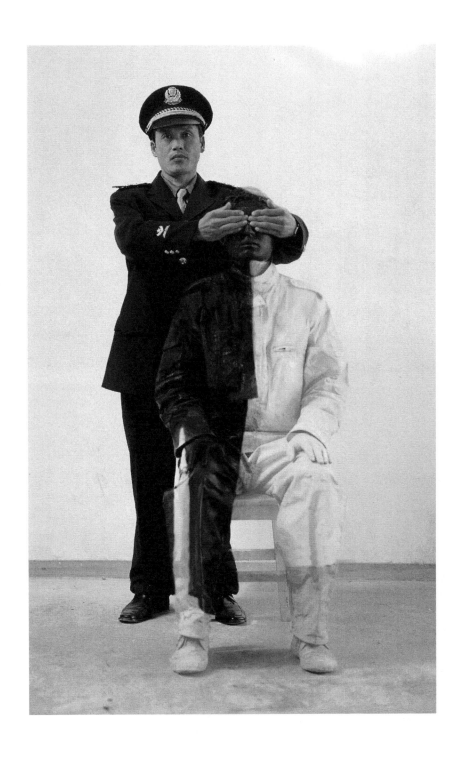

Figure 3 (*above and opposite*). Liu Bolin, *People's Policeman*. Used courtesy of Klein Sun Gallery © Liu Bolin.

body physically moved by a policeman as if powerless. Rather than painting his message of resistance in bold colors, Liu shades himself into the
message as a whisper. Ai stands in sharp contradiction to the object of
his critique; Liu creeps into the opposition, merging with the contradiction and staging his challenge from within. Furthermore, whereas Ai's
practice of visual resistance has him standing in Tiananmen Square and
"flipping off" Chairman Mao, Liu's practice of nonvisual implication has
him standing virtually invisible in front of the iconic Mao photo, his face
replacing the chairman's.[64] By quietly blending into the background and
challenging static authority in a subtle manner, Liu's style of contention
works from *within* the calm of social harmony. By contrast, Ai's style
brazenly confronts the government and its regimen of censorship. Thus,
whereas Ai has been censored and is constantly the focus of the government's gaze, Liu has been able to skate past censors thus far.

Liu's "Invisible Man" strategy therefore uses invisibility to render the
corruption, waste, and injustice that is too often blocked from public view.
Liu's style aligns with the Taoist concept and practice of *wu wei*, which
may be translated as the philosophy of "'inaction', 'non-action', or simply
'doing nothing.'"[65] There is a calm in Liu's art that seems "to act without
acting," thus implying the ancient practice of "noninterference, or letting-
go; doing nothing virtually refers to doing things strategically."[66] The calmness in *wu wei* allows for the enfolding of an antagonism —restrictions to
speech and expression in this case—so that one becomes the "master" in
the end. It is a form of "subdu[ing] the enemy without fighting."[67] Drawing out the Taoist metaphor a bit further, I would argue that when taken
together, Ai and Liu represent a quasi yin/yang in that they make up "two
changing sides of the same phenomenon."[68] As Fang explains, "Ying and
Yang are both necessary and complementary if universal events are to
be created, maintained, and developed in a harmonious way."[69] Whereas
Liu's style is closer to the yin of enfolding and changing from within, Ai's
style is closer to the yang of directly confronting a threat from without.
The style of each artist's works are examples of the contrasting voices that
can come together to ask the viewer to question the facade of harmony in
contemporary China. Both of these styles together shed light on the new
mode of social reimagining taking shape in China. Both styles on their
own are powerful, but together they represent the prospects for being

seen and heard in multivocal ways that are reconfiguring the boundaries of legitimate expression in China today.

Conclusion: The Artistry of Imagining a New China

As I have shown throughout this chapter, creative productions in art and the Internet have opened up new vistas for a social imaginary mobilized against the restrictions placed on communication in China. The mythic grass mud horse has served as an important symbol in this new social imaginary. Ai's art serves as an example of the constant breaking and re-making of the facade of harmony, the interplay between censorship and resistance as it plays out in art and on the Chinese Internet. Whereas Ai has been harmonized and rendered nearly invisible in Chinese Internet spaces, Liu Bolin's sly and neo-Taoist style of critical invisibility sheds light upon another kind of approach where there is power in "acting without acting." Together, in both artists' styles of contention—and the myriad works made by other Chinese artists and online dissidents—we find the process of harmony playing out as a constant game of making, breaking, and remaking long-standing cultural norms and communicative habits. All of this amounts to a wonderfully complex rhetorical dynamic. The cases I have examined herein confirm that political meanings, and the communicative practices that produce them, are never finally closed nor totally controllable—thus suggesting that censorship is futile. Despite the Party's attempts to dominate the communication platform, citizens have answered by persistently reinventing Chinese norms of expression, the sayable, and the doable. I have shown here that in their daily performances (whether as netizens, artists, literary critics, lawyers, or beyond), and in their bold acts of resistance, ordinary Chinese citizens have begun to complicate the facade of social harmony by making visible the political turbulence hidden beneath the surface. Across these resistance efforts—whether epic, direct, aggressive, and in-your-face, or coded, camouflaged, indirect, and subtle—a cacophony of styles and voices is reimagining civic expression, and thus reshaping the imagined boundaries of the social, in China.

NOTES

1. Murong Xuecun, "Caging a Monster" (speech delivered at the Oslo Literary Festival, Oslo, Norway, November 19, 2011), translated by Jane Weizhen Pan and Martin Merz, http://chinadigitaltimes.net.

2. Murong Xuecun, "Acceptance Speech for the 2010 People's Literature Prize," *New York Times*, Asia Pacific version, November 6, 2011, translated by Harvey Thomlinson, Jane Weizhen Pan, and Martin Merz.

3. Ibid.

4. Edward Wong, "Pushing China's Limits on Web, If not on Paper," *New York Times,* November 6, 2011.

5. For example, see Lara Farrar, "For Many Chinese Literary Dreams Go Online," CNN, February 15, 2009, http://www.cnn.com.

6. Netizens are responsibly engaged Internet users that are often labeled "dissidents" by the Party. Ya-Wen Lei, in "The Political Consequences of the Rise of the Internet: Political Beliefs and Practices of Chinese Netizens," *Political Communication* 28 (2011): 291–322, has asked about the political consequences of the rise of the Internet and netizens in China. She tells us that netizens in China are "showing [us] evidence of critical thinking and a willingness to take political actions" (310). Further, netizens have gone so far as to "constitute a formidable social force in China's politically restricted environment" (310), by "challenging authoritarian rule" (291).

7. Murong Xuecun, "I, Too, Will Stand Up for Tiananmen," *New York Times*, May 22, 2014. Murong arrived back in Beijing on July 2, and on July 6 he "posted a message online saying that I was ready to be picked up." Murong received a call two days later and surrendered himself to a local police station, where he was interrogated but eventually released; see his "Inside a Beijing Interrogation Room," *New York Times,* July 17, 2014.

8. In this one word, *Tiananmen*, I channel Louisa Lim's complication of the dangers of writing about politically sensitive topics from within China. Lim lived in China for over ten years with her family where she contemplated writing and releasing her book about Tiananmen. Since leaving China, she has published *The People's Republic of Amnesia: Tiananmen Revisited* (Oxford: Oxford University Press, 2014). Embedded in this sentiment I think of Murong's conjecture of being a "word criminal" and "coward" for waiting so long to say what must be said, and my own self-censoring in the lead-up.

9. Murong, "Inside a Beijing Interrogation Room."

10. Xi Jinping. "Chasing the Chinese Dream," *The Economist*, May 4, 2013.

11. For example, see President Xi's February 2016 state media tour to CCTV, the *People's Daily*, and Xinhua News Agency, "Xi's State Media Tour: 'News Must Speak for the Party,'" *China Digital Times*, http://chinadigitaltimes.net.

12. The grass mud horse is a Chinese phenomenon and symbol that represents contestation to censorship on the Chinese Internet.

13. Guo-Ming Chen, "Towards Transcultural Understanding: A Harmony Theory of Chinese Communication," *China Media Research* 4, no. 4 (2008): 1–13.

14. Ibid., 3.

15. Ibid., 2–3.

16. Hui-Ching Chang, "Harmony as Performance: The Turbulence under Chinese Interpersonal Communication," *Discourse Studies* 3, no. 2 (2001): 156.

17. Ibid., 155.

18. To be harmonized—this elusive pun mocks former President Hu Jintao's political rhetoric and legacy of building a "harmonious society" during his reign in China. For more examples of Chinese "resistance discourse," see the *China Digital Times*'s "Grass Mud Horse Lexicon" at https://chinadigitaltimes.net.

19. Chang, "Harmony as Performance," 156.

20. Ibid.

21. Dwight Conquergood, "Performance Studies: Interventions and Radical Research," *Drama Review* 46, no. 2 (2002): 145–56, 148.

22. Ibid., 146.

23. Erving Goffman, *The Presentation of Self in Everyday Life* (New York: Anchor Books, 1959); James C. Scott, *Domination and the Arts of Resistance: Hidden Transcripts* (New Haven, CT: Yale University Press, 1990).

24. Chang, "Harmony as Performance," 159.

25. Xiao Qiang, "The Battle for the Chinese Internet," *Journal of Democracy* 22, no. 2 (2011): 47–61.

26. Ibid., 47.

27. Ibid., 49, 59.

28. See Lijun Tang and Peidong Yang, "Symbolic Power and the Internet: The Power of a 'Horse,'" *Media, Culture & Society* 33 (2011): 675–91.

29. Baidu Baike is the Chinese equivalent to Wikipedia. In China, the mythical *Cao Ni Ma* looks like an alpaca but, through linguistic manipulation, has become

a rallying point over the struggle for unrestricted expression on the Internet. A Google Images search with the terms "grass mud horse" comes back with a plethora of appropriations.

30. Qiang, "Battle for the Chinese Internet," 52.

31. Bingchun Meng, "From Steamed Bun to Grass Mud Horse: E Gao as Alternative Political Discourse on the Chinese Internet," *Global Media and Communication* 7 (2011): 44.

32. Qiang, "Battle for the Chinese Internet," 52.

33. Ai Weiwei's *Hexie* river crab installation was a sensation at museums in New York (Brooklyn Museum), Washington, D.C (Hirshhorn Museum), Miami (Perez Art Museum), Indianapolis (Indianapolis Museum of Art), Ontario (Art Gallery of Ontario), and Tokyo (Mori Art Museum) among other cities around the world. *Hexie* was part of his *According to What?* exhibition. Most recently, a smaller version of *Hexie* has been displayed in Barcelona (La Virreina Image Center) as part of his *On the Table* exhibition.

34. Meng, "From Steamed Bun to Grass Mud Horse," 44. The six government agencies are the Information Office of the State Council, the Ministry of Industry and Information Technology, the Ministry of Culture, the State Administration for Industry and Commerce, the State Administration for Radio, Film and Television, and the General Administration of Press and Publication listed ibid., 48.

35. Ibid., 45.

36. Tang and Yang, "Symbolic Power and the Internet," 679, 680.

37. Ibid., 680, 681.

38. Ibid., 681.

39. Meng, "From Steamed Bun to Grass Mud Horse," 34.

40. Ibid., 46.

41. Ibid., 45.

42. See the *China Digital Times*'s "Grass Mud Horse Lexicon" at https://chinadigitaltimes.net.

43. Ibid.

44. Ibid.

45. Chang, "Harmony as Performance," 159.

46. Guobin Yang, *The Power of the Internet in China: Citizen Activism Online* (New York: Columbia University Press, 2009), 85.

47. Ibid., 85.

48. Such as in manifestos, documents, papers, speeches, and books. Ibid., 90.

49. Ibid., 95.

50. Weibo is the Chinese version of Twitter and Weixin (WeChat in its English version) is similar to WhatsApp.

51. Yang, *Power of the Internet in China*.

52. Hans Ulrich Obrist, *Ai Weiwei Speaks with Hans Ulrich Obrist* (New York: Penguin Books, 2011), ix–x.

53. Ai's performance art "Grass Mud Horse Covering the Middle," considered pornography, was quickly "harmonized" by the CPC's Internet censors. Images of Ai's performance art can be found with a Google Images search using the terms "grass mud horse covering the middle"; Ai's accompanying testimony has been translated as "Ai Weiwei: 'All That's Left Is a Grass Mud Horse,'" *China Geeks* (blog), June 15, 2009, http://chinageeksarchive.wordpress.com.

54. Leah Goldman, "Check Out Revolutionary Artwork by Ai Weiwei, the Guy China Has under House Arrest," *Business Insider*, June 23, 2011, http://www.businessinsider.com.

55. Translation by Charlie Custer, June 15, 2009, and retrieved from: http://chinageeksarchive.wordpress.com.

56. The image of Ai riding a grass mud horse and telling the Party's censors to "go home" can be found with a Google Images search using the terms "Ai Weiwei grass mud horse." The image is reproduced at Kyle Chayka, "Breaking: Ai Weiwei Released on Bail," Hyperallergic, June 22, 2011, http://hyperallergic.com.

57. Meng, "From Steamed Bun to Grass Mud Horse."

58. Images of Ai in Tiananmen Square with his back to the Gate of Heavenly Peace of the Forbidden City and of Ai giving "the finger" to Chairman Mao in Tiananmen Square can be found with a Google Images search using the terms "Ai Weiwei Tiananmen Square."

59. Anthony Tao as cited by Max Fisher, "Explaining Ai Weiwei's 'Grass Mud Horse' Obsession," *Washington Post*, October 24, 2012.

60. See Elizabeth Brunner, "Imagining China through the Culture Industries: The 798 Art Zone and New Chinas," this volume, for a nuanced reading of the 798 as culture industry.

61. Klein Sun Gallery, *Liu Bolin: The Invisible Man*, June 29–September 28, 2011. For this exhibition as well as Liu's various *Hiding in the City* exhibition images see http://www.kleinsungallery.com.

62. TED Talk, "Liu Bolin: The Invisible Man," February 2013, http://www.ted.com.

63. Alan Taylor, "Liu Bolin: The Invisible Man," *The Atlantic*, November 6, 2013.

64. The "Tiananmen" image of Liu standing invisibly in the place of Mao's iconic image can be accessed with a Google Images search using the terms "Liu Bolin Tiananmen."

65. Tony Fang, *Chinese Business Negotiating Style* (Thousand Oaks, CA: Sage Publications, 1999), 32.

66. Ibid.

67. Ibid., 167.

68. Ibid., 31.

69. Ibid., 30.

Imagining China through
the Culture Industries:
The 798 Art Zone and New Chinas

Elizabeth Brunner

In 2014, the Chinese government made a move to ban wordplay, alleging that it was creating "cultural and linguistic confusion" among the people of China.[1] When this story hit the United States, it ignited conversation fueled by both amazement and disdain. Why would the Chinese government ban puns in China? As the story bounced from television to radio to social media it was met with befuddled media personalities who, baffled by this edict, repeatedly made fun of the Chinese government for seeking to control its people to such a ridiculous level. Jon Stewart addressed the issue on Comedy Central's *The Daily Show*, poking fun at the Chinese government for being so overly controlling that it took away its citizen's ability to make the simplest of witticisms and, as many people from the vantage point of the United States see it, to engage in the most harmless form of critique.[2] Yet, from the perspective of the leaders of the Communist Party of China (CPC or the Party), the purpose of this law was not to prevent "cultural and linguistic confusion" at all;

rather, the government was trying to prevent netizens from developing alternative languages for activist purposes. Puns are widely used in China to circumvent censorship in a language rife with homonyms. Netizens trade widely in puns and use them as an alternative language that can (at least temporarily) elide censors, criticize the government, and raise awareness about sensitive issues. In fact, such language games are so common that *China Digital Times* publishes up-and-coming puns in its regular newsletter and keeps a database of phrases and their multilayered meanings.[3]

I open with the censorship issue for two reasons. First, I want to acknowledge the fact that censorship exists in China and is a force with which people have to contend, especially those who are politically active. Second, at the same time, this story shows how U.S. media framings perpetuate a limited understanding of how censorship operates on a daily basis.[4] Attention to censorship in China is perfectly warranted, as it is a deep and tangled problem throughout the country; yet people all over China are responding to censorship by circumventing the Party's "harmonizers" in creative ways.[5] The story of censorship in China is not that of a unilaterally effective edict; rather, it weaves in and out of government offices, dorm rooms, Weixin group chats, IKEA dolls, and the offices of software engineers. As Fan Yang argues, studying the "visibility" of messages that circumvent censors is a much more productive way of discussing the issue of censorship in China.[6] Unfortunately, when "censorship represses all Chinese people" determines how media consumers in the United States understand China, this narrative flattens the intricacy of events unfolding on the ground. Within this Orientalist imagination, outdated images of gray, staid citizens defeated by censors prevail, despite ample evidence that China is now a rapidly changing and boisterous nation brimming with creative activism. Such simplified portraits are in dire need of an update, one that acknowledges the sheer messiness and complexity of daily life in China. Indeed, if U.S.-based readers and viewers continue to approach China through the singular lens of censorship, they will miss out on the eruptive protests filling its streets and the vibrant online debates cascading across its social media. Ultimately, if we cannot embrace a more nuanced portrait, a more supple and subtle imagination, then our policies toward China will prove inadequate and our intercultural dealings will clash. I argue, then, that a subtler interpretive lens is needed to open up new ways of connecting with this emerging global partner over important environmental, social, and political issues. Accordingly, in this chapter I critically examine the ways censorship influences interpretations of a specific category of visual rhetoric: contemporary Chinese art.

Perhaps unsurprisingly, the censorship framework does not end with stories about banning puns, high-profile dissidents, or "the Great Firewall." This framework has also come to dominate how many in the United States understand the contemporary Chinese art scene. Whether addressing the censoring of Ai Weiwei from Chinese galleries[7] or the censoring of performance artist Han Bing by exiling him from Tiananmen during the enactment of his "Cabbage" piece,[8] the conclusion is all-too familiar: Chinese artists are perpetual victims of censorship. While censorship has been and continues to be a problem that *some* Chinese artists face, it is by no means the most dominant theme in contemporary Chinese art; nor has the censorship regime stifled the country's exploding metropolitan art scene. In fact, in terms of both size and levels of activity, Beijing's art spaces rival other metropolitan centers around the world.[9] CaoChangDi and Black Bridge (or Hei Qiao) offer working studios and homes to thousands of artists who gather to talk about their work, politics, and collaborations in courtyards over *chuar* and *pijiu*. The 798 art district, a former artist enclave, has in recent years evolved into a world-renowned exhibition space and shopping zone that embodies the new China: it is a place where art, commerce, tourism, and cunning political protests are entwined in vibrant networks of exchange, thus offering a living laboratory for reimagining China and its possible roles in global culture.

The 798 art district is fascinating and revelatory for several reasons. First, 798 is a highly visual space that encourages cross-cultural dialogues through painting, graffiti, architecture, design, and sculpture. With their ability to circumvent language barriers, images are a fast and effective means of provoking conversations. Second, this ability to communicate across cultures has arguably enhanced 798's success as an international tourist destination. Many thousands of people come every year to engage with the fellow visitors, local art, and unique design spaces, which means that 798 has become an important theater of communicative exchange between China and visitors from all over the globe.

Finally, I turn to art because it is a form of communication revered for its tendency to challenge authority and critique culture, and for having, as Marshall McLuhan argues, the "power to anticipate future social and technological developments, by a generation or more."[10] Thus, examining art's functions in a culture Westerners conceptualize as suppressed and riven with censorship reveals a more complex picture of how contemporary imaginations are evolving in China; at least in its high-end, privileged, consumer zones.

To develop the analysis, this chapter offers a detailed examination of the communicative interactions in 798 between cultural history, regional governance, global tourism, political economy, and local artists and their work. This examination tackles the discrepancy between pervasive Western media framings of China as a land of grim repression and the layered, rich, creative communication practices of 798's artists, allies, and enthusiasts. To that end, I first explain how the relations between art and politics communicate an image of China to the world; I do so by tracing 798's evolution from being a proud icon of the Cultural Revolution (it was a Cold War–era weapons plant) to becoming a government-sanctioned space of postmodern cultural reinvention. Second, I analyze thirty-four interviews (conducted over the course of twenty days in the summer of 2012) with Western visitors in English, which illustrate how some people from abroad are interpreting the space of 798 and using their experiences to reinterpret their views on China.[11] These interviews capture visitors' tensions between the conceptions they first held of China (largely influenced by the Western media) and their conceptions after experiencing 798's vibrant dynamic.[12] Third, I turn to interviews with six contemporary Chinese artists conducted in both English and Chinese to illustrate how the complicated terrain of 798 has helped, hindered, muddled, and intensified their experiences of being artists—and sometimes activists—in a rapidly changing China.[13] In response to the call put forward by academics and foreign policy experts to dismantle tired assumptions and Orientalist stereotypes of China, this chapter looks to contemporary China's cauldron of creativity—the cultural art scene of 798—to open up space to think closely about China's evolving social imaginaries. In doing so, I hope to honor the complexity of a country grappling with rapid economic growth, environmental degradation, resource scarcity, vanishing traditions, an influx of foreign influence, and a political system toying with reform.[14]

Tracing 798 from Electronics Factory to Creative Carnival

The 798 art zone is a vast space, inhabiting two million square feet on the northeast outskirts of Beijing. The large Bauhaus-style buildings create delicate arcs and layered angles that form gentle waves against the sky and are connected by a maze of streets, lanes, pipes, and small alleyways. This sprawling complex was conceived and constructed in the 1950s in a government-led effort to establish China as a militarily powerful and technologically focused communist nation.[15] As a symbol of national pride, 798 blossomed into a space that transformed citizens' ways of connecting with their country.[16] During its heyday in the late 1950s, the 798 factory's German motorcycle brigade rolled down the alleyways, music troupes filled the space with sound, and sporting competitions drew cheering crowds. Workers lived onsite with their families, dined together, and spent their free time with neighbors. During work hours, the cutting-edge facility whirred with the noise of machines that ended up producing all the latest in electronic designs, including the speakers for Tiananmen Square.

The success of 798 as a neighborhood of electronics factories and weapons plants, and thus as a source of national pride, was cut short by regime change, as Deng Xiaoping replaced Mao Zedong and implemented reforms that shifted the economic policies of the nation. During this period of rapid change, like many other large factory complexes that dotted the periphery of Beijing, 798 was shut down.[17] The jobless workers entitled to receive unemployment compensation posed a financial problem for the government-sanctioned managing body, the Seven Stars Group, and so, in 2001, in an effort to recoup some of their losses, they began renting out the abandoned buildings at low rates.[18] With its high ceilings and natural light, the Bauhaus-style architecture drew first dozens and then hundreds of local artist groups and art schools desperate for cheap rent and large spaces. Before long, the factory-turned-art complex was brimming with

energy, art, and conversations that quickly attracted visitors from around the world. By 2003, *Time* magazine and *Newsweek* had both dubbed 798 as a flourishing art district.[19] However, 2003 also marked the year Seven Stars stopped signing new leases, as it had very different plans for the space. By 2005, the artists' new home was scheduled to be razed.[20]

The leases Seven Stars signed were always meant to be temporary, as they had never dreamed the burgeoning artist colony would transform into a world-renowned revenue-generating tourist destination.[21] When the government-supported plans to build an "electronic city" akin to Silicon Valley became public in 2004, Chinese artist and People's Congress of Beijing representative Li Xiangqu directed a motion to save what had become a beloved home and workplace.[22] Li's fight was bolstered by Western media attention and official visits by such global figures as Viviane Reding, the European Union's Minister of Culture[23] By 2006, 798 had been rescued from its death sentence and proclaimed a Cultural Creative Industry Cluster.

In less than five years, then, the Chinese government moved from plans to demolish 798 to "designat[ing] the district the centre of China's cultural creative industry."[24] Since then, "the concept of *creative industries* has become almost mandatory in cultural policy circles around China."[25] Kelly Chen states that "it was in 1995 that the Chinese government formally invested in cultural industries through their ministry of culture," but not until 2006—the year 798 was officially protected—did China begin to witness a drastic increase in the number of cultural sites in Beijing.[26] In 2007, Hu Jintao made a formal push to develop China's "soft power" during his keynote speech to the Seventeenth National Congress of the CPC. He further made clear in his address that "Culture has become a more and more important source of national cohesion and creativity and a factor of growing significance in the competition in overall national strength."[27] One area in which this strength could be developed, he told his audience, was art and the culture industries, as this would help to

Figures 1 and 2 (*opposite*). One of the many street-level signs announcing 798 (left); the new art spaces inhabit former factory buildings that still bear the evidence of their Cold War, industrial functions.

legitimize China as a proactive global power rather than a global "factory." Between 2006 and 2008, Beijing developed twenty-three creative clusters or zones, evidencing an official move toward cultivating *creativity* rather than solely focusing on economic might in an effort to influence foreign perceptions and imaginings.[28] With the 2008 Olympics came the understanding that in order to become a global superpower, the Chinese government needed to invest not only in technological and military advancements, but also in becoming a "global cultural space."[29] Henceforward, the work of the imagination would be harnessed to the national interest as a form of consumer- and media-friendly "soft power."

Today, 798 enables the government to showcase China as an important center of world culture. Stories abound in national state-sanctioned media outlets, including *China Daily* and *Xinhua News*, and the official website of the Beijing government boasts about the struggling artist community that flourished in the face of impending doom.[30] The government's involvement in a part of Chinese culture that features controversial topics might seem curious, but 798 has been turned into a bona fide media darling, capable of garnering the global attention necessary to sway international perspectives on the country. This is likely why the CPC requires that China's Biennale—which follows in the tracks of the Venice Biennale, Art Basel, Documenta, and other world-renowned art events—be held in 798.[31] Such widespread acclaim and exposure, however, has radically altered the makeup of the district. As the CPC leveraged its investment to transform 798 from an underground art space into the face of contemporary China, more and more high-profile Western galleries—including the Pace Gallery, the Ullens Center for Contemporary Art (UCCA), and Galleria Continua—have replaced smaller independent galleries run by local artists, who are now unable to afford the ever-increasing rent. Thus we see how a modest art collective furnished the global cultural aspirations of China's central government, and how the success of this campaign continues to impact and transform the very meaning of 798 today.

As Beijing's third most visited tourist destination, behind only the Great Wall and the Forbidden City, 798 functions simultaneously as art center, revenue generator, face of contemporary China, youth hangout, and Western-friendly tourist destination, thereby offering an alternative space—compared, say, to the grim emptiness of Tiananmen Square, or to the banal classicism of the Forbidden City—for imagining a new, vibrant, thriving China.[32] Visitors to Paris and New York tend to flock to the Louvre (9.3 million in 2013) or the Metropolitan Museum of Art (6.3 million the same year).[33] However, in Beijing, *millions* of tourists choose to visit 798 each year rather than stopping at the National Art Museum of China, which is a mere stone's throw from Tiananmen Square yet saw only one million visitors in 2013.[34] A unique convergence of factors—including sensational coverage of censorship in China, the expectation of art as a combative expression of free speech, the delightful visual appeal of 798, and the highlighting of dissident art in Western media—have thus brought immense international attention to 798, even as the National Art Museum lags in attendance and importance. In this sense, 798 may be evolving, even more than the Party's officially appointed spaces, into something like a national center, a must-see emblem of where China is heading.

Reporters and scholars, faced with the question of how to situate 798 in both domestic Chinese politics and the unwieldy context of global art, often turn to the seductive free speech/censorship binary, which perpetuates tired narratives of China in the West. Tracing the history of 798, however, reveals a more nuanced picture of China's contemporary emergence, including recognizing how state interests commingle with struggling artists in ways that are both mutually beneficial and harmful; how international support of 798—often fueled by the desire for Western-style democracy to take hold in China—pushes the issue of whether an artist's district is saved to the stage of global media; and how the CPC's determination to refute stereotypes of China as backward and outdated triggers a frenzy of modernization and cultural "opening" just in time for the 2008 Olympics. All of these factors have shaped the ever-changing space that people continue to experience today. A historical perspective thus offers a way of understanding 798, and China more broadly, by addressing a series of shifting historical relations where overlapping foreign interests, Party-driven nationalism, clashing financial motives, inchoate cultural trends, and emerging social pressures intermingle as part of the ongoing drama of imagining a new China.

Meeting New Faces; or, Interview Data from 798

During the summer of 2012, I spent twenty days in the 798 arts district interviewing visitors (in English) from Germany, Australia, the Netherlands, Holland, New Zealand, Romania, the United States, and Britain. All interviewees have been anonymized. While conducting the interviews, I encountered tourists, expats, businesspeople, former Chinese citizens, professors, and study-abroad students. In total, I conducted thirty-four open-ended interviews in cafés, on street corners, and with people sitting amid the many different outdoor art installations. Three major themes emerged during these interviews, with each one illuminating particular cultural tension: (1) between a China as preimagined by Westerners versus the China they actually experience; (2) between assumptions about 798 as a free-speech bastion versus the surveillance culture witnessed in other tourist destinations; and (3) between 798 as a unique expression of "contemporary China" versus an outpost of "Westernized" commercial values. While the interview data used herein was collected in 2012, my thinking about 798, and my subsequent analysis of the data, has benefited from extensive time spent in China since then, including my immersion in Chinese language classes and ongoing dialogue with the artists driving the contemporary art scene in China.

RESPONSE #1: STRUCTURING DISCOVERIES
IN WESTERN WAYS

While resting at a café across from the UCCA, an American woman remarked that after traveling around Beijing for more than a week, the thing that surprised her most was that she "did not think that Chinese people would be happy." This candid statement exhibits a marked tension between the China she preimagined and the China she eventually experienced. This reaction, however, turned out to be more the norm than the exception. The assertion that Chinese people are "unhappy" is explicitly made in Western press outlets over and over again, as can be seen from titles like "Chinese Increasingly Unhappy with Life," "Why China Is Unhappy," "China Is Unhappy," and "China's Unhappy Rich."[35] This is yet another imagined community in China, one that is composed of somber individuals unilaterally oppressed by their government and too tired to fight back. This imaginary of Chinese people as unhappy and discontent alienates the Chinese people and fashions a place few would spend money to visit. These reportedly discontented citizens are being ruled by what the *Los Angeles Times* dubbed "gray, staid Communist Party leaders" who are robotic and out of touch with their citizens. By contrast, the United States is led by "the polar opposite," a young and charismatic President Barack Obama.[36] The rhetorical framing of China and the United States as cultural opposites creates distance between the two countries, demonstrating the power of social imaginaries to conjure real problems from partial understandings. Geographical distance and language barriers make intercultural communication difficult; those unfamiliar with China's unique cultural landscape must therefore rely on shorthand representations written by journalists, yet these tend to depict a China of the past, a nation laced with Sinophobic rhetoric, couched in images of the "Yellow Peril," and sometimes explained via a heavy-handed dose of American exceptionalism.[37] As Kent Ono and Joy Yang Jiao observe: "A discursive power struggle exists between a time-worn Orientalist image of China as a museum piece—an 'ancient civilization' and Cold War enemy—and a China under authoritarian rule but quickly becoming a modern, quasi-capitalist powerhouse with tremendous economic traction, a massive population, and a future that threatens aging and slow-to-change western-style superpowers."[38] This discursive tension is difficult to reconcile. Indeed, the interviews I conducted demonstrate a tendency for foreign visitors to 798 to rely on comfortable though outdated ways of imagining China.

If Westerners rely on tired clichés as a foundation for understanding China, then the path carved for them—China as ancient and stagnant and repressive—will serve as a broken compass for navigating China's new cultural terrain. This could explain why one visitor, perplexed by what she had witnessed in 798, remarked that she had never thought of China and modern art on the "same page, let alone the same sentence." The contemporary aspect of 798 was a shock to a number of other visitors as well, who said they only thought of China as old and ancient. Others could not but see 798 in light of the Cultural Revolution. For these visitors, 798 represented "a big step forward" for the Chinese

people from the days of Mao. The tendency to be surprised by a culturally dynamic contemporary China signals a tendency toward thinking of
the country as stuck in the past rather than evolving at an unprecedented
rate.[39] Thus, in contrast to the China imagined in foreign newspapers,
guidebooks, the Chinese tourism industry, commercials, history texts,
and countless movies and popular narratives, 798 offers jubilant scenes
of Chinese youth with wild haircuts and outrageous outfits weaving in
and out of shops as artists chat over lattes and streams of visitors flow
through the streets.[40]

Unprompted, a number of interviewees blamed the media for the
discrepancy between the China they experienced and the one they
preimagined. One interviewee remarked directly that the freedom they
found in 798 was not portrayed in Western media. This is not surprising considering that recent studies have shown newspaper coverage of
China, including highly regarded outlets such as the *New York Times*,
portrays the country, "as afflicted by an archaic authoritarian rule, unable to master rapid and comprehensive modernization, prone to seeking
unfair advantage, dominating Tibet . . . and inferior to US and western
culture."[41] One American visitor, pondering her own surprise, concluded
that the dissonance between the China she imagined and the one she
experienced in 798 arose from the disproportionate energy devoted to
stories about dissidents being punished instead of artists developing new
norms of cultural expression. The rhetorical work of imagining nations
hinges on the power of synecdoche, which converts select parts of a
culture into its overriding narratives about the nation. Within that framework, I am arguing then, following the interview cited above, that 798
serves as a powerful disruptor of older, clichéd versions of synecdoche,
offering instead new imaginings, new visions, new possibilities.

Indeed, as I sat down with interviewees day after day, those across
the table from me focused again and again on how "different" 798
was—either from what they expected to see, had seen, or had previously
imagined. Clearly, 798 offers visitors a glimpse of contemporary China
that challenges previously established notions. The graffiti-covered brick
walls, the headless sculpture of Chairman Mao, and the advertisements
for Damien Hirst's newest show; all these sights disrupt old stereotypes of
China as a land of pagodas, walls, and geishas. The communicative reach

of 798 is characterized by its distinctly immersive visuality, which makes outside visitors feel as if they are temporarily transcending language barriers. Inside the walls of 798, art, advertisements, youth culture, and kitschy wares offer a space of easy convergence between cultures. It feels both familiar and strange, at once; it seems both profoundly Chinese yet also foreshadowing of a coming world of "transculture."

While many visitors used the cultural space opened up by 798 to think China anew, others simply considered a place like 798 to be anomalous among an otherwise homogeneous China. Still others forced this "new" China into existing discourses, including those that focus on censorship and freedom of speech. China, however, cannot be bridled by binaries. It is not just new or just old; nor is it simply old on the way to becoming new. Take, for example, a street corner in the Wudaokou neighborhood of Beijing, where at any given moment you may witness a brand new BMW whizzing by a horse-drawn carriage overloaded with fruit before turning right in front of a pack of people on bicycles and electric scooters. Before the car disappears, a man on a tricycle lugs a cart so overflowing with plastic bottles that they have to be tied down in the most intricate of fashions. Simultaneously, immense waves of people are headed toward the subway, where they pay less than a single U.S. dollar to ride one of the world's largest and most modern subway systems. These are scenes of hybridity, eruption, disruption, contradiction, and splendor. China is many things at once, moving, changing, and in a constant state of transformation. It is a place that simply does not make sense when interpreted through the limited imaginaries offered to so many U.S. readers and watchers.

RESPONSE #2: THE PERSISTENCE OF BINARIES AND FREEDOM UNDER SURVEILLANCE

References to censorship arose in many street-corner conversations and relaxed strolls through galleries. After discussing their impressions of China and the space of 798, I asked visitors if they thought there was more freedom of speech in the arts district than elsewhere in China. Almost every person responded with "yes, definitely." However, the majority of people I interviewed spoke little, if any, Chinese, which complicates such a strong assertion. How could visitors know whether people elsewhere were discussing politics if they did not speak the language? Most of the support for their assertions came from visual observations. The various cartoonish representations of Chairman Mao that lined shop windows, the graffiti scrawled across walls, the lack of visible police presence, and the perceived lack of monitoring—there are, indeed, surveillance cameras on almost every block in 798—gave many the idea that 798 was much freer than other places, like Tiananmen Square or the Forbidden City. Pointing to specific art pieces, visitors elaborated on what they perceived to be overt critiques of the military or Chairman Mao as symbolizing free speech for them. Part of the lure of 798, then, is how it enables observers to watch others imagining China, making the leap from one piece of art to some larger understanding of the nation.

This being said, such observations and imaginings are never uniform. College students from both the United Kingdom and Romania saw what some considered clear signs of free speech—the critiques of Mao, for example—as merely marketable kitsch. They felt that tourists, intrigued by communism but knowing little about it, would want to buy the objects as curiosities. The student from Romania said 798 reminded her of her homeland in that the space for free speech exists but is contained. I do not have the space here to delve more deeply into this question, but it would be consistent with trends in cultural studies, communication studies, and art theory to wonder in future work about how evolving markets, kitsch, and postmodern parody both enable and constrain meaning in China's art scenes.

One American professor I interviewed, troubled by his study-abroad students' complaints about lack of access to Facebook in China, brought his class to 798 to counter the singular focus they develop on Internet censorship while in China. When students have a very limited amount of time to spend experiencing the culture, the professor found that they fixate on such restrictions. Because they cannot speak to Chinese people, their view of China becomes colored by these impositions, so 798 helps them to realize—because it is a highly visual space—that people in China can indeed express themselves creatively. For this professor, 798 broadens the students' perspective, for they, along with so many others, are surprised to find an energetic contemporary art scene anywhere in China.

With the abundance of media pointing to an oppressed China, visitors' tendency to regard 798 as an island of freedom amid a sea of oppression is unsurprising.[42] My interviews suggest that those who had spent less time in China and did not speak the language were more likely to view 798 in this polarized fashion. Moreover, I suspect that fierce adherence to the view of 798 as an exceptional outpost of free speech points to a tendency to fall back on the familiar binaries characteristic of so many U.S. imaginings. If experiencing a place like 798 abruptly shifted many interviewee's viewpoints and expanded their understandings of China, other interviewees used their experiences at 798 simply to reinforce existing stereotypes.

RESPONSE #3: ADVANCING COPYCATS AND PERCEIVED WESTERNIZATION

While interviewees repeatedly praised the uniqueness of 798, some thought it simply mimicked Western art areas, thus expressing a perception of China as a "copycat." This framing is also prevalent in political and media discourses about China. During the 2012 presidential election, both candidates—Mitt Romney and Barack Obama—alleged that China was "cheating" to win economically, in large part by stealing U.S. innovations.[43] Research and development theft by China remains, indeed, a serious problem, but its outsized presence in the media twists the way people see *all* of China. Problems arise when this framing of China as a country of copycats is echoed, as it was by visitors I interviewed, as a way to understand actual lived experiences in China. When unable to tell the difference between contemporary Chinese art and contemporary Western art, visitors assumed that Chinese art had merely stolen from other artists and thus had become "too Westernized." Interviewees remarked that they could not place what was distinctly "Chinese" about the art in 798, despite the prevalence of distinctive colors, techniques, subject matter, and materials. This tendency for the Chinese characteristics of an artwork to remain hidden is addressed in Ming Cheung's work on the topic.[44] Cheung argues that most people's inability to see past Western influences in Chinese art, despite the strong influence of Chinese culture and techniques in a given work, is largely due to the visitor's lack of exposure to Chinese art history. The artifacts, lines, brushwork, and perspectives characteristic of Chinese artists will be imperceptible to those who are unfamiliar with this visual lexicon.[45]

Based upon the perceived lack of Chinese characteristics, much of the work in 798 was viewed as a "failure," as merely an imitation of Western art. When asked what they considered to be "Chinese," one group of visitors told me that they think of ink drawings of mountains as distinctively Chinese. No one pointed out the incorporation of scholar rocks, the flat perspective, the use of black and white instead of color, or the style of the lines as "Chinese." Yet these aesthetic components align with traditional Chinese art and were prevalent in the work of the contemporary Chinese artists on display at the time. Artists were being judged by Western understandings of creativity and standards, which made success for Chinese artists difficult at best. The only work deemed remarkable was that which they perceived as leveraging a critique of communism or Mao. No interviewee pointed to or identified components of work that were linked to Chinese culture beyond these more overt and highly recognizable narratives. In summary, impoverished imaginings about contemporary Chinese art—based in part on unfamiliarity with Chinese art conventions and norms—left many interviewees grasping for understanding by calling upon clichés and stereotypes.[46]

Although some interviewees considered Chinese artists to be copycats, almost all considered 798 to represent progress for China and were excited to have found such a dynamic and Westernized space. This is evident even in a simple tongue-in-cheek statement made by one group of three German men, who said they would "judge 798" on "whether they could find a good cup of coffee." Such comments are prevalent in 798, where many visitors seem less interested in learning something about an emerging China than in finding the familiar consumerist comforts of home. Indeed, if my interviews suggest an overarching theme, it is the sheer difficulty of comprehending China on its own terms, as interviewees, again and again, seemed to fill in the gaps of their understanding by calling upon preexisting imaginings.

A MORE EXPERIENCED RESPONSE GROUP:
TEMPORARY RESIDENTS AND RETURN VISITORS

Over the course of my twenty days in 798, four of the thirty-four people I interviewed were Americans either temporarily living in China or academics conducting studies. I have chosen to focus on these individuals separately, in part, because the data tended to differ rather dramatically from the more casual visitors. Interviews with residents and regular visitors to the space were much longer and more in-depth, and as we delved deeper into the questions, I saw more nuanced perspectives of China and its politics surface. One theme that arose in these longer conversations was a frustration with what they perceived as Western misunderstandings of China, including unquestioned consumption of Chinese dissident art. These interviewees were skeptical of Chinese art they viewed as deliberately playing into Cold War rhetoric. They viewed this as a calculated move some artists make for purely financial gain. Mentioned artists included Ai Weiwei, Yue Minjun, Wang Guangyi, and the Gao Brothers. These artists consistently critique the CPC, often by highlighting widely recognized and politically charged cultural icons, such as Chairman Mao and Tiananmen Square, in their art. Two interviewees asserted that art appearing to contest the CPC was less about meaning and more about artists making profits from Western buyers.[47]

According to the numbers, Western buyers are big investors in Chinese dissident art.[48] Several dissident artists have risen to fame with their critiques of Mao and the Cultural Revolution. For example, in addition to being named *Time* magazine's person of the year in 2007, Yue Minjun's *Execution* broke the record for Chinese artists that same year when it brought in $5.9 million dollars at a Sotheby's auction.[49] *Gweong-Gweong* topped this record in 2008 when it sold for $6.9 million.[50] Ai Weiwei— *Time*'s 2011 runner-up person of the year—has also garnered a great deal of fame. *Sunflower Seeds* fetched three times the expected value, with a price tag of $559,394.[51] According to AskArt.com, between 2006 and 2011 sales of Ai's work rose from $300,000 to $1,716,330. Fellow dissident artist Wang Guangyi's artwork also made a big splash with Western buyers. *Mao-Zedong AO* sold in 2007 for $4.1 million, while Guangyi's *Coca-Cola* painting sold the same year for $1.8 million.[52] *Mao Zedong: P2*, which is a silhouette of Mao with a grid overlay that resembles the crosshairs of a gun sight, sold in 2011 for $2.4 million.[53] Playing into the political priorities of Westerners turns out to be very good business for the art industry in China.

Temporary residents and return visitors blamed the dramatic changes in the "new" 798 on this attention from Western consumers. Whereas 798 was once home to many working artists, by 2012 cafés, pizza parlors, and souvenir shops had replaced the majority of studios and galleries. For these expats, the government's involvement combined with Western underwriting posed an unwelcome trend that wrought uncomfortable changes. For them, Westernization was not a positive change but one fraught with complications for the artists and their work. The audience had changed, which meant the art being produced had changed as well. These four interviewees were therefore highly ambivalent about the Westernization of 798 and contemporary Chinese art. In fact, for the expats who lived through the changes since 2002, 798's Westernization was viewed as deeply problematic and was even met with anger and resentment. Specifically, two of the expats I interviewed openly stated they were unhappy with the transformation of studios to coffee shops and felt that 798 was nothing but a facade. Without the CPC's efforts to preserve 798, however, and its catering to Western ways of art viewing, the space was destined to become just another Silicon Valley. Recognizing that these tensions exist as one part of a larger fabric, rather than automatically judging the space as either good or bad, is a useful way to move beyond static thinking. The 798 district does challenge perspectives, but this one small district on the outskirts of Beijing cannot bear the burden of revising worn-out perceptions. Indeed, the synecdochical conversion of part-into-whole is a useful fiction, albeit one based, in part, on sheer wish fulfillment; in this case, my hunch is that 798 alone cannot bear the weight of triggering new national imaginings, either in or about China. Rather, 798 will need to be situated within a variety of enhanced communicative practices—more nuanced media coverage, a closer engagement with Chinese history, an increase in study-abroad programs, and a more thorough reading of cultural narratives—if we hope to engage an evolving nation in all its messy splendor.

Artists Unpack the Complicated Terrain of 798

In total, between 2012 and 2014, I interviewed six artists about their relations to 798. Each artist's assessment of the space was complicated by their particular understandings of art trends, neighborhood politics, national narratives, and their relationships to globalization. Indeed, over the course of their relationships with the space, they have seen 798 negotiated over and tugged at by national politics, global economics, shifting aesthetics, evolving galleries, visiting foreigners, visiting Chinese, the increasing commodification of art, and the influx of Western gallery owners and artists; all of this played into their own personal struggles with staying or leaving 798. In Beijing, as with so many other art communities, artists live on the outskirts. They take over abandoned warehouses, old villages, and factory complexes like 798 and turn them into spaces of creativity. Almost inevitably, the rent in these spaces then increases, and the artists are pushed out to find a new home, another "outskirt." The major difference between Beijing and other metropolitan centers across the globe is the pace at which this shifting of boundaries occurs. The sheer speed of Beijing's industrialization and urban expansion means that artists are forced to find new homes with alarming frequency. Thus, charting the migration of artists can lead China watchers to uncensored conversations about the country's current social problems and how citizens are confronting them. Following the artists reveals how, at the grounded, street level of daily life, people are dealing with the interplay of advancing global capitalism, resurgent Chinese nationalism, and evolving cultural trends.

In 2002, according to artist interviewees, almost every occupied building in 798 was an artist's studio or gallery. A decade later, of the 175 storefronts I counted, 114 were restaurants, cafés, or small shops, and 61 storefronts could be categorized as galleries. The numbers of artists plummeted dramatically when both numbers of visitors and gallery rents increased. Suddenly, the very artists who had once fought for the space could no longer call 798 their home. As of 2014, according to artist interviewees who had rented space there at the time, less than twenty-five artists lived in 798. Others moved to nearby abandoned warehouses to set up shop once again, where they have resorted to signing illegal leases that can be revoked at a moment's notice. The two most popular and thriving new artist enclaves are CaoChangDi and Hei Qiao. CaoChangDi is home to approximately forty galleries and somewhere between one and two hundred artists. Hei Qiao ("Black Bridge") houses an estimated two thousand artists. The movement from 798 to these new districts is thematically evident throughout the work of many artists. Annamma Joy and John F. Sherry Jr. write, "Hung (1999) suggests that the defining characteristic of contemporary experimental art is the artist's own self-positioning and re-positioning in a changing society—not style or politics."[54] Change is the one thread that runs rampant throughout contemporary Chinese art, because change is what artists experience in their own lives on a daily basis.

While all of the artists I interviewed were disappointed that 798 moved from artist complex to tourist destination, they acknowledged that these changes rippled throughout the Chinese art market with diverse repercussions. On the one hand, 798 helped establish China as an important player in the contemporary international art market. This new global face has enticed tourists, increased visibility, boosted art revenues, initiated new conversations, challenged old stereotypes of China, and offered local artists an established center for creative expression. On the other hand, it forced most of the artists out of a space they themselves founded. The introduction of big name Western galleries increased competition for artists wanting to show their work in 798, so lesser-known Chinese artists have a tougher time displaying their work in this bustling art zone. In this sense 798 fits into an evolving global narrative, wherein gentrification and advanced consumerism impact the lived realities of artists who are no longer able to afford to live in the neighborhoods they made famous and profitable.

According to one artist, 798 is no longer a space of creative possibility, but simply "ordinary business practice" for the Chinese government. This observation jells with how academics have observed that

Figures 3 and 4 (*opposite*). On the left, the gate to the Hei Qiao Artist Complex; on the right, just outside this new art space, another scene of urban destruction in preparation for development, in this case with an invading herd of goats from a nearby farm.

"the specific structural dynamics of the cultural industries sector also [chime] with wider discourses of economic innovation and competitiveness."[55] When 798 was saved and dubbed a creative cultural zone, it quickly became commodified; thereafter, tensions between artists, local government, and the leasing spaces of 798 were exacerbated. This artist believes the government does not necessarily support the art of 798 but does support the image 798 provides the country. This explains why the CPC has invested so much in 798, to attract foreigners and their revenue. From this perspective, the oppositional and inventional possibilities of 798 are at risk of being absorbed by the nationalist needs of the CPC; 798 thrives, from this perspective, as a tool for refurbishing China's international image, as a factory of positive imaginings meant to serve nationalist purposes.

Nonetheless, the changes resented by the previous artist are seen as an opportunity by another, who sees the art zone's vitality as responsible for bringing in a stream of new buyers from Europe and the United States. Indeed, people from all over the world visit 798 to purchase works of art, but now they can also buy Chinese art at international auctions. New and established collectors alike are ravenously consuming contemporary Chinese art, which can be seen turning up in European and U.S. galleries and parks around the world in places such as Germany, New York, San Francisco, London, Los Angeles, Washington D.C., and Chicago.[56] It would be fascinating in future research to try to determine how this globalizing Chinese art impacts the imaginings of international viewers: Does seeing a Chinese-made sculpture in a park in Chicago change the viewer's thinking about China? Do art patrons in Venice or Mumbai find themselves thinking differently about contemporary life in China?

As one artist put it, the question of 798's impact is not a question for Chinese people, but for foreigners. For him "China is just China. It doesn't change us too much because we have 798. While you can see more art now that 798 has changed into this art space, China is still China with or without 798." While 798 shatters old ways of understanding China, it obviously cannot represent all of China. For him, like many Chinese people I talked to, one cannot know China simply by visiting Beijing's temples, tourist stops, and trendy *hutongs*. One must learn the language and talk to people across the country playing mahjong outside convenience shops, driving a taxicab around Dalian, or fishing along the shores of Xiamen. The culture industries can offer only a single face(t) of China's diverse and contradictory social terrain: some people travel across the country and line up hours in advance to glimpse Chairman Mao's glass-encased embalmed body, while others have become so devoted to a materialistic lifestyle that they willingly buy into absurd pyramid schemes. For artists, 798 is a space of culture and change, but also a place afflicted with consumerism run rampant. It is a knotted zone of activity that both aids and marginalizes Beijing's artists. In interviews, where I gathered with several artists together around a table of home-cooked food to discuss the issues surrounding 798, no single answer emerged. The only reliable theme was the sheer complexity of daily life in a nation exploding with change.

Concluding by Opening the Red Curtain

The 798 art space is an auspicious case through which to track an evolving China because one task central to art itself is invoking new ways of thinking. Rather than offering universal proclamations, artists deploy ambiguity and contradiction to engage viewers and open up space for new conversations. Indeed, ambiguity is a forceful tactic used not only by artists, but also by protestors and by Chairman Mao. In a single piece of art—or a single furry wolf doll named Lufsig, or in speeches by Chairman Mao—meanings proliferate.[57] Take, for example, an art piece that remained on exhibit for well over a year at the UCCA in 798. This installation by artist Wang Jianwei was set on a stage that rose above the floor. On either side of the stage were navy green columns featuring a vibrant red star, a symbol of China's communist era. In between the columns were three dense layers of plastic red curtains that gleamed, reflecting the lighting of the gallery. The first two layers were pulled back to reveal a third layer. Behind the dense plastic a pool of white plastic leaked out and collected on the stage.

What was behind the red curtain?[58] What was the barrier of red—a color that represents China, happiness, politics, nationalism, and celebrations—hiding? The only thing emerging, seeping out from behind the red curtain, was that pool of white. Though white is most commonly associated with ideals of purity, goodness, and chastity in the United States, it has long represented death in China. Was death leaching out from behind the red curtain of China? Was this a nod to censorship, oppression, or other well-worn modes of seeing China? Such a conclusion would seem logical and aligns neatly with existing discourses. Yet this piece is anything but simplistic and flat. The ambiguity of the piece generates a plenitude of interpretations. If we examine the piece more closely we can see that Wang's decision to construct the curtain from plastic suggests that this barrier is somehow fake, disposable, and a contemporary construction—detached from the 1950s, when communism first took root. The China represented on stage may reference the China of the past, but it also highlights change. The oscillation between the artwork's two and three dimensionality plays with the viewer's expectations. The viewer must enter the three-dimensional space to view the piece, but once there the work is largely two-dimensional. The curtains cut off the space rather abruptly and form a flat plane. Though the piece requires three-dimensional immersion, the viewer is provided with largely two-dimensional visual stimulation. So why not paint the red curtain on a canvas? This tension between two and three dimensions mimics the tension between what China is and how it is seen. China is complex, multifaceted, and varied, but the *fake* plastic curtain, which represents a simplified and artificially constructed China, prevents people from seeing more, rendering the rest of China invisible.

If viewers turn to the gallery tag, they find an intriguing call for even further conversation. According to the UCCA's script, Wang's work is "about how to define a space of uncertainty." For Wang, the site—798— is a space of uncertainty, as is China's emerging global position. China's intense and rapid change has created clashes, openings, new directions, confrontations with the past, and prevailing uncertainty about the future. The 798 art district is an important synecdoche of China in all of these ways. Wang sees the UCCA within the larger 798 art complex as "a venue for the production of a certain kind of cultural illusion, in another word, a theatre." For Wang as well as some visitors, expats, and artists, 798's influence and face is a large and complicated production with many actors, stagehands, and lighting artists that is still very much in production: 798 is not still or complete, but a constant performance.

Wang believes that by combining memory and utopia and "by interpreting the past, we will be able to re-connect to the present and to forebode the future."[59]

Art is mobile, shifting, open. It both mirrors and influences social complexity. The themes that emerge are telling. When we look to contemporary Chinese art, we see a discourse laden with themes of change—environmental, social, religious, political, economic, and cultural. It appears as if McLuhan was right; if we look to this art as a predictor of social development, what we should see is change.[60] And we do. China's urban populations are growing at an unprecedented rate, and along with a growing population comes the transformation of cityscapes, public transportation systems, consumption practices, and living standards. These changes impact China's environmental stability. With only 7 percent of the world's freshwater but 20 percent of its population, the scarcity of clean water for drinking, crops, and livestock will put immense amounts of pressure on the government to make tough decisions between clean water and the revenue generated by factories.[61] The problems do not end here, but extend into the political realm. A recent Pew Research poll found that 33 percent of China's population considers environmental issues to be the greatest challenge facing the world today, and many people are willing to stand up and do something about it, which means that communication flows between people and their government are also changing.[62] All of these themes are readily apparent in the art being painted, sculpted, and performed across China.

Starting from 798, this chapter has sought to uncover a changing China, a China that is elaborated as imaginings are exchanged, explained, and expounded by tracing different threads. If we continue to look at China through various complex perspectives, we find Wang's deep uncertainty about the future. This deep uncertainty provides not only the fear that attends U.S. discourses about China and China's discourses about the United States, but also the space of possibility to imagine new futures where these countries collaborate on environmental, economic, and trade policies for the benefit of global citizens. I hope we can learn to inhabit these new spaces, in part by opening our minds to the wonderful social imaginaries percolating up from 798 and China's thriving contemporary art scene.

NOTES

1. Tara Branigan, "China Bans Wordplay in Attempt at Pun Control," *The Guardian*, November 28, 2014.

2. Chuck O'Neil, "A Measured Discussion of the Prohibition of Wordplay in the People's Republic of China," *The Daily Show with Jon Stewart*, Comedy Central, December 2, 2014.

3. See the "Culture" tab at *China Digital Times*, http://chinadigitaltimes.net, for a range of such stories.

4. Sensationalistic stories of censorship that create certain imaginings of China are tantalizing, dramatic, and rampant in major Western media outlets, ranging from the *New York Times* to the *Washington Post*, *Los Angeles Times*, MSNBC, CNN, NPR, and Fox News. As readers flip through front pages or scroll through search results, "censorship" and "China" are an oft-repeated refrain that portray a repressed China. For example, a Google search for "China censorship" (conducted in June 2014) produced 7,260 results in a mere sixteen-day period; a LexisNexis search for "China censorship" shows over 762 results in the mass media between 2008 and mid-2014. Additionally, blog posts, travel guides, and Twitter feed headlines—with titles like "Dim Hopes for a Free Press in China"; "Behind the Great Firewall: What It's Really Like to Log on from China"; "Tiananmen Censorship Reflects Crackdown under Xi Jinping"; "China's WeChat Messaging App Targeted in Month-long Censorship Crackdown"; "Here Are 6 Huge Websites China Is Censoring Right Now"; "The Many Faces of Chinese Censorship"; "Freedom Rock? Not in China"; and "Breaching the Great Firewall of China"—confront readers at every click. "Censorship" has become one of the dominant frameworks by which Western media explain China, thus framing it as a land of perpetual repression.

5. China has increasingly become a center for activism under communist rule. According to a 2012 Human Rights Watch report, the number of protests in China is estimated at 250–500 per day. Moreover, Censorship in China is not unilaterally successful, but a complicated and ever-changing network. VPNs, images, puns, and an endless number of homonyms are popular tools for circumventing censors.

6. Fan Yang, "Rethinking China's Internet Censorship: The Practice of Recoding and the Politics of Visibility," *New Media & Society* 18, no. 7 (2014): 1364–81.

7. The automatic turn to frame all that is Chinese through censorship has dominated not just discussions of media and websites, but discussions of contemporary Chinese art as well. For example, the world's most famous Chinese

artist, Ai Weiwei, has risen to international fame running on a platform of anticensorship art. His outspoken critiques of Chinese censorship create a point of commonality between himself and Western audiences and secure him a spot in Western media on an almost daily basis. Using his Twitter feed, Instagram, YouTube, museums, and art galleries, Ai has garnered a faithful following who align themselves with his stance including artists, activists, and ordinary people. Many of these alliances are formed through a mutual hatred of censorship and a longing for freedom of expression rather than an understanding of Ai's somewhat complicated position on various issues. For example, one of Ai's followers, David G. Hallman, stated to Al-Jazeera's "The Stream": "I can't read Chinese artist Ai Weiwei's tweets but I follow him out of solidarity with his campaign for greater democracy and artistic freedom." A similar sentiment is apparent in a post retweeted by Ai from "SunniBrown" that offered this piece of support "I love that many of us follow //aiww and many of us also don't understand a damn thing he's saying. Now that's love" (see Aiww English, March 10, 2012). Rather than "love," this blind alliance evidences how the connection with Ai Weiwei is not necessarily about his art at all, but rather his relationship with the anticensorship/pro–free speech movement. Too often, Ai's critiques of the Chinese government are highlighted while his critiques of the U.S. government fall to the wayside.

8. Austin Ramzy, "Ai Weiwei Erased from Show in Shanghai," *Artsbeat* (blog), April 29, 2014, http://artsbeat.blogs.nytimes.com; Levin, "Latest Icon in Artistic Rebellion"; Dan Levin, "The Latest Icon in Artistic Rebellion: A Cabbage," *Sinosphere* (blog), June 20, 2014, http://sinosphere.blogs.nytimes.com

9. Jennifer Currier, "Selling Place through Art: The Creation and Establishment of Beijing's 798 Art District," in *New Economic Spaces in Asian Cities: From Industrial Restructuring to the Cultural Turn*, ed. Peter Daniels, Kong-Chong Ho, and Thomas A. Hutton (Abingdon: Taylor & Francis, 2012), 184–201.

10. Marshall McLuhan, *Understanding Media: The Extensions of Man* (Berkeley: Gingko Press, 1964): 16; Gilles Deleuze, *Francis Bacon: The Logic of Sensation* (Minneapolis: University of Minnesota Press, 2003); Jacques Derrida, *The Truth in Painting* (Chicago: University of Chicago Press, 1987); Michel Foucault, *This Is Not a Pipe* (Berkeley: University of California Press, 2008).

11. All research conducted for this paper was approved by and performed in compliance with the University of Utah's Institutional Review Board (IRB Protocol #00056847). All interviews have been anonymized in this manuscript.

12. Kent A. Ono and Joy Yang Jiao, "China in the US Imaginary: Tibet, the Olympics,

and the 2008 Earthquake," *Communication and Critical/Cultural Studies* 5 (2008): 406–10; Chin-Chuan Lee, Hongtao Li, and Francis Lee, "Symbolic Use of Decisive Events: Tiananmen as a News Icon in the Editorials of the Elite US Press," *International Journal of Press/Politics* 16, no. 3 (2011): 335–56; Chin-Chuan Lee, "Established Pluralism: US Elite Media Discourse about China Policy," *Journalism Studies* 3, no. 3 (2002): 343–57.

13. The interviews in Chinese were translated by a translator of the artist's choosing.

14. Michael Pillsbury, "Misunderstanding China," *Wall Street Journal*, September 17, 2014.

15. Yue Zhang, "Governing Art Districts: State Control and Cultural Production in Contemporary China," *China Quarterly*, no. 219 (2014): 827–48.

16. Xinhua, "798 Art Factory Artists to Change Face of Beijing," *China Daily*, May 9, 2004; "The Amazing 798 Art District," *Engineering a Trip to China* (blog), July 22, 2012, http://supermanwah.wordpress.com; "Beijing's 798 District," China.org, August 10, 2014, http://www.china.org.cn/english.

17. Zhang, "Governing Art Districts."

18. Donald Morrison, "Contemporary Art Factory, Beijing," *New York Times*, July 10, 2008.

19. Wei Duan and Gang Lu, "798 Art Zone: Where Business Meets Art," *Gbtimes*, December 16, 2008, http://gbtimes.com.

20. Zhang, "Governing Art Districts."

21. Ibid.

22. Jennifer Currier, "Art and Power in the New China: An Exploration of Beijing's 798 District and Its Implications for Contemporary Urbanism," in Daniels, Ho, and Hutton, *New Economic Spaces in Asian Cities*; Zhang, "Governing Art Districts."

23. Xiao Rong, "EU Commissioner Visits 798 Factory," Nisuwang.net, December 27, 2003, http://nisuwang.net/report/b38.htm.

24. Kelly Chen, "The Rise of China's Contemporary Art Market" (School of the Art Institute of Chicago Arts Organizations in Society, 2007).

25. Michael Keane, "Culture, Commerce and Innovation in China," *China Journal*, 2009.

26. Chen, "The Rise of China's Contemporary Art Market," 11.

27. Feng Tao, "Hu Jintao Calls for Enhancing 'Soft Power' of Chinese Culture," *Xinhuanet*, November 15, 2007, http://news.xinhuanet.com.

28. Bert de Muynck, "Creative China, Cutting and Pasting?," *Moving Cities*,

November 2006, http://movingcities.org.

29. Zhang, "Governing Art Districts," 831.

30. Zhao Bing, "798 Art Festival Kicks off in Beijing," *Xinhuanet*, September 22, 2013, http://news.xinhuanet.com.

31. Zhang, "Governing Art Districts."

32. Ibid.; Currier, "Selling Place through Art."

33. Marnie Hunter, "World's Top 20 Museums," CNN, June 17, 2014, http://www.cnn.com.

34. Figures taken from *Visitor Figures 2013: Museum and Exhibition Attendance Numbers Compiled and Analysed*," special report, *Art Newspaper*, Spring/Summer 2014, http://theartnewspaper.com.

35. "Why China Is Unhappy," *Wall Street Journal*, November 14, 2011; Peter Foster, "Chinese Increasingly Unhappy with Life," *The Telegraph*, December 16, 2010; Daniel Blumenthal, "China Is Unhappy," *Foreign Policy*, May 7, 2013, http://www.foreignpolicy.com; "China's Unhappy Rich," *Wall Street Journal*, September 17, 2014.

36. Barbara Demick, "Chinese Await an Obama so Unlike Their Own Leaders," *Los Angeles Times*, November 14, 2009.

37. Ono and Jiao, "China in the US Imaginary"; Lee, "Established Pluralism"; Lee, Li, and Lee, "Symbolic Use of Decisive Events"; Terry Lautz, "U.S. Views of China: History, Values, and Power," in *The United States and China: Mutual Public Misperceptions*, ed. Douglas G. Spelman (Washington, DC: Woodrow Wilson International Center for Scholars, 2011), 9.

38. Ono and Jiao, "China in the US Imaginary."

39. To offer a comparison for perspective, in Evan Osnos's book, *Age of Ambition: Chasing Fortune, Truth, and Faith in the New China* (New York: Farrar, Straus and Giroux, 2014), he writes that China's rate of change is "one hundred times the scale, and ten times the speed, of the first Industrial Revolution, which created modern Britain" and, in 2005, "was building the square-foot equivalent of Rome every two weeks" (25).

40. Indeed, ancient China is popular, exotic, and world-renowned, with forty-seven designated UNESCO cultural sites. It also must be recognized that China promotes ancient China. Exploring China in the guidebooks and websites by climbing the remains of the Great Wall, walking through the Forbidden City filled with relics of ancient emperors, and strolling through the Summer Palace stirring up stories of Empress Dowager Cixi keeps the dream of ancient China alive.

41. Ono and Jiao, "China in the US Imaginary."

42. Ibid.

43. Charles Riley, "Tough Talk on China," *CNN Money*, October 17, 2012, http://money.cnn.com.

44. Ming Cheung, "A Study of Contemporary Chinese Art's Reaction to the Current Sociopolitical Climate in China," in *Conference Proceedings* (Ipswich, MA: International Communication Association, 2010): 1–33.

45. This observation is strengthened by the data I collected regarding visitors' knowledge of and familiarity with Chinese artists. For the vast majority of people I interviewed, Ai Weiwei was the only Chinese artist they knew, and many wanted to know where they could find him (his studio is no longer in 798, but in CaoChangDi). No one mentioned other respected and revered artists in China like Xu Bing or Yang Yongliang.

46. While I do not have the space here to conduct this line of inquiry, it would be fascinating to compare the responses of viewers in 798 to those of other art-tourists in other famous art spaces, where it would be interesting to try to discern the level of training—in specific aesthetic traditions, cultural histories, and national narratives—needed to make rich sense of more complicated pieces.

47. One interviewee called 798 the "hip version of the Silk Market." The Silk Market is a place many tourists go to buy Chinese goods that is overrun with foreigners. The high influx of tourists to the Silk Market has been met with a high density of Western eateries as well as inflated prices. This comparison highlights the Westernization of 798 as a means of attracting more business.

48. All of the sales figures in this paragraph are taken from AskArt.com, a website devoted to buyers and sellers of art that catalogues information regarding pricing, buyers, and sellers.

49. "Minjun Yue—Auction Records," AskArt.com, 2016, http://www.askart.com.

50. Ibid.

51. "Weiwei Ai—Auction Records," AskArt.com, 2016, http://www.askart.com.

52. "Guangyi Wang—Auction Records," AskArt.com, 2016, http://www.askart.com.

53. Ibid.

54. Annamma Joy and John F. Sherry Jr., "Framing Considerations in the PRC: Creating Value in the Contemporary Chinese Art market," *Consumption Markets & Culture* 7, no. 4 (December 2004): 307–48, 309.

55. Justin O'Connor and Gu Xin, "A New Modernity? The Arrival of 'Creative Industries' in China," *International Journal of Cultural Studies* 9, no. 3 (September

1, 2006): 271–283, 274.

56. See "Why Is Chinese Contemporary Art Important to Collect Today? An Interview with Larry Warsh," Artdaily.org, November 28, 2010, http://artdaily.com; Alexandre Errera, "Watch Out: Chinese Contemporary Art Is Going Global," Forbes, January 26, 2015.

57. Jacques Derrida, *Of Grammatology*, trans. Gayatri Chakravorty Spivak (Baltimore: Johns Hopkins University Press, 1998); Jacques Derrida, *Writing and Difference*, trans. Alan Bass (Chicago: University of Chicago Press, 1978); Gilles Deleuze, *Difference and Repetition* (New York: Columbia University Press, 1994); Deleuze, *Francis Bacon*; W. J. T. Mitchell, *What Do Pictures Want? The Lives and Loves of Images* (Chicago: University of Chicago Press, 2006).

58. The phrase *behind the red curtain* is and has been used to reference what is going on behind the scenes and has been used extensively in global media discourse on China. During Chairman Mao's rise to power, China became increasingly cut off from the rest of the world. Everything that happened in China happened behind the scenes of the global stage. While China has increasingly opened up its borders to the rest of the world over the past three decades, the political decisions made by Chinese government officials are still said to take place *behind the red curtain*.

59. Wall text, Ullens Center for Contemporary Art, "Yellow Signal," 798 Art District, Beijing, China, paragraph 4.

60. Gilles Deleuze, *Nietzsche and Philosophy*, rev. ed. (New York: Columbia University Press, 2006); Derrida, *The Truth in Painting*.

61. Christina Larson, "Growing Shortages of Water Threaten China's Development," Yale Environment 360, July 26, 2010, http://e360.yale.edu.

62. Pew Research Center, "Middle Easterners See Religious and Ethnic Hatred as Top Global Threat," *Global Attitudes & Trends*, October 16, 2014, http://www.pewglobal.org.

A Beijing Wolf in Hong Kong: Lufsig and Imagining Communities of Political Resistance to Chinese Unification

David R. Gruber

D ecember 7, 2013, was not the first time that Leung Chun-Ying, the Chief Executive of Hong Kong, known locally as "CY," faced rebellion and chaos at a town hall meeting. After a contentious election where many on the legislative council refused to vote,[1] and after speaking only Mandarin Chinese during his July 1, 2012, inauguration without using "one word of Cantonese," the predominant local language,[2] CY was strongly perceived as a Beijing-appointed stooge. For many in Hong Kong, CY was perceived as a wolf in sheep's clothing. And so, on July 2, his first day in office, CY was "forced to flee" his first town hall meeting, even as he attempted to reassure concerned citizens of his good-will and moderate policies. However, after the hall filled with outspoken naysayers, CY stepped off the stage, locked himself in a nearby room for an hour, and then made a speedy escape.[3] Protestors that day complained about the encroaching influence from Beijing, rising housing costs, poor environmental conditions, and CY's own alleged corruption and ties to the Communist Party in mainland China (CPC or the Party).[4] If the rhetorical work of imagining communities hinges in part on seeing elected leaders as synecdochical embodiments of the nation, then CY's taking office struck many Hong Kongers as a disaster—for he was imagined as the CPC's standard-bearer, and thus as foreshadowing of China's accelerating encroachments upon daily life in Hong Kong.

Over a year later, in early December, many of the same issues bubbled beneath the surface of Hong Kong's vibrant political community, where the question of Hong Kong–China relations dominated discussion. The prodemocracy movement had spent the past year calling CY a "wolf," as it faced down a national education policy with a clear pro-Beijing unification agenda and fought against numerous plans to eliminate the ability of Hong Kongers to vote directly for the chief executive position.[5] Many in the prodemocracy camp clearly felt embittered about what they perceived to be CY's role as a catalyst for and champion of China's escalating moves to control Hong Kong. Consequently, when CY arrived for yet another town hall meeting in December 2013, protestors gathered to confront him. Led by members of the prodemocracy League of Social Democrats, those demonstrating started yelling. Then someone threw an egg that hit Financial Secretary John Tsang square on the head. Then protestors threw "hell money"; this fake cash is usually given to dead ancestors as a ritualistic offering of thanks, but when thrown down at the feet of the living, it serves as a serious insult, ostensibly as visual evidence of the charge of corruption and greed.[6] The most notable moment of protest, however, was when a stuffed animal—a toy wolf doll, reminiscent of the notorious protagonist in "Little Red Riding Hood"—flew through the air like superman, heading straight for CY.[7] Amid the chaos, a voice punctuated the din: "Lo Mo Sai" (pinyin: "Lù mǔ xi"), a man screamed in Cantonese. This was, more or less, Lufsig, the name of the poorly translated toy that was being sold by the local IKEA. The Cantonese name sounded strikingly similar to a well-known profane statement proclaiming aggressive masculine domination, something similar to "throw your mother's cunt." From all indications, the one-pound, soft, $10 (USD) stuffed IKEA wolf, known in Swedish and English as "Lufsig," never touched CY (see Figure 1). However, after Lufsig was shown on local TV sailing through the air accompanied by the harsh profanity,[8] all of the IKEA stores in Hong Kong

Figure 1. "Lufsig Soft Toy,
IKEA." Image is used with
the permission of Inter-IKEA
Systems B.V.

sold out of Lufsig within two days.[9] Within one week, Lufsig had its own
Facebook page with thousands of "likes."[10] For reasons detailed below,
Lufsig had captured the imagination of the city's activists and would soon
become a sensation.

Indeed, in the months to follow, the doll appeared numerous times
across Hong Kong's social media sites. Photographs of local Hong
Kongers posing with Lufsig became particularly popular. Following the
incident, Lufsig was paraded in protest marches, painted into local street
art scenes, cast as a lead character in numerous homemade animations
and music videos, and promoted by some of the city's local celebrities,
including Hong Kong models and up-and-coming pop singers.[11] Much
like the grass mud horse incidents, a folkloric image with a profane linguistic twist hit a nerve. And so, virtually overnight, it seemed as if the
Hong Kong prodemocracy and anti-China movements had found their
poster child: Lufsig was a consumer hit, pop culture star, and political
sensation.

The obvious question is, why would a stuffed wolf doll sold at IKEA stores "go viral" and command so much public attention? Paper, eggs, glass, and water have all been hurled at CY in the past.[12] Many other symbols have swirled among the city's protest communities, including pink-painted tanks, Hello Kitty cartoons, and the British flag, which remains an enduring symbol of Hong Kong's century under British colonial rule (and ironically, in a postcolonial twist, a symbol of desire for British-style democracy over Chinese-style authoritarianism; the former flag of empire has become, in Hong Kong, a symbol of resistance).[13] Within this thicket of symbols, why had Lufsig become the most potent and popular? More broadly, what does Lufsig's popularity tell us about the strange rhetorical workings of national imaginations?

I propose that Lufsig's popularity is not merely about politically frustrated and good-humored Hong Kongers attaching themselves to the comedy of a toy wolf that proved seriously, if not accidentally, insulting to a derided politician. Rather, Lufsig holds much more intellectual interest and social importance in terms of protest movements than a first encounter with the story might disclose. In what follows I argue that Lufsig became a viral protest symbol precisely because of its synecdochic power, connecting Hong Konger's local identity performances with the broader, postcolonial political situation in Hong Kong. Due to its unique combination of consumer pleasure, political anger, and pop culture fun, Lufsig joined and contributed to Hong Kong's broader "social imaginary";[14] that is, Lufsig entered into a collective of material and symbolic performances, both offline and online, able to rearticulate many Hong Kongers' opposition to Beijing and highlight tensions with mainland Chinese people. Ultimately, Lufsig helped to expose public discontent with the influx of mainlanders streaming into Hong Kong and to mobilize opposition to China's attempts to assert a stronger, often unwelcomed hand in regional affairs. In short, a confluence of locally salient controversies and narrative histories enabled protesters to turn Lufsig—a likeable, sharable, and, thus, easily adoptable artifact for Hong Kongers, including netizens and other social media users—into an icon of resistance against China.

For those Hong Kongers trying to imagine new forms of dissent from China's encroachments in general and CY's leadership in particular, Lufsig was the perfect condensation symbol. The profane name, the striking wolf image referencing CY's reputation as a cunning "wolf" out to devour Hong Kong's freedoms,[15] the connection to the highly popular IKEA store, the affordability of the doll, the simple fact of being able to throw the doll without hurting anyone in the process—all of these factors added up to a highly successful protest symbol for those among Hong Kong's discontented population and those invested in the prodemocracy movement. Indeed, Lufsig could be used to mock CY and other Beijing "loyalists" without generating, in turn, any violent government backlash. Perhaps the ultimate combination of rude and cute, dangerous and cuddly, Lufsig embodies the yin and yang of political protest. As I argue in what follows, Lufsig's rhetorical power lay in its ability to be assimilated into daily enactments of relatively safe and sanctioned means of protest. A soft, cuddly vessel of political rage, Lufsig nevertheless remained a personal, playful, and consumeristic expression that served to reestablish the social imaginary of Hong Kongers as different from and more culturally savvy or affluent than those living in mainland China.

Because of Lufsig's phenomenal successes, various rhetorical redefinitions of the symbol soon arose within communities seeking to appropriate its power. The doll became a site of contested meanings, as it was reappropriated to serve the interests of Hong Kong's local pop starlets, clashing political parties, and myriad personal causes. Indeed, while CY's quick and haphazard attempts to assign his own new meanings to Lufsig failed miserably,[16] the doll was deployed on Facebook to advance the careers of rising local celebrities.[17] Why CY failed and local pop celebrities like Kashy Keegan and Lulu Tung successfully adopted Lufsig will be explored toward the end of this chapter, where I argue that Lufsig's primary appeal for Hong Kongers—its combination of protest, fun, and consumerism—overlapped nicely with the pop culture sensibilities of these stars and their fans.

Put in terms of political and rhetorical theory, the rise of Lufsig in Hong Kong illustrates the intimate connection between materiality, symbolicity, and identity in local resistance movements. If physical location and the "deployment of place" matter in protest, as Danielle Endres and Samantha Senda-Cook have pointed out, then so does the materiality and affect-ability of symbols themselves.[18] Indeed, when human bodies are physically restrained or cannot bear the weight of resistance, then the materiality of symbols—how their tangible, everyday uses make them personally salient in a situated context—proves exceptionally important. And so, in the first section of this chapter, I examine how Lufsig's materiality complements its symbolic resonances and cooperates with local identity performances. Here I show how Lufsig expresses the playfully rebellious social imaginary of Hong Kong, leading ultimately to a loveable, easily sharable object of resistance that unites protestors and embodies their grievances. Then, in the next section, I explore how Lufsig bolsters the fun of Hong Kong individuality as expressed in social media, generating a rhetoric of delight in political resistance being performed online. Put another way, if identity is an ongoing performance, as Judith Butler and Sherry Turkle, among others, have documented,[19] and if those performances have emotional potential that can be harnessed for political purposes,[20] then it is not only the moving performances or the violent, incendiary performances that can shape lives and do political work.[21] Instead, Lufsig illustrates how the joy of being a Hong Konger and showing it—or a Quebecois or a Catalonian or any political subject at all—harbors latent political energy and the capability for words and images and bodies to spread. Such performances, in other words, resonate.[22] Lufsig shows us how resistance can be not only fun but self-reflexively silly. This seems especially important to recognize in an age of "selfies," where social media performances serve to build positive bonds between like-minded people and act as entertaining sites of resistance or infectious rallying points for mass protests precisely because they are physically situated, entertaining, and simultaneously transmittable via multiple online platforms.[23] In brief, Lufsig's success is not only about how its material and symbolic resonances impel political participation offline, but also about how those resonances foster the delight of participating in political resistance online.

Lufsig: Symbolic Resonance and Material Agency

Even before being thrown at CY, Lufsig possessed some intrinsic appeal in Hong Kong, for as a stuffed animal toy, Lufsig was nicely compatible with several online and offline regional practices. For one, its furry, squishy body plays to Hong Kongers' existing obsession with stuffed animals and the regularized ritual of taking stuffed animals to major events, including graduation ceremonies and parties.[24] Photographs with stuffed animals and what Hong Kongers call "plush" regularly circulate among social media websites in Hong Kong. Taking a photograph with Lufsig or any such stuffed animal and sharing it on social media websites, outside of the ongoing protest movement, would already appear routine in Hong Kong. In addition, Lufsig's ability to be thrown across a room, once juxtaposed with a name that is an expletive in Cantonese, emphasizes the physical task of performing ongoing linguistic resistance to Mandarin speakers in Hong Kong. As Lily Kuo notes, "The intrusion of Mainland China into Hong Kong politics and culture" is "symbolized by the slow creep of Mandarin into the territory." These factors "make Ikea's toy a triple whammy: A nod to Leung's [CY's] derogatory nickname, a profane insult, and a cry of linguistic encroachment."[25] Throwing Lufsig, in physical terms, is throwing an insult in Cantonese. Thus, throwing Lufsig symbolically asserts Canton-individuality as well as palpable discontent with the ever-increasing numbers of mainland residents settling in Hong Kong.[26] As Lufsig sails through the air, it cuts through the languages spoken out by all of the non-Cantonese speakers weaving through the streets of Hong Kong. In this way, Lufsig became a grassroots advocate for preserving local linguistic cultural practices.

Further, because Lufsig holds a miniaturized grandmother figure as a way to invoke the "Little Red Riding Hood" story, Hong Kongers are able to associate Lufsig with the strict public housing policies and poor protections for the elderly in the city, conditions intermittently blamed on policies driven by mainland interests.[27] As a result, the IKEA website, read with this background knowledge, communicates amusing and poignant meanings: "Your child can have fun recreating the fairytale by rescuing the grandmother from the wolf's belly, safe and sound."[28] Taking up the lens of the Little Red Riding Hood narrative, Lufsig situates CY as engaged in the wolf's deception, positioning Hong Kongers, in turn, as living in a fairy tale wherein the wolf is ultimately exposed and killed—despite the fact that the doll and the IKEA website give no indication of who or what represents the stocky lumberjack with the axe who eventually comes to the rescue. Nevertheless, when protestors in Hong Kong throw the wolf at CY, they perform a remonstration, publicly declaring

CY as the evil antagonist in an old story about frail, vulnerable, even naive, victims who become the eventual champions. In this way, protestors send a message to CY to institute more regulations on housing and to work in favor of the elderly who often suffer as a result of high housing costs and meager social benefits. Thus merging the deep psychological power of allegory with the pointed anger of specific political crises, Hong Kongers turned Lufsig into what one observer called "an embodiment of the peoples' demands."[29]

Many protest symbols in China wield mythical stories packed with camouflaged messages that stand in for people's lived experiences and break the facade of harmony portrayed by the Chinese government. Because of their reliance on myth, these symbols—especially politically motivated versions of the grass mud horse and river crab—are able to expose government dishonesty and to express popular fears about the social conditions lingering beneath the facade of harmony, while nonetheless appearing resolutely Chinese. That the story of Little Red Riding Hood is European in origin likely indicates Hong Kong's different historical and social identifications than many mainlanders—for Hong Kongers are well known to imagine themselves not as citizens of China but as citizens of the world, with strong ties stretching back to England. The underlying meanings about everyday life in Hong Kong embodied in Lufsig illustrate the latent political power of fairy tales and mythic symbols to reveal such social imaginaries. In fact, with the story of Little Red Riding Hood in mind, Lufsig's representational status doubles: politically, the doll exposes the purported malicious intentions of CY "the wolf"; socially, the doll expresses the dissatisfaction and enflamed social consciousness of many of the people in Hong Kong, who feel that they need to protect their families and, indeed, the city itself from Chinese encroachment (what the Party calls "unification").

The political power of allegory is again evident in the "CY and Lufsig" video game, created by developer Andy Li Yu-hin one week after the first Lufsig incident.[30] Set over a classic Pac-Man interface, a miniaturized CY tries desperately to "evade his nemesis Lufsig"; in the game, CY is Pac-Man, and Lufsig takes on the role of the little ghosts chasing Pac-Man around the screen.[31] In being interposed as Pac-Man and thereby controlled by the game player, CY is subjugated to the player's whims and surrounded by many Lufsigs, visually conjuring a mob of angry protestors. As in the original Pac-Man video game, Lufsig (as the ghost) eventually catches up with CY (as Pac-Man) before the villain eats up all of the little pebbles, which could represent Hong Kong's resources or freedoms. The game thus allows the player to enact a dream of empowerment and to, once again, have fun with the idea of Lufsig. Virtualizing Lufsig in this way also usefully rematerializes its presence online, giving it a virtual embodiment in online space that parallels its offline materiality as a doll wielded by protestors who actively chase CY around the city with Lufsig in tow.

When protestors go to IKEA to buy the wolf and join the shopping crowds, or go online to play the video game, or share a photograph of Lufsig in online forums, they perform a version of the fairy tale's story of liberation from the cunning wolf while simultaneously, on another level, participating in a highly mediated act of resistance. The everyday activities of shopping and sharing, once tied to the materiality of Lufsig and embedded in the political hotbed of the Hong Kong context, add up to the compelling rhetorical power of Lufsig. This is not to mention the simple amusement of throwing Lufsig up into the air or seeing the doll pop up randomly around town. In short, Lufsig adds material agency to an already charged symbolic structure, producing both visual and auditory resistances tailored to Hong Kong's uniquely charged political situation.

Lufsig: Regional Identity and Social Media Delight

Lufsig also fits the multimodality of Internet sharing as well as the crafty, witty content expected on a friend's social media pages. There is something positively delightful about Lufsig. In some ways, Lufsig can be understood as an example of what Richard B. Gregg describes as the "ego-function" within protest movements.[32] In Gregg's conception, the rhetoric of a protest is not always purposefully directed at powerful officials with the aim of changing their minds; rather, protests also often have an ego-function, wherein the rhetoric is directed at the protestors themselves, serving two purposes. The first is to fulfill the "need for psychological refurbishing and affirmation," and the second is to allow protestors to assert "self-hood as one engages in a rhetorical act."[33] Applied to contemporary social media sharing and to the solidarity and resistance engendered through social media, an ego-function in a protest can solidify the group online, enhance an individual's social presence and currency within shared websites, and provide the opportunity for performed resistances to reach wider audiences and, perhaps, to go viral.

Reading the popularity of Lufsig through this lens of ego fulfillment highlights the ways the stuffed toy enters into ongoing social media conversations about China and the associated identity performances, often online, of Hong Kongers. As Anthony Fung notes, Hong Kongers tend to see online space as "a free and autonomous space that is separate from the highly-monitored media system and [that] allows citizens a further opportunity to engage in politics."[34] Here it should be noted that freedom within the traditional news media in Hong Kong is not always total. Fung points this out, discussing the voluntary censorship among many Hong Kong-based news agencies and the pressures they feel to continually frame Beijing in a positive light. Social media websites on the other hand—in contrast to the traditional mass media of TV, radio, and newsprint—enjoy a relative freedom that enables them to "serve as forums for the public to express its opinions, to organize actions, and to accommodate democratic engagement."[35] This has undoubtedly been the case in Hong Kong, as much of Lufsig's popularity grew up through social media sharing. More broadly, the Internet, and social media sites necessarily, have generated what Guobin Yang calls an "age of contention" in China, promoting "online activism and popular contention in general" as a response to worsening health and labor conditions under Chinese modernization.[36] For example, online censorship in China is never total, meaning social media sites have usefully expanded political conversations and exposed corruption. The online activism of Ai Weiwei and other netizens indicates that meaning is never closed. This lack of closure speaks to "the 'fraught rhetorical space' that exists between citizens and the state."[37] Although Hong Kong generally enjoys greater freedom of expression than on the mainland, the same principles apply: insofar as activism online contributes greatly to discussions in Hong Kong among people angered about overcrowding, high housing costs, and appalling water and air pollution, so these online discourses have moved both the traditional mass media and the public in new and exciting directions. In short, the Internet in Hong Kong, as in China, continues to exert a powerful influence on everyday life and on adopted forms of resistance—the rhetorical work of imagining communities is moving online.

In fact, public discourse in Hong Kong with respect to China–Hong Kong relations has been largely centered within social media sites. In 2012, for example, a Hong Konger used his cell phone to film a mainland mother and daughter eating food on the Mass Transit Railway subway train, a socially unacceptable act in the perpetually tidy Hong Kong.[38] Once posted online, the video quickly went viral, leading to a series of news articles about the influx of mainland tourists and inciting numerous online posts about mainlanders' differing behaviors, which are often considered distasteful to many Hong Kongers. Another example of such public discussion occurred in early 2014, when a Hong Konger filmed a woman from the mainland allowing her child to excrete on the street.[39] This incident, once again, ignited an Internet firestorm. Hong Kongers lashed out in social media sites against mainland visitors, declaring such actions illegal and threatening to embarrass mainlanders arriving in Hong Kong. Subsequent days saw a series of "poop protests" in Hong Kong where a small but vocal group of Hong Kongers pretended to pull down their pants and poop in public shopping areas popular with mainland tourists while declaring their presence unwanted.[40] Both incidents could be symptoms of political uncertainty and psychological destabilization in a period of growing unification with China; or such incidents might be scapegoat events for rising housing costs and other changes in the city, which are conveniently blamed on mainlanders. The incidents certainly add resonance to the arguments that public health discourses in Hong Kong hinge in part on the unfair pretense that the mainland Chinese who visit Hong Kong are dirty, unmannered, and perhaps the carriers of deadly diseases. Such discourse about bodies and daily life indicate how Hong Kongers, even while protesting the overarching political question of unification with China, are also deeply concerned about questions of everyday life, thus pointing to notions of health, class, and cosmopolitan style seemingly under siege.

Taken together, these incidents provide compelling evidence of how Hong Kongers use social media as an amplifier for complaints. Moreover, they also reveal how a segment of Hong Kongers see themselves in their shared social imaginary as different from, and more sophisticated than, many people living in the mainland.[41] It is not uncommon, in fact, to hear Hong Kongers declare themselves more cosmopolitan, fashionable, and fortunate than those who live in mainland China. These high-minded self-perceptions are not disconnected from the freedoms or the wealth that Hong Kong has enjoyed as a former British colony with a strong financial industry and a robust, even decadent, relation to free-market consumerism. The fact that Lufsig comes from IKEA stores illustrates Hong Kongers' contentment in finding a protest symbol at the mall, indicating their sense of themselves as consumer-citizens able to flaunt European goods and insider symbols as part of their identity performances. In these ways, Lufsig is a protest object tailor-made for Hong Kong. The doll's appeal lies not only in its profane name or its visual identification with CY's reputation as a wolf, but in what Lufsig suggests within the larger geopolitical context: that Hong Kongers imagine themselves aligned with Western modes of consumerism, style, protest, and freedom, not the CPC's authoritarianism and state-controlled economy.

It is no surprise, then, that when the so-called Umbrella Revolution erupted on the streets of Hong Kong in the autumn of 2014, antigovernment and prodemocracy protestors started using the emerging slogan "We are Hong Kongers" in conjunction with online images of Lufsig.[42] The slogan operates rhetorically much like Maurice Charland's constitutive rhetoric of the Quebecois. In the case that Charland examines, the people of Quebec promote the declaration of the Quebecois to "experience themselves" as a people unified and individuated.[43] The slogan "We are Hong Kongers" works discursively in much the same way, proclaiming self-identification, self-assuredness, and self-rule. In addition, the slogan mirrors the popular "We are the 99%" from the Occupy movement in 2011. Just as the Occupy slogan promotes what John Jones calls "compensatory divisions" by giving legitimacy and visibility to an overlooked group of people challenging the state,[44] so the "We are Hong Kongers" slogan forges a sense of division from the Beijing government and China more broadly. The chant invokes a joyous and unified collective imaginary— shouted both in soccer games and on the streets as "We are Hong Kong" or "We are Hong Kong People!"[45]—powerful enough to stand on its own.

The combination of the slogan "We are Hong Kongers" with Lufsig's invocation of a European fairy tale accomplishes some important
historical work as well. Indeed, the implied assertion of independence
from China and the aligning of this claim with Western consumerism
and mythology serve to counter China's triumphant historical narratives,
which are meant to justify its unification with Hong Kong. For, as is the
case with Tibet, Mongolia, and Xinjiang, so the Party has marshaled its
own histories, dating as far back as the Qin dynasty, to try to cast a net of
historical entitlement over Hong Kong.[46] In contrast to such neoimperial
Chinese claims, which argue that Hong Kong has always been and will
always be a central part of the motherland, virtually every identity symbol
in Hong Kong considered as evidence for this essay conveys a sense of the
city and its people as distant from and different from mainland China.
The perfect symbol of Hong Kong's unique culture and heritage, Lufsig
expresses the city's fashionable, postmodern image as "Asia's World City,"
one famous for having high Internet connectivity, trendy Euro-inspired
shops, and free, open-minded people.[47]

Within this historical, political, and rhetorical context, protestors
snapping photos of Lufsig and sharing them online craft visual and embodied resistances to Beijing's plans to assert "total control" over Hong
Kong (see Figure 2).[48] Through holding Lufsig, protestors portray themselves as distinct from those who live under single-party Communist rule
on the mainland, where expressions of protest are outlawed. An anti-
Communist snuggle toy, Lufsig sustains a localized identity invested in
displaying Hong Kong's relatively fun, free, happy, and largely affluent
(British) history in both online and offline ways, thus offering pointed
comparisons to life as it is imaged in mainland China. Indeed, it is hard to
look through shared online photographs of Hong Kongers holding Lufsig
and not see the sheer joy of being a Hong Konger. Just as important, this
identifying joy is simultaneously about the medium of expression: the
delight of social media, of sharing an image online that friends will love,
of receiving feedback, and of feeling like one is participating in being a
Hong Konger and becoming a part of something bigger—all of this is
fully enabled by Lufsig's circulation in online forums. Whether standing
in line among the excited, buzzing crowds at IKEA waiting to purchase
Lufsig, or watching the clever reiterations of it popping up across social

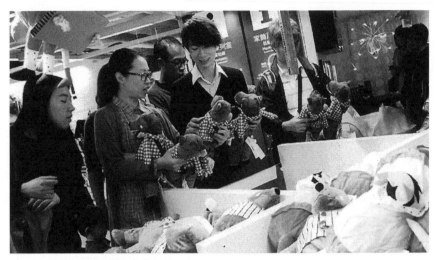

Figure 2. IKEA customers with Lufsig Doll. Photo is used courtesy of David Wong/*South China Morning Post*.

media sites, or carrying the doll at a march, or snapping one's own silly pictures with Lufsig—all of these actions cocreate strong affective bonds that add depth to the doll's material and symbolic resonances while feeding an emergent culture of protest.

The protest movement in Hong Kong, in turn, is energized by such participatory delight. Put in terms of Gregg's ego-function, the particular "psychological refurbishment and affirmation" actualized amid the rhetorical act of performing "self-hood" through Lufsig is not merely a sort of postexhaustion relief after a long hard struggle of shouting on the street during a protest.[49] It is also, in this context at least, a playful and ongoing process of shaping a defined identity within a social imaginary enabled by the possibilities of social media sharing. Consequently, the Lufsig doll, over time and over various iterations online, has sustained a positive psychological role within the protest movement, providing pointed yet delightful energy to Hong Kongers' ongoing protests against Chinese unification.

Reappropriation, Carnival, and Consumer Compatibility

Within a few days of Lufsig becoming Hong Kong's favorite protest symbol, CY wrote about Lufsig on his personal blog. He posted a picture of Lufsig sitting on his desk; in the photograph, CY sat in the background looking dutifully over some documents.[50] The photograph clearly intended to give the impression that CY was busy at work while Lufsig was merely a natural, fun part of CY's everyday office environment. In the attendant blog post, CY praised the "creativity" of Hong Kongers for appropriating Lufsig and claimed that he, too, wanted to have a Lufsig doll to give to his daughter and to support the educational fund buoyed by IKEA's sales of Lufsig.[51] In response, however, Hong Kongers pointed out that in the photograph CY was looking at a news report about a sex scandal—a detail that did not help CY's efforts to appear truly busy with official business. The seemingly minor detail also bolstered his image as a cunning, perhaps self-indulging wolf, especially in the context of mentioning love of his family. One local news site made the further observation that "Leung either kept the Lufsig the protester threw at him, made life difficult for one of his subordinates [in having to fetch the doll amid the clamoring crowds], or overpaid an online seller with taxpayers' money!"[52] Needless to say, CY's attempts to reappropriate Lufsig quickly proved fruitless.

Efforts from local Hong Kong celebrities to appropriate and benefit from Lufsig's popularity were more successful. Both Kashy Keegan, a British pop singer based in Hong Kong, and Lulu Tung, a local model, promoted Lufsig. Both celebrities were featured on Lufsig's Facebook site and/or displayed Lufsig in other publications.[53] In his personal video blog, for example, Kashy Keegan held up a Lufsig doll and declared him a "symbol against all dream killers."[54] Keegan thereby aligned himself and his dreams with Lufsig, emphasizing his own inspirational message, "Dare to dream."[55] The move allowed Keegan, as a British expat, to profit from Lufsig's popularity without himself needing to pretend to be a naturalized Hong Konger or needing to be directly involved in the protest movement. Accordingly, Lufsig, once circulated as a protest symbol, took on even broader cultural significance. By rabidly adopting nearly any mention of Lufsig in the Hong Kong region, the unknown persons running Lufsig's

Facebook site may have contributed to this subtle reappropriation of Lufsig as representing dreams in general rather than the protest movement more directly. Here, Keegan's banal pop-star message trivialized the image of Lufsig and risked damage to its political charge. In like manner, the carefree, open policy of social media appropriation of images of Lufsig converged with the impulses of self-motivated individuals wanting to redesign Lufsig for personal promotion, thus crafting messages that potentially diluted or destabilized Lufsig's political importance. The inane marketing of dreams, for example, offers a lesson about the inescapability of the self-promoting free-market mentality that underwrites many online forums, which, in mimicking the general drive of capitalism to expand to new markets, have learned that circulation can be enhanced by riding upon the energy of political resistance (even including the absorption of resistance to capitalism's products of enterprises). There can be no surprise, then, to find some online users seeking to manipulate Lufsig for their own purposes, such as in attempts to turn a symbol of political resistance into a marketing tool meant to enhance pop-star credibility and, presumably, sales of albums and other commodities.

Or consider the case of Lulu Tong, who reposted a cartoon image of a boy on his knees begging her to wear a CY Leung T-shirt instead of a soccer jersey.[56] Since Lulu built a career embodying the sexiness of soccer in Hong Kong and has often been paid to model soccer gear, the image insinuated CY's desperation for youth popularity and appeal. This cartoon image, in turn, appeared to be responsible for several online mash-ups of Lulu—who was sometimes drawn as a cute cartoon character—happily squeezing a Lufsig doll.[57] In this particular case, Lufsig proved compatible with Lulu and "sexy" enough to appear loved by the famous model or, more directly, popular enough to be associated with both Lulu and soccer in Hong Kong. Lulu's virtual embodiment as a cute cartoon character holding Lufsig also seemed to associate Lulu's cuddly, silly image with Lufsig's playfulness. In contrast, the fact that Lulu, as a cartoon, would never wear a CY T-shirt exposes CY as too mean, corrupt, and hopelessly uncool to be associated with Lulu's cartoon presence in online spaces. Whereas the Keegan example was a crude appropriation that diminished Lufsig's political potential, the various Lulu mash-ups more artfully, creatively, and productively situate Lufsig within the lively pop sensibilities of Hong Kong youth culture, which, I have argued, fuel the sense of cultural uniqueness driving resistance to Chinese unification.

In both the Keegan and Lulu cases, the online uses of Lufsig revealed the doll's compatibility with the social media habits and consumer identities of Hong Kong's pop starlet elite. In stark juxtaposition to CY, Keegan and Lulu sought to adopt Lufsig by inserting the doll into their regularly constructed online environments and interactions. That is, Keegan and Lulu maintained strong social media presences in networks where routinely sharing everyday photos and stories about their lives intersects with their overall career ambitions. Their social media identities, in other words, were already irrevocably entwined with their image development strategies. Thus, sharing an image of Lufsig was more a case of opportunity knocking than a case of defensive response. In contrast, CY's government-sponsored blog, hosted on a sterile government website and written in direct response to hostile actions taken against him as a Beijing-appointed leader, had little chance of success from the beginning.

CY's inability to reappropriate Lufsig may also be read through Lufsig's ego-function.[58] Being primarily co-opted as a way to solidify and encourage prodemocracy protestors, Lufsig was never meant to highlight a dedication to one's family or to a charity, as CY proclaimed. Reappropriating Lufsig, then, would surely prove challenging for CY. Indeed, the hasty-seeming nature of the photograph on his blog, which lacked attention to detail and appeared quickly after the inciting incident, reinforced the perception that CY was crafting ham-handed propaganda, not participating in the joyous flow in Hong Kong's online and offline cultures. Instead, his fast and haphazard response made him appear desperate to persuade Hong Kongers to think differently about Lufsig. In this way, CY unwittingly reinforced his popular image as an out-of-touch manipulator.

CY's failed reappropriation of Lufsig might be further understood through conceptualizing Lufsig as a carnival performance.[59] As James Janack explains, "the carnival," as developed by Mikhail Bakhtin, is a comic "spectacle" involving "inversions and parody," an extreme performance that "signifies the symbolic destruction of authority."[60] Although Lufsig is not the total foolish inversion of a political candidate, as in the Jesse "the Body" Ventura case that Janack explores, Lufsig nevertheless undermines authority through comedy and parody. Identifying with any such carnivalesque rhetor is tantamount to support for the middle- and working-class people not benefiting from current elite political structures. Accordingly, one can imagine that CY might have been more successful if engaging the comedy of Lufsig directly or if treating Lufsig in a satirical manner that played into the spectacle, off-setting and self-deprecating (or inverting) his own elite status. But asking audiences to resee Lufsig in terms of IKEA's educational charity or in terms of CY's good nature (in contrast to his sullied image as Beijing's anointed political elite) is less likely to be successful than situating Lufsig into its already celebrated role as a cuddly consumer product and profane symbol of protest. In this sense, the case of Lufsig illustrates how tricksters cannot be appropriated easily by elites; the doll's deconstructive and playful energies mitigate attempts to turn it into an image favorable to the status quo.

The theory of the carnival is also applicable to Lufsig insofar as Bakhtin argues that comedy and parody attract audiences while being relatively "safe" means of protest.[61] Given the free-speech laws in Hong Kong, throwing Lufsig, buying Lufsig, or taking photographs with Lufsig is, for the time being, a relatively safe form of resistance. Lufsig embodies an outrageous, funny, potent but not forbidden "expression of protest by disaffected populations."[62] As such, Lufsig generates no fear for Hong Kongers wanting to express dissent. Wielding Lufsig can actively oppose CY and his associated policies of prounification with mainland China while, at the same time, Lufsig presents no real physical threat either. Indeed, the threat that Lufsig represents stirs outside of Lufsig and lives not at IKEA but in the life experiences of those Hong Kongers feeling demoralized, exploited, and suppressed during a time of increasing unification with mainland China.

Conclusion: Imagining a Free Hong Kong

In a postcolonial region like Hong Kong, whose Chinese cultural identity has been radically altered and complicated by nearly one hundred years of British rule and whose security has been built on being an important trading port for the British and then a successful banking center for all of Asia, purchasing a protest symbol only seems right. At a time when many

Hong Kongers fear a coming transition to a less promising world, wherein the people's beloved local cultural norms and long-standing freedoms are threatened by the ruling Communist elites in Beijing, maintaining a strong sense of voice in the city, of outcry or protest, appears urgent. So does maintaining a strong identification with Europe. So does instilling leaders with a love for the life and history of Hong Kong. In stark opposition to the mandated nationalist history promulgated in mainland China, where, as Ling Chen notes, supporting the state is rooted in the "paramount importance of people's loyalty to their ruler," Hong Kongers scoff at the sense of bowing before an ultimate ruler from "heaven" (*tian*) who is endowed with "god-like stature."[63] In contrast to the Chinese sense of honoring a "mandate from heaven," Hong Kong's emergence from the British colonial situation has endowed the people with a solid sense of themselves as unique and, therefore, as content to remain a free Special Administrative Region, not a city-state absorbed into the politics and culture of mainland China.

More broadly, Lufsig demonstrates how the localized cultures and languages that contribute to a social imaginary can be superimposed upon an object, and conversely how an object can affectively stitch together that imaginary. Because of its name and face and origins, Lufsig has a voice of its own in Hong Kong; the doll no longer requires speech on behalf of the protestor, only the act of being thrown, or merely now the act of being held, or the act of appearing in a selfie. Lufsig, in this way, creates a rhetoric directed at the protestors in a call of solidarity and a rhetoric of the protestors as it embodies their discontent, all while conveying the delight of political protest in both traditional and online forms.

Despite combining symbolic resonance with a magnetic material embodiment, compatible with both online and offline cultures in Hong Kong, time will only tell whether Lufsig's efficacy as a protest symbol proves able to withstand the popular reappropriations enabled by its various presences. The affect-ability of Lufsig, its likeability, and its shareability are both its glory and potential demise. However, as Hong Kong ventures into ever more intense protests in a struggle for universal suffrage, and now grapples with political stagnation after the Umbrella Revolution protests of 2014 that showed mass defiance against Beijing's long-term agenda for full unification with mainland China, having a plush toy as a symbol of unity can serve an effective and crucial function—to ease and mitigate the threat of more dangerous, reactionary symbols one day emerging. Lufsig's role, for the time being, may be to stand in for bodies and to do the relatively nonviolent work of asserting the people's will. Lufsig acts as a particularly salient expression, a productive and performative act of Hong Kong's unique social imaginary constructed and reconstructed every day amid China's overwhelming, seemingly unstoppable, efforts to take over Hong Kong.

NOTES

1. "The Worst System, Including All the Others," *The Economist*, March 31, 2012.

2. Mark McDonald, "A Telling Language Lesson in Hong Kong," *New York Times*, July 1, 2012.

3. Walter Jennings, "New Hong Kong Chief Forced to Flee from Townhall Meeting," *Facing China*, July 3, 2012, http://facingchina.me.

4. Andrew Higgins, "Hong Kong's New Leader, Leung-Chun-ying Vows to Protect Freedoms but Faces Skeptics," *Washington Post*, March 25, 2012; Jennings, "New Hong Kong Chief Forced to Flee"; Suzanne Pepper, "Defying the Elements, Again: Reunification Day Protest," *China Elections and Governance* (blog), July 5, 2013, http://chinaelectionsblog.net; "Defying China, Thousands of Pro-Democracy Protestors Take to the Streets," Pakistan Defence, July 2, 2012, http://defence.pk.

5. The Communist government in Beijing has promised Hong Kong, as a Special Administrative Region, the right to vote for the chief executive position—the highest administrative position in Hong Kong—by 2017; however, currently the government only supports a plan where Hong Kongers can vote for two or three leaders chosen and approved by Beijing. This has caused numerous protests in the city in the past two years. For an example,, see Callum MacLeod, "Over 500 Arrested after Hong Kong Democracy Rally," *USA Today*, July 2, 2014.

6. Tom Grundy, "Politics: Why Are Hong Kongers Going Crazy for 'Lufsig' the Toy Wolf?" *Hong Wrong* (blog), December 9, 2013, http://hongwrong.com.

7. Yuen Chan, "IKEA Toy Wolf Becomes Unlikely Anti-Government Symbol in Hong Kong," *The World Post*, December 9, 2013, http://www.huffingtonpost.com; "Throw Lo Mo Sai," *i-cable TV News*, YouTube video, 1:09, posted by nelson wong, December 7, 2013, https://www.youtube.com/watch?v=tGNZov6NKio; Lily Kuo, "An IKEA Toy Wolf Is More Than Just a Way to Curse Out Hong Kong's

Chief Executive," *Quartz*, December 10, 2013, http://qz.com.

8. "Throw Lo Mo Sai."

9. "Ikea Stuffed Wolf Sells Out Amid Hong Kong Fury," *The Local*, December 10, 2013, http://www.thelocal.se.

10. "Lufsig" Facebook page, https://zh-tw.facebook.com/pages/%E8%B7%AF%E5%A7%86%E8%A5%BF-Lufsig/257718187714374; Note: Facebook remains prominent in Hong Kong. A recent *South China Morning Post* article put it as the number one social network in Hong Kong with 4.3 million active users: "Facebook Spurs More Digital Advertising," *South China Morning Post*, September 9, 2013.

11. "Lufsig" Facebook page.

12. Kelly Ip, "Security Beefed Up after Egg Throwing," *The Standard*, December 9, 2013; "HKU Poll Shows CY Leung Performing Poorly," *Coconuts Hong Kong*, December 11, 2013, http://coconuts.co/hongkong.

13. "Protestors Fill Hong Kong as New Leader Sworn In," *Wall Street Journal*, July 1, 2012.

14. Stephen Hartnett, Lisa Keränen, and Donovan Conley, "Introduction," this volume.

15. Pepper, "Defying the Elements, Again."

16. Tanna Chong, "IKEA Toy Lufsig Gets New Name After Its Claim to Fame," *South China Morning Post*, December 11, 2012; "Haha! CY Leung Befriends Lufsig," *Coconuts Hong Kong*, December 11, 2013, http://coconuts.co/hongkong.

17. See "Lufsig" Facebook page; Kashy Keegan's Facebook page, https://www.facebook.com/kashykeegan; and Lulu Tung's Facebook page, https://zh-tw.facebook.com/lulutung.

18. Danielle Endres and Samantha Senda-Cook, "Location Matters: The Rhetoric of Place in Protest," *Quarterly Journal of Speech* 97 (2011): 257.

19. Judith Butler, *Gender Trouble* (New York: Routledge, 1990); Sherry Turkle, *Life on the Screen: Identity in the Age of the Internet* (New York: Simon & Schuster, 1995). See also Lisa Nakamura, "Race in/for Cyberspace: Identity Tourism and Racial Passing on the Internet," *Humanities UCI*, http://www.humanities.uci.edu; and Jeff Grabill and Stacey Pigg, "Messy Rhetoric: Identity Performance as Rhetorical Agency in Online Public Forums," *Rhetoric Society Quarterly* 42 (2012): 99–119.

20. David Gruber, "The (Digital) Majesty of All under Heaven: Affective Constitutive Rhetoric at the Hong Kong Museum of History's Multi-Media Exhibition of Terracotta Warriors," *Rhetoric Society Quarterly* 44 (2014): 148–67; Jenny Rice, "The New 'New': Making a Case for Critical Affect Studies," *Quarterly Journal of*

Speech 94 (2008): 200–12.

21. Dustin Bradley Goltz and Jason Zingsheim, "It's Not a Wedding, It's a Gayla: Queer Resistance and Normative Recuperation," *Text and Performance Quarterly* 30 (2010): 290–312; Stephen John Hartnett, "'Tibet Is Burning': Competing Rhetorics of Liberation, Occupation, Resistance, and Paralysis on the Roof of the World," *Quarterly Journal of Speech* 99 (2013): 283–316.

22. For a rhetorical mapping of how political movements create such resonances, see Stephen J. Hartnett, "'You Are Fit for Something Better!': Communicating Hope in Antiwar Activism," in *Communication Activism*, vol. 1, *Communication for Social Change*, ed. Larry Frey and Kevin Carragee (Cresskill, NJ: Hampton, 2007): 195–246.

23. Manuel Castells, *Networks of Outrage and Hope: Social Movements in the Internet Age* (Cambridge: Polity Press, 2012); Thomas Poell, "Social Media and the Transformation of Activist Communication: Exploring the Social Media Ecology of the 2010 Toronto G20 Protests," *Information, Communication & Society* 17 (2014): 716–31; Zeynep Tufekci and Christopher Wilson, "Social Media and the Decision to Participate in Political Protests: Observations from Tahrir Square," *Journal of Communication* 62 (2012): 363–79.

24. See Chinese University of Hong Kong graduation photographs: http://cloud.itsc.cuhk.edu.hk/enewsasp/app/photodisp.aspx?articleid=7128&photoid=11042&lang=e; Lunar New Years parties images: "Lunar New Year Fairs in Hong Kong," *Isidor's Fugue* (blog), February 5, 2014, http://www.isidorsfugue.com.

25. Kuo, "An IKEA Toy Is More Than Just a Way to Curse Out Hong Kong's Chief Executive."

26. See Lucia Luo, "Dispute Over New Immigrants from the Mainland, Hong Kong Is Unhappy?" *China Hush*, May 18, 2011, http://www.chinahush.com.

27. Brian Cassey, "From Mansions, to Cages to Coffins," *The Global Mail*, June 24, 2013.

28. "Lufsig Soft Toy," IKEA, http://www.webcitation.org/6LpSF99aI. The link provided is to an archived page, as Lufsig is no longer for sale.

29. Chan, "IKEA Toy Becomes Unlikely Anti-Government Symbol in Hong Kong."

30. Amy Nip, "Cuddly Wolf Lufsig Becomes CY Leung's Virtual Nemesis," *South China Morning Post*, December 15, 2013.

31. Ibid.

32. Richard B. Gregg, "The Ego-Function of the Rhetoric of Protest," *Philosophy & Rhetoric* 4 (1972): 71–91, 71.

33. Ibid., 74.

34. Anthony Fung, "One City, Two Systems: Democracy in an Electronic Chat Room in Hong Kong," *Javnost—The Public* 9 (2002): 77–94, 78.

35. Ibid., 79.

36. Guobin Yang, *The Power of the Internet in China: Citizen Activism Online* (New York: Columbia University Press, 2011): 2–3.

37. Donovan S. Conley, "China's Fraught Food System: Imagining Ecological Civilization in the Face of Paradoxical Modernity," this volume.

38. Key, "Mainland Visitors Eating on Hong Kong Train Causes Huge Fight," *China Hush*, January 21, 2012, http://www.chinahush.com.

39. Emily Crane, "How a Chinese Toddler Urinating on a Hong Kong Street Sparked a Social Media War," *The Daily Mail*, April 28, 2014.

40. "Netizens Stage Mass Pooping at Harbour City to Protest Mainland Behaviour," *Coconuts Hong Kong*, April 28, 2014, http://coconuts.co/hongkong.

41. Ann Yip, "'Mainland Chinese Are Less Sophisticated than Hong Kong People,'" *Ann Yip* (blog), May 23, 2013, http://yipann.wordpress.com.

42. "Lufsig" Facebook page.

43. Maurice Charland, "Constitutive Rhetoric: The Case of the *Peuple Québécois*," *Quarterly Journal of Speech* 73 (1987): 133–150, 138.

44. John Jones, "Compensatory Division in the Occupy Movement," *Rhetoric Review* 33 (2014): 148–64, 148.

45. Juliana Liu, "Hong Kong–China: A Growing Football Rivalry or Just Politics?" *BBC News*, November 17, 2015.

46. On the Qin being used in this capacity, see Gruber, "The (Digital) Majesty of All under Heaven" and Yang Lu, "Qin Dynasty," *Cultural Essentials*, July 2, 2014, http://polaris.gseis.ucla.edu/yanglu/ECC_HISTORY_QIN%20DYNASTY. htm. Also see Mark D. Clifford, "Chinese History as Propaganda," *Bloomberg News*, February 19, 2003, https://www.bloomberg.com/news/articles/2003-02-18/ chinese-history-as-propaganda. More generally, regarding China's attempts to cast historical legitimacy over its contemporary geopolitical claims, see John Powers, *History as Propaganda: Tibetan Exiles versus the People's Republic of China* (Oxford: Oxford University Press, 2004); David Eimer, *The Emperor Far Away: Travels at the Edge of China* (New York: Bloomsbury, 2014); and Hartnett, "'Tibet Is Burning.'"

47. "Brand Hong Kong," 2014, http://www.brandhk.gov.hk/en/#/.

48. "Beijing Asserts Total Control Over Hong Kong in White Paper," *South China*

Morning Post, June 10, 2014.

49. Gregg, "The Ego-Function of the Rhetoric of Protest," 74.

50. "Haha! CY Leung Befriends Lufsig."

51. "Sharing," *CY Leung* (blog), December 11, 2013, http://www.ceo.gov.hk/chi/blog/blog20131211.html.

52. Ibid.

53. "Kashy," *Apple.NextMedia*, http://hk.apple.nextmedia.com/realtime/news/20131216/51998994.

54. "Lufsig" Facebook page. Also see the following article about a concert event where Kashy Keegan used Lufsig and the "dream killer" promotional slogan to raise funding for his Dreams Come True concert: Kashy Keegan, "Kashy's Hong Kong Dreams Come True Concert," *Indiegogo*, https://www.indiegogo.com/projects/kashy-s-hong-kong-dreams-come-true-concert#/.

55. Kashy Keegan's Facebook page.

56. Lulu Tung's Facebook page.

57. "Lufsig" Facebook page.

58. See Gregg, "The Ego-Function of the Rhetoric of Protest."

59. Mikhail Bakhtin, "Forms of Time and Chronotope in the Novel," trans. C. Emerson, in M. Holquist, *The Dialogic Imagination* (Austin: University of Texas Press, 1981): 84–258.

60. James Janack, "The Rhetoric of 'The Body' Jesse Ventura and Bakhtin's Carnival," *Communication Studies* 57 (2006): 199–200.

61. Ibid., 211.

62. Ibid.

63. Ling Chen, "Revolution and Us: A Cultural Rendition of Political Movements in Contemporary China," in *Chinese Communication Studies: Contexts and Comparisons*, ed. Xing Lu, Wenshan Jia, and D. Ray Heisey (Westport: Greenwood Publishing, 2002): 19.

CONCLUSION

Imagining China and the Rhetorical Work of Interpretation

We have argued in this book that imagined communities are immensely complicated, internally contradictory, rhetorically productive fictions enabling citizens to imagine themselves—across clashing senses of history and geography, class and power, gender and sexuality, race and ethnicity, religious affiliation and cultural preferences—as organically bound up in the great, unifying, ennobling thing called a nation. This process of imagining is sometimes linked to a sense of mission (as in America's "manifest destiny"), or to a sense of rejuvenation (as in Chinese President Xi Jinping's "China Dream"), or to a sense of protest (as in some Tibetans' longing for cultural autonomy within China); it is almost always wrapped up in layers of consumerism (as in the Hong Kong fever for Lufsig) and rituals of performance (as in Ai Weiwei's artistic provocations); and it is usually embodied in deeply personal ways (as in the HIV/AIDS discourse studied herein), or in proliferating concerns about the health of the public (as in China's debates about pollution, breast milk, tainted infant formula, toxic water, and pandemics)—regardless of the specific forms these imaginings assume, they are, above all else, productive. Indeed, we proposed in our introduction that the powerful logic of synecdoche, by which parts are converted into wholes and by which individuals are woven into larger communities, provides citizens with a sense of grandeur and nobility, infusing daily life with a concrete sense of collective purpose and drive. Watch a citizen of the United States waving a flag on the Fourth of July, or a citizen of China standing proudly before the immense portrait of Chairman Mao that adorns the Gate of Heavenly Peace on the north end of Tiananmen Square, and you witness an individual floating almost magically up into the collective strength of the imagined community. Nationalism is one way we transcend ourselves.

At the same time, we have also shown how imagined communities feed on darker impulses rooted in fear, racism, xenophobia, and exceptionalism. It is a short step from believing that one's imagined community is the source of all that is right and true to worrying that some other imagined community, or internal "pollutant," poses an immediate existential threat.[1] If participating in what we saw Fredric Jameson call "the great fantasm" of nationalism is how we transcend our messy and complicated daily lives, it is simultaneously how we identify our enemies and justify violence against them.[2] In this way, America's master trope of "manifest destiny" became the warrant for over a century of genocidal adventurism against indigenous people around the globe, all launched in the name of God, Progress, and Nation. Surveying a century's worth of unbridled national expansion in the name of Progress, and spurred in particular by the slaughter in the name of democracy and God known as the Spanish-American War, Mark Twain quipped that "the Finger of God was visible in it all, as usual."[3] When it comes to the available means of imagining the nation, Twain was lamenting, God comes cheap. In a parallel manner, China's master trope of "reunifying the motherland," driven by a neo-Confucian sense of "harmony," has justified the repression of political dissent and, in the case of Tibetan Buddhists and Uyghur Muslims, the slow and steady destruction of ethnic and religious differences in the name of national progress and development. As we saw in Xing Lu's chapter, Chairman Mao's rhetorical legacy has played a foundational and justifying role for Chinese leaders for more than forty years, as virtually every cultural action, political purge, or military push has been justified since Mao's death as honoring the legacy of the Great Helmsman. Whether God or Mao, Progress or Rejuvenation, we find reasons where we can to support the deeds we feel compelled to perform in the name of the nation. And so, within the rhetorical work of imagining the nation, violence and repression operate as the flip side of transcendence—imagined communities are both ennobling and grand but also enraging and deadly.

By way of example, let us turn to the South China Sea, where as many as a dozen nations claim ownership over the contested waters, islands, reefs, and barely submerged rocks that dot the world's most heavily trafficked commercial thoroughfare. As Robert D. Kaplan observes in *Asia's Cauldron*, "more than half of the world's annual merchant fleet tonnage passes through" the South China Sea, where "China's 1.3 billion people converge with the Indian subcontinent's 1.5 billion people."[4] No other place on Earth sees more people competing for more resources, held in more complicated zones of contested sovereignty with more potentially dangerous consequences.[5] Since roughly 1949, China's national imaginary has included its "nine-dash line," a boundary drawn on post–World War II maps (but never before then), wherein the People's Republic of China (PRC) claims the entire South China Sea as its territory. To contest that expansive act of rhetorical invention, the Philippines brought a suit to the Permanent Court of Arbitration at the Hague charging that China's imagined community infringed upon the Philippines' sovereignty. The Hague released its findings in July 2016, concluding that "there was no evidence that China had historically exercised control over the waters or their resources."[6] A stinging rebuke to the Communist Party of China (CPC or the Party), the findings said, in essence, that China's national imaginary was too fictional, that no historical evidence or legal precedent could be found to support its claims over the disputed territory.[7]

Embodying the historically fueled sense of disrespect that we have called "traumatized nationalism," the CPC erupted. According to Chinese Foreign Minister Wang Yi, "This arbitration is imbued with question marks and fallacies in terms of procedure, legal application, fact finding and evidence gathering."[8] Dismissing both the court's findings and its right to render them, Chinese President Xi Jinping said, "China's territorial sovereignty and marine rights in the South China Sea will not be affected by the so-called Philippines South China Sea ruling in any way."[9] In fact, the CPC questioned the very legitimacy of the court, using *China Daily* to assert that the findings were further evidence of the United States "instigating trouble by proxy" in order "to challenge China's sovereignty."[10] The *Global Times* used even more fiery language, calling the court "a pawn of the US" and its findings "a farce."[11] If, as the *New York Times* noted, the Hague's findings offered a "conspicuous test of Beijing's respect for international law and multilateral institutions," then it would seem the CPC failed the test.[12]

More broadly, the South China Sea controversy in general, and the Hague's findings in particular, raise important questions about grounding, that is, the processes of reasoning and justification that underwrite our imagined communities. For the CPC, the "nine-dash line" stands as a statement of intentions, a declaration of ambitions, a forward-looking claim to sovereignty bathed in a reconstructed, fantastical history. Whether it is factually rooted in historical practice or legal precedent is irrelevant, however, as the CPC has stated again and again that the line demarcates the "inherent" and "ancient" and "non-negotiable" edge of China's sovereignty.[13] The CPC's claim is therefore both clear and tautological: Our imagined community is a fiction of our own making, on our own terms, and, as a synecdochical fragment of the whole, we refuse to compromise on any aspect of it, for to do so would call the entire apparatus of the nation-state into question—in this case, the fiction is foundational, the nation stands upon the rhetorical act of invention.

The case of China's statements about the South China Sea illustrates how the rhetorical work of imagining the nation strives to turn the murky and contested details of history into something that stands beyond interpretation, almost like nature itself, thus converting a contingent set of choices about the past into sovereign claims about the present. The stakes within this process are high, for within this language game the greatness and even the very future of the "China Dream" hinges on the sanctity—the legitimacy—of the nine-dash line, making any critique of it not only rhetorically explosive but also, and alarmingly, a possible precursor to war. From the Philippines' perspective, the line is an act of extravagant national invention on the part of the PRC, further evidence of how each imagined community impinges upon the rights of others. From the perspective of the United States and its allies, the Hague's findings are more than fictional; they are legally binding and supranational, as if this one form of rhetorical invention (international law) trumps all others. Yet for the CPC, as we have shown here, such talk is just another riff on the centuries-old theme of imperial hubris, wherein foreign powers allocate to themselves the power and right to adjudicate whose fictions will be sovereign and whose will be scrapped, like faded scribbles on a trampled page. The South China Sea controversy illustrates, then—as we hope the preceding chapters have as well—how the rhetorical processes of imagining the nation carry life-and-death consequences. If words can heal and empower, so they can defame and kill. In this case, a line drawn on a map may well spur a regional war. The imagined community, then, albeit rooted in overlapping fictions, is experienced as real, as a living, breathing, daily entity worth fighting and even dying for.

• • •

The chapters in this book, considered together, have sought to unpack the multilayered senses in which China, as both an imaged community and a sovereign nation-state, interpenetrates with the lived realities of globalization and the conflicting national imaginaries flowing out of the United States, Tibet, Hong Kong, and elsewhere. We saw these themes played out in fascinating detail in the case studies that comprise Part One of this book. We first mapped out contemporary Chinese political rhetoric from the heyday of Chairman Mao's rule up through President Xi Jinping's resurgent nationalism, showing how the process of imagining China is always part recollection of the past, part slicing-and-dicing of useful fictions from the present, part fantasy about the desired future, and part appropriation of existing cultural artifacts. The age of globalization means, however, that no cultural entities exist in neat seclusion, suggesting that even as President Xi tries to improvise a new sense of Chinese nationalism, so his bold assertions about the coming Chinese Dream rub many of China's neighbors the wrong way—for each imagined community thrives, at least in part, by diminishing the glory of others. The opening chapter thus tackled the complicated dance of national imaginings in China, wherein political rhetoric often feels less like the prudent discussion of policies and statecraft and more like the staging of immense, and immensely complicated, theaters of wish fulfillment.

The next chapter expanded upon this theory by showing how the plight of Chen Guangcheng, the celebrity "barefoot lawyer," forced Chinese national imaginings and U.S. national imaginings about China onto a crash course. In this theater of dissonant charges and countercharges, the PRC found itself defending China's besmirched honor while Chen and his allies blasted the Communist regime for its violations of U.S.-style human rights. Still, as Chen's rhetoric became more and more heated, and especially when he began to publically criticize his U.S. hosts too, it began to seem that perhaps his prophetic version of human rights was out of touch with the sheer complexity of China–U.S. relations, wherein hundreds of millions of lives, entire markets, and international security rest upon the United States and China not pushing each other too far into a corner. Chen's fascinating case thus points to the limits of national imaginings, which at some point confront the pragmatic and strategic needs of states.

The third chapter extended that thesis even further, showing how the national imaginings driving China's "liberation" of Tibet, the national imaginings fueling Tibetans' resistance to what they call China's colonization of their lands, and the intermingling of these forces with a wide array of international observers, supporters, critics, and activists has led to a cacophonous mish-mash. In this case, the PRC has spent more than sixty years trying to instill its Chinese national imagining in the Tibetans, who still, even now, imagine themselves as someday being free and independent. Ironically, this chapter showed how the Tibetans' resistant national imaginings have found fertile ground in exile communities and foreign allies, where any sense of Tibetan nationalism is increasingly detached from the land, or space on a map, suggesting the emergence of a unique form of postnational nationalism, an imagined community united less by physical proximity and language than imagined solidarity with a set of ideals.

Taken together, these chapters enabled readers to watch as the indigenous, Mao-based rhetoric of Chinese political discourse encountered the startling cultural changes launched by China's post-Mao "opening and reform," a series of radically different versions of human rights in the United States, and then a proliferating global community of pro-Tibetan supporters who envision their nation as transcending all physical boundaries. The chapters in Part One thus progressed from analysis of domestic political rhetoric in China to a comparison of national imaginings in China and the United States and on into a global labyrinth where the very meanings of nations are in question.

Part Two then turned to the embodied, ecological, and emotive senses of the imagined nation as a site of constructed risk and safety, danger and security. These chapters showed how even as nationalism serves as a transcendent and unifying vision, so the imagined community also bears the material imprint of its collective action—the nation is, in this sense, embedded on and in our bodies. As we saw in Donovan S. Conley's chapter, China's breakneck development on its road to rejuvenation entails more than one billion souls collectively raising one another out of poverty, but doing so while using more concrete in just three years than the United States used in the entire twentieth century.[14] The economic miracle of China's modernization is therefore inescapably enmeshed with an ecological disaster, as the modern, wealthy, urban, sophisticated vision of the China Dream is being built upon a landscape scarred by too much development, too little conservation, air that is often toxic, and water that is often undrinkable. The paradox of modernity then, is that the rapid development pursued through large-scale industrialization and urbanization projects has prompted an ecological crisis that has become crucially important to China's citizens as they navigate their everyday lives.

Zhuo Ban's chapter then showed how the embodied nationalism of the China Dream has turned sour for millions of mothers, who, even as they enjoy the new urban pleasures of modern China, also imagine their bodies as, literally, contaminated and therefore as incapable of fulfilling their desire to breastfeed their babies. In that same vein of thinking about how national imaginings are embodied in notions of risk and safety, we saw in Huiling Ding and Jingwen Zhang's chapter how if you imagine HIV/AIDS as a moral punishment, rather than, say, a medical condition, then a series of traditional Confucian values about assumed filial piety risk turning those infected with the disease into family pariahs, thus making it very hard to feel sutured into the warm embrace of the nation. And as we saw in Lisa Keränen, Kirsten Lindholm, and Jared Woolly's analysis of avian influenza discourses, such national imaginaries about risk—Where is the "bird flu" coming from? How is it spreading? Who is responsible? Can it be stopped?—occur in conversation with global imaginaries about health and security. In the case of the "bird flu," this entailed the emergence of two contradictory narratives: one, coming largely from Hong Kong, about the alleged health and safety of that city compared to the petri-dish filthiness of China's booming megacities; another, coming largely from the CPC, about the PRC's magnificent handling of the health crisis, which was positioned as additional evidence of the Party's managerial genius, health care competence, and political acumen.

What unites these chapters, along with their focus on the embodied complications of daily life, and how these material experiences collide with national imaginings, is how China is facing a serious legitimacy crisis: If your people feel contaminated, or under siege from pandemics, or simply unsure about their water and air, then it is difficult for the grand narrative of the nation to feel legitimate. In our introduction, we discussed Benedict Anderson's realization in his *Imagined Communities* that the sense of "fraternity," "community," and "deep, horizontal com-radeship" holding the nation together worked "regardless of the actual inequality and exploitation" found in particular communities.[15] Yet here, in Part Two of our study, we reach the limits of that theory, as the actual inequality prompted by China's escalating ecological and health crises is clearly undermining the promises embedded within the China Dream. The rhetorical work of imagining the nation is and must be fictional, but as these chapters show, even fictions can only contradict daily life so much before they begin to buckle and crack.

Recognizing that our sense of ourselves and our places within the nation are formed largely through interactions with proliferating new media technologies and evolving global markets, Part Three closed the book with three chapters addressing the essential questions of *when to speak* and *where to connect* and *how to engage*. These are questions about representation, dissemination, and organization, that is, of the mediating and shaping roles that culture plays in the rhetorical process of imagining the nation and assenting to its legitimacy. For example, Patrick Shaou-Whea

Dodge's chapter used debates about the postmodern artistic productions of Ai Weiwei and Liu Bolin to dive into the wonderfully slippery and nuanced world of dissent on the Chinese Internet, where language games—based in large part on the complexity of the tones that make Chinese such a gorgeous and layered language—lead to mythical creatures like the "grass mud horse" being turned into challenges to the China Dream and rallying cries for netizens globally. Such rhetorical inventions are flowering, as was shown in Elizabeth Brunner's chapter, in China's booming arts districts, wherein playful political dissent, sly rhetorical subterfuge, and artistic genius and bombast are folded into the international networks of consumption that both drive the creativity of and homogenize the messages produced in these arts spaces. As these chapters demonstrate, the delicate balance between dissent and censorship, creativity and consumption, and frivolity and style hinges in no small part on some of the foundational questions of political representation: How is the self portrayed and performed as both a stable and heterodox figure? How is the self situated within the immense structures that make up the nation? And how do viewers and consumers insert themselves into these questions, so that the synecdochical logic of part-to-whole convergence feels somehow organic and authentic?

Our authors have shown, then, that national imaginaries are tenuously ambivalent fictions, at once fragile and overpowering, partial and transcendent. If the political logic of synecdoche offers the promise of emergence, an almost magical process of transformation where disparate parts are folded into a harmonious unity called the nation, then our authors have also shown how our daily, lived realities can call that longed-for emergence into question. Indeed, our authors have shown how the synecdochic process is never closed or finished. Slippages occur, and tensions arise, particularly if the China Dream starts to feel more like repression, or contamination, or sheer imperial hubris. As David Gruber's chapter shows, this slippage between the lived experience of daily life and the totalizing promises of the nation can sometimes find expression in odd and even comic ways. In the case of Hong Kong's Lufsig fever, a stuffed toy doll came to symbolize the hopes of a generation of youth who reject China's encroaching influence over their city. Merging consumerism, pop culture, online activism, silly memes, and ongoing protests following the Umbrella Revolution, the rhetorical work of imagining a resistant and proudly independent Hong Kong falls onto the fluffy shoulders of a child's toy—such are the mysteries of identification and projection. Taken as a whole, Part Three illustrated the infinite ways artists, activists, and netizens bend and twist the national imaginary in subtle, creative, and provocative ways. These chapters remind us that the rhetorical work of imagining is ongoing to the extent that lived conditions—including access to resources and information and pathways to better futures—fail to satisfy. Moreover, these chapters remind us that acts of imagining are always infused with the pulse of hope, even if that hope sounds like rage or sarcasm or whispering.

• • •

Imagining China makes no assumptions about providing definitive answers to, or interpretations of, the questions raised above. Rather, we hope herein to have provided our readers with useful frameworks for engaging in the rhetorical work of interpretation, of making sense of the apparently infinite flow of words and images jostling for our attention. If, as we believe, relations between China and the United States will help to determine the fate of international relations in the twenty-first century—including shaping our evolving global discourses about HIV/AIDS, debates about the ecological health of the planet, worries about the military fate of the South China Sea, and interest in the ever-changing practices of millions of online netizens, just to name a few—then surely this rhetorical work of interpretation stands among the most urgent of our time. With that claim in mind, nothing would make us happier than to witness an eruption in rhetorical studies of national imaginings within and between China and the United States, with future scholars hopefully expanding our scope of interest to ask such questions as "How does the rhetorical work of imagining the nation stand in Vietnam, or the Philippines, or Singapore, or Australia, or any of the dozens of other Asian nations impacted by China's rise?" "What is China's rapid modernization doing to international imaginaries regarding markets and consumers and our notions of economic justice?" "Considering how China's government treats its internal minorities, and considering how China has moved so dramatically into development projects across Africa and South America, what will China's rise mean for the rhetorical work of interpreting how different cultures and ethnicities interact and influence each other?" The list of such projects could go on and on; there is literally no end to the fascinating and important questions awaiting the collective attention of communication scholars, for as we have shown here, the rhetorical work of imaging the nation—whether American or French or Japanese or Malaysian—will henceforward, in our age of globalization, need to take into consideration the fantastic, confusing, exciting, sometimes alarming, and delightful return of China to global prominence.

NOTES

1. Mary Douglas, *Purity and Danger: An Analysis of the Concepts of Pollution and Taboo* (New York: Routledge, 2002).

2. Fredric Jameson, *The Political Unconscious: Narrative as a Socially Symbolic Act* (Ithaca, NY: Cornell University Press, 1981), 79.

3. Mark Twain, "The Fable of the Yellow Terror" (assumed 1904), as printed in *The Devil's Race Track*, ed. John S. Tuckey (Berkeley: University of California Press, 1966), 369–72, 371.

4. Robert D. Kaplan, *Asia's Cauldron: The South China Sea and the End of a Stable Pacific* (New York: Random House, 2015), 9.

5. Sections of this and the following paragraphs are pulled from collaborative research by Stephen J. Hartnett and Bryan R. Reckard.

6. "PCA Press Release: The South China Sea Arbitration (The Republic of the Philippines v. The People's Republic of China)," Permanent Court of Arbitration (The Hague), July 12, 2016, http://www.pca-cpa.org.

7. Ibid.

8. "Political Manipulation behind Arbitral Tribunal Will be Revealed," *China Daily*, July 27, 2016.

9. "South China Sea: Tribunal Backs Case against China Brought by Philippines," *BBC News*, July 12, 2016.

10. Yi Fan, "Let Reason and Cooperation Prevail in South China Sea," *China Daily*, June 4–5, 2016, 5.

11. "Pawn" from Ren Yan and Liu Xin, "China Rejects Arbitration Ruling," *Global Times*, July 13, 2016, 1–2, 2; "farce" from Zhang Junshe, "US Iraq Tricks Reused in Tribunal Award," *Global Times*, July 13, 2016, 15.

12. Jane Perlez, "Decision Day Nears over South China Sea," *New York Times*, July 8, 2016, A4.

13. For representative examples, see the Xinhua news release of January 30, 2014, wherein the Party argues that "Diaoyu Island and surrounding islands have been Chinese territory since ancient times" ("China Voice: Japan's History Education Tricks 'False and Dangerous,'" *Xinhuanet*, http://news.xinhuanet.com); virtually identical claims can be found in "Sino-Japanese Economic Ties Chill Amid Political Disputes," *People's Daily*, September 17, 2013; in Wu Xia, "WSJ Should Not Serve as Mouthpiece for Japan," *People's Daily*, November 5, 2013; and in dozens of other *People's Daily*, *Global Times*, and *Xinhuanet* releases.

14. Niall McCarthy, "China Used More Concrete in 3 Years Than the U.S. Used in the Entire 20th Century [Infographic]," *Forbes*, December 5, 2014.

15. Benedict Anderson, *Imagined Communities: Reflections on the Origin and Spread of Nationalism* (1983; London: Verso, 2006), 7.

Acknowledgments

Edited books are team projects that depend upon sprawling networks of collaboration, friendship, and shared labor. To that end, the editors of *Imagining China* would like to thank a number of people who have made this book possible.

At Michigan State University Press, we are grateful for the visionary leadership of Martin Medhurst, who, by founding and overseeing this series, continues to shape the field of communication by shepherding cutting-edge work into press. Julie Loehr continues to be the best editor in chief in the business. We are especially grateful to the anonymous reviewers who pushed this book toward greater clarity and coherence. For her expert help with images, thanks to Annette Tanner; for her relentless copyediting, thanks to Kristine Blakeslee; for her indexing work, thanks to Dawn Martin. The collective life of the mind depends on nonprofit presses thriving—so thanks to MSU Press and everyone who supports it.

At the University of Colorado Denver (CU Denver), Stephen

Hartnett and Lisa Keränen thank the remarkable team of scholars, administrators, students, and staff who have made such a deep and fun-filled commitment to the internationalization of higher education and the study of globalization. We are grateful for the support and friendship of colleagues Sonja K. Foss, Barbara J. Walkosz, Hamilton "Dou Dou" Bean, Steve Thomas, ej Yoder, and Tony Smith. Our work has enjoyed the support of a series of deans of CU Denver's College of Liberal Arts and Sciences, including Daniel Howard, Laura Argys, and Pamela Jansma. Our teaching, research, and travel have been enriched by fantastic students, travel companions, and occasional collaborators Andrew Gilmore, Jeremy Make, Benjamin Nichols, and Bryan Reckard. Our work in China has been facilitated by CU Denver Office of International Affairs allies and friends John Sunnygard, Alana Jones, Jessica Tharp, Carolyn North, Clay Harmon, Joanne Wambeke, and Weijia "Peyton" Wu. We send hugs and wishes for faster Internet service to our International College of Beijing (ICB) superstars Kirsten Lindholm, Jared Woolly, Jeffrey Golub, Dongjing Kang, Fan Zhang, Haoxiang "Edward" Liu (and his lovely parents), Kuan-Yi "Rose" Chang, James Wu, and Chairman Feng Meng, Dean Huang, and Deputy Dean Xu. At ICB, we owe a special debt of gratitude to Patrick Shaou-Whea Dodge, who for the past decade has been a fun-loving cultural ambassador, collaborator, global teacher, and adventurer. We still think he cheated at cards on that overnight train from New Delhi to Dharamsala, but he also brought the beer, so all is forgiven. And finally, we send our love and appreciation to Michelle Médal, the World's Best Program Assistant, who has done enormous behind-the-scenes work to make our teaching, research, and travel possible.

At the University of Nevada, Las Vegas (UNLV), Donovan Conley thanks his chair and valued colleague David Henry for allocating department resources—in the form of Professional Development Funds for research faculty—that supported three separate rounds of summer travel, even when there was little early sense of where I was going or what might come from doing so. Thanks also to the dean of the College of Urban Affairs at UNLV, Rob Ulmer, for continuing to champion this broad collaboration. I also wish to thank UNLV for granting a sabbatical leave during the spring of 2014, when I wrote my chapter for the book.

Thanks also to Sara VanderHaagen, who stepped in as interim graduate coordinator while I was on leave, taking on a hefty administrative load far sooner than she ought to have. For her help with the seemingly endless string of bookings, cancellations, rebookings, phone calls, emails, receipt printings, document filings, and general institutional advocacy, I offer a heartfelt thank you to Donna Ralston, our administrative assistant, who in the most literal sense made possible my contributions to the project. A special thank you also goes out to Gabriela Tscholl for her wonderfully efficient work as a research assistant during crucial phases of writing and editing. Finally, to my sweetie and partner in all things, Amy, for cheerleading and being the reason to come home: so many kisses.

The chapters collected here were first presented in a series of workshops, preconferences, and panels that the editors organized in 2013, 2014, and 2015 in conjunction with the annual conventions of the National Communication Association (NCA) and the Western States Communication Association (WSCA)—thanks to those organizations for supporting this work and thanks to our authors, who have grown those conference presentations into these book chapters.

In addition to the NCA and WSCA conferences noted above, versions of the chapters collected here were presented in preliminary form before the following bodies:

- The Department of Communication at the University of Colorado Denver;
- The Department of Communication at the International College of Beijing;
- The School of Media and Communication at the University of Shenzhen;
- The Department of Communication and Culture at Indiana University; and
- The 2015 and 2016 conferences on "Communication, Media, and Governance in the Age of Globalization," which were cohosted by the Faculty of Journalism and Communication at the Communication University of China (CUC), the National Journalism and Communication Discipline Supervisory Committee of China, CU Denver, and the NCA. Special thanks go to Patrick

Shaou-Whea Dodge from the ICB and Zhi Li from the CUC for all of their hard work organizing these two fantastic gatherings.

At each of these marvelous institutions and venues, our authors benefited from the energies, insights, and support of students, faculty, and staff—thanks to everyone who helped push those formative presentations toward the chapters that appear here.

If edited books represent sprawling networks of collaboration, friendship, and shared labor, then they also provide testimony to the labyrinth of funding sources that make independent intellectual production possible. To that end, we would like to acknowledge these forms of financial support:

- "Alternative Modernities, Postcolonial Colonialism, and Contested Imaginings in and of Tibet," by Stephen J. Hartnett, was produced with the support of grants from the CU Denver Center for Faculty Development and the Waterhouse Family Institute for the Study of Communication and Society at Villanova University.
- "China's Fraught Food System: Imagining Ecological Civilization in the Face of Paradoxical Modernity," by Donovan Conley, was produced with the support of a sabbatical leave from the College of Urban Affairs, UNLV.
- "Imagining the People's Risk: Projecting National Strength in China's English-Language News about Avian Influenza," by Lisa Keränen, Kirsten Lindholm, and Jared Woolly, was produced with the support of a CRISP grant from the CU Denver College of Liberal Arts and Sciences.
- "Imagining Dissent: Contesting the Facade of Harmony through Art and the Internet in China," by Patrick Shaou-Whea Dodge, was produced with the support of Professional Development Funds from the ICB and the CU Denver College of Liberal Arts and Science's Dean's Fund for Excellence.
- "Imagining China through the Culture Industries: The 798 Art Zone and New Chinas," by Elizabeth Brunner, was produced with the support of Hu Qinwu, who provided housing and hospitality during a long summer of data collection in Beijing, and a Foreign Language and Area Studies (FLAS) Fellowship.

Finally, we are grateful for the network of friends and collaborators who have deepened our engagement with China over the past ten years. In addition to all of the friends at the ICB named above, we send our gratitude to super collaborators Qingwen Dong, Xing "Lucy" Lu, and Michelle Murray Yang, who have done so much to help NCA members learn about China; travel agent extraordinaire Daisy Ye; Zhengzhou University's tireless and witty associate dean, Zhiwei "James" Wang; the CUC's Zhi Li, Dean Gao, and President Hu, who have done so much to build bridges of collaboration between the United States and China; Shenzhen University's Xiaohui Pan and Dean Wang, who always spice up meetings with their laughter and fresh lychee fruit picked from the trees of that beautiful campus; the University of Shanghai for Science and Technology's Yufang Zhang, who so boldly announced to a class, "thank you, Dr. Hartnett, for your talk, but you are totally wrong!" (to which the students laughed and clapped before tearing into another rip-roaring debate); and our good friends at Shandong University, Ke, Tina, and Mei Mei Li. In this era of globalization, it really does take a village to conduct international research, so we appreciate the assistance, intellectual camaraderie, and friendship of those involved with our work and studies abroad. May this book, like all the travels and conferences and meetings and seminars that have gone into it, stand as testament to the simple truth that the United States and China can and should be friends.

About the Contributors

Zhuo Ban is an Assistant Professor in the Department of Communication at the University of Cincinnati. Her research brings a global, critical perspective to Organizational Communication and Public Relations via analyses of globalized supply chains, offshore labor politics, and corporate social responsibility discourses. Her work has been published in *Management Communication Quarterly*, the *Journal of Applied Communication Research*, and the *Journal of International and Intercultural Communication*.

Elizabeth Brunner is an Assistant Professor of Communication at Idaho State University. She has studied at Nankai University in Tianjin and Tsinghua University in Beijing. Her scholarship focuses on social movements in the United States and China, with an emphasis on the use of social media in environmental activism. She has published essays on visual rhetoric, new media, civic engagement, and transnational social movements.

Donovan Conley is an Associate Professor and Graduate Coordinator in the Department of Communication Studies at the University of Nevada, Las Vegas. A scholar of rhetoric, his research examines the intersections of materiality and aesthetics through the prism of taste. His recent work can be found in *Communication and Critical/Cultural Studies, Pre/Text,* and *Critical Media Studies.*

Huiling Ding is an Associate Professor of Technical Communication in the Department of English at North Carolina State University, where she directs the Master of Science in Technical Communication program. Her research focuses on intercultural professional communication, health communication, scientific communication, and comparative rhetoric. Her most recent book is *Rhetoric of a Global Epidemic: Transcultural Communication about SARS.*

Patrick Shaou-Whea Dodge is an Associate Professor Clinical Track at the University of Colorado Denver's International College in Beijing, where he has lived and worked since 2007. He is a member of the National Communication Association's Task Force on Fostering International Collaborations in the Age of Globalization. His work has been published in *Communication and Critical/Cultural Studies,* the *Journal of Communication, Intercultural Communication Studies, Women & Language,* and the *International Journal of Intercultural Relations.*

Mohan J. Dutta is Provost's Chair Professor and Head of the Department of Communications and New Media at the National University of Singapore (NUS), where he is also an Adjunct Professor at the Interactive Digital Media Institute. He is the Founding Director of the NUS Center for Culture-Centered Approaches to Research and Evaluation (CARE), directing research on community-based projects of social change. He teaches and conducts research in globalization, political economy of communication, postcolonial studies, and participatory social change.

David R. Gruber is a Senior Lecturer in the School of English and Media Studies at Massey University, Auckland, New Zealand. His research bridges rhetoric, technical communication, and digital media studies, and has been published in *Rhetoric Society Quarterly, Public Understanding of Science,* the *Journal of Medical Humanities,* and others. His work in various forms of media and interactive exhibits has been featured in *HyperRhiz.net* and *The New Everyday.*

Stephen J. Hartnett is a Professor of Communication at the University of Colorado Denver; he served as the 2017 president of the National Communication Association. His eight books include the award-winning *Executing Democracy,* vol. 2: *Capital Punishment & the Making of America, 1800–1845,* the coedited *Working for Justice: A Handbook of Prison Education and Activism,* and *Globalization and Empire: The U.S. Invasion of Iraq, Free Markets, and the Twilight of Democracy.*

Leonard C. Hawes is a Professor of Communication at the University of Utah, where he is the Director of the Peace and Conflict Studies program. He teaches classes on globalization, cultural studies, and conflict resolution. Based on research in the United States and Denmark, and building upon a career of conflict mediation, he is completing a book addressing alternative means of peace building in conflict-riddled communities.

Lisa B. Keränen is an Associate Professor and Chair of the Department of Communication at the University of Colorado Denver, where she is a University President's Teaching Scholar. She has worked with her department's International College Beijing for the past decade. She is a past president of the Association for the Rhetoric of Science, Technology, and Medicine and writes about health rhetoric. Her book *Scientific Characters: Rhetoric, Politics, and Trust in Breast Cancer Research* received the 2011 Marie Hochmuth Nichols Award for Outstanding Scholarship in Public Address.

Kirsten N. Lindholm is the Department of Communication's Associate Program Chair and an Instructor at the University of Colorado Denver's International College of Beijing, where she has lived and worked since 2013. Lindholm is a passionate advocate for international education and also serves as CU Denver's China Operations Coordinator for the Office of International Affairs. Her research interests include intercultural communication and critical media studies.

Xing Lu, Professor of Rhetoric and Communication at DePaul University, is the author of the award-winning *Rhetoric in Ancient China, Fifth to Third Century B.C.E.* Her other books include *Rhetoric of Chinese Cultural Revolution: The Impact on Chinese Thought, Culture, and Communication*; *Introduction to Speech Communication* (in Chinese); *The Rhetoric of Mao Zedong: Transforming China and Its People*; and two co-edited volumes on Chinese communication studies.

Jeremy Make is a public health consultant at John Snow, Inc., where he works on health communications campaigns around the United States. He once drove a golf kart around America searching for the artist in all of us; the award-winning documentary that resulted is available at www.kARTacrossamerica.com. He has taught the art of communication in various settings for more than a decade to undergraduate, medical, and incarcerated learners.

Kent A. Ono is a Professor of Communication at the University of Utah. His books include *Contemporary Media Culture and the Remnants of a Colonial Past*; *Asian Americans and the Media* (coauthored with Vincent Pham); and *Shifting Borders: Rhetoric, Immigration, and California's Proposition 187* (coauthored with John Sloop). Ono will serve in 2020 as the President of the NCA.

Jared Woolly is an Instructor of Multimedia Journalism at Virginia Tech University, where he teaches digital news gathering and production. Before this appointment, he spent four years teaching communication and journalism for the University of Colorado Denver's International College Beijing (ICB), where he was the founding director of the ICB's Media Learning Laboratory. Before entering academia, Woolly spent a decade working in broadcast journalism.

Michelle Murray Yang is an Assistant Professor in the Department of Communication at the University of Maryland. She is the author of

American Political Discourse on China (2017); her research has appeared in a variety of journals, including the *Quarterly Journal of Speech, Rhetoric & Public Affairs,* and the *Journal of Intercultural Communication Research.*

Jingwen Zhang is an Assistant Professor of Communication at the University of California, Davis. Her research focuses on health communication, persuasive technology, and social media, using both qualitative and quantitative methods deployed in partnerships with researchers from the fields of computer science, medicine, public health, and social work and policy. Her recent work has been published in *Preventive Medicine Reports, Annals of Behavioral Medicine,* and *Sexual Health.*

Index

A

Aaltola, Mika, 278, 279

Acheson, Dean, xxxi

activism: artists and, 313, 317, 321, 342, 404; in China, 8, 47, 52, 65–66, 72, 76, 81–83, 320, 364 (n. 5); conversion and, 50; harassment and, 73; HIV/AIDS and, 239; in Hong Kong, 373, 403; lawyers and, 48, 68–69, 212–13, 312; online, 320, 380, 404; synecdoche and, x, 52, 79, 83; Tibetan, 119, 120, 123, 127 (n. 24), 400; transnational, 118; U.S. aid to, 80–81; wordplay and, 339, 340. *See also* Ai Weiwei; Chen

Guangcheng; Liu Xiaobo

Age of Empire, The (Hobsbawm), xxi

Agres, Ted, 189

Ahmad, Aijaz, 126 (n. 16)

Ai Weiwei (artist): activism of, 304, 305, 322, 365 (n. 7), 380; censorship of, 322, 323, 324; detainment of, 305, 321; grass mud horse meme and, 305, 337 (n. 56); as human rights activist, 321; ideology of, 322; internet use by, 304, 313, 322, 324, 380; netizens and art of, 322; performance artwork of, 305, 323–25, 328, 395; "798" studio of, 368 (n. 45); social media used by, 365

China Agricultural University, 182

China Daily (newspaper), 134 (n. 95); arts reporting by, 346; avian flu articles in, 171, 275, 277, 279–84, 286–88; CPC-created English articles in, xxxiv, 171, 273, 293, 346, 398; censorship and, 273; cyberwar and, xviii; health risk reporting by, 201, 275, 277, 279–81, 293; nationalist rhetoric in, xviii, 286, 398; political cartoons in, xxxii, xliv (n. 89); on South China Sea dispute, 398

China Digital Times (online news), 316, 317, 319, 340

"China Dream" (trope), 31, 33, 105, 196, 395, 401–3; "nine-dash-line" and, 397, 398

China Fantasy, The (Mann), xii

China Illustrata (Kircher), xxix–xxxi, xliv (n. 82)

"China miracle," 23, 177, 179, 186, 200 (n. 18), 401

China Mirage, The (Bradley), xii, xxix

China National Human Development Report, 2013, 191

"China in the US Imaginary" (Ono and Jiao), xxvii, xxix

Chinese Academy of Social Sciences, 191, 192

"Chinese Dream" of Xi, 31, 33–34, 36, 38, 59, 399

Chinese Foreign Ministry, 48, 55, 66, 397

Chinese medicine, 232 (n. 47)

Chinese society: censorship and

being harmonized in, 305, 322, 325, 333, 335 (n. 18), 337 (n. 53); as democracy, xi; digital, xi; "harmony" in," 178, 194, 200 (n. 13), 304, 308, 315; nationalism of, xi; religion in, 4

Chow, Rey, xxxiii

Christianity, xxix, xxviii, xxxi, xxxiii, 4, 260

Chung, Daniel, 76

civil society, xi, xvii, 6, 58, 197, 203 (n. 63); Chinese paradoxes of, 169, 177–78, 190, 193, 195–96, 199; as a Great Community, 195; postmodern, 118; public sphere and activity, 195; rhetoric of, 195; state activities in, 194; transparency and, xvi, 72, 171–73, 189, 195, 275

class, xxiii, 113, 176; allegiances, xxi; imagining and, xxii, 131 (n. 56); bourgeoisie, xx, 15, 19–20, 27; Mao on Marxist struggles and, xx, 15–16, 19–21, 26–27, 38, 177, 183; proletarian, 15, 19–21, 27, 75; in Tibet, 111, 115; working, xix, xxii, 20, 27, 388

climate change, 55, 176–77, 272

Clinton (President), ix

Clinton, Hillary, xv, 54, 65, 82

Cohen, Jared, xvii

Cohen, Jerome, 50

Cold War, 92; China and, xviii, xxxi, 306, 342, 349; mentality of, x, 51, 56, 57; modernity after, 6, 103, 104, 344, 345; "pivot" as revised containment from, 51, 56, 57; rhetoric, xxxi, 6, 19, 355

"officialese" (CPC), 16, 24, 31
"Old Lhasa," *101*
Olympics (Beijing, 2008); formula
    poisoning during, 186; global
    imaginings and, xxvii–xxviii,
    346–47; propaganda for, 328
"On the People's Democratic
    Dictatorship" (Mao), 22
"one-child policy," 48, 206, 213, 232 (n.
    54), 261
online forums. *See* Breastfeeding;
    BBS; HIV/AIDS online forum;
    Internet
Ono, Kent A., xxvii, xxix, 349
Opium Wars, xxix, xxxi, 36
Oriental Other, 171, xxx
Oriental Pearl TV Tower, *148, 149*
Orientalism, xxx, xxxvii, 278; Acheson
    and, xxxi; discourse, xxviii–xxix;
    China images and, xxxii–xxxiii,
    52, 340, 342, 349; communication
    reduces, xxxvi; conversion to
    Christianity and, xxxi; fashion
    industry and, xliv (n. 81); Said
    on, xxviii–xxix, 126 (n. 16); in U.S.
    universities, xxxi
Orientalist Romanticism, xxix;
    simplification and, xxx–xxxi
"orphans of the Cold War" (Knaus), 92
Orphans of the Zhao (play), 34
Orwell, George, 16
Oslo, Norway, 73, 311
Osnos, Evan, 196, 198; *Age of
    Ambition: Chasing Fortune, Truth,
    and Faith in the New China*, 367
    (n. 39)

Other, xxvii, xxxii–xxxiii, 4, 9, 272; bird
    flu and, 277, 282, 292–93; Chinese,
    171; imagined, xxxvi, 239; Oriental,
    xxx
Overholt, William, 30

P

pagoda, *158, 159*, 350
Palmer, Brian, 178
"paradoxical modernity," 169, 177–78,
    186, 190, 194, 196, 276
Pastreich, Emanuel, xv
Peking University, 51, 57, 157, 159
"people, the," xxvii, 275; Chen and,
    78; Mao's trope of "serving," 17, 18,
    20–21, 24, 26–29, 38; reality and,
    xxiii, xxv
People's Communes, 26
People's Daily (newspaper), x, xvii,
    xviii, xl (n. 28), 134 (n. 95); activist
    Chen in, 81; bird flu articles in, 171,
    273, 279, 281, 286; CPC-created
    English reporting in, xxxiv, xl (n.
    29), 273; on "pivot" policy, 55
People's Liberation Army, 51, 145
People's Policemen (Liu), 328, 330–31,
    332
People's Republic of China. *See* PRC
"People's War," xviii, xl (n. 33)
Perdue, Peter, 94, 126 (n. 18)
performance, 11, 333; Lufsig as
    carnival, 385, 387–88; "harmony"
    and, 304, 315–16; rhetorical, 196,
    308
performance art: of Ai Weiwei, 305,
    322–25, 328, 337 (n. 53), 395; of

Stoler, Ann Laura, 94, 126 (n. 18)

"storm of progress," 8, 91, 95–96, 101, 103, 106–8, *107*

Strategic and Economic Dialogue (U.S.–China), 64, 68

Stuckey, Mary, xxvi

Students for a Free Tibet, 123, 131 (n. 54)

Summer Palace, *146*, *147*

Sunnylands Estate, California, ix, x, xiii, xv, xxxvii (n. 1)

sustainability, xii, 100, 169, 177, 191, 192

Suzhou, China, *152*, *153*, 282

Sweet, Derrick, xxvi

Sweet Freedom's Song (Branham and Hartnett), xxvi

swine flu (H1N1), 285

synecdoche: Burke on, xix, xxii–xxv, 17, 62, 63; Chen Guangcheng's definitions of, xiv, xix–xx, 62–63, 396, 403; imagining communities rely on, xiv, xxii, xxvii, 350, 396; logic of, 403; Lanham on, xix; Marxist conversion and, xxi; nationalism and, xx; "798" as, 306, 350, 362; for social problems, 170, 306

synecdoche, types of: Ai Weiwei as, 321–22, 325; breast milk, 170; breastfeeding risk, 212; Chinese soldiers as, *150*, 151; for free expression, 325; for human rights, 65, 67–68, 72, 325; invisibility as, 305; Liu Xiaobo as human rights, 61–62, 80, 328; "representation"

as, 63; "798" as, 306, 350, 362; *Tiananmen*, 334 (n. 8); violated rights as, 5–6, 47–53, 60, 64–68, 72, 80, 83

T

Taiping Rebellion, 37

Taiwan, xxxv, 55, 76, 161

Tao, Anthony, 324–25

TAR (Tibet Autonomous Region), 92–93, 106, 109, 111–13, 115–16; closing of, 123, 128 (n. 33); monasteries, 143

Tate, Nathan, xxx–xxxi

tautology, xxiii, xxv, xxxvi, 398

TCM (traditional Chinese medicine), 289, 290

Telegraph, The (newspaper), 72, 77

television, 17, 100, 372, 380; BBC News and, 33; CPC-run, 119, 134 (n. 95); on Mao, 12; Oriental Pearl tower, *148*, *149*; Xi's use of, 34

Terrill, Robert, 61

Terrill, Ross, 13

terrorism, xviii, xl (n. 33), 58, 108, 123; rhetoric of, 129 (n. 41)

Thompson, Kim, 279

threat construction, xii, xvi, xxx, xxxvi, 151; DSB as, xxxviii (n. 9); professional, xi, xxxviii (n. 14)

Three-Anti Campaign, 32, 44 (n. 68)

"Three Represents, The" (Jiang), 26–27, 43 (n. 52)

Tiananmen, 334 (n. 8)

Tiananmen Square, *107*, Ai Weiwei's art in, 337 (n. 58); closed by Deng,